The Pennsylvania Continentals

The Pennsylvania Line

Regimental Organization And Operations, 1776-1783

By John B. B. Trussell, Jr.

Illustrated by
Charles C. Dallas, Jr.

Commonwealth of Pennsylvania

Pennsylvania Historical
And Museum Commission

Harrisburg, 1977

Contents

Maps and Chart

Preface

L IKE the Continental Army as a whole, the regiments of the Pennsylvania Continental Line evolved over a period of several years. The inevitable expansion, over-expansion, contraction, and restructuring resulted in a somewhat tortuous progress which, with the duplication of designations and the kaleidoscopic regroupings, has led to considerable confusion with regard to the activities of entire units, not to mention the specific individuals who comprised them. The problem has been compounded by the fact that historical treatment of the Continental Army has tended to be restricted to senior officers and the formations they led, with units smaller than brigades seldom getting more than passing attention except, perhaps, when employed in detached status on some minor operation.

From the standpoint of the serious student of military history, however, it is important to look deeper. The existence of the phenomenon which could be called "organizational personality" is well established. To a large extent, a given unit's character *as* a unit is shaped by the character and attitude of its commander. But any substantial degree of homogeneity among the men who make up the unit is a factor which is at least equally influential. To consider extreme cases, a Continental organization consisting chiefly of frontiersmen and an equivalent organization consisting of townsmen and farmers from long-settled regions could be expected to differ markedly in discipline, skills, stamina, and general "toughness." This has been recognized by many historians; but, in default of any previously available information, they have been prone to assume — erroneously — that practically all Pennsylvania regiments were made up of western backwoodsmen, armed with rifles. The facts are that few Pennsylvania counties, east or west, were able to raise more than one or two companies for any given regiment; that the sparse population of the frontier areas could not support large numbers of units even if the threat of Indian attack had permitted more than a relative handful of men to be spared to the Army; and that the rifle, while invaluable for scouts, rangers, and outposts, had distinct and serious limitations for close combat in a pitched battle. In several different Pennsylvania regiments there were indeed companies from the western part of the State, and there was one entire regiment (although perennially under-strength even for the times) of western Pennsylvanians. By no means all of these particular troops were riflemen, however. Furthermore, the rifle companies which did exist were not composed exclusively of frontiersmen.

On another level, the student of biography or genealogy trying to thread his way through such records as are available to track down the activities of any but the more prominent historical figures of the Continental Army can quickly find himself lost (or, worse, misled) in a labyrinth of organizational confusion. Aside from the fact that the basic Pennsylvania military organization began as a "battalion" and was then renumbered and redesignated (but not restructured) as a "regiment,"* the companies within these organizations were identified only by their commanders' names. But company commanders were promoted or killed; they resigned or were cashiered or were rendered supernumerary by reorganization ("deranged" was the expression used at the time). Consequently, a soldier listed in Captain White's Company in 1777 might be listed in Captain Brown's Company in 1778 and in Captain Black's Company in 1779; but in all likelihood, he was serving with the same body of men — that is, in the same company under a succession of captains — throughout the entire period.

This book attempts to come to grips with the questions of regional origin and unit continuity in an effort to trace each regiment's organizational development. After a chapter surveying the evolution and combat operations of the Pennsylvania Continental Line as a whole, successive chapters examine each of the Pennsylvania Continental regiments in turn, considering the regiment organizationally, company by company, and then outlining the regiment's operational experience.

In some cases, the county in which a given company was initially recruited has been identified in the published *Pennsylvania Archives*. In other cases, the authorization to recruit a particular regiment specified the county or counties from which men were to be recruited. In a few others, the place of residence of the men is shown on the surviving muster rolls.

For a substantial number of companies, however, no such information has been provided. In the attempt to make a reasonable guess regarding the regional origin of such companies, the assumption has been made that the original company commander, who necessarily functioned as the chief recruiting officer for his own company, would have obtained most of his men from the area where he lived. A further assumption is that men appointed to captaincies would have been of

*The terms "battalion" and "regiment" were essentially interchangeable, except that from late 1776 on, the term "regiment" was the one more usually employed. So far as official designations were concerned, the seven one-year Pennsylvania Continental units were called battalions; the units which replaced them were called regiments.

some substance, and therefore their residences could be identified by checking the tax rolls of the immediate pre-war years. All instances in which these perhaps questionable assumptions have provided the only means of suggesting a unit's geographical identity are expressly identified in the text.

As for the sustained identity of companies under successive company commanders, the method employed has been a detailed comparison of the existing muster rolls. Although the records are incomplete, a surprising but convincing degree of continuity has been found to prevail in most organizations. To clarify the identity of a company, it has been arbitrarily assigned a letter designation, as in modern military usage. This designation has been assigned solely for the purposes of this book; companies were not in fact designated by letters until many years after the Revolutionary War.

Inevitably, the only specific details concerning many companies are those relating to their captains. Considering the probable role of the captain in influencing the "personality" of his company, both by obtaining his men in a particular region and by the style of leadership he provided, these cases are presented without apology and with the thought that details concerning the service of the company commander are not unenlightening concerning the company itself.

It must be kept in mind that the organizations which made up the Continental Army were extremely small by modern standards; and moreover, that only a fraction of the authorized strength was usually present for duty. Until the fall of 1775, battalions were standard only in approximate terms, even in theory. Whereas most battalions of that time had eight companies (although of varying strength), the first Pennsylvania organization to be formed—Thompson's Rifle Battalion—had nine, each with four officers, four sergeants, four corporals, a drummer, and sixty-eight privates, for a total of eighty-one officers and men.[1] When fixed organization developed, battalions originally retained the eight-company structure, with a company made up of three officers, four sergeants, and sixty-eight privates, totalling seventy-five personnel.[2] Pennsylvania battalions formed during late 1775 and early 1776 were more nearly standard than Thompson's Battalion, following the eight-company pattern except that each of the companies was authorized four corporals in addition to the other enlisted men.[3] In time, this structure gave way to a somewhat larger organization, and with the 1777 reconstitution of the old battalions into the new regiments the Pennsylvania organizations were formed in eight companies, each company with four officers, four sergeants, four corporals, one drummer, one fifer, and seventy-six privates. On May 27, 1778, a new structure for the whole Army was established by Congress. This increased the number of companies per regiment from eight to nine, but reduced the company strength to three officers, three sergeants, three corporals, one drummer, one fifer, and fifty-three privates. Furthermore, only six of the companies were to be commanded by captains: one company was nominally commanded by the colonel of the regiment, with a "captain-lieutenant" performing the actual duties of company commander; a second company was commanded by the regiment's lieutenant colonel; and a third by the regiment's major. Still another organizational structure was adopted on January 1, 1781.[4] However, this had little impact on the Pennsylvania Line, because the mutiny of the Pennsylvania regiments on that day resulted in their personnel being grouped, for tactical purposes and on what appears to have been an *ad hoc* basis, into three provisional battalions, without regard to the six remaining regiments to which, on paper, they were assigned.

From the above, it can be seen that the authorized strength of a battalion (or regiment) varied from as many as 728 to as few as 582. In actual fact, the numbers present for duty were much smaller—totaling, typically, no more than 250 personnel altogether.[5]

Further points relating to organization concern regulations governing the status of officers.

For one thing, officers' commissions were regimental—they applied to specific positions in specific organizations. This meant that when an officer was taken prisoner, he continued to occupy his authorized position, even though he was no longer able to perform its duties. Consequently, the position necessarily remained unfilled until the official incumbent was exchanged, died, or resigned following exchange. Thus, in a number of cases, key positions remained for all practical purposes vacant, not infrequently for years.

Similarly, when a captain, for example, was detailed to duty on the staff of a higher headquarters as, say, "Brigade Major," he had not actually been promoted; in fact, he continued to hold his captaincy in his parent regiment, thus precluding the promotion of anyone to perform the duties which he was no longer carrying out.

Still a third matter pertaining to officers which related to organization is that the reorganization of May 27, 1778, prescribed that there would be no more promotions to the grade of colonel. An officer advanced thereafter to command of a regiment was simply designated as "Lieutenant-Colonel Commandant."

Aside from the conventional units, two special organizations should be mentioned. These are the "Flying Camp" and the "Invalid Corps."

The "Flying Camp" was created in July, 1776, as a reserve or pool of organizations, to reinforce the Continental Army on an emergency or temporary basis. It consisted primarily of local, militia-type units called up from the colonies of the Middle Atlantic region. Although the unit structure remained relatively constant, the individual personnel comprising it fluctuated, departing on the expiration of their prescribed limited tours of duty and being replaced by others, until the tours of those men also expired. The members of the Flying Camp, although provided by individual colonies, were paid by Congress. In the case of Pennsylvania, some units in the full-time service of the colony (as distinct from short-term volunteers or from militia in State service, and from Continentals in the service of Congress) were briefly made available to the Flying Camp.[6]

The "Invalid Corps," authorized on July 20, 1777, consisted of men incapacitated by wounds or illness for service in combat units. Its function was to perform duty in garrisons, hospitals, arsenals, and magazines.[7]

It must be emphasized that this book concentrates on the Pennsylvania organizations which were or became part of the Continental Army. The Pennsylvania militia is not treated.

Although volunteer units, called "Associators," existed in Pennsylvania for emergency, short-tour service from 1775 until 1777, there was no militia organization until an act was passed on March 17, 1777, by the Assembly, and implemented by the Supreme Executive Council. Simply stated, that act provided for the enrollment of all able-bodied white males between the ages of eighteen and fifty-three. These were organized in local "training companies," and each man was assigned to one of eight "classes." When militia services were needed, the members of one or more classes from specified counties were ordered into service for a maximum of two months. Although the militia of a given county might be called up more than once, the second call would not apply to a class which had already served until an entire cycle of all eight classes had been completed. The system had the advantages of equalizing the obligation of military service and of avoiding the depopulation of any particular area of military-age men. It had the disadvantage, however, of insuring that men called for militia duty not only had no military experience from previous call-ups but also, as they came from the same class but from different localities, had never trained or worked together before.[8]

As a final explanatory comment, it is hoped that this book may be useful as a reference work. Accordingly, it is heavily documented. To avoid extensive distractions, however, only explanatory footnotes are provided on the same page as the text. Footnotes which merely cite the authority for a given statement refer to the listings which will be found at the back of the book.

A particular word is called for with regard to the computer analysis which provided the basis for Appendix E, Personnel Data. Generous support and invaluable assistance were provided by Col. James B. Agnew, U.S. Army Military History Institute, Carlisle Barracks, Pennsylvania, and by Col. Louis F. Dixon, Major Darryl L. Steiner, Lt. Frank G. Bilotta, and Lt. James R. Wallis, of the Automatic Data Processing Division of the U.S. Army War College, also at Carlisle Barracks. Their unfailing help and encouragement are gratefully acknowledged.

Acknowledgement is also due to the members of the Pennsylvania Historical and Museum Commission and its Executive Director, Mr. William J. Wewer, for the approval they gave to this study and its publication; to those who supervised and gave encouragement, Mr. Harry E. Whipkey, Director of the Bureau of Archives and History, Mr. William A. Hunter, Chief of the Division of History, now retired, and his successor, Dr. John Bodnar; and to Mr. Harold L. Myers, Associate Historian, who, with the assistance of Mr. George R. Beyer, Associate Historian, directed the publication.

Chapter I

The Pennsylvania Continentals: from Cambridge to Charleston

AFTER fighting broke out between British troops and Massachusetts colonists at Lexington and Concord on April 19, 1775, men flocked in from the New England colonies to assemble at Cambridge, blocking British movement inland from Boston. On June 14, 1775, the Second Continental Congress, sitting at Philadelphia, voted to take these troops into its own service, and two days later elected a Virginian, George Washington, to command this newly created "Continental" army.

Also on June 14, Congress voted to raise ten companies of riflemen, enlisted for twelve months' service. Six of these companies were to consist of Pennsylvanians. Response was so great, however, that the six were increased to eight, and then to nine. Collectively, they comprised the Pennsylvania Battalion of Riflemen—better known, from its original commander's name, as "Thompson's Rifle Battalion." This was the beginning of what at its peak strength would reach a total of seventeen and a half combat regiments, a service support regiment, and ultimately a provost company which Pennsylvania would furnish to the Continental Army.

The companies of Thompson's Battalion reached Cambridge individually during the month of August. On its arrival, the unit was officially designated (but almost never called) the 2d Continental Regiment. The Pennsylvanians, serving as outposts, took part in a number of brushes with British patrols and raiding parties but saw no major action. On September 11, however, two companies were detached to become part of a force under Col. Benedict Arnold which started on a move through the wilderness of northern Maine, with the object of invading Canada and capturing Quebec.

While Arnold's force struggled painfully through Maine and the rest of Thompson's Battalion continued its vigil near Boston, a new Pennsylvania unit for the Continental Army began to take shape. This was the 1st Pennsylvania Battalion, authorized on October 12, 1775. Four days later, the Pennsylvania Council of Safety directed the formation of an artillery unit, Procter's Artillery Company. Unlike the infantry organizations, the artillery company was not intended to join the Continental Army but to defend the State—specifically, to guard the Delaware River approaches to Philadelphia. Two months later, however, on December 9, three more Pennsylvania infantry battalions for the Continental Army were authorized. These were the 2d, 3d, and 4th Battalions, with the 5th Battalion being added on December 15.

With Thompson's command, Pennsylvania was now committed to furnishing six battalions to what could be called the national forces, but only Thompson's organization was actually in the field. Furthermore, it was soon to suffer a substantial blow. On December 31, the American forces in Canada launched what proved to be a disastrous attack on Quebec, and the two Pennsylvania companies were for all practical purposes wiped out.

For the army at Cambridge, January 1, 1776, brought a largely administrative reorganization. For the Pennsylvanians, still known as Thompson's Battalion, it merely meant a change in official designation whereby their unit ceased being the 2d Continental Regiment, becoming instead the 1st Continental Regiment. In a more substantive development three days later, on January 4, still another unit from Pennsylvania was authorized. This was to be the 6th Pennsylvania Battalion, the last of the organizations enlisted for only twelve months.

Late in the same month, the companies of the 1st Pennsylvania Battalion began leaving for New York City. Within a short time after all of them had arrived, the battalion was ordered to move up the Hudson, continuing by way of Lake George and Lake Champlain to join the American forces still in Canada.

Meanwhile, Pennsylvania authorities were concerned about the security of the Province itself. Pennsylvania as yet had no militia;

Philadelphia, as the principal city in America, had considerable strategic significance; and Washington at Cambridge was much too remote to be of help if Pennsylvania were threatened. Accordingly, on March 5, 1776, the Pennsylvania Council of Safety passed a resolution to form two infantry organizations to remain under its own control, not to be furnished to the Continental Army. They were specifically for the defense of Pennsylvania, and were to be enlisted not for twelve months but until January 1, 1778. These units were the Pennsylvania State Regiment of Riflemen ("Miles's Regiment") and the Pennsylvania State Battalion of Musketry ("Atlee's Battalion").

By March 13, the 2d Pennsylvania Battalion followed the 1st Pennsylvania Battalion to New York and, like it, was redirected to Canada. These two would be followed, as the units were recruited and equipped, by the 4th and 6th Pennsylvania Battalions.

But while the force-strength in Canada was being built up, Washington was anticipating an imminent British evacuation of Boston. Concluding that New York City would be the enemy's next objective, on March 14 he started Thompson's Battalion southward to join the forces he was beginning to assemble on Manhattan.

As the spring progressed and the Continental strength in New York grew, the situation in Canada was deteriorating. On May 6, the Americans still at Quebec began a withdrawal up the St. Lawrence River. Thus far, only the 1st Battalion of the Pennsylvania troops had actually reached the force before Quebec, but five companies of the 2d Pennsylvania Battalion had come to within three miles of the city when they met the advance guard of the retreating army. The rest of the 2d Battalion, still on the way from New York, made contact with the main force on May 24, at Sorel, where an assembly point was established. Within two weeks, three companies of the 4th Pennsylvania Battalion and all of the 6th Pennsylvania Battalion had also arrived there.

Almost immediately, a task force was formed to attack what had been a lightly manned British outpost at Three Rivers, part way back down the St. Lawrence toward Quebec. Included in the task force were the 2d, the 6th, the three companies of the 4th, and elements of the 1st Pennsylvania Battalions. Unknown to the Americans, Three Rivers had been substantially reinforced. Aside from that, the attack which took place on June 9 was bungled and the result was another disaster. Casualties were relatively light, but substantial numbers of Americans were captured. The British, however, did not pursue, and survivors straggled back to Sorel over the next four or five days. Thoroughly alarmed, the American army then began a retreat southward along the Sorel River toward Lake Champlain.

During the same month, strength continued to be built up at New

York City. The 3d and 5th Pennsylvania Battalions arrived and were assigned the task, with other units, of building a defensive work near Kingsbridge, overlooking the Hudson, which was to be named Fort Washington. Also during June, on the 27th, still another Pennsylvania unit was formed. This was the "German Regiment." Although four of its companies were raised in Maryland (five were eventually from Pennsylvania), it was officially assigned as part of Pennsylvania's quota for the Continental Army.

All told, Pennsylvania now was providing eight organizations for the Continental forces: with the force withdrawing from Canada were the 1st, 2d, 4th, and 6th Battalions; in New York City and its vicinity were Thompson's Battalion and the 3d and 5th Battalions; and, still in process of formation, there was the German Regiment. Miles's Regiment, Atlee's Battalion, and Procter's Artillery Company remained under the control of the Pennsylvania State authorities.

But the enlistments of Thompson's Battalion were due to expire on June 30. Originally, the American forces had been raised primarily as a form of active protest against resented Crown policies. But now, with the war aim about to be changed to independence, it was clear that the struggle would be much longer than had first been envisioned. Twelve-month enlistments were obviously inadequate. From this time on, Congress decided, men would be enrolled for two years (later changed to three years or the duration of the war). A new organizational structure also began to evolve. And when on July 1, 1776, the men of what had been Thompson's Battalion re-enlisted, the unit they joined was what would later be designated as the 1st Pennsylvania Regiment of the Continental Line.

On that same day, the force retreating from Canada reached Crown Point. There, the 6th Pennsylvania Battalion was assigned the mission of establishing an outpost line to block the advancing British. The rest of the force, including the 1st, 2d, and 4th Pennsylvania Battalions, moved on to Fort Ticonderoga and went into garrison.

In Pennsylvania, the possibility of Indian trouble on the frontier led the Continental Congress to share the concern of the Pennsylvania Council of Safety for the State's security, and on July 15, it directed the formation of a Continental regiment (eventually to be designated the 8th Pennsylvania) for service in the west. The need was intensified by the fact that Washington, sure of a British attack on New York, was calling for reinforcements; to meet this obvious need, Miles's Regiment, Atlee's Battalion, and a detachment of Procter's Artillery Company were relieved of their purely State-defense missions and made available to the Continental Army. Before the middle of August, the two infantry organizations had been moved to Long Island, joining the

1st Pennsylvania Regiment, which was already there; and the artillery detachment had been assigned to the garrison of Fort Washington. About the same time (on August 14), the Pennsylvania Council of Safety increased Procter's command to a two-company battalion.

On August 22, the long-expected British threat began to develop when Gen. William Howe started moving some seventeen thousand British and Hessian troops from Staten Island to Long Island. The actual attack was launched on August 27, with two enemy columns making a diversionary frontal assault on the American center and right, while a third column, undetected, swung around to strike and roll up the American left flank. The result was a major defeat. Miles's Regiment and Atlee's Battalion lost heavily, especially in officers and men taken prisoner. The 1st Pennsylvania Regiment, which also took part in the battle, suffered less severely.

On the following two days the situation remained relatively quiet, as Howe did not resume his attack. The 3d and 5th Pennsylvania Battalions, brought from Fort Washington, were among the reinforcements which Washington rushed to Long Island. By the night of August 29, however, he realized that his only hope was to try to evacuate his army across the East River to Manhattan. The remnants of Miles's Regiment and Atlee's Battalion were withdrawn that night. The other three Pennsylvania units, formed in a brigade under Brig. Gen. Thomas Mifflin, were assigned the mission of holding the line of defenses to cover the retreat of the rest of the army.

During the night, an aide brought orders for Mifflin's force to make its own retreat, and the men began the march toward the boats. But while they were on their way they were met by General Washington, who accused Mifflin of abandoning his position without authorization. Mifflin convinced him that the brigade was acting under instructions, but Washington said that a dreadful mistake had been made and ordered the men back to the line. Untrained and undisciplined as the Pennsylvanians still were, it is greatly to their credit that they reversed direction and reoccupied the defenses. It was their great good fortune, also, that their movements had been undetected. By dawn, when all the rest of the army had escaped, they successfully made their way to the river and were safely ferried across.

The 3d and 5th Battalions returned to Fort Washington. The 1st Pennsylvania Regiment and what was left of Miles's and Atlee's men, now consolidated provisionally into a single State battalion, were stationed near the upper end of Manhattan Island.

While Washington realigned his forces, the German Regiment arrived to join his army. There was a certain amount of skirmishing, including an unsuccessful engagement between elements of the German

Regiment and a British raiding force at Montresor's (now Randalls) Island, New York, but no action of any consequence occurred.

Back in Philadelphia, on September 16 a quota of twelve Continental regiments was assigned to Pennsylvania. The plan adopted was to build the new organization on the foundations of the old. Thompson's Battalion, already re-enlisted, would as previously noted become the 1st Pennsylvania Regiment. As many as possible of the twelve-month volunteers would be re-enlisted in the new versions of what had been their old units. Under this system, the 1st Pennsylvania Battalion became the 2d Pennsylvania Regiment, the 2d Pennsylvania Battalion became the 3d Pennsylvania Regiment, and so on through the 6th Pennsylvania Battalion, which became the 7th Pennsylvania Regiment. The organization formed for frontier defense, which as yet had no number, became the 8th Pennsylvania Regiment. Only the German Regiment retained its old name.

The program did not occur all at once, as some one-year enlistments would not expire for several months. However, the basis was established for beginning the formation of new organizations so that, it could be hoped, minimum time would elapse between the mustering out of an old battalion and the deployment to the field of the new regiment replacing it.

As for the State organizations, the provisional battalion made up of what was left of Miles's and Atlee's commands was not an immediate problem, as the enlistments of its men had more than a year to run. Procter's Artillery Battalion, having been enlisted for only twelve months, was a different matter, but the organization was authorized to continue after its year of service ended, this time being enlisted for the same period as applied to Continental troops.

On the northern New York front, the British under Gen. Guy Carleton moved by ship along Lake Champlain to invade Valcour Island. With a fleet of small craft the American troops at Fort Ticonderoga had built, Col. Anthony Wayne attacked Carleton on October 11, 1776, and, in a running fight that lasted into October 13, drove the British off. Both the 2d Pennsylvania Battalion and the 6th Pennsylvania Battalion suffered some loss in this action, and it is likely that the 1st Pennsylvania Battalion and the 4th Pennsylvania Battalion were also represented in the force. This bought only a brief delay, however, for by October 14 the British advanced close enough to Crown Point to force the 6th Pennsylvania Battalion to abandon its outpost line and fall back to join the garrison at Fort Ticonderoga. With the approach of winter, however, it was clear that there would be no more offensive operations in that area until spring. At the same time, it would be unsafe to denude the Ticonderoga garrison, and as the battalions' enlistments began to run out (those of the 1st Pennsylvania Battalion expired on October 27), the men agreed to their officers' requests that they stay on until replacement units could arrive.

In keeping with the new organizational program, authority to begin recruiting the 9th, 10th, 11th, and 12th Pennsylvania Regiments had been granted before October 25. As yet, however, these units existed only on paper.

As for Washington's army, it saw action again on October 28, when Howe's troops attacked the Americans at White Plains, New York. The only Pennsylvania unit which is documented as taking part is the provisional State battalion, composed of what had been Miles's and Atlee's units. Within about two weeks, the whole army except for the garrison of Fort Washington moved across the Hudson to eastern New Jersey. The army was still in that area when, on November 16, a major enemy attack stormed and overran Fort Washington, capturing virtually the entire garrison, including most of the members of the 3d and 5th Pennsylvania Battalions, the detachment of Procter's Artillery, and a number of men detached for service there from the 1st Pennsylvania Regiment, the German Regiment, and the provisional State battalion.

After this disaster, with the British in pursuit, Washington began a retreat through New Jersey toward Pennsylvania. Following the loss of Fort Washington, only three Pennsylvania units remained assigned to Washington's army—the 1st Pennsylvania Regiment, the German Regiment, and (although not technically a Continental organization) the provisional State battalion. On December 1, the British came close to the position the Americans were occupying at New Brunswick, but contented themselves with cannonading the American lines from a distance. Washington withdrew his troops before an attack could develop and headed toward the Delaware River, crossing it on December 8 and moving on to the general area of McKonkey's Ferry.

With the situation having grown desperate, units in other areas began to be relieved of their missions and sent to join the forces along the Delaware. A provisional company of Procter's Artillery Battalion, under Capt. Thomas Forrest, was withdrawn from the Philadelphia defenses and assigned to Washington's army. New Jersey militia and Pennsylvania volunteers (called "Associators," as the State still had no militia organization) added to the strength of the army. It was with this mixed force that, during the night of December 25-26, Washington moved back across the river and carried out his early-morning attack on the Hessian garrison at Trenton. Aside from the Associators, the Pennsylvania units which took part were the 1st Pennsylvania Regiment, the German Regiment, the remnant of Miles's and Atlee's organizations, and the detachment of Procter's Artillery.

While the troops at Trenton got ready for the British counterattack that they could be sure would come, Congress was busy with still further organizational expansion. On December 27, a number of "additional" (unnumbered) Continental regiments were authorized. The two related to Pennsylvania would come to be known as "Patton's" and "Hartley's" Regiments. And on January 1, 1777, a new mounted regiment, to become the 4th Continental Light Dragoons, was added to Pennsylvania's quota.

The expected British attack came on January 2, when Lord Charles Cornwallis led a force southward from Princeton. With his main force, Washington held a position behind Assunpink Creek, flowing into the Delaware just south of Trenton. Helping to defend this line were the provisional State battalion and such elements as could be hastily thrown together of five of the new Pennsylvania regiments which were still being organized—the 2d, 4th, 10th, 11th, and 12th. A second detachment of Procter's Artillery, under Major Procter himself, had also arrived.

To gain time to strengthen this defense, Washington sent forward a delaying force consisting of two regiments—the 1st Pennsylvania and the German Regiment—supported by the Pennsylvania artillery detachment under Captain Forrest. Throughout almost the entire day, these troops contested the British advance, compelling Cornwallis' men to fight for every inch of progress. But eventually the Pennsylvanians were pushed through the town, finally reaching and crossing the bridge to the questionable security of the line behind Assunpink Creek. Before dark, the British made three unsuccessful assaults on the bridge, but when night fell it was still in American hands.

Washington was already preparing a daring stroke. While Cornwallis remained at Trenton, the Americans disappeared undetected from his front, making a night march along a road paralleling the one Cornwallis had used, and fell upon the weakened British garrison at Princeton at dawn. The engagement was bitter, and the sound of musketry and cannon fire brought Cornwallis hurrying back from Trenton. But by the time he arrived, the Americans had defeated the enemy garrison, occupied the town, and then moved northward beyond reach. Within the next few weeks, Washington had established his army in winter quarters in and around Morristown, New Jersey. For all practical purposes, both armies suspended operations except for minor raiding and patrolling until spring could bring better weather.

Meanwhile, as the enlistments of the three Pennsylvania battalions remaining at Ticonderoga ran out (the 1st Pennsylvania Battalion had reached home by the first week of December), these units started back to Pennsylvania. The last to leave—the 6th Pennsylvania Battalion—

would return home on March 15. As for the new regiments, the need for their services with the main army was compelling. Although the 8th Pennsylvania Regiment had been raised explicitly for service on the western Pennsylvania frontier, it had already been ordered to New Jersey. Before long, most of Procter's Artillery Battalion had reached Morristown. The 1st Pennsylvania Regiment and the German Regiment were already there, and the other new regiments, as they were recruited up to approximately full strength, arrived as the winter wore on.

And Washington had made still another request of Pennsylvania. The army had a desperate need for fabrication and repair of weapons and equipment. To meet that requirement, on January 16 he asked for the formation of what was called the Regiment of Artillery Artificers, which would combine many of the functions of ordnance and quarter-master depot support. Less than a month later, on February 6, the Pennsylvania Council of Safety expanded Procter's two-company artillery battalion to an eight-company regiment. It was considered a State unit, but on February 28 it was authorized to serve anywhere in the United States.* Before the end of spring, Washington's army in New Jersey included the 1st through the 12th Pennsylvania Regiments, the German Regiment, the artillery regiment, Patton's Regiment, and presumably Hartley's Regiment, although probably all of them were still below their prescribed manning levels. The survivors of Miles's and Atlee's units, although not yet back with the main army, were in the process of being reorganized into the Pennsylvania State Regiment.

As the weather grew better, the raiding and patrolling on the loosely held front in New Jersey picked up in tempo. On April 12, the 8th Pennsylvania, near Bound Brook, was surprised and somewhat battered. The 12th Pennsylvania was also engaged that day, and on April 12 or 13, a detachment of the 4th Continental Artillery, with two guns, was captured when a British force under Cornwallis made a sudden assault from New Brunswick. Part of the 1st Pennsylvania was in a skirmish near Piscataway about April 20, and Patton's Regiment was engaged on April 25 at Amboy.

During this period, the 3d, 6th, 9th, and 12th Pennsylvania Regiments were assigned to the brigade commanded by Brig. Gen. Thomas Conway. The 1st, 2d, 4th, 5th, 7th, 8th, 10th, and 11th Regiments, along with Hartley's Regiment, were divided between the two brigades

---

*The Pennsylvania State Artillery Regiment did not officially become a Continental unit (as the 4th Continental Artillery) until September 3, 1778. However, it was regarded as part of the Continental Army, and functioned as such, from February 28, 1777, on. Therefore, for convenience, it will henceforth be referred to as the 4th Continental Artillery.

comprising the division under Brig. Gen. Anthony Wayne. Patton's Regiment was in the brigade commanded by Brig. Gen. Charles Scott, whose other regiments were from the Virginia Line. The German Regiment was with a group of Maryland regiments in a brigade under a French volunteer, Brigadier General Prud'homme de Borre. The Pennsylvania State Regiment, formally organized on May 1, 1777, eventually reached New Jersey and was assigned to the Virginia brigade of Brig. Gen. George Weedon, in Maj. Gen. Nathanael Greene's division. These organizational arrangements continued substantially in effect throughout the remainder of 1777.

Meanwhile, small-scale engagements continued. On May 8, the 12th Pennsylvania was involved in a skirmish at Bonhamtown; and on May 10, in another at Piscataway. There was another fight in the area on May 26. On June 14, at Somerset Court House (now Millstone), the 1st Pennsylvania had a short fight, followed by another near New Brunswick on June 22. The 12th Pennsylvania was in action again at Short Hills on June 26.

On May 12, the leading elements of the newly organized 4th Light Dragoons had reached Morristown, dismaying the civilians with their red coats until Washington ordered the color changed. Within a few weeks, another organizational development took place when Washington formed a special task force of riflemen, under Col. Daniel Morgan, which was sent to reinforce Maj. Gen. Horatio Gates, who was facing an invading British army from Canada under Gen. John Burgoyne. With this task force were one company of the 1st Pennsylvania, one company of the 12th Pennsylvania, and three detachments from the 8th Pennsylvania.

A few weeks later, unsure of what direction General Howe would take from New York City, Washington sent the 4th Continental Artillery to Trenton, to be ready to move either south or north, as the situation might dictate. By late August, it seemed clear that the British, who had taken to sea, would approach Philadelphia by way of Chesapeake Bay. Accordingly, on August 24 Washington marched his army through Philadelphia and on toward Wilmington, Delaware, to meet and try to block the enemy.

The British landed at Head of Elk (now Elkton), Maryland. On September 3, at Iron Hill, the 10th Pennsylvania and elements of the 2d and 11th Pennsylvania Regiments were among the troops who took part in an engagement with a British reconnaissance force at Cooch's Bridge. Washington then withdrew northward and deployed his army on the east side of Brandywine Creek, barring Howe's further advance toward Philadelphia. Conway's and De Borre's brigades were part of the force holding the American right flank. Wayne's division and Procter's artillery, on the left, held the high ground at Chadd's Ford, covering the main road from the British camp toward Chester. Weedon's brigade was in reserve with the rest of Greene's division, behind Wayne. The defensive line covered what Washington believed were all the fords across the Brandywine.

But Howe learned of another ford, north of the American right. On the morning of September 11, he sent Gen. Wilhelm von Knyphausen to make a demonstration against Chadd's Ford. With the rest of his army he marched undetected to the northern ford, then swung south and struck the American right flank. De Borre fled ignominiously, but the other units on the flank put up a vigorous resistance, finally being forced to retreat by superior enemy numbers and the exhaustion of their ammunition. Weedon's brigade was rushed to cover their withdrawal, holding back the British pursuit. At that stage, Knyphausen drove across the creek at Chadd's Ford and beat back Wayne's men who, after a bitter fight, joined the army's retreat to Chester.

Washington regrouped and began an effort to block the British farther to the north. Wayne's division, however, was detached and given the mission of harassing the enemy rear. Before Wayne could launch any attacks, the division was surprised and temporarily scattered on the night of September 19-20, near Paoli. Then, by a feint toward the American supply depot at Reading, Howe outmaneuvered Washington and crossed the Schuylkill. On the morning of September 26, a British and Hessian detachment marched into Philadelphia.

Howe remained with the bulk of his army at Germantown. Against his position there, early on October 4, Washington launched a complex attack. With Wayne's division on the left, Conway's brigade in the center, and Maj. Gen. John Sullivan's division (of which the German Regiment was now a part) on the right, he hurled a frontal attack toward the center of the British line. Meanwhile, Greene led a force, including the Pennsylvania State Regiment, in a wide swing to the north. Greene was to circle around and then veer southward and roll up the British right flank.

Unfortunately, Greene's column got lost and arrived late. Moving through fog toward the center of the village, some of the troops in Greene's flanking column mistook Wayne's left brigade for the enemy and opened fire. Wayne's men, in turn, thought they were being encircled and, just as they were about to break the British center, began a retreat, leaving Conway's left flank in the air. As Conway's men also withdrew, Sullivan's division, for the same reason, had no alternative but to withdraw as well.

The Battle of Germantown was a defeat for Washington's army. On

October 7, however, the troops under Morgan, with Gates in upstate New York, helped win a major victory at Bemis Heights. After General Burgoyne surrendered ten days later at Saratoga, Morgan and his task force started back to rejoin the main army in Pennsylvania.

They arrived in time to move into the line where Washington had deployed his army, along three hills at Whitemarsh, north of Philadelphia. On December 5, Howe began a cautious advance toward the American position. There was some fighting involving outposts that day and again on December 6. But the British never launched an attack against the main position and, on the afternoon of December 8, started back toward Philadelphia.

The American army remained in place for two more days. Then, on December 11, Washington started his troops westward. After crossing the Schuylkill, they made camp at Gulph Mills. From there, on December 19, they moved on to Valley Forge for what was to be their winter encampment.

Except for the Regiment of Artillery Artificers, mostly at Carlisle, all the Pennsylvania Continental organizations—the 1st through the 13th* Pennsylvania Regiments, the German Regiment, Hartley's and Patton's Regiments, the 4th Continental Artillery, and the 4th Continental Light Dragoons—were at Valley Forge at this time. The 13th Pennsylvania, however, was drastically weakened when the enlistments of many of its men expired on January 1, 1778, although for the time being it continued to exist as a skeleton regiment. On February 26, 1778, the German Regiment was transferred from the Pennsylvania Line to the Maryland Line. On March 8, the 8th Pennsylvania was redeployed to the west, its new mission being to try to provide security against growing Indian raids on the frontier. On March 20, the 4th Continental Light Dragoons (one of the few cavalry units to be kept at Valley Forge, as most of the rest had been stationed in New Jersey to ease the demand for forage in the Valley Forge area) was sent to Trenton. And on May 27, Congress authorized a modified organization for the Continental Army.

This gave rise to the formation of a new Pennsylvania Continental unit—a company of provost guards, organized and equipped as light dragoons, under Capt. Bartholomew von Heer. On the other hand, it also provided for regrouping what had become badly understrength regiments, the change scheduled to take effect on July 1. The 13th Pennsylvania would be absorbed by the 2d Pennsylvania, the 12th Pennsylvania by the 3d Pennsylvania, and the 11th Pennsylvania by

*The Pennsylvania State Regiment had been formally transferred to the Continental Line on November 12, 1777, as the 13th Pennsylvania Regiment.

the 10th Pennsylvania. This would render a number of officers super-numerary, and these, in the terminology of the times, were "deranged" and left the service.

Before that reorganization actually went into effect, the British (now under Gen. Henry Clinton) evacuated Philadelphia, and on June 18 started across New Jersey toward Sandy Hook, where they were to take ship for New York City. The 4th Continental Light Dragoons stayed close on their rear, keeping Washington informed of the enemy move-ments while he followed with the rest of the army.

The leading elements of the main American army caught up with the enemy at Freehold, New Jersey, on June 28, and brought on the Battle of Monmouth.

In this confused engagement, in which American units were com-mitted piecemeal, not all the Pennsylvania organizations saw much ac-tual fighting. In the first phase, when Anthony Wayne led an attack against the British rear guard, Patton's Regiment and the 9th and 13th Pennsylvania Regiments were involved. Later, when Wayne stopped a British counterattack, the 3d Pennsylvania was part of the scratch force under his command. The 2d and 11th Pennsylvania Regiments were in a provisional brigade under Lt. Col. Aaron Burr which charged the base of a salient the British had established and drove the enemy back. The other Pennsylvania regiments apparently were with the main body of the army farther to the rear. The 1st, 4th, 6th, 7th, 10th, and 12th Pennsylvania Regiments arrived in time to see only limited action toward the end of the day; and Hartley's Regiment, on duty in Philadel-phia, was not present. The 4th Continental Artillery, likewise assigned to Philadelphia, also was not present, although some if its cannoneers seem to have been on hand, attached to other artillery units. The 4th Continental Light Dragoons, however, kept on the enemy's heels when Clinton withdrew on June 29, following all the way to Sandy Hook.

During July, the American army moved into the area along the New Jersey-New York border. The reorganization was put into effect. Some time during the summer, the 4th Pennsylvania and the company of the 1st Pennsylvania which had served with Morgan in 1777 were detached and assigned to duty along the New York frontier in the vicinity of Schoharie. The 4th Continental Light Dragoons took up patrol duties, ranging through northern New Jersey from a base at Hackensack.

Meanwhile, the 8th Pennsylvania had been operating along the West and North branches of the Susquehanna, trying to cope with the In-dian threat. The western part of the frontier, however, was still un-protected. On July 14, therefore, Hartley's Regiment was ordered to

Sunbury to take over from the 8th Pennsylvania so that the latter regiment could go on to Fort Pitt.

The 4th Continental Artillery, which officially became a Continental unit on September 3, was largely back in its original positions, manning the defenses of the Delaware River. The rest of the Pennsylvania regiments remained with Washington.

Toward the end of the month, on September 21, Hartley's Regiment began a three-week sweep to the north through territory where Indians had been raiding. Reinforced by militia, the regiment started from Sunbury and moved almost to the New York border. On September 26, its advance guard had a brush with a small party of Indians. Three days later, on September 29, the force had a sizable engagement with Indians and Tories near Wyalusing, driving the enemy into a disorderly retreat. By October 5, the expedition was safely back at its Sunbury base.

As October wore on, the Pennsylvania troops on the New York frontier—the 4th Pennsylvania and the one company of the 1st Pennsylvania—carried out an operation against the Indians in their area. They saw no combat, but burned a number of Indian towns and destroyed the food supplies they found.

These efforts were of little effect in preventing Indian attacks through such a large area, and on October 24, Patton's Regiment was ordered to Sunbury to reinforce Hartley's Regiment. Farther west, the 8th Pennsylvania was assigned to an expedition under Brig. Gen. Lachlan McIntosh which advanced down the Ohio River and on to the Muskingum, building forts and seeking to put the Indians on the defensive.

On December 16, an order was issued for Patton's and Hartley's Regiments to be consolidated and to be redesignated as the 11th Pennsylvania Continental Regiment. As there had been an 11th Pennsylvania up until July 1, 1778, the unit now formed was thenceforth known as the "New" 11th Pennsylvania, and the former organization was, retroactively, given the unofficial designation of the "Old" 11th.

During the winter of 1778-1779, the "New" 11th Pennsylvania remained at Sunbury and the 8th Pennsylvania returned back up the Ohio to Fort Pitt. The 4th Pennsylvania was still in the Schoharie vicinity and the 4th Continental Artillery in the Delaware River forts. The 4th Continental Light Dragoons, however, were moved to Durham, Connecticut. All the other Pennsylvania combat units—the 1st, 2d, 3d, 5th, 6th, 7th, 9th, and 10th Pennsylvania Regiments and Von Heer's Provost Troop—were in or near Middlebrook, New Jersey.

There was little change in these dispositions until May, 1779, when an expedition was formed under Maj. Gen. John Sullivan, to strike a major blow against the Iroquois who at British and Tory instigation were raiding in New York State and into Pennsylvania. On May 20, 1779, the 4th Continental Artillery received orders to join this expedition, which was to assemble over the next several weeks at Wyoming. The "New" 11th Pennsylvania was also soon ordered to join the expedition. The 4th Pennsylvania and the company of the 1st Pennsylvania, which were near Schoharie, were part of a force which was ordered to rendezvous with Sullivan's men at Tioga Point, when the expedition had traversed northern Pennsylvania to the New York border.

In the meantime, there was activity on other fronts. On July 11, the 4th Continental Light Dragoons hurried to Norwalk, Connecticut, to drive off a British amphibious raid. They arrived in time to inflict some losses on the enemy, but not soon enough to keep the town from being burned. A few days later, on July 16, Wayne carried out a successful night attack on Stony Point, a few miles down the Hudson from West Point. With him were all or parts of the 5th, 6th, 9th, and 10th Pennsylvania Regiments. Wayne withdrew his troops from Stony Point soon after capturing it—it was too exposed to be held—but the psychological value of the action was substantial.

On July 31, Sullivan's expedition began its march from Wyoming, moving up the North Branch of the Susquehanna, advancing cautiously but encountering no opposition. Then, on August 11, the 8th Pennsylvania and militia reinforcements, under the 8th's colonel, Daniel Brodhead, began a similar advance up the Allegheny River, heading toward the New York border. Although Sullivan's and Brodhead's expeditions roughly coincided in time and had identical purposes, the impossibility of communicating through a wilderness prevented any actual coordination. Their effects, however, were mutually reinforcing.

On August 13, having reached the Chemung, the "New" 11th Pennsylvania constituted the chief part of a force of Sullivan's men which pushed toward Newtown (now Elmira), New York, and attacked and drove off an Indian and Tory force. The Americans then returned to Chemung.

Two days later, on August 15, Brodhead's advance guard fought a brisk skirmish with a group of Indians on the Allegheny River.

While Sullivan's men were still at Chemung, they were joined by the column from New York, which included the 4th Pennsylvania and the one company of the 1st Pennsylvania. These Pennsylvania units, with the "New" 11th, were among the organizations assigned to the leading element of the force (the "Light Infantry Corps"), under Brig. Gen. Edward Hand.

A week later, the entire force started forward. On August 29, near Newtown, the Americans attacked a breastwork manned by Indians and Tories. The 4th and "New" 11th Pennsylvania Regiments and the 1st Pennsylvania's detached company, supported by a bombardment from the 4th Continental Artillery, assaulted the breastworks while other troops tried to move around the flank to cut off the enemy rear. However, the Indians were so terrified by the artillery that they fled before the encircling force could get into position.

This was the last actual engagement of Sullivan's expedition, although a small scouting force of Americans was later cut off and annihilated. The expedition pushed on into New York State, burning the Indians' villages and destroying their crops. This operation, which ended with the return of the force to Wyoming on October 7, completely shattered the Iroquois confederation and put an end to effective attacks on the New York and northern Pennsylvania frontiers. Brodhead's expedition, although it probably did not get across the New York line, employed similar tactics and, within its limits, achieved comparable results. Brodhead and the 8th Pennsylvania, having covered a shorter distance, returned to Fort Pitt on September 14.

By October 15, eight of the Pennsylvania regiments were at West Point in the division commanded by Maj. Gen. Arthur St. Clair; they were organized into two brigades: the 1st, 2d, 7th, and 10th Pennsylvania Regiments were under Brigadier General Wayne; and the 3d, 5th, 6th, and 9th were under Brig. Gen. William Irvine. The 8th Pennsylvania was at Fort Pitt. The 4th and the "New" 11th Pennsylvania Regiments were in Brig. Gen. Edward Hand's brigade, now redeployed to winter quarters in New Jersey. By the time winter came on, the regiments which had been at West Point had moved into camp at Morristown, New Jersey. The 4th Continental Light Dragoons were still in Connecticut. The 4th Continental Artillery was dispersed in various locations, part being with Washington, part at Carlisle, and part along the Delaware.

Patrol activity continued in the New Jersey area. On March 23, 1780, 1st Pennsylvania troops were in a skirmish at Paramus. The 7th Pennsylvania fought at New Bridge, New Jersey, on April 16, being brushed aside by a British force which went on to surprise and overrun an outpost including elements of the 2d, 3d, 5th, 6th, 9th, and 10th Pennsylvania Regiments at Paramus. Another skirmish between outposts, this time involving the 2d Pennsylvania, occurred on May 18, also in the vicinity of Paramus.

There were some redispositions later in the spring. On May 20, the 4th Continental Artillery company at Carlisle left for Fort Pitt, arriving on June 25. During the same period, the enlistments of many of the men of the 8th Pennsylvania expired, and recruits proved almost impossible to acquire. The strength of the forces in the west rapidly declined.

Small engagements continued. The 2d Pennsylvania was in a fight at Connecticut Farms, New Jersey, on June 7, and the 9th Pennsylvania fought at Springfield, New Jersey, on June 23.

Then, General Wayne planned a large-scale raid near the Hudson. While Irvine's brigade stood ready to meet reinforcements that might come across from New York, other regiments would seal off landward approaches, and two more regiments, with artillery support, would attack a Tory-held blockhouse at Bergen Heights, New Jersey. This would leave the 4th Continental Light Dragoons free to drive off the herds of cattle and horses the Tories had assembled in nearby pastures.

The attack took place on July 21. The blocking forces, consisting of the 3d, 5th, 6th, 7th, and 10th Pennsylvania Regiments, performed their functions; the dragoons rounded up the stock successfully; but the light-caliber cannon balls fired at the blockhouse by the detachment of the 4th Continental Artillery bounced off the walls. Even so, the 1st and 2d Pennsylvania Regiments, assigned to assault the building, got out of hand and stormed fruitlessly at the enemy position despite the hopelessness of the undertaking. The result was a considerable casualty list. The blockhouse was not taken, but the cattle and horses were driven off as planned.

Two months later, back in brigade command, Wayne marched with Washington to Hartford, Connecticut, to greet the French force under Count Rochambeau which had recently arrived. The Americans returned to Tappan, New York, and almost immediately, on September 25, received urgent orders from Washington. Having just discovered Benedict Arnold's treason, he sent instruction for Wayne to rush to West Point to reinforce the garrison there against a possible British attack. Wayne started at once with the 1st, 2d, 3d, 7th, and 9th Pennsylvania Regiments, making a frenzied forced march which covered the winding, hilly sixteen miles in the remarkably short time of four hours. In the event, no attack materialized, but the speed with which Wayne's brigade reacted represented an impressive achievement.

By early December, the army moved into winter quarters at Morristown. The 4th and "New" 11th Pennsylvania Regiments joined the 1st, 2d, 3d, 5th, 6th, 7th, 9th, and 10th Pennsylvania infantry regiments and the bulk of the 4th Continental Artillery. What was left of the 8th Pennsylvania was still at Fort Pitt, with one company of the 4th Continental Artillery. The 4th Continental Light Dragoons were divided, part at West Point but most at Lancaster. Effective on January 1, 1781, the eleven infantry regiments—now all badly under strength— were to be consolidated into six.

Pay was badly in arrears. The men were as hungry and ragged as ever. But new grounds for resentment had developed. For one thing, the enlistment commitment which had been extended from two years to three years or the duration of the war had been interpreted by the troops to mean whichever came sooner. Now that the three years had been completed, Congress ruled that the "duration of the war" provision was the binding one. To make matters worse, new recruits were being paid bounties which greatly exceeded anything the men already in the service had received. And adding insult to injury, felons were being released from prison to join the army.

On January 1, 1781, all the Pennsylvania units at Morristown mutinied against their officers. It began with the men of the "New" 11th Pennsylvania and spread to the other organizations. When some regiments demurred, they were threatened with the cannon of the 4th Continental Artillery until they joined the mutineers. There was little actual violence, although one officer was killed when he tried to halt a soldier by force.

The men were not defecting to the enemy; they wanted the discharges to which they believed themselves entitled. Some of them wanted to go home, but a considerable number merely wanted the opportunity to re-enlist under the more liberal current terms. Indeed, when Sir Henry Clinton sent two agents to approach the mutineers, who had moved to Princeton, and persuade them to join the British, the Pennsylvania soldiers turned the agents over to their officers to be hanged as spies.

After some weeks of haggling, the discharges were granted. By January 29, over half the men of the Pennsylvania Line had left the service. Even with re-enlistments, there were no more than 1,150 men remaining to man the six regiments of infantry and one each of artillery, cavalry, and artificers which, officially on January 17, 1781, were authorized under the "new arrangement."

In fact, the infantry structure remained largely a paper organization. So far as tactical organization was concerned, the men who were still available were formed into three provisional battalions which began to assemble at York during the month of May. They were joined there by the bulk of the 4th Continental Artillery (except for the company remaining at Fort Pitt). The 4th Continental Light Dragoons were assembling at Lancaster.

At York, another protest broke out over pay. Wayne, in no mood to brook another mutiny, convened a drumhead court martial and summarily executed the ringleaders. On May 26, he started with two of the provisional infantry battalions (the third was not yet organized) and the artillery to join Lafayette in Virginia. By the end of June, part of the 4th Light Dragoons had also reached Virginia and had been attached to Wayne's command.

The Pennsylvanians shared in the harassment of Cornwallis' force as it moved from Charlottesville toward the peninsula formed by the James and the York rivers. Then, on July 6, Wayne fell into a well-prepared ambush which Cornwallis set near Green Spring. Thinking that he was striking only the enemy rear guard, and that the main body of British had already crossed the river, he led an assault toward some timber, only to be counterattacked by Cornwallis' full strength which had been concealed in the woods. Instead of retreating, however, Wayne boldly struck to the front and cut his way through to meet Lafayette, who was approaching as fast as his men could march. Cornwallis then crossed the James to Portsmouth.

Not long after this, on July 29, the 4th Continental Artillery company at Fort Pitt was ordered to move to the Falls of the Ohio to join a force under Brig. Gen. George Rogers Clark. The purpose was to launch an attack against Detroit. The plan was eventually abandoned, and the artillery company got back to Fort Pitt on December 26.

Meanwhile, the 4th Continental Light Dragoons had been assembled at Williamsburg, Virginia, on October 1. They moved on to take part in the siege of Yorktown, along with the two provisional infantry battalions that were in the field, and the bulk of the 4th Continental Artillery.

After Cornwallis surrendered at Yorktown on October 19, the Pennsylvania units, joined now by the third provisional infantry battalion, were ordered south to join the forces under Maj. Gen. Nathanael Greene. They reported to him at Round O, South Carolina, on January 4, 1782. Immediately, the 4th Continental Light Dragoons and a detachment of the 4th Continental Artillery, assigned to a command under Anthony Wayne, were sent to deal with British troops in the vicinity of Augusta, Georgia. The other Pennsylvanians remained in South Carolina.

The war was not over in the south, although it had deteriorated into a guerrilla conflict. There were occasional skirmishes and small battles; and these, with disease, took a continuing toll. In Georgia, there was somewhat more action as Wayne's men pushed the British back into Savannah, but that city was evacuated on July 12, 1782. The Pennsylvanians with Wayne then moved up the coast to join the Pennsylvania troops, including the provisional infantry battalions and the rest of the 4th Continental Artillery, which were helping to besiege Charleston. On December 14, the British evacuated that city and the war in the south was essentially over.

By this time, the three Pennsylvania infantry units were so reduced in strength that they were consolidated into a single battalion. The 4th Continental Light Dragoons were disbanded on December 15, leaving only what remained of the infantry, the artillery, and the provost troop (the latter unit serving with Washington's headquarters in the north) still on duty. Finally, in June of 1783, the Pennsylvanians in South Carolina were sent home, where the men were placed on furlough. Without returning to duty, they were mustered out, the last of them leaving the service by early December, 1783.

Chapter II

The Pennsylvania Rifle Battalion
1st Pennsylvania Regiment

ORGANIZATION

The Pennsylvania Rifle Battalion ("Thompson's Battalion of Riflemen")

On June 14, 1775, as part of the action by Congress in establishing an army in the service of all the colonies collectively, authority was issued to raise special companies, to be armed with rifles rather than muskets. Originally, six such companies were to be recruited in Pennsylvania, two in Maryland, and two in Virginia. A week later, on June 22, the Pennsylvania contingent was increased to eight companies, formed into a battalion. The recruiting efforts were so successful that within three weeks enough men had enlisted to form still another company, and thereupon, on July 11, Congress authorized the battalion to have a strength of nine companies.[1]

21

The original commander of the organization, which existed in this configuration until July 1, 1776, was William Thompson, of Carlisle. He was commissioned colonel on June 25, 1775, remaining in command until he was promoted to brigadier general on March 1, 1776, when he was replaced by Edward Hand, of Lancaster, who was promoted from lieutenant colonel.[2]

Colonel Hand, who had been the organization's first lieutenant colonel, commanded the battalion during the remainder of its existence.[3] He was replaced as lieutenant colonel by James Chambers, who was promoted from captain.[4]

The battalion had the services of a major during only part of its existence. When it was formed, Robert Magaw, of Carlisle, was commissioned as major. On January 3, 1776, however, he was promoted to colonel and appointed to the command of the 5th Pennsylvania Battalion.[5] The vacant majority was left unfilled.

The companies of the battalion were as follows:

• [Company A], originally commanded by Capt. James Chambers. The company was recruited from the part of Cumberland County which later became Franklin County. When Captain Chambers was promoted to lieutenant colonel, on March 7, 1776, he was replaced as company commander by James Grier, promoted from first lieutenant of the company.[6] This unit reached Cambridge, Massachusetts, August 7, 1775. Aside from skirmishing and sniping, it first came under fire on August 26-27 at Ploughed Hill, where it was bombarded by British cannon on Bunker Hill while serving as part of a covering force for troops entrenching the area.[7] The rest of its service was in conjunction with the operations of the battalion as an entity.

• [Company B], commanded by Capt. Robert Cluggage and enlisted in Bedford County.[8]

• [Company C], commanded by Capt. Michael Doudle (or Doudel). This unit was raised in what was then York County, including what is now Adams County, the enlistments taking place "principally at Samuel Gettys' Tavern,"[9] now Gettysburg. It reached Cambridge on July 25, 1775, and four days later was involved in a skirmish at Charlestown Neck, losing one man captured. Soon afterward, poor health forced Captain Doudle to resign, and Henry Miller was promoted from first lieutenant of the company to replace him.[10] Evidently, the men of this company earned a reputation for insubordination and indiscipline, at least in garrison, for when companies were chosen to go on an expedition invading Canada, Lieutenant Colonel Hand wrote (on September 23, 1775) that "The General [presumably Washington] refused peremptorily to take the York company."[11]

• [Company D], commanded by Capt. William Hendricks, was enlisted in Cumberland County. It reached Cambridge on August 9, 1775,[12] and was with Company B at Ploughed Hill on August 26-27.[13] It was one of the two Pennsylvania units assigned to the Canadian expedition on September 5, 1775.[14] On November 3, during the march through Maine toward Quebec, the company's first lieutenant, John McClellan, died from what appears to have been pneumonia. A few weeks before, he had written to Captain Chambers, in Cambridge, that "...It is your indispensable duty to thank God for not permitting the devil to put it into General Washington's head to send you here."[15] The company took part in the unsuccessful assault on Quebec on December 31, 1775, when Captain Hendricks and two enlisted men were killed and 2nd Lt. Francis Nichols and fifty-nine enlisted men were captured,[16] virtually wiping out the company.

• [Company E], commanded by Capt. John Lowdon. This organization was raised primarily in Northumberland County, although some of its men came from what is now Union County.[17] After assembling at Northumberland, where it was formally enlisted on June 29, 1775, the company went down the Susquehanna by boat, probably as far as Harris' Ferry (modern Harrisburg), then marched overland to Reading, which it reached on July 13. After drawing equipment, it left a week later and moved by way of Bethlehem, across northern New Jersey and southeastern New York and then through Connecticut to Prospect Hill, near Boston, Massachusetts. It reached the camp there about September 1. The company served part of the time at Dorchester, and took part in the fight at Lechmere's Point on November 9.[18]

• [Company F], commanded by Capt. Abraham Miller, was enlisted in Northampton County. On November 9, 1775, Captain Miller resigned, and Charles Craig was promoted from first lieutenant of the company to replace him.[19] This company reached Cambridge during the first part of August, 1775,[20] serving in the engagements in which the rest of the battalion also took part.

• [Company G], commanded by Capt. George Nagel. The men of this unit were enlisted at Reading, Berks County.[21] The company reached Cambridge on July 18, 1775.[22] In early September, when thirty-two men of Company H staged a mutiny (see below), Nagel's Company surrounded them and stood guard while the mutineers were arrested.[23] The company also took a part in a skirmish between the battalion and a British landing party at Lechmere's Point on November 9.[24] Some months later, on January 5, 1776, Captain Nagel was promoted major, 5th Pennsylvania Battalion, and Morgan Conner was promoted from first lieutenant to fill the vacancy which was created. However, Conner was sent to the Southern Department on March 9, 1776, and command (but not promotion) devolved upon 1st Lt. David Harris.[25]

• [Company H], commanded by Capt. James Ross. This company was recruited in Lancaster County and arrived in Cambridge on August 18, 1775.[26] The discipline of this unit appears to have been exceptionally slack, and the men were insubordinate and defiant of authority. In September, when a sergeant was confined for neglecting his duties and "murmuring," the men began to threaten to release him forcibly from arrest. At this, the battalion adjutant, 3d Lt. David Ziegler, placed the ringleader under arrest, then went to report his action to Colonel Thompson. While Ziegler was gone, some of the troops carried out their threat and released the ringleader of the protest (although not, apparently, the sergeant). Colonel Thompson and several other officers recaptured the released prisoner and sent him under escort to the main guard enclosure at Cambridge, a mile or so away. For a short time, there was a surface quiet; but after about twenty minutes, thirty-two men of Company H, with loaded rifles, announced that they intended to break into the main guard and rescue their comrade, and started on the run toward the main camp. Word was hastily sent to General Washington, who threw some five hundred armed troops around the main guard enclosure, alerted two other regiments, and with Generals Charles Lee and Nathanael Greene hurried to the Pennsylvanians' camp. Meanwhile, the mutineers had lost some of their boldness and had taken cover on a wooded hill about half a mile away. Washington ordered them to lay down their arms and they obeyed. Then Company G surrounded them. The two other regiments, with fixed bayonets, moved up; two leaders of the mutiny were bound and all thirty-two mutineers were marched off to confinement. On September 12, they were tried by a court martial, convicted of "disobedient and mutinous behavior" — and fined twenty shillings each! Another soldier, Private John Leaman, of Company G, was also convicted, but in addition to the fine was awarded six days' confinement.[27] Despite its rowdiness in garrison, this company behaved well in action, fighting effectively at Lechmere's Point on November 9, and sustaining several losses.[28]

• [Company I], commanded by Capt. Matthew Smith, was recruited in the part of Lancaster County which became Dauphin County. [29] After reaching Cambridge, it took part in the action at Ploughed Hill on August 26-27, 1775. One of its members, Private William Simpson, of Paxtang, was wounded there when he was hit in the foot and ankle; although his leg was amputated, infection set in and he died a few days later, becoming the battalion's first fatal casualty.[30] This company was one of the two Pennsylvania units assigned to the Canadian expedition on September 5.[31] Apparently one factor in its selection was that it had been a disruptive influence at Cambridge, for on September 23, Lieutenant Colonel Hand wrote that "Had Smith's company been better behaved, they might probably have saved themselves a disagreeable jaunt."[32] Certainly, the experience must have had extremely "disagreeable" aspects. On the approach march through "the wilderness" (Maine), one man died; and in the attack on Quebec on December 31, 1775 (during which Captain Smith was not present), the company lost seven men killed and thirty-five—over half its strength present for duty—captured. However, almost all of these were speedily paroled; they had reached New York by September 11, 1776, although they were not officially exchanged until 1778.[33]

During August, 1775, Thompson's Pennsylvania Rifle Battalion was redesignated, becoming the 2d Continental Regiment,[34] and on January 1, 1776, it received still another title, becoming the 1st Continental Regiment.[35] On March 14, 1776, it was reassigned from Cambridge to the New York City area. There (less the two companies which had gone to Canada), it spent the remaining period of its men's enlistments, performing beach patrol duty on Long Island.[36]

The battalion's uniform was practical in design for a skirmishing force, if not perhaps suitable in color. According to an observer in Cambridge, the men wore white hunting shirts and round hats.[37]

1st Pennsylvania Regiment

Effective on July 1, 1776, while still on Long Island, the Pennsylvania Rifle Battalion was re-enlisted as what was eventually designated the 1st Pennsylvania Regiment. Colonel Hand remained in command until his promotion to brigadier general on April 1, 1777. He was replaced by James Chambers, transferred from command of the 10th Pennsylvania Regiment, who continued with the 1st Pennsylvania Regiment until January 1, 1781.[38]

At the time the 1st Pennsylvania Regiment was formed, of course, Chambers was its lieutenant colonel, as he had been in Thompson's Rifle Battalion. On March 12, 1777, however, he was promoted to colonel, 10th Pennsylvania Regiment, but returned to the 1st Pennsylvania within a matter of weeks (on April 12, 1777).[39] To replace him as lieutenant colonel, James Ross was promoted from major of the regiment. On June 11, 1777, Ross was transferred to the 8th Pennsylvania Regiment.[40] Richard Butler, lieutenant colonel of the 8th Pennsylvania Regiment,[41] was transferred to fill this vacancy,[42] but apparently never joined the unit; instead, he became colonel of the 9th Pennsylvania Regiment.[43] His replacement in the 1st Pennsylvania was Thomas Robinson, who was promoted from major, 5th Pennsylvania Regiment. Robinson continued as lieutenant colonel of the 1st Pennsylvania for the duration of the war.[44]

As of July 1, 1776, there had been no major of Thompson's Rifle Battalion since Robert Magaw's promotion and transfer to the 5th Pennsylvania Battalion the previous January. Effective on September 25, 1776, James Ross was promoted from captain to fill this vacancy.* As noted above, Ross was promoted to lieutenant colonel on March 12, 1777, and Henry Miller was promoted from captain to major in his place, serving in that position until July 1, 1778, when he became lieutenant colonel of the 2d Pennsylvania Regiment.[45] The new major of the 1st Pennsylvania Regiment was James Moore, promoted from captain, 5th Pennsylvania Regiment, who remained with the 1st Pennsylvania throughout the remainder of the war.[46]

All of the company commanders of Thompson's Rifle Battalion initially remained with the regiment except William Hendricks (killed at Quebec), Morgan Conner (transferred), and John Lowdon. Fourteen of the battalion's junior officers also joined the 1st Pennsylvania Regiment;[47] and the enlisted men's records, fragmentary as they are, show that at least 240 non-commissioned officers and privates continued in the new organization. In time, this included a number of the men captured at Quebec, who re-enlisted following their formal exchange.[48]

The companies of the 1st Pennsylvania Regiment, with designations corresponding to those used for them in the section treating Thompson's Rifle Battalion, were:

- [Company A] (originally from the modern Franklin County), commanded by Capt. James Grier until October 23, 1777. On that date, he was promoted to major, 10th Pennsylvania Regiment,[49] and was replaced by Thomas Buchanan, promoted from captain-lieutenant. Although Buchanan remained on the regiment's rolls until his resignation on September 26, 1779,[50] he apparently did not continue in command of this company; following the army reorganization of May 27, 1778, this unit became the Colonel's Company of the regiment,[51] serving nominally under the direct command of Col. James Chambers.

- [Company B] (originally from Bedford County) continued under Capt. Robert Cluggage. However, on October 6, 1776, Cluggage resigned in protest at being passed over by the promotion to major of Capt. James Ross.[52] The lack of muster rolls makes it impossible to tell who succeeded him as company commander. However, by the early fall of 1778 this unit was the Major's Company of the regiment, so remaining for the duration of the war.[53] As such, it was commanded by Major James Moore.

---

*PA(5), II, 627. Ross was junior as a captain to both Robert Cluggage and Matthew Smith. As a result, the two resigned their commissions.

- [Company C] (originally from York and the modern Adams counties) also continued to serve under the officer who had last commanded it in Thompson's Rifle Battalion. This was Capt. Henry Miller. There is no record showing who took over command when Miller was promoted to major on March 12, 1777, but by the latter part of 1778 this company became the Lieutenant Colonel's Company of the regiment. Its commander from that time on was Lt. Col. Thomas Robinson.[54]

- [Company D] of Thompson's Battalion (originally from Cumberland County) had been for all practical purposes wiped out in the Quebec assault of December 31, 1775. When the 1st Pennsylvania Regiment was formed, therefore, this company had to be re-created almost *in toto*. The new Company D, which drew some men from several of the older companies and therefore could not be said to have had any particular county affiliation, was commanded by Capt. James Wilson, who had been a second lieutenant in Thompson's Rifle Battalion and initially a first lieutenant in the 1st Pennsylvania Regiment. Recruitment of this company probably took some time, for Wilson was not promoted to captain until January 16, 1777. He remained in command until the end of the war.[55]

- [Company B] (orginally from Northumberland County) was commanded by Capt. James Parr. Between June and November, 1777, this company was on detached service, forming part of the special task force under Col. Daniel Morgan which was sent to reinforce Maj. Gen. Horatio Gates, opposing the British force under Gen. John Burgoyne advancing through northern New York. After taking part in the campaign which ended with Burgoyne's surrender at Saratoga in October, 1777, the company returned to duty with its parent regiment. By October, 1778, however, it was again detached for service on the New York frontier, remaining to take part in the campaign of Maj. Gen. John Sullivan against the Iroquois in the summer and fall of 1779.[56] Meanwhile, Parr had been promoted to major and transferred to the 7th Pennsylvania Regiment on October 9, 1778,[57] and command of the company passed to Capt. Michael Simpson,[58] who continued in this position until January 17, 1781.[59]

- [Company F] (originally from Northampton County) continued under Capt. Charles Craig,[60] who held the command until December 31, 1776.[61] He was replaced by Capt. Samuel Craig,[62] who continued as company commander during the rest of the war.[63]

- [Company G] (originally from Berks County) was under David Harris, who had commanded it in the battalion as a first lieutenant but was promoted to captain on September 25, 1776. He resigned on October 20, 1777,[64] and was replaced by William Wilson,[65] who commanded the company for the remainder of the war.[66]

- [Company H] (originally from Lancaster County) was con. manded by Capt. James Ross. When Ross was promoted to major on September 25, 1776, he was replaced by James Hamilton.[67] However, on December 24, 1777, at New Brunswick, New Jersey, Captain Hamilton was taken prisoner. Following his exchange, he was promoted on December 10, 1778, to major, 2d Pennsylvania Regiment.[68] It appears that this company was then put under the command of David Ziegler, who as a third lieutenant had been adjutant of Thompson's Rifle Battalion, later being promoted to second lieutenant in the battalion and appointed first lieutenant in the 1st Pennsylvania Regiment when it was formed. He was promoted to captain on December 8, 1778, remaining in that capacity throughout the rest of the regiment's existence.[69]

- [Company I] (originally from what is now Dauphin County), initially commanded by Capt. Matthew Smith. Along with Robert Cluggage, he resigned his commission in protest over the promotion to major of Capt. James Ross,[70] his resignation taking effect in November, 1776.[71] Like Company D of Thompson's Rifle Battalion, this company had suffered so heavily in the attack on Quebec on December 31, 1775, that it was almost a completely new unit when the 1st Pennsylvania Regiment was formed. It appears to have been commanded briefly by John Holliday, who was promoted from first lieutenant with an effective date of rank of September 25, 1776, but who was taken prisoner at Fort Washington, New York, on November 16, 1776, and seems never to have returned to duty with the regiment. In any case, he resigned his commission on March 1, 1778.[72] While he was a prisoner, however, he would have been carried against the regiment's authorized strength in captains, so no one could be promoted in his place. Even after his resignation, the captaincy remained vacant until John McClellan (not, of course, the 1st Lt. John McClellan of the battalion's Company D who had died during the Canada campaign) was promoted from first lieutenant on October 1, 1779. Captain McClellan continued with the regiment for the duration of the war.[73]

Following the mutiny of the Pennsylvania Line on January 1, 1781 (in which the men of the 1st Pennsylvania Regiment took part), the regiment was in effect disbanded, although it was one of the six regiments retained on paper.[74] Those of its members remaining in the army were scattered among one of three battalions which were sent to serve in the southern theater.

Summary

The Pennsylvania Rifle Battalion ("Thompson's Battalion of Riflemen") consisted of companies from all sections of the Commonwealth except the extreme southeast around Philadelphia. Thus, although areas which currently were or recently had been frontier regions were strongly represented, there was also some input from localities which had been settled and peaceful for a comparatively long time.

The 1st Pennsylvania Regiment seems to have retained to a very marked degree the company structure, personnel, and organizational personality of the Pennsylvania Rifle Battalion. Comparison of the battalion's muster rolls with those which have been preserved for the regiment shows that large numbers of the individual members of companies of the battalion remained together in the same companies of the regiment. It can be concluded with some confidence, therefore, that with the exception of the two companies (one from Cumberland County, the other from what is now Dauphin County) decimated at Quebec, the regional identifications of the companies of the Pennsylvania Rifle Battalion carried over to their corresponding companies of the 1st Pennsylvania Regiment.

OPERATIONS

The Pennsylvania Rifle Battalion ("Thompson's Battalion of Riflemen")

As noted previously, the companies of this organization moved individually to join the army under General Washington which was based at Cambridge, Massachusetts, while it laid siege to Boston in the summer of 1775. The men made a considerable impression, both in their appearance and their marksmanship. One observer noted that physically, they were exceptionally robust, with a substantial number topping six feet, and their skill with their rifles was said to make their fire accurate at ranges beyond two hundred yards.[75]

Although one account states that Company E did not arrive until about September 1 (see above), another says that the entire battalion was assembled by August 18, at which time it had present for duty a strength of 43 officers and 755 enlisted men.[76] As riflemen, the Pennsylvanians were assigned to man the outpost line, and were therefore made exempt from routine guard and fatigue details. Their special status went to the men's heads, and they became unruly and insubordinate to a degree that was noteworthy even in the collection of undisciplined men who comprised the army at that time. The situation reached a head in September when, as previously described, thirty-two men of one company staged a minor mutiny. Apart from the punishments awarded to the men involved, the battalion as a whole was placed on guard and fatigue rosters along with the other troops from that time forward.[77]

Meanwhile, over half the command had seen action at Ploughed Hill when the British launched an attack on August 27 against entrench-ments which the Americans had dug the previous day.[78] Elements of the battalion were also engaged in a number of minor skirmishes on a more or less continuing basis. Then, on September 5, the companies under Captains Hendricks and Smith were assigned to the expedition for invading Canada, leaving Cambridge on September 11.[79] A short time later, on September 23, the strength of the battalion at Cambridge was reported as being 35 officers and 518 enlisted men present for duty; another 49 men were sick, and one soldier was on detached service. Evidently, sickness increased, for about a month later, on October 27, the total of enlisted men present for duty had dropped to 471.[80]

There was an engagement of some magnitude on November 9. On that day, a British force covered by naval gunfire as well as artillery support from British-occupied Bunker, Breed's, and Copp's hills, landed on Lechmere's Point, which, at high tide, became an island. The Pennsylvania battalion was rushed to meet this attack. Wading through the water up to their armpits, the men stormed the enemy position and drove the British back into their boats.[81]

Total strength at Cambridge of the Pennsylvania battalion on Jan-uary 1, 1776, was 693 officers and men. As of that date, the unit was designated as the 1st Continental Regiment. As such, it was later authorized a regimental color, described by Colonel Hand in a letter of March 8 as having on "a deep green ground, a tiger partly enclosed by toils, attempting the pass, defended by a hunter armed with a spear (in white), on crimson field the motto Domari nolo."[82]

The Pennsylvania Rifle Battalion was redeployed from Cambridge, leaving on March 14, to New York City, which it reached by way of Hartford, Connecticut, two weeks later. On April 5, a week after arriv-ing, three companies were assigned the mission of patrolling the Long Island shoreline. They saw some action almost at once when they cap-tured a small British naval landing party which had come ashore, ap-parently to reconnoiter. A few days later, the remaining four com-panies joined the three already on Long Island, where the whole bat-talion was assigned to the brigade commanded by Brig. Gen. John Sul-livan. At this point, the battalion's strength had dropped to 507 officers and men.[83] It remained on this mission until, on June 30, 1776, the enlistments of the men ran out.

As for the two companies which had left for Canada with Benedict Arnold's expeditionary force on September 11, 1775, they marched to Newburyport, Massachusetts, and from there, on September 19, the whole force of over a thousand men boarded transports which took them to the Kennebec River and then upstream to a shipyard, where bateaux had been built for their use. The expedition transferred to the bateaux and on September 22 started farther up the river to an outpost called Fort Western (Augusta, Maine).[84] From there, progress was slower, as portages were fairly frequent. Much of the time, too, the bateaux could be used only for carrying supplies, and except for steersmen the troops proceeded on foot along the river banks. As riflemen, the two Pennsylvania companies served as an advance guard. On October 29, the force reached the Chaudière.[85] By this time, the commander of the rearmost of the expedition's two battalions had abandoned the operation, returning to Cambridge with his five hundred troops and a large part of the supplies. Despite a severe shortage of rations, increasingly cold weather, and difficult terrain, the rest of the command continued toward Canada. By November 4, when they reached the first Canadian settlements, the men were starving; and when they arrived at a French hamlet and were able to get food, several men so gorged themselves that they died.[86]

From that point on, the advance to the St. Lawrence River was easier. At that river, by the night of November 13, enough canoes were collected to ferry the force to the other bank, although several trips were required before all the troops had crossed. Two days later the force had reached the Plains of Abraham before Quebec. After several days of pointlessly deploying outside the walls of the city, Arnold withdrew on November 18 to Point Aux Trembles, twenty-odd miles away, to await the arrival of Gen. Richard Montgomery, who after capturing Montreal reached Point Aux Trembles on December 1. The following day the combined force marched back to Quebec. A battery of American artillery was brought up and for several days cannon fire was exchanged while the American riflemen sniped at sentries on the city's walls. Then, on the night of December 31, the assault on the city was launched. It was a disaster, with many killed and many more captured. As for the Pennsylvanians, both companies were for all practical purposes destroyed.

1st Pennsylvania Regiment

The 1st Pennsylvania's initial major action as a regiment was at the Battle of Long Island, on August 27, 1776. Earlier in the month it had been relieved from the mission of beach patrol.[87] When the British army was ferried across from Staten Island to Long Island on August 22, the 1st Pennsylvania Regiment met the enemy forces near Flatbush but was unable to lure them into an attack and was too badly outnumbered to launch an attack of its own. The Pennsylvanians did keep the enemy under close observation, however, and there was fairly continuous sniping and minor skirmishing until the morning of August 26.[88]

The regiment was actually in contact only with the center of three British columns. On their right (to the west) there was another column, of which they would have been aware. But the third column, of which the Americans had no knowledge, was making a wide swing to the east, and during the night of August 26-27, cut north through an unguarded pass in the range of hills called Brooklyn Heights, then struck due west to hit the American left flank. This was the signal for a general attack by all British forces.

During the action which followed, the 1st Pennsylvania saw hard fighting. At one point, a considerable part of the regiment was surrounded, but drove off the attackers long enough to escape the trap. The regiment did lose a number of men, both as casualties and prisoners.

The Americans fell back behind prepared defenses extending from Gowanus Bay to the East River, and there was no further significant action for the next two days. On August 29, Washington decided to evacuate his army to Manhattan. The Pennsylvania troops, under the command for this operation of Brig. Gen. Thomas Mifflin, were to form the rear guard.[89]

The 1st Pennsylvania held its position until about 2 A.M. on August 30, when orders arrived for it to move through Brooklyn to the boats. Carrying out these instructions, the men had gone a good part of the way toward the river when they came upon General Washington. Recognizing Colonel Hand, Washington expressed surprise that Hand of all people would abandon his post. Hand protested hotly that he was acting under orders. Washington then said that there must have been some mistake. The Pennsylvanians thereupon turned back and succeeded, undiscovered by the British, in regaining their position.[90] Eventually they received valid orders to withdraw and, under cover of a dense fog, reached the boats and were ferried safely to Manhattan. From there, the regiment moved to Kingsbridge, a few miles north of New York City.[91]

No record has been found to show whether the 1st Pennsylvania Regiment fought at the Battle of White Plains, New York, on October 28, 1777. However, one of its men was wounded near White Plains on October 27,[92] in what may have been a preliminary encounter, and some of its personnel were detached for service with the garrison of Fort Washington, and were taken prisoner when the British attacked and captured the position in the war's next major operation, which took place on November 16.[93]

During Washington's retreat through New Jersey across the Delaware to Pennsylvania, the 1st Pennsylvania Regiment was assigned to the brigade commanded by Brig. Gen. Hugh Mercer. For the crossing of the Delaware on Christmas night, 1776, and the attack on Trenton, New Jersey, however, it was reassigned to a brigade under a French volunteer, Brigadier General Roche de Fermoy.[94] This brigade marched with the left-flank column of the American army; about a mile north of Trenton, it broke off from the column to head east to the Princeton road, then swung south toward Trenton.

After the attack had begun and the Hessian commander, Col. Johann Rall, led a force in an attempt to break out toward Princeton, the 1st Pennsylvania Regiment was one of two units (the other was the German Regiment) which, on Washington's orders, charged forward and blocked the Hessian move.[95] As the Hessians fell back, the Pennsylvanians drove ahead, firing from a range of no more than fifty paces, until the Hessian units began to surrender.[96]

After this victory, Washington remained for several days in Trenton. Because Lord Cornwallis and two British brigades were barely ten miles away in Princeton, Fermoy's brigade, including the 1st Pennsylvania Regiment, was posted at a point where the Princeton road crossed Five Mile Run, about halfway between the two towns. On January 2, 1777, Cornwallis started from Princeton with a reinforced brigade to attack the American army.

The advance elements of the British force approached Five Mile Run at about 10 A.M. At the time, Colonel Hand was acting in command of the brigade in the absence of General de Fermoy, who had left abruptly for Trenton. Under Hand's orders, the American riflemen took the British under a galling attack, firing from cover, inflicting substantial losses and slowing the enemy advance so greatly that it was about 3 P.M. before Cornwallis finally reached prepared American defenses about half a mile northeast of Trenton. Almost single handed, except for some support from Capt. Thomas Forrest's Pennsylvania artillery detachment, Hand's force stubbornly continued to delay the British advance through Trenton. Another hour had passed before this outpost guard was compelled to withdraw over the bridge across Assunpink Creek, behind which the rest of the American army held strong entrenchments. Here the remaining American cannon came into play and three successive British attempts to take the bridge were beaten off with heavy losses. By this time it was dark, and the action broke off.[97]

During the night, Washington moved his army stealthily out of the Trenton area and, by a somewhat more circuitous route than the one the British held, started toward Princeton to attack the reduced British garrison there. By dawn on January 3, the advance guard was within three miles of its objective. Meanwhile, two of the three British regiments in the town had started for Trenton to escort a convoy carrying supplies to Cornwallis. When the British and American columns ran into each other a heavy fire fight developed, in which the 1st Pennsylvania Regiment played an important part, continuing to pursue when the British finally broke, and taking most of the prisoners who were captured that day.[98]

Realizing that Cornwallis would soon arrive from Trenton, Washington had evacuated Princeton by early afternoon. From there, the army moved into what were to be its winter quarters at Morristown, New Jersey. Possibly it was during this period that the 1st Pennsylvania was authorized its organization uniform. This was supposed to be a brown coat with green facings. As the other Pennsylvania infantry regiments had pewter buttons, probably this was the case with the 1st Pennsylvania as well. For field service, however, this unit continued to wear hunting shirts,[99] sometimes ornamented with fringe.*

The 1st Pennsylvania Regiment is next mentioned about April 20, 1777, when at least some of its personnel took part in an engagement in the vicinity of Piscataway.[100] It fought again on June 14, when it was involved in a skirmish at Somerset Court House (now Millstone, New Jersey),[101] some ten miles south of Morristown. A few days later, on June 22, it helped drive British troops out of New Brunswick.[102] By this time it had been assigned to the 1st Brigade of the division commanded by Brig. Gen. Anthony Wayne.[103]

The summer of 1777 was spent in marching and counter-marching to meet the various tentative and anticipated movements of the British forces under Gen. William Howe in New York. It was at this time, too, that Captain Parr's Company was detached to go with Col. Daniel Morgan's task force to reinforce Maj. Gen. Horatio Gates. This unit took part in the Saratoga campaign, which ended on October 11, and then rejoined the regiment in Pennsylvania. During the fighting in upstate New York, on one occasion Colonel Morgan told Private Timothy Murphy, one of Parr's men who was an especially fine marksman, to bring down the British Gen. Simon Fraser, and Murphy picked off the general with his first shot.[104]

In the meantime, Washington had moved his army south to try to block General Howe's advance on Philadelphia. The first engagement of this campaign was the Battle of Brandywine, fought on September 11, 1777. In that action, the 1st Pennsylvania Regiment with the rest of

---

*According to a General Order issued by Washington on October 2, 1779, all Continental infantry wore white or light-colored breeches or "overalls" and white-buttoned blue coats, faced and lined with a contrasting color denoting the region from which they came. For Pennsylvania Continental infantry regiments, along with Delaware, Maryland, and Virginia infantry units, the lining and facing were red. Of course, it is doubtful that any regiments were ever fully uniformed according to regulation.

Wayne's division was posted to cover Chadd's Ford, which was assumed to be where the British main thrust would be made. However, General Howe carried out a diversionary action at Chadd's Ford while his main attack swung upstream for several miles, crossed the Brandywine undiscovered, and then drove southward to crush the American right flank. The enemy forces at Chadd's Ford then stormed across the creek. Under extremely heavy pressure, the 1st Pennsylvania helped bring off some of the American cannon which had been abandoned by their crews. It then fell back to another defensive position, holding in place until the division was ordered to withdraw to Chester.[105] During the battle, it had some fourteen casualties, about equally divided between killed and wounded.[106]

The regiment was again in action on the night of September 19-20, when a British force surprised Wayne's division at Paoli. Parts of the 1st Pennsylvania, in particular a detachment under Capt. James Wilson, helped cover the retreat of the main body of the division.[107]

At the Battle of Germantown, on October 4, the 1st Pennsylvania took part in the thrust of Wayne's division just to the left of the Germantown Road. The American frontal assault was about to smash the center of the British line when the American division under Maj. Gen. Adam Stephen approached from the left rear and, mistaking Wayne's men in the dense fog for a British force, opened fire. This, combined with the sound of firing from well to the rear where a surrounded British regiment was holding out, convinced Wayne's men that they had been encircled and they began to retreat, causing the whole American line to fall back.

The regiment was present at Whitemarsh, deployed in the first line of the American defense when the British approached in early December. However, it was not involved in such skirmishing as took place.[108]

The 1st Pennsylvania Regiment spent the winter of 1777-1778 at Valley Forge. Then, when the British evacuated Philadelphia on June 18, 1778, and started across New Jersey to rendezvous at Sandy Hook with transports that would take them to New York, the Americans followed as rapidly as possible. The leading elements of the American army caught up with the British army on June 28, at Monmouth Court House (modern Freehold). The 1st Pennsylvania was not part of the advance force which was involved in the initial part of the engagement. As the main body of the army came onto the field, however, the regiment was ordered forward late in the action with the 7th Pennsylvania and one other Pennsylvania regiment (possibly the 3d Pennsylvania), all under Anthony Wayne, to pursue withdrawing British forces. They inflicted considerable casualties until British reinforcements came up;

Wayne's troops fell back to a hedgerow, where they received a British charge, again inflicting heavy casualties (in this fighting, Capt. William Wilson's Company G, on the regiment's right flank, captured the colors of one of the British battalions) but being forced by superior numbers to withdraw.[108] One account lists the regiment as having one officer and two enlisted men wounded,[110] but Colonel Chambers reported two killed and four wounded, all by splinters from fence rails which were struck by the crossfire of cannons between which the regiment lay.[111]

Soon after this operation, Parr's Company was again detached from the 1st Pennsylvania to help guard the New York frontier against the Indians. The rest of the regiment spent the remainder of the year in the New Jersey-New York border area. The regiment seems to have spent the winter of 1778-1779 in the vicinity of Middlebrook, New Jersey.[112] There is no record of its activities during the spring and summer which followed, but the company on the New York frontier took part in Maj. Gen. John Sullivan's campaign against the Iroquois during the summer and fall. Private Timothy Murphy again earned recognition in this operation when, on September 13, he killed and scalped an Indian, bringing the total of enemy fighters he had personally killed during the war to thirty-three.[113]

The 1st Pennsylvania as a whole, although now reduced to a strength of only 256 officers and men, was part of Wayne's brigade in the garrison of West Point as of October, 1779.[114] It soon moved from there, however, to spend the winter of 1779-1780 (with all companies having been reunited) at Morristown.[115]

The spring and summer of 1780 brought a resumption of scattered engagements with British and Tory forces. The largest of these occurred on July 21, near Bergen Heights, New Jersey, when Wayne led two brigades (one of them including the 1st Pennsylvania Regiment) in an attack on a blockhouse at Bull's Ferry. While the American force ineffectually bombarded the blockhouse with light cannon, British reinforcements started across the Hudson. Irvine's American brigade held off this force while the other brigade kept the blockhouse under small arms fire. Wayne eventually decided to withdraw his force, but the men of the 1st Pennsylvania, their fighting blood up, recklessly disregarded the orders and pleas of their officers and stormed up to the blockhouse to try to break their way in. Troops of the 2d Pennsylvania followed suit. Finally, realizing that there was no way they could get into the blockhouse, the two regiments withdrew, but only after losing, between them, fifteen men killed and forty-nine wounded.[116]

The impetuosity of the troops had cost the now badly understrength regiment severely, and became a matter of official notice in Washington's report on the engagement to Congress; with some tact, he described their performance as an "act of intemperate valor."[117] When their officers were finished with them, the men of the 1st Pennsylvania were no doubt somewhat abashed. In any case, there is no further mention of the regiment for several months. It was with the force which, under Wayne, marched with Washington's army to meet the newly arrived French troops under Lt. Gen. Comte de Rochambeau at Hartford, Connecticut, on September 21, and then returned to the vicinity of Tappan, New York.[118] On September 25, when Washington reached West Point and discovered Benedict Arnold's betrayal, he hurriedly sent word to Wayne to rush reinforcements to him from Tappan in case the British were planning an immediate assault. The 1st Pennsylvania was part of the brigade under Brig. Gen. William Irvine which left shortly after midnight on September 26 and in a gruelling forced march over sixteen miles of twisting roads through the mountains reached the threatened garrison in the remarkably short time of four hours.[119]

Despite its past loyalty, by the time the 1st Pennsylvania reached its winter encampment at Morristown in December, its men were finally nearing a saturation point with regard to further endurance of hardships, deprivation, and the indifference of Congress. When the mutiny of the Pennsylvania regiments broke out on January 1, 1781, the 1st Pennsylvania joined in. Since it was the oldest of the Pennsylvania units, a particularly large number of its members had long service, and in the settlement which was eventually reached, a substantial number of them took their discharges. Although the 1st Pennsylvania was one of the six regiments of the Pennsylvania Line which were retained, it did not actually exist as a unit: many of the officers and men nominally assigned to it were on furlough, and the bulk of those who were available for duty were dispersed among the three new battalions which were formed for deployment to Virginia. Finally, in November or December, 1783, the 1st Pennsylvania was formally disbanded at the time that the Continental Army as a whole was mustered out.

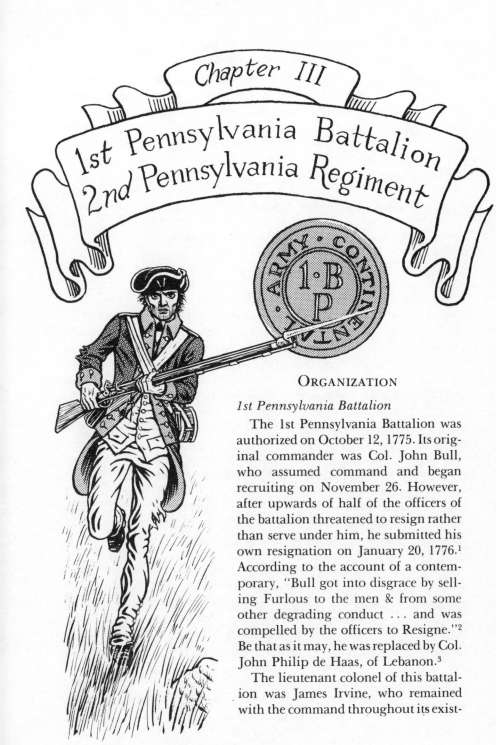

Chapter III

1st Pennsylvania Battalion
2nd Pennsylvania Regiment

ORGANIZATION

1st Pennsylvania Battalion

The 1st Pennsylvania Battalion was authorized on October 12, 1775. Its original commander was Col. John Bull, who assumed command and began recruiting on November 26. However, after upwards of half of the officers of the battalion threatened to resign rather than serve under him, he submitted his own resignation on January 20, 1776.[1] According to the account of a contemporary, "Bull got into disgrace by selling Furlous to the men & from some other degrading conduct ... and was compelled by the officers to Resigne."[2] Be that as it may, he was replaced by Col. John Philip de Haas, of Lebanon.[3]

The lieutenant colonel of this battalion was James Irvine, who remained with the command throughout its existence. Similarly, the battalion's major—Anthony James Morris—served in that capacity until the battalion was mustered out.[4]

Like all the numbered battalions of Pennsylvania troops raised during late 1775 and early 1776, this organization had eight companies. Only two company muster rolls have survived, however, so there is no way of identifying the regional origins of the companies except through the assumption that the men of each company were recruited in the counties where their original captains resided. The battalion's companies were as follows:

• [Company A], commanded by Capt. William Allen, Jr. As he was promoted to lieutenant colonel and transferred to the 2d Pennsylvania Battalion on January 4, 1776,[5] he did not actually serve with the unit. On the other hand, even by early January, recruiting would have been well advanced, and it is probable that he had a considerable hand in it. He himself was a resident of Philadelphia,[6] although as of October, 1776, he held lands in Northampton County.[7] His replacement as company commander was Capt. Benjamin Davis,[8] who may be the Benjamin Davis listed as a land warrantee in Northampton County in 1774;[9] that fact, however, would not necessarily make him a resident of that county. Captain Davis commanded the company from the date of his promotion from first lieutenant (January 5, 1776) until the battalion ceased to exist.[10]

• [Company B], commanded by Capt. Jonathan Jones, of Berks County. This company was one of the American units which took part in the engagement on June 9, 1776, at Three Rivers, in Canada, where a number of its men were captured.*

• [Company C], commanded by Capt. William Williams. Thanks to the number of Welsh settlers in Pennsylvania, this was a fairly common name, and a number of men called William Williams lived in Philadelphia County on the eve of the American Revolution.[11] Collateral evidence concerning their identities, however, makes it seem more likely that Captain Williams was the man of that name who owned land in Berks County in 1773.[12]

• [Company D], commanded by Capt. Josiah Harmar. According to the article on Harmar in *The Dictionary of American Biography*, he was a resident of Philadelphia. This company was part of a force under Colonel de Haas which, on May 25, 1776, reinforced the troops under Benedict Arnold at La Chine, in Canada, when Arnold was seriously threatened by a British and Indian force from Detroit. As of October 20,

---

*PA(5), II, 63. The date of this attack is variously given as June 9 and June 10. See Tucker, p. 39.

1776, the company was part of the garrison of Ticonderoga.[13] Captain Harmar was still with Colonel de Haas and the remnants of the battalion at New Germantown, New Jersey, on December 8, 1776.[14]

• [Company E], commanded by Capt. Thomas Dorsey, who in 1774 had been a resident of Philadelphia.[15] This company was one of the first elements of the battalion to leave for Canada, departing Philadelphia on January 22, 1776. Before February 15, it had moved beyond Albany, New York, but by that time it had lost nine men by desertion and had left fourteen more hospitalized at Albany.[16] Since its authorized strength was only seventy-six men, it was now down to no more than fifty-three non-commissioned officers and privates, plus its three officers. Captain Dorsey was still with what was left of the battalion at New Germantown, New Jersey, on December 8, 1776.[17]

• [Company F], commanded by Capt. William Jenkins, of Philadelphia.[18] This company is mentioned as having passed through Three Rivers, on its way to join the main army before Quebec, on March 12, 1776. Falling back with that force, it took part in the June 9 attack on the enemy troops now garrisoning Three Rivers. On August 5, Captain Jenkins was granted leave,[19] apparently not returning to the battalion, as he resigned his commission on September 6.[20] He would seem to have been replaced as company commander by 1st Lt. Jacob Ashmead.[21]

• [Company G], commanded by Capt. Augustin Willet. Captain Willet lived in Bucks County.[22] The only specific references to this company are that it was serving with the battalion at St. John's, Canada, on June 16, 1776, and that it was at Ticonderoga as of October 20.[23]

• [Company H], commanded by Capt. Marien Lamar, of Philadelphia.* This company was part of a detachment under Colonel de Haas which, on May 25, 1776, reinforced Benedict Arnold at La Chine.[24] It was at St. John's on June 16, and at Ticonderoga on October 20.[25] Meanwhile, on September 20, Captain Lamar had been appointed major of the newly authorized 4th Pennsylvania Regiment.[26] There is no information as to who replaced him as company commander during the brief time that the battalion remained in existence.

The prescribed uniform of the battalion was a brown coat, faced with green (buff, according to some accounts), with pewter buttons stamped "No. 1," buff breeches, white stockings, and black half-gaiters. In the field, the men wore hunting shirts and overalls made of linen or deerskin, depending on season and availability.[27]

---

*PA(3), XIV, 271. The statement that "he was probably from Northampton County" — see PA(5), II, 1031, Note — would seem to be in error.

2d Pennsylvania Regiment

The 2d Pennsylvania Regiment was formed around a nucleus of personnel from the 1st Pennsylvania Battalion, with some 339 of the enlisted men of the old unit joining the new organization when the battalion was mustered out in December, 1776.[28]

Colonel de Haas briefly commanded the regiment, but was promoted to brigadier general on February 21, 1777.[29] He was replaced by James Irvine, who was transferred from command of the 9th Pennsylvania, and who had served until October 25, 1776, as lieutenant colonel of the 1st Pennsylvania Battalion. He was carried as commander of the 2d Pennsylvania Regiment (apparently never joining) for only three months, resigning from the army on June 1, 1777.[30] To replace him, Henry Bicker was promoted from lieutenant colonel, 6th Pennsylvania Regiment. Bicker held the command for over a year. On July 1, 1778, however, the 2d Pennsylvania Regiment absorbed the 13th Pennsylvania Regiment; as Col. Walter Stewart, of the 13th Pennsylvania, was senior to Bicker, Stewart became the regimental commander and Bicker, thus rendered supernumerary, left the army.[31] Colonel Stewart remained in command for the rest of the war.[32]

The original lieutenant colonel of the 2d Pennsylvania Regiment was Anthony James Morris, who had been major of the 1st Pennsylvania Battalion. On March 12, 1777, he was promoted to colonel and transferred to the 9th Pennsylvania Regiment. The new lieutenant colonel was Jonathan Jones, promoted from major. His health, damaged during the Canadian expedition, made it impossible for him to continue serving,[33] and he resigned his commission almost immediately — on April 5, 1777.[34] The lieutenant-colonelcy remained vacant for more than a year, not being filled until the organizational reshuffling of the whole army on July 1, 1778. On that date, Henry Miller was promoted from major, 1st Pennsylvania Regiment,[35] but after less than six months — on December 8, 1778 — he resigned.[36] This brought the promotion from major of John Murray, who continued as lieutenant colonel of the regiment until January 17, 1781.[37]

The first major of the 2d Pennsylvania Regiment was Jonathan Jones, who had been a captain in the 1st Pennsylvania Battalion. As noted above, he was promoted to lieutenant colonel on March 12, 1777. At that time, William Williams (another company commander from the 1st Pennsylvania Battalion) was promoted from captain to replace him. Williams was wounded and taken prisoner at the Battle of Germantown on October 4, 1777; he was exchanged on April 20, 1778 (some accounts state that he escaped), and at that time was promoted to lieutenant colonel, 3d Pennsylvania Regiment. The majority remained vacant from that time (as a matter of practical reality, it had been vacant since Germantown) until July 1, 1778, when it was filled by John Murray. He had been major of the 13th Pennsylvania Regiment, which was now consolidated with the 2d Pennsylvania. Upon his promotion to lieutenant colonel on December 10, 1778, he was succeeded as major by James Hamilton, promoted from captain, 1st Pennsylvania Regiment, who remained with the regiment for the rest of the war.[38]

Of the captains who were serving in the 1st Pennsylvania Battalion at the time its men's enlistments expired, only William Williams became a captain in the 2d Pennsylvania Regiment, and he was very soon promoted to major. (Captains Benjamin Davis,[39] Thomas Dorsey,[40] and Augustin Willet[41] resigned on January 1, 1777; Capt. Jonathan Jones was appointed to the new regiment as its first major; [42] and Capt. Josiah Harmar became major of the 3d Pennsylvania Regiment.[43]) However, six of the original captains of the new regiment had been lieutenants in the old battalion.

The practically complete absence of any continuity of company commanders between the battalion and the regiment, even apart from the lack of battalion muster rolls, makes it impossible to establish any identification between companies of the battalion and corresponding companies of the regiment. A number of factors, moreover, make it difficult to associate specific companies of the regiment with the particular captains who commanded them, even though some company muster rolls for the regiment have survived: the regiment experienced at least two major reorganizations (one when the entire organizational structure of Continental regiments was altered on May 27, 1778, and a second when the 13th Pennsylvania was absorbed on July 1, 1778); both reorganizations resulted in several captains of the original 2d Pennsylvania Regiment becoming supernumerary and leaving the army; captains were in some cases shifted from one company to another; and the available muster rolls do not represent complete coverage of all companies throughout the whole period of the regiment's existence. However, a comparison of the muster rolls which are available, together with data from existing rosters of officers, permits reasonably sure identification of most of the companies at the various stages of the regiment's service.

The regiment's companies (not necessarily corresponding to the companies bearing the same designations in the battalion) were as follows:

• [Company A], commanded by Capt. John Patterson, presumably one of the four men of that name living in Philadelphia in 1774.[44] He had been a second lieutenant in the 1st Pennsylvania Battalion and served as a captain, 2d Pennsylvania Regiment throughout the war.[45]

• [Company B], commanded by Capt. John Bankson, of Philadelphia.[46] He had been a first lieutenant in the 1st Pennsylvania Battalion. On October 14, 1778, he became the regiment's Quartermaster and Inspector, probably vacating command of his company.[47] The name of the officer who succeeded him is not known, but by July 1, 1780, this unit had become the "Colonel's Company" of the regiment — nominally coming under the immediate command of Col. Walter Stewart but actually under Capt. John Irwin (or Irvine), who had been promoted from captain-lieutenant in May, 1780.[48] It is important to note that as of September 9, 1778, another unit of the regiment had been the "Colonel's Company" (see Company D, below).

• [Company C], commanded by Capt. William Williams, of Berks County. As he had been a company commander in the 1st Pennsylvania Battalion, it is likely that some of the men of his former unit joined his company when the regiment was organized. Upon his promotion to major on March 12, 1777, he was replaced by Capt. Joseph Howell,[49] probably one of the men of that name living in Philadelphia in 1774.[50] Howell had served as a captain in Atlee's State Battalion of Musketry[51] until he was captured at the Battle of Long Island on August 27, 1776. Following his exchange on December 9, 1776,[52] he was appointed captain in the Pennsylvania State Regiment (which became the 13th Pennsylvania Regiment), and on July 1, 1778, was transferred to the 2d Pennsylvania Regiment. On August 27, 1778, he became the Regimental Paymaster,[53] but resigned on October 1.[54] Lack of muster rolls makes it impossible to determine who succeeded him as company commander.

• [Company D], commanded by Capt. Roger Staynor, of Philadelphia. He had been a first lieutenant in the 1st Pennsylvania Battalion. On September 26, 1777, while visiting his home, he was taken prisoner when British and Hessian troops occupied Philadelphia. He was not exchanged until November 4, 1780, and never returned to duty.[55] The company was then commanded by Capt. Peter Gosner,[56] who was still in command on September 9, 1778, even though as of that date the unit was listed as the "Colonel's Company" of the regiment.[57] As already noted, by May of 1780 this company was no longer the "Colonel's Company." Although Captain Gosner remained with the regiment until January, 1781,[58] this company was not under his command in April, 1780; its commander at that time is listed as being Capt. John Bankson,[59] who apparently had assumed command in addition to or in lieu of his duties as Regimental Quartermaster and Inspector. It may be that Captain Gosner had been shifted to the command of Company C.

• [Company E], commanded by Capt. George Jenkins, of

Philadelphia.[60] After Captain Jenkins was wounded at Paoli on September 20, 1777, he did not return to duty.[61] The unit became the "Major's Company" of the regiment, and after the absorption of the 13th Pennsylvania Regiment by the 2d Pennsylvania Regiment on July 1, 1778, it came under Major John Murray, of what is now Dauphin County. Major Murray had been a captain in Miles's State Rifle Regiment and major of the Pennsylvania State Regiment,[62] continuing in the same position when that organization became the 13th Pennsylvania Regiment and becoming major in the 2d Pennsylvania Regiment when it absorbed the 13th Pennsylvania.[63] On Murray's promotion to lieutenant colonel on December 10, 1778,[64] this company did not become the "Lieutenant Colonel's Company" but continued as the "Major's Company," coming under the command of Major James Hamilton, who at this time was promoted from captain, 1st Pennsylvania Regiment.[65] Major Hamilton is shown as commander of this company through May, 1780,[66] and remained on the regiment's rolls until the organization was officially disbanded.[67]

• [Company F], initially commanded by Capt. Jacob Ashmead, of Germantown, Philadelphia County.[68] He had been a first lieutenant in the 1st Pennsylvania Battalion,[69] and apparently succeeded to command of a company when Capt. William Jenkins resigned (see above). There is some basis for assuming, therefore, that Company F of the regiment was initially the same in personnel composition as Company F of the battalion. In the regiment, this company lost heavily by desertion in the spring of 1777 (of twenty-eight privates on its muster roll of May 3, 1777, no less than twelve are marked as having deserted).[70] By July, 1778, recruits and men transferred from the 13th Pennsylvania had made this company virtually a new organization.[71] At some time during the winter of 1779, Ashmead was transferred to command another unit (see Company H, below), and Capt. John Cobea, promoted from first lieutenant on March 11, 1779,[72] took over command of the company,[73] continuing in that position until January, 1781.[74]

• [Company G], commanded by Capt. Samuel Tolbert, whose prewar residence is not known. He had been a first lieutenant in the 1st Pennsylvania Battalion.[75] He is shown as commander of this company as of Septermber 9, 1778, and again as of June 1, 1780, although the company appears to have been for a time shortly preceding the latter date under the temporary command of Capt. Jacob Ashmead.[76]

• [Company H], whose original commander cannot be firmly identified. It may have been Capt. Christopher (or Christian) Staddel (or Staddle),[77] whose pre-war residence is not known. He had been a first lieutenant in the 1st Pennsylvania Battalion. In any case, he left the army on July 1, 1778.[78] By September 9, 1778, the company was nominally under Capt. John Marshall, of what is now Dauphin County.[79] Marshall had commanded a company in Miles's State Rifle Regiment[80] and its successor organizations, the Pennsylvania State Regiment[81] and the 13th Pennsylvania Regiment,[82] and took over this company of the 2d Pennsylvania Regiment when the 13th Pennsylvania was absorbed. However, he resigned from the army on September 25, 1778,[83] and by April, 1779, the company was under Capt. Jacob Ashmead, who was still commanding it in August, 1779.[84] On May 16, 1780, Ashmead resigned his commission.[85] There is no record of who succeeded him.

• [Company I], which was the ninth company, added to the regiment as a result of the reorganization of May 27, 1778. This unit became the "Lieutenant Colonel's Company" of the regiment, and as of September 9, 1778, was under Lt. Col. Henry Miller.[86] A number of the men in this company had been in Capt. John Robb's Company of the 13th Pennsylvania prior to the merger of July 1, 1778,[87] originally the company Robb had commanded in the Pennsylvania State Regiment,[88] coming initially from a company of Miles's State Rifle Regiment that appears to have been raised around Sunbury.[89] Lieutenant Colonel Miller resigned in December, 1778, and the company then came under the new lieutenant colonel, John Murray, who remained with the regiment until January 1, 1781.[90] As of mid-1780, however, the actual commander of the company was Capt.-Lt. John Stoy,[91] who remained on duty with the unit until January 1, 1781.[92]

Prior to the standardization of all Continental infantry uniforms in October, 1779, this regiment — made up as it was of men from different parent organizations — seems to have been dressed in a mixture of uniforms: the brown of the 1st Pennsylvania Battalion, the red-faced blue coat of the Pennsylvania State Regiment, along with hunting shirts and vari-colored civilian clothing.[93]

Summary

Despite the complexity of this unit's organizational history, it seems likely that in its original configuration, the 1st Pennsylvania Battalion, it was recruited primarily in the city and what was then the county of Philadelphia and in the neighboring areas of Berks, Bucks, and possibly Northampton counties. After the 2d Pennsylvania Regiment was formed, the regional composition undoubtedly became more varied. In April, 1778, some men were recruited in Lancaster and York counties. Parenthetically, a substantial number of these recruits were not native-born: of one list of twenty-three, eight were natives of Germany, four of Ireland, one of England, the remaining ten being American-born.[94] Of forty men in the Lieutenant Colonel's Company in mid-1780, seventeen had been born in America but eleven were born in Ireland, five each in Germany and England, and two in Scotland. The seventeen native Americans were mostly from Pennsylvania, but one was from Delaware and another from New Jersey; also, these Pennsylvanians were from relatively scattered counties — four from Lancaster, two each from Berks, Chester, Northumberland, Philadelphia, and York, and one each from Northampton and what is now Lebanon.[95]

The absorption of the 13th Pennsylvania Regiment on July 1, 1778, would surely have brought a considerable change in the regional complexion of the 2d Pennsylvania Regiment, as the members of the 13th Pennsylvania were residents of counties throughout the State (see Chapter XVII).

OPERATIONS

1st Pennsylvania Battalion

The 1st Pennsylvania Battalion, functioning for the most part in company detachments, served in the campaign in Canada between January and July, 1776. On January 22, the first company of the battalion to leave Pennsylvania (Captain Dorsey's) started for New York City, from which point it moved by sloop up the Hudson to Albany, New York. It was quickly followed by five more companies. In the case of all six of these units, the combination of sickness and desertion sharply reduced their strength; half of the men lacked weapons which were capable of being fired, and almost all had to be issued shoes, socks, and cold weather clothing.[96]

From Albany, the route followed by the companies in question was Fort Edwards-Fort William Henry (later renamed Fort George)-Fort Ticonderoga-Crown Point, mostly by sloop and bateaux but partly on foot. Proceeding north by Lake Champlain, they went on by way of the Sorel River to the St. Lawrence, then northeast down the St. Lawrence to Three Rivers, the first elements of the battalion passing that point on March 1. From there, they went on for ninety more miles to join the American army deployed near Quebec. By March 30, a total of four companies of this battalion, mustering 225 men, were at Quebec; as of April 12, two other companies had not yet left Fort George; and the remaining two, with Colonel de Haas, were still en route from New York.[97]

Before the laggard companies could come up, the attempt to take Quebec was abandoned, and on May 6 the American army began a withdrawal up the St. Lawrence past Three Rivers, which it reached on May 15, to Sorel. A detachment, under Benedict Arnold, was nine miles farther upstream at La Chine. On May 25, word was received that Arnold was being seriously threatened by a large British and Indian force.

Colonel de Haas had now reached the field, and he was sent with some four hundred men from several units, including the companies of his own battalion under Capt. Josiah Harmar and Capt. Marien Lamar (D and H) to reinforce Arnold. Their arrival caused the British to fall back. Arnold wanted to take the offensive and ordered De Haas to attack a nearby Indian village, but De Haas refused.[98]

In the meantime, British forces had begun a cautious pursuit from Quebec, and early in June, scouts reported that an eight hundred-man advance guard of mixed British Regulars and Canadian militiamen was now at Three Rivers, well beyond ready supporting distance of its main army. On June 7, Brig. Gen. William Thompson moved from Sorel with some three thousand men to attack Three Rivers.[99] Included in this force were Capt. Jonathan Jones's and Capt. William Jenkins' companies (B and F) and possibly others of the 1st Pennsylvania Battalion.[100]

The operation was a disaster. The American approach was discovered, and on the morning of June 9 (June 10, according to some versions), as the troops marched along the river bank, they were taken under naval gunfire from British frigates in the St. Lawrence. To escape, they pushed inland, bogging down in a dense swamp which held them trapped for four hours. The units became separated, many of them never reaching the enemy.[101] Those who did make contact found that the British garrison at Three Rivers had been strongly reinforced. Outnumbered, the Americans were soon driven back into the swamp, trying to escape. Substantial numbers were cut off and captured. Fortunately, the British made no pursuit, and the survivors straggled back individually and in small groups to Sorel, some of them not arriving until June 14.[102]

On June 15, the Americans began a retreat southward from Sorel up the Sorel River,[103] reaching St. John's on June 16. In the meantime, British troops had moved toward Montreal, threatening to encircle Arnold's command (including Colonel de Haas and his detachment). Only just in time, Arnold's force escaped the trap, and by a forced march joined the main army at St. John's, also arriving on June 16. At this point, all eight companies of the 1st Pennsylvania Battalion were finally united for the first time since their enlistment.[104] But the British were on their heels, and the Americans promptly resumed their retreat. On June 18, they halted for a time at Isle Aux Noix, up the Sorel River. There the battalion was swept by illness, which struck Colonel de Haas, all the field officers, and a number of the men. On June 25, the army began moving to Isle la Motte, sailing from there on June 27 for Crown Point, where it arrived on July 1. After something more than a week's stay, on July 10 the bulk of the force — including the 1st Pennsylvania Battalion — moved on to Ticonderoga. As of August 24, the battalion mustered 521 personnel, 157 of whom were listed as sick.[105]

By that time, the four Pennsylvania battalions of the expedition were formed into a brigade under Col. Arthur St. Clair.[106] The 1st Pennsylvania Battalion remained at Ticonderoga through the fall, enduring shortages of weapons and equipment. On October 20, the unit's total strength was reported as being 540—245 below its authorized manning level. Colonel de Haas offered the view at that time that "there is not the least reason to think that any of the men will reenlist at this place." Even so, although the enlistments were due to expire on October 27, the men agreed to remain for three more weeks to help safeguard Ticonderoga. By that time it was clear that winter would prevent any British offensive, so on November 13 the 1st Pennsylvania Battalion was relieved and sent home. By December 8, a remnant of the unit was at New Germantown, New Jersey, the bulk of the men having been mustered out.[107]

2d Pennsylvania Regiment

Despite the pessimism of Colonel de Haas, 340 of the total of approximately five hundred enlisted men who had served at Ticonderoga did join the 2d Pennsylvania Regiment when it was formed, although one man failed to pass muster,[108] presumably on physical grounds. Recruiting began at once, and there is evidence that Colonel de Haas and elements of the new regiment had joined Washington's army at Trenton in time to take part in the Battle of Princeton on January 3, 1777, serving in the brigade commanded by Brig. Gen. Thomas Mifflin. However, they could have formed only a small contingent, as the five Pennsylvania Continental "regiments" in that brigade together totaled only some five hundred men.[109]

During the winter months at Morristown, New Jersey, which followed, the regiment built up its strength. Colonel de Haas was replaced by Col. James Irvine, and he in turn by Col. Henry Bicker, although Bicker did not actually join from his former command until some time in October. In the meantime, as part of Brig. Gen. Anthony Wayne's division, the 2d Pennsylvania Regiment operated under the senior officer present for duty, Major William Williams.[110] He led it in the patrol actions in New Jersey during the spring and summer, including the engagement at Bound Brook on April 12 or 13[111] and a skirmish at Amboy, on April 25, in which one officer was killed.[112] He was also in command at the Battle of Brandywine (September 11, 1777), the affair at Paoli (September 20, 1777), and the Battle of Germantown (October 4, 1777), where he was wounded and taken prisoner.[113] Detachments from the regiment also took part in the engagement between American outposts and a British scouting force at Iron Hill, on September 3, 1777.[114]

At Brandywine, the 2d Pennsylvania Regiment was part of the force guarding Chadd's Ford until the British diversionary force stormed across the creek and compelled Wayne to withdraw his division. It sustained some casualties at Paoli, where one of its officers was killed.[115] At Germantown, it was in the left-flank element of the force making the attack against the British center, falling back with the division when other American troops fired on it by mistake. By this time it had suffered extensive losses. With the capture of Major Williams, Capt. Joseph Howell became acting regimental commander; only one other captain (Christian Staddel), nine junior officers, three officers of the regimental staff, and seventy-four enlisted men were present for duty at the end of October; seventeen more enlisted men were reported as sick, and twenty-four others as being on detached service.[116] Such men as could be mustered, however, were present at Whitemarsh in early December, posted to the right of the center of the first line of the American defenses. The British made an abortive assault early in December, but did not come within range of this part of the line.[117]

Although sickness was a major problem during the winter while the regiment was at Valley Forge, the command was apparently brought up to something more nearly approximating reasonable manning levels. On June 19, 1778, it left Valley Forge in Wayne's division to pursue the British across New Jersey, and on June 28 took part in the Battle of Monmouth. In that battle, its principal service was as part of a provisional brigade under Lt. Col. Aaron Burr, when it made a charge from the left flank on a British force trying to cross a causeway across a swamp to attack the American center. The British were halted, but artillery fire forced the Americans to withdraw, sustaining several casualties.[118] However, only two men of the regiment were wounded.[119]

As already noted, on July 1 the 2d Pennsylvania Regiment absorbed the 13th Pennsylvania, whose colonel (Walter Stewart) became commander of the consolidated regiment. Under him it operated in the area along the New Jersey-New York border, moving early in December to Middlebrook, New Jersey, for the winter of 1778-1779.[120] There is no record of any particular action involving the regiment during the summer of 1779, but in October it was at West Point in Anthony Wayne's brigade, and its strength is shown as 452 officers and men.[121] From there, it moved to winter quarters at Morristown, New Jersey.[122]

With the spring of 1780, the 2d Pennsylvania Regiment was once again involved in a succession of minor skirmishes and patrol actions. One of these, which cost the life of one of the regiment's junior officers, took place on May 18, at Paramus, New Jersey.[123] Another was at Connecticut Farms, New Jersey, on June 7.[124] It was also at the blockhouse at Bergen Heights on July 21, where the regiment joined the 1st Pennsylvania in driving forward in a hopeless attack, despite the attempts of the officers to restrain the men[125] (see Chapter II). In this action, two of its lieutenants were mortally wounded,[126] although it is not clear whether they became casualties before the actual assault or while it was taking place.

The regiment was also with Wayne on the September 21 march to Hartford, Connecticut, to greet General Rochambeau, and the return to Tappan, New York,[127] and it was with the troops making the forced march from Tappan to West Point to reinforce the garrison there on September 25 after Benedict Arnold's defection was discovered.[128]

In December, the 2d Pennsylvania moved to Morristown, New Jersey, to begin another winter. It was there, on January 1, 1781, that the mutiny broke out among the Pennsylvania troops. At first, the men of this regiment refused to side with the revolt, but when they were threatened at bayonet point, and cannon were brought up, they joined the mutineers.[129]

The reorganization which followed this event perpetuated a 2d Pennsylvania Regiment among the six regiments retained to comprise the Pennsylvania Line. However, this establishment existed primarily on paper. Regimental personnel who remained in the army served chiefly in one of the three provisional battalions which were formed in the spring of 1781 for operations in Virginia and, later, in South Carolina. As a regiment, the 2d Pennsylvania ceased to exist as a functioning organization.

Chapter IV

2nd Pennsylvania Battalion
3rd Pennsylvania Regiment

Arthur St. Clair

ORGANIZATION

2d Pennsylvania Battalion

Authority to raise the 2d Pennsylvania Battalion was issued on December 9, 1775, and on January 3, 1776, Col. Arthur St. Clair was appointed its commander.[1] Upon his promotion to brigadier general on August 9, 1776, command passed to Joseph Wood, promoted from lieutenant colonel.[2]

The officer who first became lieutenant colonel of the battalion was William Allen, Jr., promoted from captain, 1st Pennsylvania Battalion.[3] He was the son and namesake of the man who had been chief justice of Pennsylvania until 1774. While the Allens opposed British oppression, they favored reform rather than a complete break with the Crown.[4] Accordingly, when the Declaration of Independence was issued, Lieutenant Colonel Allen resigned his commission, effective July 24, 1776,[5] later becoming lieutenant colonel of a Tory battalion in the British service.[6] He was replaced as lieutenant colonel of the 2d

Pennsylvania Battalion by Joseph Wood, promoted from major.[7] When Wood was promoted to colonel to succeed Arthur St. Clair, Thomas Craig was promoted from captain, effective September 29, 1776.[8]

The battalion's first major was Joseph Wood. When he was promoted to lieutenant colonel, he was replaced as major by William Butler, promoted from captain on September 7, 1776.[9]

The eight companies of the battalion were as follows:

• [Company A], enlisted primarily from Northampton County, was initially commanded by Capt. Thomas Craig. When Captain Craig was promoted to lieutenant colonel in September, 1776, he was succeeded as company commander by Capt. Rudolph Bunner,[10] transferred from command of Company D[11] (see below). This company took part in the attack on Three Rivers, in Canada, on June 9, 1776.[12]

• [Company B], enlisted from the vicinity of Greensburg, Westmoreland County, was first commanded by Capt. William Butler. As noted, Butler was promoted to major on September 7, 1776. The new company commander was Capt. James Chrystie (or Christie),* promoted from first lieutenant of Company E[13] (see below). This company also fought at Three Rivers.[14]

• [Company C], commanded by Capt. John Brisban. Information on where this company was recruited has not been found. Brisban himself was probably from Northampton County, as he was commanding a State company there[15] after leaving the Continental service on September 2, 1777. Company C evidently fought at Three Rivers, as Brisban was wounded in that engagement.[16]

• [Company D], commanded by Capt. Rudolph Bunner. In 1774, Rudolph Bunner lived in Philadelphia.[17] As noted above, in the fall of 1776 he was transferred to command Company A,[18] being replaced in Company D by Samuel Moore,[19] promoted from first lieutenant of Company G[20] (see below). Like the previously mentioned companies, this unit took part in the action at Three Rivers.[21]

• [Company E], originally commanded by Capt. Stephen Bayard.[22] Again, there is no information regarding the area in which this company was recruited, but Bayard himself had been a resident of Philadelphia in 1774.[23] There is also no information indicating specific combat operations in which the company may have participated.

• [Company F], commanded by Capt. John Huling.[24] Like the preceding unit, no information concerning the company's origin has been found. Captain Huling, however, would appear to be the John

---

*PA(5), II, 97. However, the *date* given in the preceding reference for Butler's promotion to major (*October* 7, 1776) is incorrect. See Heitman, p. 138 and PA(5), II, 911.

Huling who lived in Berks County in 1767[25] and 1768.[26] This company was one of those which is known to have fought at Three Rivers.[27]

• [Company G], commanded by Capt. John Reese.[28] Although there were several contemporaries named John Reese, Captain Reese would seem to be one of the two men of that name living in Philadelphia or Philadelphia County in 1774.[29] This company fought at Three Rivers on June 9, 1776.[30]

• [Company H], commanded by Capt. Samuel Watson.[31] Captain Watson's pre-war residence is not known, although conceivably he could have been the man of that name living in Bedford County in 1774.[32] Initially commissioned as a first lieutenant in the 1st Pennsylvania Battalion, he was promoted to captain and transferred to the 2d Pennsylvania Battalion shortly after its organization. He died at Three Rivers on May 21, 1776,[33] and was replaced by Thomas L. Moore, promoted from first lieutenant of Company D.[34]

The enlistments of the members of the 2d Pennsylvania Battalion expired on January 5, 1777, but the organization did not leave Fort Ticonderoga for home until January 24,[35] being discharged after returning to Pennsylvania.

The only information regarding the uniform of this battalion is taken from the descriptions of men who deserted from it. One was wearing a blue coat with buttons marked "2 B. P." and a red waistcoat, another wore a hunting shirt, and a third a brown military coat.[36]

3d Pennsylvania Regiment

Recruiting for the new 3d Pennsylvania Regiment had begun as early as December, 1776. However, as members of the 2d Pennsylvania Battalion returned from Ticonderoga, a considerable number joined this regiment, which was accepted in the Continental Army on March 12, 1777.[37]

The first commander of the 3d Pennsylvania Regiment was Col. Joseph Wood, continuing in the position he had held in the 2d Pennsylvania Battalion. He resigned in July, 1777,[38] finding himself unable to serve because of the wounds he had received on October 11, 1776,[39] in the battle on Lake Champlain between the Americans' improvised fleet and the British ships trying to land troops on Valcour Island, when he had been hit in his left leg and arm.[40] Thomas Craig was then promoted from lieutenant colonel to command the regiment, holding that position throughout the rest of the war.[41]

Craig had been the last lieutenant colonel of the 2d Pennsylvania Battalion, and held the same position when the 3d Pennsylvania Regiment was formed. Replacing him as lieutenant colonel when he was promoted to command the regiment was Rudolph Bunner, promoted from major. When Bunner was killed at the Battle of Monmouth, on June 28, 1778, his successor was William Williams, promoted from major, 2d Pennsylvania Regiment. Williams appears to have resigned from the army on April 27, 1780, when he was replaced by Lt. Col. Christopher Stuart, of the 5th Pennsylvania Regiment.[42]

The original major of the 3d Pennsylvania Regiment was Josiah Harmar, promoted from captain, 1st Pennsylvania Battalion. Within a short time (on June 6, 1777), he was promoted to lieutenant colonel, 6th Pennsylvania Regiment, and Rudolph Bunner became major in his place. When Bunner was promoted to lieutenant colonel (on August 1, 1777), John Huling was promoted from captain; but with the reorganization of July 1, 1778, Huling was rendered supernumerary and "deranged." The officer who replaced him was Thomas Langhorne Byles, who had been a captain in the 3d Pennsylvania Battalion. Byles was killed in action at Paramus, New Jersey, on April 16, 1780. To take his place, William Alexander was promoted from captain, 7th Pennsylvania Regiment, remaining in this position for the rest of the regiment's existence.[43]

The eight captains of the original 3d Pennsylvania Regiment had also commanded companies in the 2d Pennsylvania Battalion. These were Rudolph Bunner, Stephen Bayard, John Huling, John Reese, John Brisban, Thomas L. Moore, James Chrystie, and Samuel Moore.[44] However, comparison of available muster rolls indicates a certain amount of shifting around of captains.

Two groups of rosters for this regiment have survived. One is for the period of August-September, 1778; the other is dated in the April-May period of 1780. Thus, both relate to the period after the date (July 1, 1778) when the 3d Pennsylvania Regiment absorbed the 12th Pennsylvania Regiment (see Chapter XIII). The latter organization had been recruited in Northampton and Northumberland counties, mostly on the West Branch of the Susquehanna River.[45] The only muster roll of the 12th Pennsylvania is extremely fragmentary,[46] but it does include the names of eighteen soldiers who can be identified on the 3d Pennsylvania Regiment's rosters. These men were spread among several 3d Pennsylvania companies rather than remaining together.

By the late summer of 1778, Captain Bunner had been promoted to major and lieutenant colonel and had been killed in action (see above); Captain Bayard had been promoted to major, 8th Pennsylvania Regiment; Captain Huling had been promoted to major, 9th Pennsylvania Regiment;[47] Captain Reese had resigned (on December 31, 1777);[48] and Captain Brisban had also resigned (on September 2, 1777).[49] The enlisted veterans of the 2d Pennsylvania Battalion had been extensively scattered among the companies of the 3d Pennsylvania Regiment; but, to a considerable extent, several of the companies retained a nucleus of their original members.

The companies of the regiment were as follows:

• [Company A], made up of men from several of the old companies, also contained recruits and probably men formerly in the 12th Pennsylvania Regiment. When the regiment was first formed, this may have been the company commanded from July 4, 1777, to April 9, 1778 (when he resigned), by Capt. Henry Epple.[50] It is equally possible, however, that Epple commanded Company F or Company G, instead (see below). It is likely, although not certain, that this unit became the "Colonel's Company" of the regiment after July 1, 1778, remaining nominally under Col. Thomas Craig's direct command.[51]

• [Company B] was by the late summer of 1778 under Capt. Thomas Butler. He had been a first lieutenant in this company in the 2d Pennsylvania Battalion.[52] He had particularly distinguished himself by rallying retreating troops at the Battle of Brandywine on September 11, 1777, and remained in command of this company until January 1, 1781.[53]

• [Company C] was commanded by Capt. William Craig, who had been an ensign and second lieutenant in Company F of the 2d Pennsylvania Battalion,[54] and was promoted from first lieutenant on July 4, 1777.[55] He resigned his commission on June 1, 1779.[56] It cannot be established with certainty who then took over command of this company, as muster rolls of 1780 do not cover all of the companies for which rolls were prepared in 1778, and no men listed in the 1778 roster of this unit can be found listed in the rolls which do exist for 1780.

• [Company D] was under Capt. Samuel Moore, who had succeeded to its command in the 2d Pennsylvania Battalion (see above). However, he became a supernumerary by reason of the absorption of the 12th Pennsylvania Regiment on July 1, 1778, and the company came (at least, by April, 1780) under the command of Capt. Isaac Budd Dunn. In the 2d Pennsylvania Battalion, Dunn had been a second lieutenant in Company E[57] and a first lieutenant in Company A.[58] As he held rank as a captain from October 6, 1776 (although apparently on staff duty rather than commanding a company), he was senior enough at the time of the 1778 reorganization to displace Samuel Moore.[59] When the mutiny of the Pennsylvania Line on January 1, 1781, effectively ended the existence of the 3d Pennsylvania Regiment, Dunn became aide-de-camp, in grade of major, to Maj. Gen. Arthur St. Clair, serving in that capacity to 1783.[60]

• [Company E] was commanded by Capt. James Chrystie, who had been the commander of Company B in the battalion. Chrystie was a native of Edinburgh, Scotland, who had arrived in Pennsylvania only in

1775.[61] Apparently a popular commander, he brought many of the men from his company of the 2d Pennsylvania Battalion into the 3d Pennsylvania Regiment,[62] although he himself was, by 1778, commanding a different company from that in which most of his former soldiers were serving. He continued in command of Company E throughout the war.[63]

• [Company F] may have been under Capt. Henry Epple from July 4, 1777, to April 9, 1778 (see Company A above). It appears to be the unit which eventually was assigned to Capt. John Reily, who was transferred to the 3d Pennsylvania Regiment from the 12th Pennsylvania on July 1, 1778.[64] Reily, however, refused to join the 3d Pennsylvania,[65] and was replaced by John Marshall (not to be confused with the Capt. John Marshall mentioned in Chapter III), promoted from captain-lieutenant.[66]

• [Company G] may originally have been commanded by Capt. Henry Epple (see Company A above). After July 1, 1778, it became the "Major's Company" of the regiment. It thus was commanded by Major Thomas L. Byles. He had been a captain in the 3d Pennsylvania Battalion and was taken prisoner at Fort Washington on November 16, 1776. Following his exchange, he was appointed major, 3d Pennsylvania Regiment, effective July 1, 1778.[67] After he was mortally wounded at Paramus, New Jersey, on April 16, 1780, he was replaced by Major William Alexander, promoted from captain, 7th Pennsylvania Regiment. Major Alexander retained command of this company throughout the rest of the war.[68]

• [Company H] was commanded by Capt. Thomas L. Moore, who had eventually been its commander in the 2d Pennsylvania Battalion. On May 12, 1779, he was promoted to major, 9th Pennsylvania Regiment,[69] being replaced as company commander by John Henderson, promoted from captain-lieutenant.[70]

The new organizational structure adopted in 1778 provided for a ninth company, to be commanded by the regiment's lieutenant colonel. In the 3d Pennsylvania, this company was formed of men from existing companies, men transferred from the 12th Pennsylvania Regiment, and recruits. Until April, 1780, it was commanded by Lt. Col. William Williams, after which it was under Lt. Col. Christopher Stuart.[71]

Deserters from the 3d Pennsylvania Regiment were not uniformly clad. Some wore brown coats, others blue faced with red. Apparently, veterans of the 2d Pennsylvania Battalion often continued to wear their old uniforms, as one deserter from the 3d Pennsylvania Regiment was wearing 2d Pennsylvania Battalion buttons, but with the numbers scratched out.[72]

Summary

The personnel of the battalion's Company A and Company C, largely from Northampton County, appear to have been diffused throughout several companies of the regiment; Company B of the battalion, from Westmoreland County, and Companies D, E, and G (apparently from Philadelphia), Company F (apparently from Berks County), and Company H (possibly from Bedford County) remained relatively intact in the regiment. Absorption of the 12th Pennsylvania Regiment on July 1, 1778, scattered more men from Northampton County and men from Northumberland County through the command. Thus, both the battalion and the regiment combined troops drawn from the northern and western frontier areas with those from the vicinity of Philadelphia, leaving the counties in between represented scantily or not at all.

OPERATIONS

2d Pennsylvania Battalion

As was the case with the other Pennsylvania units deployed to support American operations in Canada during the early part of 1776, this battalion was dispatched piecemeal to New York City as rapidly as its companies could be organized. By March 13, Lieutenant Colonel Allen was at New York, supervising the further movement of the battalion's advance contingent and arranging for the quartering of the companies that had not yet arrived from Pennsylvania. Almost exactly a month later, on April 12, five companies of the battalion were at Fort Edwards, leaving on April 19 for Fort George. Pushing ahead, on May 6 the detachment of the 2d Pennsylvania Battalion under Allen had come within three miles of Quebec when it made contact with the American army—just in time to join it in its withdrawal up the St. Lawrence River.[73]

At least one of the battalion's companies (Company H) may have been with the force which was dropped off at Three Rivers while the main body of the army continued to Sorel, for it was at Three Rivers on May 21 that Capt. Samuel Watson died.[74] At the time, orders were already on the way for the Three Rivers detachment to rejoin the main army, and this force reached Sorel on May 24. Colonel St. Clair and the rest of the battalion had previously arrived at Sorel (on May 16). Although the 2d Pennsylvania Battalion was now finally assembled in one place, it appears to have continued to operate in two elements, one under St. Clair and the other under Allen. In any event, for the attack on Three Rivers in early June, Colonel St. Clair commanded the force of some seven hundred troops initially scheduled to make the assault, while Allen and the remaining companies of the battalion were part of the larger force under Brig. Gen. William Thompson which almost immediately followed to reinforce them.[75]

The fiasco which took place was outlined in Chapter III. In the confused action, General Thompson was taken prisoner and Colonel St. Clair, as the next senior officer, was left in command. However, he had stumbled over a tree root, injuring his foot so painfully that he did not feel able to continue functioning, and the command devolved upon Col. Anthony Wayne. Although a considerable number of Americans broke and fled and still more, having got lost in the swamp, never got into action, Lieutenant Colonel Allen held his 2d Pennsylvania Battalion companies with Wayne's own organization (a detachment of the 4th Pennsylvania Battalion); and these, with elements of other units, made a fighting withdrawal of sorts, preventing the situation from becoming even more of a shambles than it actually did. In a letter to Benjamin Franklin, Wayne later claimed with little modesty but considerable justification that "I believe it will be Universally allowed that Col. Allen and myself saved the Army in Canada."[76]

As noted in Chapter III, the army retreated up the Sorel to St. John's, and thence via Isle Aux Noix to Isle la Motte, then to Crown Point, and finally to Ticonderoga, which the 2d Pennsylvania Battalion reached on July 10. There, on July 20, St. Clair was put in command of the 4th Brigade (comprising the four Pennsylvania battalions) of the army, which was now commanded by Maj. Gen. Horatio Gates, and Joseph Wood took charge of the 2d Pennsylvania Battalion.[77] On August 24, 1776, the battalion's strength consisted of 56 officers and 429 men, but 161 of the enlisted personnel were sick. Some of the battalion, at least, took part in the naval engagement against Gen. Guy Carleton's British force on Lake Champlain on October 11-13, for Colonel Wood was wounded in that action.[78]

By November 29, the battalion total had dropped from 485 to 426. Despite the miserable conditions and severe shortages, the troops voluntarily remained past their scheduled discharge date (January 5, 1777) until fresh units could arrive to replace them.[79] The 2d Pennsylvania Battalion did not leave Ticonderoga, therefore, until January 24, reaching Pennsylvania in mid-February. The men of the battalion had subsisted for months on nothing but "Bread or Flower, & Salt Pork or Beef," according to a March 3 petition they submitted to the Pennsylvania Council of Safety, asking for back pay due them, and were "in a Raged Dirty Condition, Enough to affright an Indian from Inlisting."[80]

3d Pennsylvania Regiment

Despite the hardships the men reported, "many" of them promptly re-enlisted, joining the 3d Pennsylvania Regiment,[81] which was then organized and recruited up to strength. When it joined the army in New Jersey in late winter or early spring of 1777, it was assigned to the brigade formerly commanded by Brig. Gen. Thomas Mifflin but now under Brig. Gen. Thomas Conway,[82] an Irish-born volunteer from the French army. During the operations in New Jersey in the spring and summer of 1777, the regiment took part in the engagements at Bound Brook, on April 12 or 13,[83] and at Short Hills, on June 26.[84]

As part of Conway's brigade, the regiment was in the right-flank wing of Washington's army at the Battle of Brandywine on September 11, 1777, and thus shared in receiving the initial surprise attack of the main body of the British army. Although Conway's brigade fought steadfastly, the American defenses eventually crumbled and men began to leave the battlefield. It was at this point that Capt. Thomas Butler performed exceptional service in rallying fleeing troops and thereby received a personal commendation from General Washington.[85]

The regiment fought next at the Battle of Germantown, on October 4, when Conway's brigade had a conspicuous part in the action. It was the center unit of the three forces making a frontal attack down the Germantown Road. This attack was on the verge of smashing through the British line when the left-flank element (Wayne's division) was fired on from the rear by other American troops and began to fall back, leading the way for the rest of the assault force to follow.

At Whitemarsh, with other elements of Conway's brigade, the 3d Pennsylvania Regiment was in the second line of the American defense. It was not involved in any fighting when the British approached and then withdrew in early December.[86] The 3d Pennsylvania was at Valley Forge during the winter of 1777-1778. It also took part in the Battle of Monmouth, on June 28, 1778.

In that engagement, Lt. Col. Rudolph Bunner was killed, having "very much distinguished himself on the field."[87] Although it is not certain, this regiment may have been one of the units making up the force under Anthony Wayne which, late in the action, first pursued the withdrawing British and then held a defensive position against a heavy counterattack until forced by superior numbers to retreat.[88] Contrary to another account,[89] however, it was not one of the three units which, a little earlier, Lt. Col. Aaron Burr had led in an attack on British forces threatening the American center. Aside from Lieutenant Colonel Bunner, the regiment had only one man wounded.[90]

Shortly after this battle, on July 1, 1778, the 3d Pennsylvania absorbed the 12th Pennsylvania Regiment.

It spent the following winter in camp at Middlebrook, New Jersey, and the summer of 1779 in patrolling the area of the New Jersey-New

York border, at least some of its members taking part in Anthony Wayne's July 16 assault on Stony Point, New York.[91] As of October 15, it was based at West Point. At that time, it was in the 2d [Pennsylvania] Brigade, under Brig. Gen. William Irvine, as part of the over-all command of Maj. Gen. Arthur St. Clair. Its strength in officers and men was 394.[92] By the time winter came, the regiment was at Morristown, New Jersey.[93]

The 1780 campaign season early brought part of the 3d Pennsylvania into combat. By April 16, Major Byles and a detachment of about two hundred troops were stationed at Paramus, New Jersey, in an area reputed to contain numerous British sympathizers. Perhaps with information provided by such people, a British infantry and cavalry force estimated to number six hundred men launched a surprise attack soon after dawn on April 16, drove off many of the Americans, and soon surrounded the house where Byles had established headquarters. Some of Byles's men obeyed his orders to continue firing, but others called for quarter. The British, shouting that this was treachery—even though Byles called out that he had not authorized anyone to surrender—broke their way into the building. Byles then tried to yield formally, but was mortally wounded in what appears to have been an act of deliberate brutality.[94]

The regiment as a whole was involved in the attack on the Bergen Heights Blockhouse three months later, on July 21. As part of Irvine's brigade, it was with the troops which moved to block the approach of a British relief force coming across the Hudson, and thus did not take part in the fruitless and costly assault on the Blockhouse itself[95] (see Chapter II).

After marching with Washington's army to Hartford, Connecticut, on September 21, 1780, the 3d Pennsylvania was back at Tappan, New York, on September 25. It was part of the force which was rushed that day to West Point to guard against a possible British thrust following Benedict Arnold's treachery.[96] How long it remained at West Point is not known, but in December it had been moved to Morristown, New Jersey, where its men took part in the mutiny that began on January 1, 1781.[97]

Although there was a 3d Pennsylvania among the six Pennsylvania regiments which were retained in the new structure which was then established, the organization which had operated as the 3d Pennsylvania Regiment since early 1777 ceased in effect to exist. Many of its men were discharged. Those who were not, or who re-enlisted, were for the most part distributed among the three provisional battalions of Pennsylvania Continentals which were redeployed to the southern theater of operations.

3rd Pennsylvania Battalion
4th Pennsylvania Regiment

Lambert Cadwalader

ORGANIZATION

3d Pennsylvania Battalion

The 3d Pennsylvania Battalion, like the 2d and 4th, was authorized on December 9, 1775. While most of its officers were residents of Philadelphia, the enlisted men were recruited not only from throughout Pennsylvania but also from New Jersey, Delaware, and Maryland.[1] Thus, it is not justifiable to attribute any precise regional identity to this battalion or to any of its component elements, although in general it seems to have been drawn to a considerable extent from the southeastern area of Pennsylvania.

The original commander of the battalion was Col. John Shee. Following his resignation on September 25, 1776, he was replaced by Lambert Cadwalader, who was promoted from lieutenant colonel.[2]

Lambert Cadwalader had been the original lieutenant colonel of the battalion. His replacement in that position was Daniel Brodhead, who was administratively transferred from Miles's State Rifle Regiment,[3] but seems never to have joined the unit.

The original major of the battalion was Henry Bicker. He was transferred on October 25, 1776, to the newly-authorized 10th Pennsylvania Regiment, and Capt. William West was promoted in his place.[4]

The eight companies of the battalion were:

• [Company A], commanded by Capt. William West. When West was promoted to major on October 25, 1776, Matthew Knox was promoted from first lieutenant to replace him.[5]

• [Company B], commanded by Capt. Alexander Graydon.[6]

• [Company C], commanded by Capt. David Lennox.[7]

• [Company D], commanded by Capt. Thomas Langhorne Byles.[8]

• [Company E], commanded by Capt. Joseph Hubley.*

• [Company F], commanded by Capt. Walter Stewart. Captain Stewart was appointed aide-de-camp to Maj. Gen. Horatio Gates on May 26, 1776. He was replaced as company commander by George Tudor, promoted from first lieutenant on June 13, 1776.[9]

• [Company G], commanded by Capt. Peter Scull, until he was appointed brigade major on March 23, 1776. Joseph Davenport was promoted from first lieutenant to replace him as company commander.[10]

• [Company H], commanded by Capt. Henry Allice. Captain Allice resigned his commission on February 27, 1776. Evan Edwards was promoted from first lieutenant on March 23, 1776, succeeding to command of this company.[11]

Presumably because practically all the members of the battalion were taken prisoner at Fort Washington, New York, on November 16, 1776 (see below), almost no muster rolls of this organization have survived. A comparison of the few records which do exist has identified the name of only one enlisted man who served both in the 3d Pennsylvania Battalion and what is traditionally regarded as its successor unit, the 4th Pennsylvania Regiment. However, the fact that considerable numbers of the officers of both organizations were the same men gives some basis for the view that the 4th Pennsylvania Regiment was formed on a nucleus of the 3d Pennsylvania Battalion. Further, because the men of the battalion had enlisted for only one year, those who were captured at Fort Washington (and who survived the rigors of imprisonment) were released on the expiration of their enlistments in January, 1777.[12] Thus, many of them may have joined the 4th Pennsylvania Regiment, which was then in process of being formed. There are no data, how-

---

*PA(5), II, 126. Captain Hubley is mentioned only once, on the battalion roster, and there is one reference to a private as belonging to Hubley's company. Hubley is not listed at all in Heitman.

ever, from which to determine any link between specific companies of the battalion and corresponding companies of the regiment.

The uniform of this battalion seems to have included a hat laced with white tape, a brown coat faced with white and bearing pewter buttons stamped "No. 3," and buckskin breeches.[13]

4th Pennsylvania Regiment

When the 4th Pennsylvania Regiment was formed in January and February, 1777, Col. Lambert Cadwalader was appointed its commander, and held this position throughout the war. However, he had been taken prisoner at Fort Washington on November 16, 1776; and while he was promptly released, he was placed on parole, and was never formally exchanged. Thus, actual command devolved upon Lt. Col. William Butler,[14] who was formally designated "Lieutenant-Colonel Commandant" on January 22, 1779,[15] continuing in that capacity throughout the life of the regiment.

The original major of the regiment was Marien Lamar, promoted from captain, 1st Pennsylvania Battalion. When he was killed in the engagement at Paoli on September 20, 1777, he was replaced by Major Thomas Church, transferred from the 5th Pennsylvania Regiment. Major Church continued in this capacity until January 1, 1781.[16]

The companies of the 4th Pennsylvania Regiment were as follows:
• [Company A], commanded by Capt. Edward Scull, of Berks County. He resigned from the army on May 11, 1779,[17] and was replaced by William Henderson, who according to the records was promoted from first lieutenant on May 16, 1778.*
• [Company B], commanded by Capt. William Gray, of Northumberland County.[18] Gray had been a lieutenant in Capt. Casper Weitzel's Company (recruited around Sunbury) of Miles's State Rifle Regiment. Taken prisoner at the Battle of Long Island on August 27, 1776, he was exchanged on December 8, 1776,[19] and was appointed captain in the 4th Pennsylvania Regiment on January 3, 1777, continuing in this position until January 1, 1781.[20]
• [Company C], commanded by Capt. Benjamin Fishbourne, whose pre-war residence has not been identified. He also had seen prior service, having been Paymaster, 2d Pennsylvania Battalion before his appointment, on January 3, 1777, as captain, 4th Pennsylvania Regiment. In April, 1779, he became aide-de-camp to Brig. Gen. Anthony

---

*PA(5), II, 1032. The years given for Scull's resignation and Henderson's promotion are incompatible. Either Scull resigned in 1778 or Henderson was not promoted until 1779. PA(5), II, 1032, however, states categorically that Henderson was promoted to fill the vacancy created by Scull's resignation.

Wayne, on whose staff he served until June 3, 1783.[21] While serving in detached status, Fishbourne was presumably carried against the authorized strength of the regiment. Apparently, however, Fishbourne's company was taken over by Capt. Henry Bicker, Jr., who had been adjutant of the 3d Pennsylvania Battalion, had been captured at Fort Washington on November 16, 1776,[22] and had been exchanged on May 8, 1778. He was promoted captain, 4th Pennsylvania Regiment, with a date of rank (possibly assigned retroactively) of May 15, 1778. He continued with the regiment as a captain throughout the rest of its existence.[23]

• [Company D], commanded by Capt. John McGowan (or McGowen). He had been captain of a company from Northampton County in Miles's State Rifle Regiment[24] before being assigned, on January 3, 1777, to the 4th Pennsylvania Regiment. In September, 1777, he was appointed brigade major,[25] thus vacating command of his company. Presumably, it was this company which was taken over by Capt. Adam Bettin. Bettin was a veteran of the 3d Pennsylvania Battalion, in which he had been a first lieutenant and with which he had been captured at Fort Washington on November 16, 1776. Following his exchange on May 8, 1778,[26] he was assigned to the 10th Pennsylvania Regiment as a captain-lieutenant, but at some unspecified date was promoted to captain and reassigned to the 4th Pennsylvania Regiment.[27] When the mutiny of the Pennsylvania Line broke out on January 1, 1781, he was killed by a mutineer.[28]

• [Company E], commanded by Capt. Benjamin Burd, of Bedford County.[29] After serving as a third lieutenant, second lieutenant, and first lieutenant in Thompson's Rifle Battalion and then in the 1st Pennsylvania Regiment, Burd was appointed captain, 4th Pennsylvania Regiment, effective January 3, 1777. However, it is not clear that he ever joined this unit; and in any case, on March 14 he was commissioned lieutenant colonel of the 3d Continental Light Dragoons.[30] It would appear that Company E was the unit which, after July 3, 1777, was commanded by Capt. John Mears, of Berks County, until May 26, 1778.[31] When Capt. George Tudor of the 3d Pennsylvania Battalion, captured at Fort Washington on November 16, 1776, was exchanged on May 10, 1778,[32] Captain Mears was thereby rendered supernumerary, so he left the army and Tudor took over the company.[33] There is no indication of who replaced Tudor as company commander when he was promoted, on April 17, 1780, to be major, 5th Pennsylvania Regiment.[34]

• [Company F], commanded by Capt. William Cross, of Hanover, in York County.[35] He had been a third lieutenant and second lieutenant in Thompson's Rifle Battalion and a first lieutenant in its successor organization, the 1st Pennsylvania Regiment. From January 1 through June 2, 1777, he was a first lieutenant in the 4th Continental Light Dragoons, being appointed captain, 4th Pennsylvania Regiment on June 3, 1777. He served in this capacity until May 14, 1779, when he resigned.[36] His replacement as company commander was Capt. David Brown, promoted from captain-lieutenant on May 27, 1779. Brown resigned on April 17, 1780,* and was replaced by William Sproat, promoted from captain-lieutenant, who continued in command of the company until January 17, 1781.[37]

• [Company G], commanded by Capt. Robert Connelly, of Northumberland County.[38] He had been a second lieutenant in the 3d Pennsylvania Battalion, but apparently was not present at Fort Washington when the bulk of the battalion was taken prisoner. On January 3, 1777, he was appointed captain, 4th Pennsylvania Regiment, but he became supernumerary and left the army on August 31, 1778.[39] The name of his successor has not been established.

• [Company H] was the "Major's Company" of the regiment. When the new organizational structure was adopted after May, 1778, the commander of this unit was Major Thomas Church, who served as this company's commander from the summer of 1778 until January 1, 1781.[40]

• [Company I] was the "Lieutenant Colonel's Company" of the regiment. Lt. Col. William Butler was the nominal commander of this unit throughout its existence. Direct command, however, was held by a succession of officers holding the rank of captain-lieutenant. These were David Brown, from May 16, 1778, to May 27, 1779;[41] William Sproat, to May 11, 1780; and Thomas Campbell, from May 11, 1780,[42] until January 1, 1781.[43]

The only information pertaining to the uniform of this regiment concerns the clothing worn by three deserters, one reported in April, 1777, and two in June, 1778. In the earlier case, the man was unshod, but was wearing woolen stockings, linen drawers, and a hunting shirt. The 1778 deserters were more completely clad, in both cases having "Wilton" coats, coarse shirts, and trousers.[44]

On the subject of deserters from the 4th Pennsylvania, a list of twenty-four such men[45]—dated June 6, 1781, presumably consisting of soldiers who had re-enlisted after the mutiny—provides some insight into what may have been the enlisted composition of the organization, as it gives the ages of twenty men, the civilian occupations of twelve, and the birthplaces of twenty-three. The ages range from 16 to 49, distributed as follows: 16, 1; 20, 1; 22, 2; 25, 4; 27, 1; 28, 1; 29, 2; 30, 5; 31, 1; 40, 1; 49, 1.

---

*Heitman, p. 124. The date (1779) given in PA(5), II, 1032 and 1033 is clearly in error.

Five of these men were tailors, five were shoemakers, one was a bricklayer, and one other was a tobacconist. Five were born in Pennsylvania, two in England, one in Germany, one (surprisingly) in Spain, and nineteen in Ireland.

The fact that these men were deserters means that they cannot be considered as necessarily representing a cross-section of the regiment. For, common as desertion was in the Continental Army, it still was not the action of the majority of the soldiers. At the same time, while the proportion of foreign-born men on this list is extremely high (probably higher than in the regiment as a whole), it is still generally consistent with such sparse facts as are available about the national backgrounds of the members of the Pennsylvania Continental organizations.

Summary

There was a considerable carry-over of officers from the 3d Pennsylvania Battalion to the 4th Pennsylvania Regiment. There may well have been a comparable carry-over of enlisted men, but records have survived in such limited quantities that no documentation of such a link is possible. In any event, it is clear that many of the members of the 4th Pennsylvania Regiment would have been new recruits.

Of the regiment's original company commanders, Captain Scull was from Berks County, Captain Gray and Captain Connelly were from Northumberland, Captain McGowan was from Northampton, Captain Burd was from Bedford, and Captain Cross was from York. Captain Fishbourne's residence is not known, and it is likely that neither the Lieutenant Colonel's Company nor the Major's Company would have been recruited by their commanders. Both from the residences of the company commanders (to the extent that they are known), however, and the specific service for which this organization was selected (see below), it seems probable that the members of the 4th Pennsylvania Regiment—in contrast to the members of its parent organization, the 3d Pennsylvania Battalion—were largely recruited in the "frontier" areas of the State.

OPERATIONS

3d Pennsylvania Battalion

The 3d Pennsylvania Battalion left Pennsylvania for New York City on June 15, 1776, arriving by companies between June 20 and June 25. With the 5th Pennsylvania Battalion, it was sent to the vicinity of Kingsbridge, New York, where it helped to build Fort Washington. This was not only heavy labor but involved considerable discomfort because of the large clouds of dust that were raised and hung in the air.[46] There was no place to sleep except on the ground, which was often damp; and, as discipline was poor and little training had been provided, there was probably little attention to proper field sanitation. In any case, illness was rife, and a contemporary account claims that almost half of the men of the battalion became too sick to perform duty.[47]

When the Battle of Long Island took place on August 27, the 3d Pennsylvania Battalion was sent to New York City, moving early the next morning to Brooklyn. All through August 28 and August 29, it held the left flank of the American entrenchments protecting Brooklyn, being engaged in continual skirmishing. It was part of the Pennsylvania brigade under Brig. Gen. Thomas Mifflin which formed the rear guard covering the withdrawal of the main army to Manhattan on the night of August 29-30. With that brigade, it obeyed a mistaken order to evacuate its position, and was approaching the boats when General Washington discovered the error, and the brigade turned back to reoccupy its entrenchments, finally leaving Long Island only between 6 A.M. and 7 A.M. on August 30. On the following day, it reinforced a new defensive position some eighteen to twenty miles from New York City, above the Bronx River, while other units straggled in. Then the battalion was returned to Fort Washington.[48]

By October 7, the 3d Pennsylvania Battalion was under Lieutenant Colonel Cadwalader, Colonel Shee being absent on a leave from which he never returned, resigning his commission while absent (the effective date—September 25, 1776—was assigned retroactively). The strength of the command at this time was 541; but 98 men, though present, were sick, 107 more were absent, sick, and 6 were on detached service.[49]

When the British attacked Fort Washington on November 16, the 3d Pennsylvania Battalion was assigned to man three defensive lines, their right flanks anchored on the Hudson; the most advanced of these was about a mile and a half south of the fort itself, the second a half mile closer in, and the third (as yet incomplete), another half mile closer still. Driving against them were the British 3d Brigade and a Hessian regiment, the whole under Hugh, Earl Percy. Then another British column landed from the Harlem River, striking at an angle that would take it behind the rearmost of the three American lines and cut the battalion off from the fort. At the first report of the landing attempt, Colonel Cadwalader sent Capt. David Lennox and his Company C to block it, but Lennox soon found that he was facing the entire 42d Regiment of Foot.* Company C, soon reinforced by about two more companies, inflicted heavy losses on the landing force, but was unable to

---

*This was the Royal Highland Regiment, which ultimately became the modern Black Watch. See Philip R. N. Katcher, *Encyclopedia of English, Provincial, and German Army Units, 1775-1783* (Harrisburg: Stackpole Books, 1973), pp. 52-53.

keep the British from getting ashore. Simultaneously, Lord Percy's columns drove ahead, forcing the main body of the 3d Pennsylvania Battalion to withdraw to the second line of defense. Even there, it was about to be cut off, but orders arrived directing the battalion to fall back into the fort; however, some men—including Capt. Alexander Graydon and probably most of his Company B—were captured in the process of retreating. Company C and its reinforcements, on the left above the Harlem River, were also ordered back. Then, after tightening their encirclement, the British sent in a demand for surrender, which the Americans saw no choice but to accept.[50] As a result, almost all of the 3d Pennsylvania Battalion, along with the rest of the garrison, became prisoners of war.[51]

4th Pennsylvania Regiment

When the 4th Pennsylvania Regiment was organized around the remnants of the 3d Pennsylvania Battalion, it joined Washington's main army in New Jersey for the campaign of 1777. Some elements of the regiment seem to have been present at the Battle of Princeton on January 3, 1777.[52] The command was involved in the engagement at Bound Brook on April 12 or 13,[53] and probably saw other action during the spring, for as of June 30, 1777, it had lost seventeen men killed and fifteen prisoners of war. At that time, besides the 33 commissioned officers, only 196 men were present for duty; 40 more were sick, 121 had deserted, and 28 were on detached service.[54]

On September 11, 1777, it fought at the Battle of Brandywine as part of Brig. Gen. Anthony Wayne's division. In that action it helped to cover Chadd's Ford until an enemy force under General Knyphausen stormed across Brandywine Creek and drove the division from its position.

Nine days later, on September 20, the regiment took part in the action at Paoli, when the British conducted a surprise night attack on Wayne's camp. In this engagement, Major Lamar was killed, his last words before he was struck down being a vain plea to the fleeing American troops to "Halt, boys, and give these assassins one fire!"[55]

On October 4, 1777, the 4th Pennsylvania Regiment with the rest of Wayne's division took part in the Battle of Germantown. It was part of the force which made up the left-flank element of the frontal assault on the British center; it was about to smash through when it was fired on from the left rear by American troops. The whole division then broke off its attack and retreated, leading the rest of the assaulting column to fall back as well.

During these operations and the weeks that followed, the regiment suffered considerably. A number of officers and men had been wounded at Germantown, and by November 1, the regiment had an enlisted strength of only 159—and forty of these were sick and another fifty on detached service, leaving only sixty-nine men present for duty.[56] Even so, the 4th Pennsylvania was present at Whitemarsh, in the first line of the defense, although it saw no action.[57]

The 4th Pennsylvania Regiment spent the winter of 1777-1778 at Valley Forge, then took part in the pursuit of the British army across New Jersey, fighting at the Battle of Monmouth on June 28, 1778, where it was with the advance wing of the army[58] but was in limited contact with the enemy and lost only one man wounded.[59] Not long afterward, it was detached from Washington's immediate command to be based on Schoharie, New York, from which it would help defend the frontiers in upstate New York against Indian attacks.

In furtherance of this mission, in October, 1778, it carried out a deep penetration raid, during which it burned a number of Indian towns but suffered only one casualty, when a soldier was killed by a sniper.[60] On completing this operation, it mustered 14 officers and 190 enlisted men, of whom 54 were too sick for duty and 12 were detached.[61] It remained in the New York frontier sector during the first half of 1779. By June 13 of that year, its strength had grown to 15 officers and 228 enlisted men. Of these, only 13 were sick, but 32 were on detached service.[62] Later in the summer, initially with the brigade commanded by Brig. Gen. James Clinton, it took part in the expedition under Maj. Gen. John Sullivan against the Iroquois; but on making junction with Sullivan's main force at Tioga Point, it was transferred to the brigade of Brig. Gen. Edward Hand. With that organization, it fought at the only substantial engagement of the campaign, the Battle of Newtown (modern Elmira), New York. This occurred on August 29, 1779. In this action, Sullivan's troops defeated and drove off a mixed force of Tories and Indians. Hand's brigade played a crucial part. Supported by detachments of the 4th Continental Artillery, it kept the enemy preoccupied on the front while other troops attempted to carry out an enveloping maneuver, swinging around to the right to hit the enemy on his left rear. Considerable loss was inflicted, but the Tories and Indians were able to escape to the rear.[63] Later in the campaign a scouting force including a corporal and five privates of the 4th Pennsylvania Regiment was cut off and massacred by Indians at Genesee, New York (across the Genesee River and some miles west of the modern town of Geneseo), on September 13.[64]

After the campaign against the Iroquois, the 4th Pennsylvania was reassigned to Washington's main army, spending the winter of 1779-1780 at Morristown, New Jersey.[65] It remained in Hand's brigade at least until March 25, 1780, when it was shown as having 117 men present for duty,[66] but was no longer under Hand when it comprised part of the force which on September 25 marched from Tappan, New York, to West Point at the time of Benedict Arnold's treachery.[67] By December, it had gone with the rest of the Pennsylvania Line for another winter encampment at Morristown.

When the mutiny of the Pennsylvania troops broke out on January 1, 1781, the men of this regiment at first refused to take part. Indeed, one detachment, under Capt.-Lt. Thomas Campbell of the Lieutenant Colonel's Company, began a charge to try to recapture the cannon which the mutineers had seized, but faltered before making contact. A mutineer then attacked Lieutenant Colonel Butler, who, in order to save his life, dodged among the huts. Racing around the other side to cut Butler off, the mutineer came face to face with Capt. Adam Bettin, who raised his spontoon (a type of short-shafted halberd with which officers were armed) against the man. The mutineer shot Bettin through the body, wounding him mortally.[68] At that, the men of the 4th Pennsylvania joined the mutiny.

On the reorganization of the Pennsylvania Line which was put into effect after the mutiny, the 4th Pennsylvania was one of the six infantry regiments which were retained. However, it no longer existed as an actual regiment. Such of its members as remained in the army were pooled with the other Pennsylvania troops and distributed among the three provisional battalions which were sent to Virginia for the Yorktown campaign, and then to South Carolina. There, they took part in some of the guerrilla skirmishes and the siege of Charleston, remaining to perform garrison duty until June, 1783, when they were returned to Pennsylvania and, eventually, demobilized with the rest of the Continental Army.

Chapter VI

4th Pennsylvania Battalion
5th Pennsylvania Regiment

Anthony Wayne

ORGANIZATION

4th Pennsylvania Battalion

Authorized on December 9, 1775, for one year's service, the 4th Pennsylvania Battalion was recruited primarily in Chester County (which at that time included what is now Delaware County), but drew some personnel from Bucks County and possibly from Lancaster County as well. The formal date of enlistment was January 5, 1776, and the battalion began assembling at Chester on February 9.[1]

The colonel of this organization throughout its existence was Anthony Wayne. He was subsequently promoted to brigadier general—on February 21, 1777[2]—but that was after the battalion had been disbanded.

The lieutenant colonel of the battalion from its formation to its mustering out was Francis Johnston.[3]

The 4th Pennsylvania Battalion had two majors. The first was Nicholas Hausegger. After Hausegger was appointed colonel of the

German Regiment on July 17, 1776,[4] he was replaced by Persifor Frazer. However, Frazer's promotion from captain did not become effective until September 24, 1776.[5]

The companies of the battalion were:

• [Company A], commanded by Capt. Persifor Frazer. The company was assembled at Chester in March, 1776, remaining until it left on May 16, arriving at Long Island on May 19. It spent the next six weeks seeking out and arresting Tories. On June 29, the company started by boat for Albany, New York, which it reached on July 2. After a short stay, it left on July 4 to cover the seventy miles (sixty of them on foot) to Fort George, arriving there on July 7. The company then moved to Ticonderoga, where it was based throughout the remainder of its service.[6] After Frazer's promotion to major, Joseph Potts succeeded to command of this company,[7] being promoted from first lieutenant.[8]

• [Company B], commanded by Capt. Thomas Robinson. This was one of the first companies of the battalion to be equipped. It served briefly on Long Island, but by May 16, 1776, it was at Albany.[9] It was part of the force taking part in the engagement at Three Rivers, in Canada, on June 9, 1776.[10] According to Capt. John Lacey, who was not altogether an impartial reporter, Captain Robinson was a particular crony of Colonel Wayne; Lacey said of Robinson that "when any extra duty is required, he is sure to be sick, and never fails to faint at the sight of human blood."*

• [Company C], commanded by Capt. John Lacey. This unit was raised in Bucks County,[11] and was the first company of the battalion to be fully equipped and to leave Pennsylvania for New York City, arriving on March 28.[12] On April 13, following the arrival of Company B, both units were stationed on Long Island.[13] The company was selected for service in Canada and had reached Albany by May 10. Captain Lacey was not with it at this time, having been sent back to Pennsylvania on an administrative task; the company was actually commanded by another of Wayne's favorites, Capt. James Moore, whose own company had not left Long Island, as it had not yet received weapons. Lacey deeply resented being displaced, and described Captain Moore as "a Bully; he is of profligate and debauched morrels. . . ."[14] The substitution of Moore for Lacey also gave rise to resentment among the troops; on May 12, two sergeants of the company were convicted by a court martial of "encouraging sedition" and were reduced to private, and there were several desertions.[15] Moving northward, the company remained under Captain Moore even though Captain Lacey

---

*Lacey, p. 353. As will be shown, Lacey had considerable reason to be resentful of Wayne, and had a perhaps understandable dislike for any of Wayne's special friends.

had rejoined the command—Wayne, in what seems a preposterous action, ordered Lacey to serve as a "volunteer" so that Moore could retain command until Moore's own company should arrive. Company C was part of the force at Three Rivers on June 9; but Samuel Smith, its first lieutenant, asserted that "the company never came within reach of the enemy's muskets."[16] Lacey said that Smith also reported that ". . . the Vallient Capt Moore ran at the first fire of the Enemies Cannon, without returning a shot, being at too great a distance for the fire of Muskets to do any execution."[17]

- [Company D], commanded by Capt. Caleb North.[18]
- [Company E], commanded by Capt. Thomas Church.[19] This company was armed with rifles, in contrast to the others, which had muskets.[20] It served on Long Island, at Albany,[21] and in the engagement at Three Rivers.[22]
- [Company F], commanded by Capt. Frederick Vernon.[23]
- [Company G], commanded by Capt. James Moore.[24] As previously noted, Captain Moore spent most of the campaign in charge of Company C rather than of his own unit. While Company G was still in New York, it was briefly under Captain Lacey, presumably being commanded by its first lieutenant after Lacey left for Albany (on May 22, 1776[25]) until it reached Ticonderoga on July 17, when Captain Moore resumed command.[26]
- [Company H], commanded by Capt. James Taylor. Captain Taylor was from Lancaster County,[27] and it is possible that he recruited many of his men from that area.

After the first companies began to leave Chester in late March, the battalion was not reunited until July 17, 1776, when Companies A, D, F, G, and H arrived at Ticonderoga to join the three which were already in the field.[28] It remained at Ticonderoga as part of the garrison, continuing on duty past the legal expiration of enlistments (January 5, 1777) until replacements arrived, leaving for Pennsylvania on January 24. Although the men were mustered out, "a large proportion" promptly re-enlisted, joining the newly formed 5th Pennsylvania Regiment.[29] A comparison of muster rolls, although they are incomplete for both the battalion and the regiment, shows that at least 107 men of the regiment were veterans of the parent organization.

According to one account of the battalion's uniforms, "Our Regimental Coats were Deep blew faced with white, white Vests & Overalls edged with blew Cloth." This was "a very beautiful uniform, but on experience we found [it] much better adapted for parades than utility in the hardships of a Camp, as they too easily became soiled, and hard to clean."[30] Evidently, the prescribed uniform was either not standard or gave way to whatever the men could obtain, for a deserter from this battalion is described as wearing buckskin breeches and a brown coat faced with blue silk.[31]

5th Pennsylvania Regiment

As noted, the 5th Pennsylvania Regiment was largely officered and manned by veterans of the 4th Pennsylvania Battalion. It was commanded during the entire span of its existence by Col. Francis Johnston, who had been lieutenant colonel of the battalion.[32]

The regiment's first lieutenant colonel was Persifor Frazer,[33] who had been a captain in the battalion and then its major. He was captured on September 16, 1777, soon after the Battle of Brandywine, while making a reconnaissance in Aston Township of the present Delaware County. He remained a prisoner, being held at Philadelphia, until March 17, 1778, when he escaped. He returned to the regiment and was acting as its commander at the Battle of Monmouth, on June 28, 1778,[34] but resigned his commission on the following October 9.[35] He was replaced as lieutenant colonel by Francis Mentges, promoted from major of the 7th Pennsylvania Regiment. Mentges remained with the 5th Pennsylvania Regiment for the rest of the war.[36]

The first major of the 5th Pennsylvania Regiment was Thomas Robinson, who had been a captain in the 4th Pennsylvania Battalion. He was wounded at the Battle of Brandywine, on September 11, 1777,[37] after which he was promoted to lieutenant colonel and transferred to the 1st Pennsylvania Regiment, with a date of rank (assigned retroactively) of June 7, 1777.[38] He was succeeded as major by James Taylor, promoted from captain on September 23, 1777, but Taylor soon resigned—on April 3, 1778.[39] His replacement was Christopher Stuart, who had been a captain in the 5th Pennsylvania Battalion,[40] and as such had been taken prisoner at Fort Washington, New York, on November 16, 1776. After he was exchanged (in January, 1777), he was promoted to major and eventually assigned to the 5th Pennsylvania Regiment, but with an antedated date of rank.[41] On April 17, 1780, he was promoted to lieutenant colonel of the 3d Pennsylvania Regiment, being replaced in the 5th Pennsylvania by George Tudor, promoted from captain, 4th Pennsylvania Regiment.[42]

Originally, the 5th Pennsylvania Regiment had eight companies, as follows:

• [Company A], commanded initially by the same officer—Capt. Joseph Potts—who had succeeded Persifor Frazer as its commander in the battalion. Potts was wounded and taken prisoner at the Battle of Brandywine, on September 11, 1777, and never rejoined the regiment.[43] A comparison of names on the muster rolls shows that with the reorganization of July 1, 1778, the men of this unit became the bulk of the "Major's Company" of the regiment,[44] and therefore were under the command of Major Christopher Stuart until April 17, 1780, after which the company was commanded by Major George Tudor.

• [Company B], commanded by Capt. Benjamin Bartholomew, who had been a first lieutenant in the 4th Pennsylvania Battalion. Although he was wounded at the Battle of Brandywine, he remained in command of the company throughout the war.[45]

• [Company C], from Bucks County, was commanded at first by Capt. Alexander Johnston. He resigned his commission on January 23, 1778,[46] after which the company came under Charles McHenry,[47] promoted from first lieutenant. McHenry became supernumerary on July 1, 1778,[48] when this unit became the "Colonel's Company" of the regiment,[49] nominally under Col. Francis Johnston. The actual commanders were Capt.-Lt. Job Vernon, until his promotion to captain on June 13, 1779,[50] and then (until the end of the war) Capt.-Lt. John Barkley.[51]

• [Company D], commanded by Capt. John Christie, of Chester County.[52] He had been a first lieutenant in the 4th Pennsylvania Battalion and was appointed captain upon the organization of the 5th Pennsylvania Regiment. He continued as company commander until the regiment was mustered out.[53]

• [Company E], commanded initially by Capt. Thomas Church,[54] who had also commanded it in the battalion. He was promoted to major of the regiment on March 1, 1777, and was replaced as company commander by Samuel Smith, promoted from first lieutenant. Smith had been a first lieutenant in the 4th Pennsylvania Battalion. He continued as captain of this company for the remainder of the war.[55]

• [Company F], which continued under its captain from the 4th Pennsylvania Battalion, Capt. Frederick Vernon, until June 7, 1777, when Vernon was promoted to major and transferred to the 8th Pennsylvania Regiment.[56] It appears that the company then came under Capt. Robert Gregg,[57] who was promoted from first lieutenant on the same date that Frederick Vernon was promoted to major. He had been a first lieutenant in the 4th Pennsylvania Battalion, but became supernumerary as a captain on July 1, 1778.[58] Although conclusive evidence has not been found, it appears that this unit then became the "Lieutenant Colonel's Company" of the regiment. If so, it would have been briefly under Lt. Col. Persifor Frazer and, after October 9, 1778, under Lt. Col. Francis Mentges.

• [Company G], which also continued for a time under its captain in the 4th Pennsylvania Battalion, Capt. James Moore. When he was promoted to major and transferred to the 1st Pennsylvania Regiment on September 10, 1777,[59] he was replaced as company commander by

Isaac Seeley (or Seely), of Cumberland County,[60] who was promoted from first lieutenant, having also served in that grade in the 4th Pennsylvania Battalion. On March 22, 1778, Seeley was appointed brigade major;[61] but as he did not thereby vacate his captaincy, no one could be promoted in his place, and he was still carried as commander of the company as of September 9, 1778[62] and again on March 24, 1780.[63] He was taken prisoner at Paramus, New Jersey, on April 16, 1780, and apparently was never replaced. In actual fact, the company was probably commanded by its first lieutenant.

• [Company H], also initially under its commander from the battalion, Capt. James Taylor. He was promoted to major on September 23, 1777. His replacement was Thomas Boude,[65] who was promoted from first lieutenant, having served as a second lieutenant in the 4th Pennsylvania Battalion.[66] Although Boude is listed as captain of this company as of September 9, 1778,[67] his actual promotion seems not to have taken place for almost two years, as it was awarded for gallantry in the attack on Stony Point, New York, on July 16, 1779.[68] However, the date of rank assigned to him was the date when Taylor's promotion created a vacant captaincy in the regiment. Boude remained in this position for the rest of the war.[69]

A ninth company was added to the 5th Pennsylvania Regiment on March 24, 1777. This was an organization which had been formed as an independent company. At the time of its incorporation into the 5th Pennsylvania Regiment, it was commanded by Capt. William Oldham. On January 9, 1779, Oldham resigned,* apparently being replaced by Job Vernon, although Vernon's promotion from captain-lieutenant did not take effect until June 13, 1779.[70]

A number of the deserters from the 5th Pennsylvania Regiment are reported as being dressed in brown coats (one of them faced with white) and a diversity of leather breeches or white overalls. Several others wore blue coats with white facings. Headgear was also varied, some men having round hats, others broad felt hats, still others beaver hats, and one man had a "fashionable wool hat." Some of the hats were cocked, and one was "turned up behind." A few men had hunting shirts, but of differing colors (including one of yellow and another of purple), and several wore "sailors' jackets"—one gray, one blue, and two green. Other deserters from this regiment wore civilian clothing.[71]

Summary

With the exception of Captain Oldham, all company commanders of

---

*Heitman, p. 419. His name is given in PA(5), III, 8 as *John* Oldham, but in all other references—PA(5), III, 27, 28, 33, and 37 as well as Heitman—as *William* Oldham.

the 5th Pennsylvania Regiment had held commissions in the 4th Pennsylvania Battalion. This fact, together with the extent of re-enlistment in the regiment by veterans of the battalion, gives weight to the likelihood that the regiment retained a strong Chester (and modern Delaware) County flavor—except, of course, for Company C (Bucks County) and Company H (possibly Lancaster County). All the same, recruits brought in as the war progressed would have injected a certain amount of regional diversity. For example, a roster of sixteen newly enlisted men which is dated January 12, 1779, shows six from York County, one from Philadelphia, and nine from Lancaster County.[72]

OPERATIONS

4th Pennsylvania Battalion

Soon after the 4th Pennsylvania Battalion was formed in the winter of 1776, Colonel Wayne received orders (on February 22, 1776) to send each company to New York City as soon as it was equipped.[73] It was some time, however, before these orders could be carried out, for it was a month before the first unit (Company C) had been assembled, armed, and dispatched, traveling by boat from Chester, Pennsylvania, to Trenton, New Jersey, and thence overland to New York.[74] This company was soon joined by Companies B and E. All three were stationed on Long Island.[75]

Even for these units, armament was incomplete, and the men had no military training and little discipline. Captain Lacey complained that between the time he left Chester and reached Trenton he was "almost weryed to Death in keeping the Company in order," for "we were all young, and...quite Novices in Military matters, had every thing to learn, and no one to instruct us who knew any better than ourselves."[76]

On May 2, 1776, Wayne and two of the three companies of the battalion that had first reached New York were sent to Albany, on the way to join the American forces in Canada, and were soon followed by the third. The remaining five companies had either just arrived on Long Island or were still on the way from Pennsylvania.[77] Only after the three leading units reached Albany did they finally complete their full issue of arms.[78]

As mentioned earlier, Captain Moore had been placed in temporary command of Company C (one of those sent to Albany) during Captain Lacey's absence in Pennsylvania, and the men were showing considerable resentment at the change. Lacey returned to New York on May 11, finding orders to stay in command of Moore's Company until it got arms and, with the other units of the battalion, was ordered to Canada. He also began to receive disturbing reports from Albany. "My mind was continually harrowed up to the highest pitch of Mortification," he wrote, "by repeated accounts...that my Company was deserting, that they had refused to March under Cap.ᵗ Moore, that numbers [were] under Guard & twenty absent at one time...."[79]

While Lacey stewed in New York, Companies B, C, and E moved on from Albany into Canada, but did not make contact with the American forces there until late May. By early June they were at Sorel, where most of the American troops were by then concentrated.[80]

From there, Wayne and his three companies were attached to the force which carried out the disastrous attempt to destroy the British outpost at Three Rivers on June 9. As the attackers slogged their way through the swamp on their approach march, Wayne's troops were the first to emerge and catch a complete view of the unexpectedly reinforced garrison they had been sent to strike. With characteristic daring, Wayne threw forward a body of skirmishers and followed through to drive in the British outpost line. However, this offensive move was not supported by the main body of Americans, and the 4th Battalion companies were unable to hold what they had gained. Most of the rest of the American force was in utter confusion. Brig. Gen. William Thompson, in over-all command, had been cut off and, along with Col. William Irvine, was about to be captured; Colonel St. Clair had been injured; and Wayne found himself in command. To prevent a complete rout, he formed a covering force of his own companies and elements of the 2d Pennsylvania Battalion (see Chapter III), which successfully protected the survivors of the retreating American army.[81]

Lacey, who had reached Sorel but was still kept from command of his company, had been put in charge of a lieutenant and "Ten Riffler men" and sent to scout toward Three Rivers and help stragglers to find their way back to the base camp. They "Proceeded through most Horrid Swamps, were almost devoured by Muskeetoes of a Monsterous size and innumerable numbers," but eventually made contact with some of the retreating troops, whom they escorted back to Sorel.[82]

Following this defeat, the Americans retreated from Sorel to St. John's. The men of the 4th Pennsylvania Battalion helped form the rear guard, slowing down to permit the American force withdrawing from Montreal to regain the main column.[83] The next stage of the retreat took the force to Isle Aux Noix, where almost half the men of the battalion became ill,[84] suffering from fevers, dysentery, vermin, and smallpox.[85] From there, they withdrew to Crown Point, which they reached on July 1, and by July 10, to Ticonderoga.[86] There they were joined a week later by the battalion's other five companies.[87]

During the next several months while the command helped garrison Ticonderoga, there were occasional alarums and excursions, but no actual combat except for the naval engagement off Crown Point on October 11-13, in which the 4th Pennsylvania Battalion may have taken part. The men suffered severely from shortages and illness, and although Wayne worked hard to instill some discipline and provide a degree of training, there were substantial morale problems. Among the officers, not the least of these was the running controversy between Wayne and Captain Lacey, who with some justification considered himself the victim of "the Caprice of...an unjust tyrent."[88] At length, however, the arrival of reinforcements permitted the battalion to leave on January 24, 1777, almost three weeks after the expiration of its enlistment, to return to Pennsylvania to be mustered out.[89]

5th Pennsylvania Regiment

Reconstituted as the 5th Pennsylvania Regiment, this organization was part of Wayne's division with Washington's army during the spring and summer of 1777. It saw action near New Brunswick, New Jersey, on June 22,[90] and probably in several of the other skirmishes of that summer, for as of August 14, 1777, it had lost forty-seven men killed and captured. It had 372 officers and men present for duty, 74 sick, 57 on detached service, and had lost 189 men by desertion.[91]

It fought at the Battle of Brandywine on September 11, 1777, in the position just above Chadd's Ford, sustaining a number of casualties. It was also present at the engagement at Paoli on September 20, when an ensign was killed[92] and two privates were wounded.[93] It fought again at the Battle of Germantown, on October 4, taking part in the frontal assault on the British center. All this had its impact on personnel strengths, and by November 3 the regiment's officer strength was down to 21; it had only 157 enlisted men for duty, with 50 more listed as sick, 56 on detached service, and two on furlough.[94] It was in the first line at Whitemarsh, with the rest of Wayne's division, but did not come under attack when the British briefly advanced in December.[95]

The regiment spent the winter of 1777-1778 at Valley Forge. It was next in combat at the Battle of Monmouth, on June 28, 1778. It was committed late in the action, and its only casualty was a first lieutenant wounded.[96] During the remainder of the year, it saw no particular action, going into camp for the winter at Middlebrook, New Jersey.

Elements of the 5th Pennsylvania Regiment, at least, took part in the assault on Stony Point, New York, on July 16, 1779, and the whole organization (numbering 342 officers and men) was at West Point on October 15, 1779, as part of Brig. Gen. William Irvine's brigade of Maj. Gen. Arthur St. Clair's division.[97]

During the winter of 1779-1780, the 5th Pennsylvania Regiment was with the main army at Morristown, New Jersey, and was still there as late as May 7, 1780.[98] Presumably, it was with Irvine's brigade in providing a blocking force against British reinforcements during the assault on the Blockhouse at Bergen Heights, New Jersey, on July 21, 1780, but it reported no casualties in that engagement. It does not seem to have been with the troops making the forced march to reinforce the West Point garrison on September 25. However, it was with the main army at Morristown when the Pennsylvania troops mutinied on January 1, 1781. Initially, in response to its officers' orders, it formed to resist the mutineers; but when the rebellious soldiers fired a cannon over the heads of the men in ranks, most of them broke formation and joined the mutiny.[99]

Although the 5th was one of the six Pennsylvania regiments retained on the rolls after the mutiny, many of its men were discharged. The remainder were dispersed among the three provisional battalions formed for service in the southern theater, fighting at Green Spring[100] and Yorktown, and later serving in South Carolina.

Chapter VII

5th Pennsylvania Battalion
6th Pennsylvania Regiment

Josiah Harmar

ORGANIZATION

5th Pennsylvania Battalion

The 5th Pennsylvania Battalion was authorized on December 15, 1775.[1] Its officers were appointed in early January, 1776, and the men were recruited during the winter.

The battalion's first commander was Col. Robert Magaw, of Carlisle,[2] who was promoted from major of Thompson's Rifle Battalion.[3]

Joseph Penrose was lieutenant colonel of the battalion until October 25, 1776, when he was appointed colonel of the 10th Pennsylvania Regiment.[4] No replacement was named.

The unit's first major was George Nagel,[5] promoted from captain in Thompson's Rifle Battalion.[6] On October 25, 1776, he was promoted to lieutenant colonel and transferred to the 9th Pennsylvania Regiment,[7] being replaced in the battalion by John Beatty,[8] promoted from captain effective October 12, 1776.[9]

The battalion's companies were the following:

• [Company A], commanded by Capt. John Beatty and raised chiefly in Bucks County.[10] When Beatty was promoted to major on October 12, 1776, he was replaced as company commander by John Priestly, promoted from first lieutenant.[11]

• [Company B], commanded by Capt. John Miller, largely recruited from the city and county of Philadelphia but including a number of men from New Jersey and a contingent from Northumberland County.[12] Captain Miller was mortally wounded at Fort Washington, New York, on November 16, 1776. His nominal replacement was John Morgan, promoted from first lieutenant,[13] but as the members of the battalion had practically all been taken prisoner, the company could never actually have functioned under Morgan's command.

• [Company C], commanded by Capt. Samuel Benezet. It consisted primarily of men from the Philadelphia area, but included men from adjacent counties, all the neighboring states, and several men from Northumberland County.[14]

• [Company D], commanded by Capt. Christopher Stuart, and made up of men from Philadelphia and the surrounding areas in Chester (which included Delaware County), Bucks, and Lancaster counties.[15]

• [Company E], commanded by Capt. John Spohn. This was predominantly a Berks County organization.[16]

• [Company F], commanded by Capt. Nathaniel Vansandt, comprising men from Philadelphia and Bucks, Berks, and Chester counties, with some representation from Lancaster and Northumberland counties.[17]

• [Company G], commanded by Capt. Peter Decker, essentially from Berks County.[18]

• [Company H], commanded by Capt. John Richardson. The men of this unit were largely from Philadelphia and Chester County.[19]

Descriptions of the clothing worn by deserters from this battalion indicate that the prescribed uniform featured a brown coat faced with red, with buttons marked "5th B. P."[20]

Like the 3d Pennsylvania Battalion, the 5th Pennsylvania Battalion was part of the garrison of Fort Washington, New York, where most of its members were taken prisoner on November 16, 1776. The enlisted men were released within a few weeks, however, and substantial numbers of them appear to have joined the 6th Pennsylvania Regiment. Although the muster rolls for both the battalion and the regiment are incomplete, no less than twenty-three of the same names show up on the rosters of both organizations. In part, this re-enlistment rate can be attributed to the previously mentioned early release of the men captured at Fort Washington, and in part to the fact that a considerable number of the members of the battalion were absent, sick, at the time of the engagement. With one exception, however (see Company G below), little correlation can be found between the regional origin of the companies of the battalion and that of the companies of the regiment in which the battalion's veterans enlisted.

6th Pennsylvania Regiment

Actual recruiting of the 6th Pennsylvania Regiment appears to have begun in January and February, 1777. Colonel Magaw was carried as the regimental commander, but he remained a prisoner of war — indeed, he was not exchanged until October 25, 1780[21]—so throughout its existence the 6th Pennsylvania Regiment was actually commanded by its lieutenant colonel.

The regiment's first lieutenant colonel was Henry Bicker, promoted on December 5, 1776, from major, 10th Pennsylvania Regiment. On June 6, 1777, he became colonel of the 2d Pennsylvania Regiment,[22] Josiah Harmar being promoted from major, 3d Pennsylvania Regiment to take his place. Harmar continued in command until August 9, 1780, when he became Lieutenant-Colonel Commandant of the 7th Pennsylvania Regiment.[23] From that time until the reorganization of the winter of 1781 (which in effect eliminated all Pennsylvania Continental infantry regiments as operational units), the lieutenant-colonelcy of the 6th Pennsylvania Regiment appears to have remained vacant.

The first major of the regiment was Samuel Benezet, promoted from captain, 5th Pennsylvania Battalion,[24] who had missed being taken prisoner at Fort Washington by virtue of being absent, sick, at the time.[25] His appointment as major was made on February 14, 1777, but he seems never to have joined the regiment, and evidently resigned his commission.[26] His replacement was Jeremiah Talbot, promoted from captain, 7th Pennsylvania Regiment on September 22, 1777. He continued in this position until January 1, 1781.[27]

The organizational history of the companies of the 6th Pennsylvania Regiment is confused by the facts that muster rolls are incomplete, at least one captain carried on the strength of the regiment was permanently on detached service, and some of the dates given for the service of captains of the 6th Pennsylvania Regiment are incompatible with the number of companies authorized. All told, exclusive of five captains of the 5th Pennsylvania Battalion who continued to be carried as captains of the 6th Pennsylvania Regiment although still prisoners of war, fifteen officers are listed as serving as captains with the regiment at one time or another between January, 1777, and January, 1781.

When the regiment was formed, the captains assigned for duty were

Jacob Humphrey (or Humphreys), Company A; Jacob Bower (or Bauer), Company B; Robert Wilkins, Jr., Company C; John McGowan, Company D; Walter Cruise, Company E; James Waugh, Company F; Jacob Moser (or Mouser), Company G; and Luke Brodhead, Company H.[28] A ninth captain was also assigned, although apparently he never had a company. This was Jeremiah Lochrey, who had been commissioned from civilian life on February 15, 1777.[29] However, on August 19, 1777, Lieutenant Colonel Bicker reported that "This gentleman drawed upwards [of] 1,000 dollars, came to Camp without a recruit & returned home immediately."[30] Apparently, Lochrey rejoined at a later date, but in October, 1777, while under arrest, he deserted.[31]

A ninth company was added, in fact, on July 1, 1778. This was Company I, commanded by Capt. John Doyle.[32] The increase in the number of companies was only one of the changes which took place at this time, as five of the incumbent company commanders (McGowan, Cruise, Waugh, Moser, and Brodhead) became supernumerary and left the army.[33] They were replaced by three officers (Captains Hawkins Boone, John Nice, and Walter Finney) transferred from other organizations. Still another captain, John Savage (or Savidge), who apparently had been promoted earlier to fill an unidentified vacancy in the regiment, left the army on September 7, 1778.[34]

To the extent that information is available, it appears that the following company organization prevailed in the 6th Pennsylvania Regiment:

• [Company A], commanded by Capt. Jacob Humphrey,[35] apparently from Chester County.[36] He continued as a captain in this regiment until the end of the war.[37]

• [Company B], commanded by Capt. Jacob Bower,[38] also of Chester County.[39] Formerly a captain in the Flying Camp, he was appointed captain, 6th Pennsylvania Regiment on February 15, 1777, remaining in that capacity throughout the war.[40]

• [Company C], commanded by Capt. Robert Wilkins, Jr.,[41] likewise of Chester County.[42] He had been a first lieutenant in Capt. Christopher Stuart's company (D) of the 5th Pennsylvania Battalion,[43] and was captured at Fort Washington on November 16, 1776, but was exchanged in January, 1777, and immediately appointed captain in the 6th Pennsylvania Regiment. He remained in this position until January 1, 1781.[44]

• [Company D], commanded by Capt. John McGowan, of Lancaster.[45] He is not the John McGowan who served in the 4th Pennsylvania Regiment (see Chapter V), and his name does not appear in Heitman. He became supernumerary on June 21, 1778, and left the army.[46] It is not clear which of the captains joining the 6th Pennsylvania Regiment from other units at this time took over his company.

• [Company E], commanded by Capt. Walter Cruise,[47] whose pre-war residence is not recorded. However, he had been a corporal in Capt. Michael Doudle's Company C (enlisted in York County) of Thompson's Rifle Battalion.[48] On June 29, 1775, he had been taken prisoner near Boston, not being released until December, 1776. In the meantime (in July, 1776), he had been commissioned as a second lieutenant in the 1st Pennsylvania Regiment. On February 15, 1777, he was promoted to captain, 6th Pennsylvania Regiment, but was rendered a supernumerary on June 21, 1778.[49] Again, it cannot be determined who took over his company.

• [Company F], commanded by Capt. James Waugh.[50] His pre-war residence is also unknown, and he had no service prior to his appointment as a captain, 6th Pennsylvania Regiment on February 15, 1777. He became supernumerary on June 21, 1778,[51] and his replacement is unknown.

• [Company G], commanded by Capt. Jacob Moser.[52] The muster rolls of this company, which are relatively comprehensive, make it clear that the men comprising it were drawn largely from Berks County, but that at least six of its members were veterans of Capt. Christopher Stuart's Philadelphia-area company (D) of the 5th Pennsylvania Battalion. After Captain Moser became supernumerary on July 1, 1778,[53] the company was assigned to Capt. Hawkins Boone, who was transferred on paper from the 12th Pennsylvania Regiment when the bulk of that organization was absorbed by the 3d Pennsylvania Regiment. Boone never actually joined his new unit, as he had been on detached service on the frontier, at first with Col. Daniel Morgan's task force and then with Col. Thomas Hartley's "Additional" Regiment, since the summer of 1777, and was killed by Indians at Fort Freeland on July 29, 1779.[54] Meanwhile, the company listed as under his command in the 6th Pennsylvania Regiment was presumably under a lieutenant. At any rate, the existing muster rolls indicate that this company was later split up, its men going in approximately equal numbers to the "Lieutenant Colonel's Company" and the "Major's Company" of the regiment (see below).

• [Company H], commanded by Capt. Luke Brodhead,[55] of Northampton County.[56] Brodhead had been a third lieutenant and second lieutenant in Miles's State Rifle Regiment, and was wounded and captured at the Battle of Long Island on August 27, 1776. He was exchanged on December 8, 1776, and appointed a captain, 6th Pennsylvania Regiment on February 15, 1777. On June 21, 1778, he left the service,[57] apparently because his health continued to suffer from the effects of his wound.[58] Once more, it is not apparent who became commander of the company.

• [Company I], commanded by Capt. John Doyle,[59] of Philadelphia.[60] This was originally an independent company, but was attached to the "Old" 11th Pennsylvania Regiment on December 16, 1777. When that organization was absorbed into the 10th Pennsylvania Regiment on July 1, 1778, this company was transferred to the 6th Pennsylvania Regiment, where it remained, under Doyle's command, for the rest of the war.[61]

Aside from Captain Boone, the two other captains who were transferred to the 6th Pennsylvania Regiment on July 1, 1778, cannot be associated with any particular one of the four companies (D, E, F, and H) whose command was vacated at that time. One of these companies would have become the "Lieutenant Colonel's Company" (actually under Capt.-Lt. William McElhatton[62] from July 1, 1778 to July 1, 1779, when he was transferred to the Invalid Corps;[63] and from then on, under Capt.-Lt. Isaac Van Horn,[64] promoted from first lieutenant on that date[65]); and the other the "Major's Company," under Major Jeremiah Talbot.

Two other names of captains remain unaccounted for. These are John Savage, who was promoted from first lieutenant on January 1, 1778, but for whom no vacancy can be identified and who retired on September 7, 1778;[66] and Thomas Bull. Although Bull is listed as a company commander as of September 9, 1778,[67] he was actually a prisoner of war at the time, having been captured at the Battle of Monmouth on the preceding June 28; his promotion to captain did not take place until November 1, 1778; he was not released until February, 1780; and he never returned to duty.[68]

The only references to the uniform of the 6th Pennsylvania Regiment mention a deserter wearing a brown coat with no facings, and other deserters dressed in hunting shirts.[69]

Summary

It seems clear that the 5th Pennsylvania Battalion was manned chiefly by soldiers from the eastern counties of the State and from Philadelphia, although there were fairly substantial contingents of men from Northumberland County in several of the companies. On a purely speculative basis, it may be suggested that Colonel Magaw, who was from Carlisle and began his service with Thompson's Rifle Battalion (composed of considerable numbers of men from the frontier areas), may have deliberately introduced these men with the purpose of providing some leavening of experienced riflemen and hard-bitten fighters into as many companies as possible. But it is obvious that the battalion as a whole, contrary to some accounts,[70] was not a "western" unit.

Considering the geographic origins of the bulk of the original company commanders of the 6th Pennsylvania Regiment, it is not unreasonable to assume that the regiment retained much of the regional character of the battalion as a Philadelphia-area organization, although the surviving records are too sparse to reveal a conclusive pattern. It does seem clear, however, that at some time between the summer of 1779 and the summer of 1780 the regiment's company strength was reduced, through consolidation, from nine companies to eight.

OPERATIONS

5th Pennsylvania Battalion

By May 28, 1776, while the 5th Pennsylvania Battalion was still in Pennsylvania, it had reached a strength of 598 officers and men.[71] On June 15, 1776, it was sent, along with the 3d Pennsylvania Battalion, to New York City, then moved upriver along the Hudson to Kingsbridge. There it helped build and garrison Fort Washington, sharing in the sufferings and hardships of the 3d Pennsylvania Battalion (see Chapter V). On August 28, it was ordered to New York City and then to Brooklyn. It helped cover the retreat of the main army from Long Island on August 20, then moved northward to help strengthen the army's defenses above the Bronx River. Ordered back to Fort Washington, it remained there through the fall. As of October 7, 1776, its strength in personnel present for duty was only 394; an additional 120 were absent, sick.[72] Colonel Magaw, as the senior officer present, was in command of the entire garrison.[73]

Early in November, the adjutant of the 5th Pennsylvania Battalion, Capt. William Dement (or Demont), deserted to the British, carrying detailed information of defensive works and troop dispositions which greatly facilitated the successful British attack of November 16, 1776.[74] As a consequence of this engagement, almost all of the garrison— including 237 of the enlisted men and a large proportion of the officers of the 5th Pennsylvania Battalion[75]—were taken prisoner.

6th Pennsylvania Regiment

After the 6th Pennsylvania Regiment was formed, it became part of Washington's main army, assigned to Brig. Gen. Thomas Conway's brigade. Like the other American elements in the area, it ranged in comparatively small detachments, fighting when it encountered a British force on a similar patrolling mission. The one such engagement by the 6th Pennsylvania Regiment which is of record took place on May

26 or May 27, in the vicinity of Middletown, New Jersey, when one of the regiment's second lieutenants was killed.[76]

The regiment took part in the Battle of Brandywine, on September 11, 1777. As part of Conway's brigade it was on the American right flank, where the main weight of the British blow fell. Although it was involved in the fierce fighting around the Birmingham Meeting House until forced by superior numbers and exhausted ammunition to retreat, it reported only two casualties from this battle—a sergeant and a private, both wounded.[77]

As Conway's brigade was not assigned to Wayne's division, the 6th Pennsylvania Regiment was not present at Paoli on September 20, 1777, but one of its men, presumably on detached service with one of Wayne's regiments, was wounded in the British surprise attack on that occasion.[78]

At the Battle of Germantown, on October 4, 1777, however, the 6th Pennsylvania Regiment, with the rest of Conway's brigade, advanced between Wayne's division on the left and Sullivan's division on the right, making up the center element of the force carrying out the frontal assault on the middle of the British defensive line. When Wayne's men began to fall back after being mistakenly fired on from the left rear by other American troops, Conway's brigade found its left flank uncovered, and also withdrew. The regiment lost one private killed and an ensign, a sergeant, and a private wounded.[79]

At Whitemarsh, the 6th Pennsylvania was in the second line of the American defenses,[80] and was not engaged.

Like the other Pennsylvania Line regiments, it spent the winter of 1777-1778 at Valley Forge, and was with the main body of Washington's army following the British forces from Philadelphia across New Jersey in June of 1778. Apparently, it was not heavily engaged with the enemy at the Battle of Monmouth on June 28, its only known losses being the previously mentioned capture of Lt. Thomas Bull and the wounding of one private.[81]

The regiment stayed in the area of the New Jersey-New York border, spending the winter of 1778-1779 at Middlebrook, New Jersey. The following summer, it was at West Point for a time, then formed part of the force which stormed Stony Point on July 16.[82] By October 15, it was in Brig. Gen. William Irvine's brigade at West Point, where its strength is shown as 244 officers and men.[83]

After surviving the winter of 1779-1780, probably at Morristown, New Jersey, the 6th Pennsylvania took part in the fighting in New Jersey in the spring and summer of 1780. The most costly of these actions took place at Paramus, where parts of the regiment were with the force that was surprised by a British raiding party early on April 16. The 6th Pennsylvania's share of the casualties that day was one private killed and a first lieutenant and two privates captured.[84] The regiment was also present at the attack on the Blockhouse at Bergen Heights on July 21. Here it was part of the blocking force holding off British troops while the actual assault on the Blockhouse took place. In this action, one of its men was blinded by a musket ball.[85]

The 6th Pennsylvania Regiment was not with the troops who reinforced West Point on September 25, but some of its members, traveling in boats on the Passaic River, were attacked by a Tory detachment at Brown's Ferry, New Jersey, on October 6, 1780, and one 6th Pennsylvania soldier was wounded.[86]

The regiment was at Morristown again in December. There, its members joined in the mutiny of all the Pennsylvania troops on January 1, 1781.[87] After the settlement of the mutineers' complaints, those of the men of the 6th Pennsylvania who remained in the service were distributed among the three provisional battalions sent to the south, although the regiment as such remained nominally in existence until 1783, when the army as a whole was disbanded.

Chapter VIII
6th Pennsylvania Battalion
7th Pennsylvania Regiment

ORGANIZATION

6th Pennsylvania Battalion

The 6th Pennsylvania Battalion was authorized on January 4, 1776. The original plan to recruit the battalion exclusively in Cumberland County was modified during the period of actual organization, with six of the eight companies being raised in Cumberland County and the remaining two in York County.[1]

William Irvine was appointed colonel of the battalion. He continued to hold that position throughout the organization's existence.[2]

The lieutenant colonel of the battalion, again for the duration of its service, was Thomas Hartley.[3]

Initially, James Dunlop was the battalion's major, but apparently he did not serve with the organization continuously. Although Dunlop was not promoted and transferred (to the 10th Pennsylvania Regiment) until October 25, 1776,[4] David Grier had already been promoted— seemingly irregularly—to be the battalion's major with an effective date of June 1, 1776.[5]

The companies of the battalion were as follows:

- [Company A], raised in Cumberland County, commanded by Capt. Abraham Smith.[6]
- [Company B], commanded by Capt. Samuel Hay,[7] of Cumberland County.[8]
- [Company C], commanded by Capt. Jeremiah Talbot.[9] By inference, it is clear that this company was recruited in Cumberland County.
- [Company D], commanded by Capt. William Rippey.[10] Although not explicitly so identified, this definitely was another of the Cumberland County companies.
- [Company E], commanded by Capt. James Armstrong Wilson,[11] and also raised in Cumberland County. Captain Wilson was captured at Isle Aux Noix, in Canada, on June 24, 1776.[12] The company's first lieutenant, Samuel McFerren, was taken prisoner at the same time, and the only other officer of the company present for duty, Ensign Joseph Culbertson, was killed.[13] Probably this company was placed for command purposes under one of the other captains.
- [Company F], commanded by Capt. Robert Adams[14] and recruited in Cumberland County. Captain Adams was killed at Isle Aux Noix on June 24, 1776.[15] To replace him, Lewis Bush, formerly first lieutenant of Company E, was promoted to captain.[16]
- [Company G], raised in York County, was commanded by Capt. David Grier.[17] On Grier's promotion to major on June 1, 1776, the company was put under the command of William Alexander, promoted from first lieutenant of Company D.[18]
- [Company H], commanded by Capt. Moses McClean[19] and also raised in York County.[20] Captain McClean was taken prisoner on June 24, 1776, at Isle Aux Noix, and not exchanged until March 27, 1777,[21] by which time the battalion's term of service had expired. As he had been carried against the battalion's authorized strength throughout the time he was a prisoner, no one could be promoted to replace him. The company's first lieutenant, John Edie, and its second lieutenant, John Hoe, had both been captured at Three Rivers on June 9, 1776,[22] so it is likely that this company, as well as Company E, was simply attached to one of the other units of the battalion.

On the return of the 6th Pennsylvania Battalion to Carlisle in March, 1777, large numbers of its members enlisted in the 7th Pennsylvania Regiment, the battalion's successor unit. While the muster rolls of the two organizations give less than a definitive picture, a comparison of those rolls shows 139 enlisted veterans of the battalion serving in the regiment. As the initial strength of the battalion had been 710[23] and as it sustained considerable losses from disease and enemy action, together with experiencing the inevitable desertions, it appears that upwards of at least one fourth of the survivors of the 6th Pennsylvania Battalion joined the 7th Pennsylvania Regiment. This fact, combined with an unusually extensive list of rosters for the regiment, provides exceptionally strong documentation for the continuity not only between the battalion and the regiment but also between the specific companies of the two organizations.

The battalion's uniform consisted of a blue coat and breeches, the coat "turned up" with red, and a small round hat, bound with braid or tape.[24]

7th Pennsylvania Regiment

Col. William Irvine had been captured at the fiasco at Three Rivers on June 9, 1776. Although he was paroled on the following August 3, he was not formally exchanged until May 6, 1778, and thus did not assume command of the 7th Pennsylvania Regiment until that date. However, he did serve as colonel of the regiment for the year intervening between that time and his promotion to brigadier general on May 12, 1779.[25]

In the meantime, when the regiment was first formed, Major David Grier had been promoted to lieutenant colonel,[26] replacing Lt. Col. Thomas Hartley, who had been appointed colonel of an "additional" Continental regiment on January 1, 1777,[27] and it was Grier who actually commanded the 7th Pennsylvania Regiment until he was wounded at Paoli on September 20, 1777. He did not return to duty;[28] and from that time until Colonel Irvine was exchanged, the senior officer present would have acted as regimental commander. When Colonel Irvine was promoted to brigadier general on May 12, 1779, Lt. Col. Morgan Conner, of Hartley's Regiment, was transferred to the 7th Pennsylvania Regiment. However, as this was after the date when Congress had banned any further promotions to the grade of colonel, he was not promoted; rather, he was designated as Lieutenant-Colonel Commandant. He commanded the regiment until December 2, 1779, when he began a six months leave, but was lost at sea in January, 1780.[29] No replacement was named until August 8, 1780, when Josiah Harmar was transferred from his assignment as lieutenant colonel of the 6th Pennsylvania Regiment to become Lieutenant-Colonel Commandant of the 7th Pennsylvania Regiment, a position which he then held until January 17, 1781.[30]

The first major of the 7th Pennsylvania Regiment was Samuel Hay,[31] who had been a company commander in the 6th Pennsylvania Battalion.[32] On February 21, 1778, he was promoted to lieutenant colonel and assigned to the 10th Pennsylvania Regiment.[33] He was not replaced until October 9, 1778, when James Parr was promoted from captain, 1st Pennsylvania Regiment. Parr continued to hold this position for the rest of the war,[34] although during much of that time he was on detached service with organizations operating on the frontier against the Indians.

The companies of the 7th Pennsylvania Regiment can be confidently identified with their parent companies of the 6th Pennsylvania Battalion, due to the recurrence of large numbers of the same names on the respective muster rolls.

• [Company A], commanded by Capt. John Alexander,[35] who in the battalion had been first lieutenant of this company under Capt. Abraham Smith.[36] Captain Smith had left the army when the 6th Pennsylvania Battalion was mustered out[37] and Alexander was promoted in his place, retaining command until January 17, 1781.[38]

• [Company B], commanded by Capt. Samuel Montgomery.[39] This company's commander in the battalion, Capt. Samuel Hay, was promoted to major in the 7th Pennsylvania Regiment when it was formed. Montgomery, who had served in the 6th Pennsylvania Battalion as an ensign and second lieutenant, was promoted to fill the vacancy. He commanded this company for the remainder of the war.[40]

• [Company C], initially commanded in the regiment, as it had been in the battalion, by Capt. Jeremiah Talbot. He was promoted to major, 6th Pennsylvania Regiment on September 27, 1777.[41] The company then came under Andrew Irvine, who was promoted from first lieutenant,[42] having previously been a second lieutenant in the 6th Pennsylvania Battalion. He continued as company commander until January 17, 1781.[43]

• [Company D], which in the battalion had been under Capt. William Rippey, was in the regiment placed under Capt. Alexander Parker,[44] as Rippey resigned his commission on March 20, 1777.[45] Parker, who had been a second lieutenant and first lieutenant in the 6th Pennsylvania Battalion, commanded this company until January 17, 1781.[46]

• [Company E], commanded by Capt. Robert Wilson.[47] In the battalion, he had been a second lieutenant in the same company,[48] when it had been commanded by Capt. James Armstrong Wilson until his capture on June 24, 1776. Capt. Robert Wilson was wounded at Paoli on September 20, 1777, and resigned his commission on March 1, 1778.[49] Subsequently, this unit became the "Major's Company" of the regiment, and as such was commanded, at least nominally, by Major James Parr.

• [Company F], commanded by Capt. William Bratton.[50] In the battalion, this company had been under Capt. Robert Adams until he was killed, and then under Capt. Lewis Bush. As Captain Bush did not join the 7th Pennsylvania Regiment, transferring instead to Hartley's Regiment, this company was assigned to Captain Bratton. He had been first lieutenant of the same company in the 6th Pennsylvania Battalion.[51] On April 17, 1779, he resigned from the army,[52] and was replaced by William Miller, promoted on that date from captain-lieutenant of Company H.[53]

• [Company G] continued for a time under Capt. William Alexander,[54] who had been promoted to command it when its original commander, Capt. David Grier, had become major of the battalion. On April 11, 1780, Alexander was promoted to major, 3d Pennsylvania Regiment.[55] His successor as company commander was Capt. Samuel Kennedy,[56] who had been an ensign and second lieutenant in the 6th Pennsylvania Battalion and a second lieutenant, first lieutenant, and captain-lieutenant in the 7th Pennsylvania Regiment. Kennedy continued as commander of Company G until January 17, 1781.[57]

• [Company H], commanded by Capt. John McDowell.[58] In the battalion, this company had been under Capt. Moses McClean until he was taken prisoner. McClean was exchanged on March 27, 1777, but left the army at that time,[59] and McDowell, who had been a first lieutenant in the 6th Pennsylvania Battalion, was appointed in his place. McDowell was a physician by profession, and on February 2, 1778, he resigned his captaincy to accept appointment as Surgeon, 6th Pennsylvania Regiment.[60] Company H then became the "Lieutenant Colonel's Company" of the regiment, operating under the actual command of Capt.-Lt. William Miller,[61] who was promoted to captain on May 12, 1779,[62] and transferred to command Company F. As the Lieutenant Colonel's Company, this unit then came under Capt.-Lt. John Bush,[63] who had been an ensign in the 6th Pennsylvania Battalion and a first lieutenant in the 7th Pennsylvania Regiment prior to his promotion to captain-lieutenant. He served as commander of this company until January 17, 1781.[64]

• [Company I] was an additional unit, formed to bring the regiment up to its full complement of nine companies as provided by the reorganization of May 27, 1778. It was commanded by Capt. William Lusk.[65] He had been an ensign in the 6th Pennsylvania Battalion and a first lieutenant in the 7th Pennsylvania Regiment. He was promoted to captain, having been a captain-lieutenant for less than a month, on May 12, 1779. He commanded this company until January 17, 1781.[66]

Many of the men of the 7th Pennsylvania Regiment continued to wear the same "regimentals" they had been issued when serving in the 6th Pennsylvania Battalion. One deserter, however, had a blue coat faced with white instead of red, and others were dressed in a diversity of red, brown, and other colors of coats, and one wore a white hunting shirt.[67]

Summary

Companies G and H of the 6th Pennsylvania Battalion were raised chiefly in York County, and the other companies primarily in Cumberland County. A substantial number of men from the battalion re-enlisted when the 7th Pennsylvania Regiment was formed, a statistically significant number joining the companies of the regiment corresponding to those in which they had served in the battalion. Thus, the 7th Pennsylvania Regiment's Companies G and H continued to be essentially York County units, and the other companies were manned mainly by Cumberland County residents. The one possible exception was the regiment's ninth company, Company I. This was filled by detachments from a number of the older companies, plus new recruits. All the same, it undoubtedly had the same regional character, if not the specific identification with one county or the other, which marked the other companies of the organizatibn.

OPERATIONS

6th Pennsylvania Battalion

The 6th Pennsylvania Battalion, then at Carlisle, received orders on March 14, 1776, to join the forces at New York City.[68] Evidently, it was rapidly uniformed and equipped, for by April 24 the entire battalion had arrived as ordered; but on April 26 it was directed (along with three companies of the 4th Pennsylvania Battalion) to go to Albany to join the army attacking Canada. The battalion reached Albany on May 10, leaving three days later. On May 24, as part of a force under Brig. Gen. John Sullivan, it passed Lake George; it reached Chambly on June 3, and joined the main army at Sorel the next day. On June 5, with other troops under the over-all command of Brig. Gen. William Thompson, it was sent on to Nicolette to reinforce troops under Col. Arthur St. Clair. It was this force which was involved in the fiasco at Three Rivers on June 9.[69]

In that action, seventy-eight of the members of the 6th Pennsylvania Battalion were killed or captured.[70] Among the prisoners was the battalion commander, Col. William Irvine.[71] It was a party of retreating members of Company A, under Capt. Abraham Smith, that the detachment of ten riflemen under Capt. John Lacey found and guided back to Sorel following the defeat[72] (see Chapter VI).

The survivors of the battalion, with the rest of the American force, fell back to Isle Aux Noix. While still camped there, on June 24, Captains McClean, Adams, and Rippey, along with Lieutenants Samuel

McFerren, Abdiel McAllister, and John Hoge, Ensigns William Lusk and Joseph Culbertson, and four privates, decided to leave camp "to fish and disport themselves," going across the lake to a point about a mile away from camp but still within sight. Although Captain McClean suggested that they should take their weapons, the others ridiculed the idea, and they went unarmed. After a time, they went into a nearby house and were drinking spruce beer when they were attacked by a group of Indians who had been watching their movements. Captain Adams, Ensign Culbertson, and two of the enlisted men were killed and scalped "in a most inhuman and barbarous manner." Captain Rippey and Ensign Lusk escaped capture, but all the others were taken prisoner. This was seen from the camp on the island and a force quickly came to help, but did not arrive in time to prevent the captives from being carried off.[73] Rippey had avoided capture because he was a short distance away in the woods when the Indians rushed the house. Lusk escaped because, when the raid began, he climbed into the loft of the house, pulling up the ladder and closing the trap door behind him.[74]

The American force at Isle Aux Noix retreated to Crown Point, which it reached on July 1. While the other troops moved on to Ticonderoga, the 6th Pennsylvania Battalion remained behind, forming the outpost for the army. For the next three and a half months it continued in this mission, having occasional brushes with the enemy and sustaining some casualties. Lieutenant Colonel Hartley's orders were to hold on unless faced by a major attack, in which case he was to retreat; and on October 14, with the main British army approaching, he set fire to the houses at Crown Point and its vicinity and fell back to Ticonderoga.[75]

The battalion stayed at that post, as part of the garrison, until the men's enlistments ran out. It then returned to Carlisle, where it was mustered out on March 15, 1777.[76]

7th Pennsylvania Regiment

With so large a proportion of veterans re-enlisting, the 7th Pennsylvania Regiment was ready for field duty in a short time. It may have seen some combat very shortly after it joined the main army, for as of June 17, 1777, at Middlebrook, New Jersey, a strength report lists a total of fourteen men dead, although it is not clear how many of these may have died of disease. Of the remaining 389 personnel, 60 had deserted and 83 were sick. What with furloughs, absence without leave, and recruiting details, only 37 officers and 220 men were present for duty.[77]

As part of one of the brigades under Brig. Gen. Anthony Wayne, the 7th Pennsylvania Regiment marched south with Washington's army in

August. It fought at the Battle of Brandywine on September 11, 1777, where it helped in the unsuccessful effort to block the advance of the enemy troops under Knyphausen across Brandywine Creek at Chadd's Ford, reporting one soldier killed.[78]

It was much more badly battered in the British surprise attack at Paoli on September 20, when it was so located that it found itself bearing much of the brunt of the assault.* Lieutenant Colonel Grier suffered a bayonet wound in the chest and Capt. Robert Wilson one in the side, although neither was especially serious (Lieutenant Colonel Grier, however, never returned to duty with the regiment). Capt. Andrew Irvine (then still a first lieutenant) was stabbed seventeen times; although he was not incapacited from further duty, he never fully recovered and died soon after the war. All told, sixty-one of the regiment's enlisted men—half of those who had been present for duty—were killed or wounded.[79]

Despite these casualties, the 7th Pennsylvania Regiment fought again, at the Battle of Germantown, on October 4, 1777. In that action it took part in the frontal assault on the British center. No reports list any of its personnel killed, but a first lieutenant[80] and three enlisted men[81] were wounded before the regiment fell back with the rest of Wayne's division when fired on from the rear by other American troops.

All this seriously eroded the regiment's strength. By November 1, 1777, it had only 17 officers and 105 enlisted men present for duty. Eighty more men were sick and thirty others were on detached service. The senior officer present was Captain Talbot.[82]

The regiment was present, disposed in the American first line, at Whitemarsh in December, 1777, but did not see any fighting.[83] After spending the winter of 1777-1778 at Valley Forge, it fought at the Battle of Monmouth, on June 28, 1778. There, it appears to have been one of the three Pennsylvania regiments which comprised the hastily gathered force which Anthony Wayne led in an attack, late in the afternoon, against withdrawing British forces, and then in the defense of a position along a hedgerow against a strong British counterattack.[84] However, only one of its members, Sgt. John Hays,[85] was a casualty, and at the time he was wounded he had been detached, because of his previous experience as a cannoneer, for service with an artillery unit. According to legend, it was his wife, Mary Ludwig Hays ("Molly Pitcher"), who

*Major Hay, in a letter to Colonel Irvine, was critical both of General Wayne and the 1st Pennsylvania Regiment. He said that the troops were not alerted to the British approach, and charged (without apparent justification) that "the General had full intelligence of their designs two hours before they came out." He also said that the 1st Pennsylvania "stood only one fire and retreated." PA(5), III, 202.

took his place on the gun crew when he was wounded, thereby becoming the heroine of Monmouth.[86]

Unlike many of the other regiments, the 7th Pennsylvania was little affected by the reorganization of July 1, 1778, and none of its officers became supernumerary. It continued in Washington's army, helping to keep watch on the British in New York and to counter the enemy raids into New Jersey. It apparently spent the winter of 1778-1779 at Middlebrook. In the summer of 1779, at least some of its elements were in the force which attacked Stony Point, New York, on July 16. By October 15, with its strength listed as 247 officers and men, the regiment was part of the garrison at West Point, serving in Anthony Wayne's brigade of St. Clair's division,[87] but it probably spent the winter of 1779-1780 at Morristown, New Jersey.

Part of the 7th Pennsylvania saw action when an outpost including some of its members at New Bridge, New Jersey, was struck by a large force of Hessian infantry and cavalry on April 16, 1780, and 1st Lt. Samuel Bryson (who had also been wounded at the Battle of Germantown) was wounded and captured. The same enemy force then moved on to strike the American outpost at Paramus, where another 7th Pennsylvania officer, 1st Lt. John Bryson, was also wounded and captured.[88]

The regiment was part of the force with which Wayne attacked the Blockhouse at Bergen Heights, New Jersey, on July 21, 1780. It was not in the actual assault on the fortification, however, being posted to protect the line of retreat in case British troops tried to cut the Americans off,[89] and apparently sustained no losses. It was still under Wayne two months later, when it took part in the forced march from Tappan, New York, to strengthen the West Point garrison at the time that Benedict Arnold's defection was discovered on September 25.

With most of the other units of the Pennsylvania Line, the 7th Pennsylvania began the winter of 1780-1781 at Morristown. There, on January 1, 1781, its men joined the mutiny of the other Pennsylvania troops.[90] In the reorganization which followed, this regiment was disbanded, its officers either leaving the service or being transferred to one of the six regiments that were retained. The bulk of the enlisted men were discharged, although some of them re-enlisted, serving in one of the three new provisional battalions which were sent to the southern theater of operations.

Chapter IX

8th Pennsylvania Regiment

Daniel Brodhead

ORGANIZATION

THE 8th Pennsylvania Regiment, the first of the Pennsylvania Continental regiments formed without prior existence as a battalion, had an irregular organizational history; much of its service was remote from the main army and the center of activity; and its company personnel records are virtually nonexistent. It thus cannot be described in the same sort of detail as most of the other units of the Pennsylvania Line.

It was authorized on July 15, 1776, for the specific purpose of manning Presqu'Isle, Le Boeuf, and Kittanning, to provide protection against Indian attacks in the western frontier area. Seven of its companies were recruited in Westmoreland County; the eighth company was raised in Bedford County.[1] Because all but two of the original company commanders whose pre-war residences can be identified were from Bedford County, however, it is not possible to identify with assurance which captains commanded companies from which county.

The first commander of the regiment was Col. Aeneas Mackey (or Mackay),[2] who had been an officer in the British Army during the

French and Indian War, after which he had settled in Westmoreland County.[3] Following his death on February 14, 1777,[4] he was replaced by Daniel Brodhead, who was promoted from lieutenant colonel, 4th Pennsylvania Regiment, and given command of the 8th Pennsylvania, retaining this position until January 17, 1781.[5]

The regiment's lieutenant colonel was George Wilson,[6] but he also died in February, 1777. He was replaced by Richard Butler, who was promoted from major of the regiment. But on June 9, Lieutenant Colonel Butler was transferred to Col. Daniel Morgan's special task force of riflemen supporting Major General Gates's force in northern New York.[7] The new lieutenant colonel of the regiment was James Ross, transferred in grade from the 1st Pennsylvania Regiment. Within three months — on September 22, 1777 — he resigned his commission.[8] To replace him, Stephen Bayard (Colonel Mackey's son-in-law[9]) was promoted, continuing as lieutenant colonel of the 8th Pennsylvania until January 17, 1781.[10]

Richard Butler had been the regiment's first major. When he was promoted to lieutenant colonel on March 12, 1777,[11] Stephen Bayard was promoted from captain, 2d Pennsylvania Battalion and transferred to the 8th Pennsylvania.[12] Bayard's subsequent promotion to lieutenant colonel brought the promotion and transfer of Frederick Vernon from captain, 5th Pennsylvania Regiment. Major Vernon served with the 8th Pennsylvania Regiment until January 17, 1781.[13]

The eight original companies, whose commanders all had commissions dated August 9, 1776, were:

• [Company A], commanded by Capt. David Kilgore, a resident of Bedford County.[14] He served only until January, 1777.[15] Apparently it was this company which was taken over by Capt. Michael Hufnagel. Captain Hufnagel had formerly been adjutant of the 1st Pennsylvania Regiment. He ranked as a captain in the 8th Pennsylvania from March 16, 1777,[16] but had been listed as a captain on the regimental roster as early as December 16, 1776.[17] In any case, he became supernumerary on July 1, 1778.[18] It is not clear who replaced him.*

• [Company B], commanded by Capt. Samuel Miller. Probably Captain Miller was the man of that name residing in Bedford County in 1773.[19] His name is on the list of the regiment's company commanders dated November 1, 1777.[20] He died on January 10, 1778,[21] but his name

---

*The reorganization of 1778 made four of the captains of the 8th Pennsylvania Regiment supernumerary, and there was already one vacant captaincy in the regiment. Five captains of other regiments which had been absorbed by various units were transferred to the 8th Pennsylvania at this time, but the lack of any relevant company muster rolls prevents establishment of the captain-for-captain replacements.

is also on the regiment's list of company commanders dated December 10, 1778, although it bears the notation (obviously incorrect), "supposed to be deserted."[22] There is no indication that anyone was promoted to replace him. After July 1, 1778, this company was presumably assigned to one of the officers transferred from other regiments.

• [Company C], commanded by Captain Van Swearingen. From February 3, 1776, until he was commissioned in the 8th Pennsylvania Regiment on August 9, 1776, Captain Swearingen commanded an independent company in the State service,[23] formed to defend Westmoreland County against Indians.[24] In the summer of 1777, he was put in command of one of three detachments, formed of picked riflemen drawn from all companies of the regiment, which were attached to a special task force under Col. Daniel Morgan and sent to reinforce Maj. Gen. Horatio Gates.[25] While on this assignment, on September 19, 1777, near Bemis Heights, New York, Swearingen was wounded and, with a number of others, taken prisoner by Indian elements of a British-Indian force which raided Morgan's camp at Stillwater.[26] Before the Indians could kill Swearingen, he was rescued by a British soldier, who took him to the British commander, Gen. Simon Fraser. Swearingen refused to give answers when Fraser interrogated him, at which Fraser threatened to hang him. Swearingen is reported to have replied, "You may, if you please." Fraser, with his bluff called, had Swearingen put in with the other prisoners.[27] There is no record of Swearingen being exchanged, but he resigned from the army on August 10, 1779.[28] Until that time, he was carried on the regimental rolls.[29] Upon Swearingen's resignation, John Crawford was promoted to fill the vacancy thus created. Captain Crawford had joined the 8th Pennsylvania as a second lieutenant on August 9, 1776, being promoted to first lieutenant on April 16, 1777. He served with the regiment as a captain from August 10, 1779, to January 17, 1781.[30]

• [Company D], commanded by Capt. James Piggott. Commissioned as a captain of Pennsylvania Associators on April 6, 1776, Piggott became a captain in the 8th Pennsylvania Regiment when it was formed. He resigned his commission on October 22, 1777.[31] John Finley was promoted from first lieutenant to replace him, and continued as a captain in the 8th Pennsylvania until January 17, 1781.[32]

• [Company E], commanded by Capt. Andrew Mann (or Man). Captain Mann was commissioned on August 9, 1776. Although Heitman's *Register* shows him only as a second lieutenant,[33] this is evidently an error, as the 8th Pennsylvania's records repeatedly list him as a captain.[34] He is shown as being sick in quarters on May 2, 1777,[35] and he died some time in June of that year.[36] He was replaced by Thomas T.

Cook, who was promoted from first lieutenant, but became super-numerary and left the army on January 31, 1779.[37]

• [Company F], commanded by Capt. Wendel Oury, a resident of Bedford County in 1773.[38] He resigned his commission on October 11, 1777.[39] To replace him, Nehemiah Stokely was promoted from first lieutenant, but became supernumerary on January 31, 1779.[40] Which of the transferred captains took over this company is not known.

• [Company G], commanded by Capt. Moses Carson.[41] Carson deserted to the enemy on April 21, 1777 (on February 23, a 1st Lt. Richard Carson of the 8th Pennsylvania Regiment, presumably a relative, had also deserted).[42] Apparently, his replacement was Matthew Jack, promoted from first lieutenant. Captain Jack, however, had recently (on April 12 or 13) been seriously wounded at Bound Brook, New Jersey, when his rifle burst, causing him to lose his left hand. He never returned to duty, and left the army — presumably as a super-numerary — on January 31, 1779.[43] There is no information concerning which of the captains later transferred into the 8th Pennsylvania Regiment succeeded to command of this company.

• [Company H], commanded by Capt. James Montgomery. This James Montgomery would appear to have been a resident of West-moreland County.[44] Although two Pennsylvania officers of this name are listed in Heitman,[45] neither of them is this individual, as one was a second lieutenant in the 2d Pennsylvania Battalion and the other was a captain of an independent artillery company. The James Montgomery of the 8th Pennsylvania Regiment, however, is on several of the regiment's lists of company commanders in 1776 and 1777.[46] He died on August 26, 1777[47] — the same date given in Heitman for the artillery captain, which makes it seem likely that Heitman has confused two men as being a single person. Again, no information identifying a replacement has been found; the vacancy created by Captain Montgomery's death was probably not filled until the five captains from other regiments joined the 8th Pennsylvania.

• [Company I], commanded by Capt. Samuel Brady. This unit was not part of the regiment's original structure, but was added when a ninth company was authorized. It was part of Capt. John Doyle's in-dependent company, organized on July 6, 1776,[48] in which Brady was the first lieutenant. In November, 1776, however, this part of Doyle's Company was detached from its parent unit, eventually becoming the ninth ("Colonel's Company") component of the 8th Pennsylvania, with Brady being promoted to captain-lieutenant. On August 2, 1779, the resignation of one of the captains transferred from another regiment—Capt. James Francis Moore (see below) — brought Brady's promotion to captain. He continued in command of this company, however, until January 17, 1781.[49]

Five captains were transferred into the 8th Pennsylvania Regiment from other organizations, effective July 1, 1778, although apparently they did not join their new unit until early 1779 and did not thereby displace the supernumerary officers of the regiment until that time. The specific companies to which these newly arrived captains were assigned are not known. The officers, however, were:

• Capt. Samuel Dawson, from the "Old" 11th Pennsylvania Regiment.[50] He died at Fort Pitt on September 6, 1779.[51] Whatever company he took over, no one was promoted to replace him.

• Capt. James Francis Moore, from the 13th Pennsylvania Regiment. He resigned on August 2, 1779,[52] and as noted above, Samuel Brady was promoted to fill the vacancy that was created.

• Capt. John Clark, from the 12th Pennsylvania Regiment, who remained in the 8th Pennsylvania until January 17, 1781.[53]

• Capt. James Carnaghan, from the 13th Pennsylvania Regiment, also continued in the 8th Pennsylvania until January 17, 1781.[54]

• Capt. Joseph Lewis Finley, from the 13th Pennsylvania Regiment. After July 20, 1780, he was on detached duty as brigade major, but was carried on the regiment's rolls as a captain until January 17, 1781.[55]

Summary

About all that can be said about the organizational history of the 8th Pennsylvania Regiment is that it was recruited chiefly in Westmoreland County, with one company from Bedford County. Much of the time, its elements were widely scattered, serving in detachments or as separate companies. It spent the bulk of the war on the frontier, where supervision was loose, administration lax, and recruiting apparently so difficult in a relatively sparsely populated area that strength fell too low to justify promotions to fill officer vacancies. If the number of officers who died is any indication, there must have been an abnormally high mortality rate from other than combat causes, for during the regiment's existence it lost a colonel, a lieutenant colonel, and four captains to illness.

OPERATIONS

After the regiment was recruited, it was assembled at Kittanning, where it remained until at least November 26, 1776. On December 4, orders (directed by Congress on November 22) arrived, instructing the regiment — now first officially designated as the 8th Pennsylvania — to march to join Washington's army wherever it might be found. These orders apparently were not well received, causing resentment in an organization already not noted for discipline or subordination. In a letter to a member of Congress on December 5, Lt. Col. George Wilson expressed his personal willingness to comply, adding "But as Both ye Officers and Men understood they Ware Raised for ye Defence of ye Westeran Frontiers, and their fameleys and substance to be Left in so Defenceless a situation in their absence, seems to Give Sensable trouble, altho I Hope We Will Get over it, By Leaving sum of ower trifeling Officers behind who Pirtend to Have More Witt than seven men that can Rendar a Reason." He went on to say, with what would prove to be foresight, that "We are ill Provided for a March at this Season, But there is nothing Hard under sum Sircumstances."[56] Men were poorly equipped and supplied, and if there was a prescribed uniform, it was not available for general issue; some men of this regiment are described as wearing hunting shirts, and others as having brown coats with brown facings.[57]

The regiment, less Captain Kilgore, who gave up his appointment, left Kittanning on January 6, 1777,[58] arriving some six weeks later at Quibbletown (now New Market), New Jersey. Lieutenant Colonel Wilson had not underestimated the difficulties of the march. Indeed, during February, both he and Colonel Mackey died. By June 9, when a new command structure had taken effect, the original strength of 684 men had been reduced by 36 men captured, 14 missing, 51 dead, 15 discharged, and 126 deserted.[59] Among the deserters were a captain, two first lieutenants, and an ensign. In addition, a second lieutenant and an ensign had been dismissed the service,[60] for reasons that are not recorded.

During that winter and spring, the 8th Pennsylvania Regiment was at Bound Brook, New Jersey. There, on April 12 or 13, it sustained several losses when it was defeated by a British surprise attack.[61] It was during the following summer that the three special detachments of riflemen from all companies were formed, commanded respectively by Captain Swearingen, 1st Lt. Basil Prather, and 2d Lt. John Hardin, for service with Col. Daniel Morgan on the northern front.[62]

The rest of the regiment remained with Washington's army, in Wayne's division. As such, it fought at the Battle of Brandywine on September 11, 1777, helping to cover Chadd's Ford but being driven back by an enemy force under Gen. Wilhelm Knyphausen. In this engagement, Major Bayard was wounded; a cannon ball struck him "on the head and shoulder, and tumbled him over on the ground for near two rods. Deponent [1st Lt. Gabriel Peterson] helped him up on his feet — he was frantic, and seemed much hurt, but being much engaged at that time deponent could not render him any assistance."[63]

The 8th Pennsylvania Regiment was part of the force under Anthony Wayne which was surprised at Paoli on September 20. It fought again at the Battle of Germantown, on October 4. There, with Wayne's division, it was in the frontal assault directed against the British center. It was also present, in the first line but not engaged, at Whitemarsh, in early December.[64]

By November 1, not long before moving to Whitemarsh, the regiment had lost its lieutenant colonel (Lieutenant Colonel Ross had resigned), and its present-for-duty strength was down to 18 officers and 153 enlisted men. Also present, but reported as sick, were twenty-eight enlisted men. Aside from the colonel, the major, and two staff officers, the regiment had only two captains and six lieutenants — four captaincies were vacant, one of the remaining captains authorized being a prisoner and the other, presumably, among the 139 personnel on detached service. There were seventy-seven men absent, sick, and fifty-nine enlisted men were listed as prisoners of war.[65]

It began the winter encampment at Valley Forge in mid-December, 1777. Apparently, not all the vacancies were filled at Valley Forge, although the troops who had been with Morgan did return. But troubles on the frontier were increasing, and on March 8, 1778, before the 8th Pennsylvania could get any benefit from the training which Gen. Friedrich von Steuben was about to initiate, the regiment was ordered to move to Fort Pitt.[66]

Having returned to the west, the regiment shared in providing security for the region. Then, on July 12, it was sent along the West Branch of the Susquehanna River to counter British-inspired raids by Indians against settlements in that area and in the Wyoming Valley. By late July, the regiment's headquarters were at Muncy. Colonel Brodhead, however, had split his force into company-size elements to patrol in separate areas. One of these, under one of the two Captains Finley (more likely, Capt. John Finley, as Capt. Joseph Lewis Finley might not yet have had time to join from his former regiment), ranged as far as Penn's Valley, where it based itself on Potter's Fort. There, on July 24, two of its soldiers were killed by a small party of Indians scouting near the fort.[67]

At this time, Hartley's Regiment was already on the way from Washington's army to relieve the 8th Pennsylvania in the West Branch Valley, and when it arrived, Colonel Brodhead moved his troops back to Fort Pitt.[68] Later that year, the regiment was part of a force which, under the commander of the Western Department, Brig. Gen. Lachlan McIntosh, made a probe down the Ohio River. The troops suffered greatly from the winter weather and from a lack of supplies and clothing which was extreme even for the Continental Army. Colonel

Brodhead considered the expedition to be ill-conceived and badly managed. In particular, he objected to the construction at the mouth of Beaver Creek of Fort McIntosh, which he called a "very romantic Building . . ., built by the hands of hundreds who would rather have fought than wrought,"[69] and later referring to it as "The Hobby Horse he [McIntosh] built at Beaver Creek."[70] But after the one fort was finished, the force pushed on to the head of the Muskingum and built Fort Laurens.[71]

The following year, the regiment having returned to Fort Pitt, Colonel Brodhead replaced General McIntosh as Department Commander, but still retained command of the 8th Pennsylvania. Throughout the department as a whole, Brodhead reported, Indian raids were almost a daily occurrence, and he was anxious, in his words, "to check the Caitiffs who keep the Inhabitants in one continual alarm."[72] But the regiment was widely scattered in order to provide local security. In mid-April, over a hundred men were at Fort Laurens, fifty more were divided between Wheeling and Holliday's Cove, and most of the rest were providing the entire garrison of Fort McIntosh.[73] It was not until late May that Brodhead was able to get Washington's permission to launch an offensive against the Indians, and not until early August could he assemble the regiment and the necessary militia reinforcements.[74] In the meantime, there were occasional brushes with Indian raiders. The most substantial of these took place around the middle of June, 1779, when Captain Brady's company pursued a small war party which had raided some settlements; Brady's men killed several Indians and recovered the stolen property.[75]

What came to be called "Brodhead's Expedition" set out from Fort Pitt on August 11, 1779. Counting militia as well as the 8th Pennsylvania, it numbered 605 men. It went up the Allegheny River by canoe past Fort Armstrong (Kittanning) to the point where the Mahoning Creek empties into the river — about ten miles beyond Kittanning. After being held up there for four days by heavy rains, the troops left their canoes and marched overland, finally striking the Allegheny again well to the north, near Tionesta. At this point the advance guard of twenty-three men—soldiers and Delaware Indian allies—under 1st Lt. John Hardin, of the 8th Pennsylvania, unexpectedly made contact with thirty or forty Indians coming down the river. The Indians beached their canoes and prepared to fight; Hardin deployed his men; and Colonel Brodhead, who was not far behind, quickly brought up the bulk of his force. It was a short engagement. Seven Indians were killed and the rest fled, carrying a number of wounded. Two soldiers and one of the Delawares in the advance guard were slightly wounded.[76]

This proved to be the only combat of the entire expedition. Colonel Brodhead took his troops well to the north, probably to within twenty miles of the New York border, and then started back. The men burned the hastily abandoned Indian towns along the way and destroyed what Brodhead estimated as at least five hundred acres of corn. Instead of returning to Fort Pitt the way they had come, the troops traveled by canoe down the Allegheny,[77] reaching their home station on September 14.[78]

Throughout this period, including the time on the Ohio, the discipline became, if possible, even worse, and the regiment experienced a spate of courts martial. As soon as the force returned to Fort Pitt, the regiment was reduced severely in strength by the expiration of a large number of enlistments. Recruiting was very difficult in competition with the regiments in nearby western Virginia, as Virginia paid a substantially higher enlistment bonus than Pennsylvania. In the summer of 1780, many of the men remaining in the 8th Pennsylvania had to be discharged because their three-year enlistments now expired. As of July 30, 1780, the regiment's enlisted strength present for duty was only 143 men; four men were listed as sick, two on furlough, two on detached service, and three had deserted. Although all field and staff positions were full, only two captains, three lieutenants, and four ensigns were still on the officer roll.[79]

Thus, while still nominally assigned to garrison Fort Pitt, and therefore not present at Morristown to take part in the mutiny of January 1, 1781, the 8th Pennsylvania Regiment had, to a very large extent, ceased to exist. In brief, for this unit, the reduction of the Pennsylvania Line to six regiments which followed the mutiny was essentially a formalization of an existing situation rather than an inactivation of a viable organization.

Chapter X
9th Pennsylvania Regiment

ORGANIZATION

THE 9th Pennsylvania Regiment was one of the units which came into being on October 25, 1776,[1] and began recruiting after its officers were appointed about mid-November.

The first colonel appointed was James Irvine, who was promoted from lieutenant colonel, 1st Pennsylvania Battalion. But before long (on March 12, 1777), he returned to his former unit (now the 2d Pennsylvania Regiment) as its commander, and was replaced as commander of the 9th Pennsylvania by Anthony James Morris, the lieutenant colonel of the 2d Pennsylvania Regiment.[2] Morris declined the appointment, although he did not do so until June 7, 1777,[3] and the regiment was left in the interim without a permanent commanding officer. However, when Morris finally refused the command, it was given to Richard Butler,[4] who had formerly been lieutenant colonel of the 8th Pennsylvania Regiment. As noted in Chapter IX, Butler was serving at this time with Col. Daniel Morgan's special task force in the Saratoga campaign. He did not join his new command until Morgan's task force returned to Washington's army from Saratoga, but he served with the 9th Pennsylvania from that time until January 17, 1781.[5]

To fill the lieutenant colonelcy, George Nagel was promoted from major, 5th Pennsylvania Battalion. He served with the 9th Pennsylvania until February 7, 1777, when he was promoted to colonel and assigned to the 10th Pennsylvania Regiment.* The lieutenant colonelcy of the 9th Pennsylvania remained vacant until July 1, 1778, when Lt. Col. Caleb North was transferred from the "Old" 11th Pennsylvania upon its absorption by the 10th Pennsylvania Regiment. North continued as lieutenant colonel of the 9th Pennsylvania from that time until January 17, 1781.[6]

The first major of the regiment was John Patton, who had previously served as a major in Miles's Pennsylvania State Rifle Regiment. He could have spent little if any time with his new unit, however, for on January 11, 1777, he was appointed colonel of an "additional" Continental regiment. His replacement was Matthew Smith, who had formerly been a captain in Thompson's Rifle Battalion and then in the 1st Pennsylvania Regiment, but Smith also resigned promptly, effective February 7, 1777.[7] The first major actually to serve as such with the 9th Pennsylvania Regiment, therefore, was Francis Nichols, who was promoted from captain. He held the position until his resignation, on May 12, 1779.[8] His replacement was Thomas Lloyd Moore, promoted from captain, 3d Pennsylvania Regiment, who remained with the 9th Pennsylvania until January 17, 1781.[9]

The two senior captains of the 9th Pennsylvania Regiment spent too little time in that capacity to have had much effect on forming companies. They were Jacob Gerhard Derick (or Dirks), who transferred to the 4th Continental Artillery on March 3, 1777; and Francis Nichols, who (as noted above) became major of the regiment on February 7, 1777.

The eight original companies of the 9th Pennsylvania were:

• [Company A], commanded by Capt. Joseph Erwin, apparently the man of that name who lived in Cumberland County,[10] although he may have been a resident of Westmoreland County (see Chapter XVII). Formerly a captain in the Pennsylvania State Regiment (and, before that, in Miles's State Rifle Regiment), he was commissioned a captain in the 9th Pennsylvania Regiment on November 27, 1776. He became supernumerary on July 1, 1778.[11] With the reorganization which took place at that time, this unit became the "Colonel's Company" of the regiment.[12] The captain-lieutenant in direct command from January 27 until October 10, 1779, was William Vanlear.[13] Subsequently, until

*An ambiguity exists, in that PA(5), III, 380, 469 gives this date as February 7, 1778. Also, Joseph Chambers was carried as colonel, 10th Pennsylvania, from February 7 to April 12, 1777, so that Nagel and Chambers overlap each other. Nevertheless, because it was on February 7, 1777, that a number of other personnel changes in the 9th and 10th Pennsylvania Regiments took place, and because the *Pennsylvania Archives* are inconsistent on the point, it seems more likely that Nagel's transfer and promotion took place in 1777, not 1778; and that on some unknown basis he was granted an *effective* date of rank of February 7, even though the promotion probably did not take place in fact until April 12. See Chapter XI.

January 17, 1781, the company was under Capt.-Lt. Stephen Stephenson.[14]

• [Company B], commanded by Capt. Matthew Henderson, of Philadelphia.[15] Commissioned directly on November 14, 1776, he commanded this company until the reorganization of July 1, 1778, rendered him supernumerary.[16] A comparison of muster rolls shows that this unit then became the "Lieutenant Colonel's Company" of the regiment.[17] Hence, it came directly under Lieutenant Colonel North.

• [Company C], commanded by Captain, later Major, Francis Nichols. In 1774, he held considerable land in Northumberland County,[18] although he may not have actually resided there. Originally a second lieutenant in the Cumberland County company (Company D), under Capt. William Hendricks, of Thompson's Rifle Battalion,[19] he had been taken prisoner at the assault on Quebec on December 31, 1775. He was exchanged on October 10, 1776, and appointed captain in the 9th Pennsylvania Regiment on December 16, 1776, but with an antedated date of rank. When he was promoted to major on February 7, 1777,[20] he retained nominal command of his company, which was thus the "Major's Company" of the regiment. However, as of September 10, 1778, actual command was being exercised by 1st Lt. William Vanlear.[21] As noted, Nichols resigned from the army on May 12, 1779. His company, as the "Major's Company," would then have come under his replacement, Major Thomas Lloyd Moore, who continued to command it until January 17, 1781.[22] Although Francis Nichols was the original company commander, the facts that he was promoted so soon and that he was appointed on the basis of service in another organization reduce the likelihood that the men of his company were recruited from the area of his pre-war residence. The only enlisted man of his company whose residence has been identified was from Philadelphia.

• [Company D], commanded by Capt. John Nelson. Although there were several contemporaries of this name, it seems likely that this individual was the John Nelson living in Philadelphia in 1774.[23] He had been captain of an independent company which, when the 9th Pennsylvania was formed, was incorporated into that regiment.[24] Instead of bringing all of his men with him, however, he accepted money for transferring some of them to the 7th Pennsylvania Regiment, which apparently was competing none too scrupulously for recruits. Nelson was tried and convicted by court martial and cashiered,[25] effective May 15, 1777.[26] To replace him, George Grant, of Sunbury[27] (formerly a lieutenant in Miles's Rifle Regiment[28]), was promoted from first lieutenant. Captain Grant died on October 10, 1779, at which time William Vanlear was promoted from captain-lieutenant to take his place. Vanlear continued as company commander until January 17, 1781.[29]

- [Company E], commanded by Capt. Thomas Gourley, whose pre-war residence is unknown. For what it is worth, the only enlisted man of the company whose residence is shown was from Chester County.[30] Like George Grant, Gourley had been a lieutenant in Miles's State Rifle Regiment, in which he served in a company raised in Lancaster County.[31] He resigned his commission on May 23, 1778,[32] but apparently no one was promoted to fill the vacancy, a number of the men of this company being scattered among five other companies of the regiment.
- [Company F], commanded by Capt. Joseph McClellan. This may be the Joseph McClellan living in Chester County in 1774.[33] He had been a captain in Atlee's Pennsylvania State Battalion of Musketry, and after receiving his appointment to the 9th Pennsylvania Regiment on January 1, 1777, continued in the service until January 17, 1781.[34]
- [Company G], commanded by Capt. Thomas Bartholomew Bowen, who was perhaps the Thomas Bowen of Chester County.[35] He also had seen prior service, in his case as a captain in Miles's State Rifle Regiment. Although he became paymaster of the 9th Pennsylvania Regiment on October 15, 1778,[36] he seems to have performed that function as an additional duty. In any event, he continued to be listed as a company commander as of May, 1780,[37] and January 1, 1781.[38]
- [Company H], commanded by Capt. John Davis. His pre-war residence is unknown, but he had been a captain in Miles's State Rifle Regiment. He served as a captain in the 9th Pennsylvania Regiment from November 15, 1776, to January 17, 1781.[39] The bulk of the enlisted men of his company were from Philadelphia and from Chester County, although there was also some representation from Berks, Lancaster, Cumberland, and York counties.[40]

After the reorganization of the Continental Line, directed on May 27, 1778, a ninth company was added, as follows:

- [Company I], commanded by Capt. John Pearson, apparently the John Pearson who lived in Chester County in 1774.[41] Pearson had been a captain in the "Old" 11th Pennsylvania Regiment which, on July 1, 1778, was absorbed into the 10th Pennsylvania Regiment. Being excess to the authorized strength of the consolidated organization, Captain Pearson was assigned to the 9th Pennsylvania, with which he remained until January 17, 1781.[42]

Two other officers were carried as captains against the strength of the 9th Pennsylvania Regiment. These were Capt. Robert Caldwell and Capt. William Mackey. However, the relations of both with the regiment are ambiguous. Captain Caldwell, as a first lieutenant in the German Regiment, had been captured at Fort Washington, New York, on November 16, 1776. Although he was appointed a captain in the 9th Pennsylvania Regiment on November 29, 1776, he remained a prisoner of war until January 20, 1779, and on March 20 of that year accepted appointment as a captain of marines.[43] Captain Mackey, while serving as a first lieutenant in the "Old" 11th Pennsylvania Regiment, was wounded and captured at the Battle of Brandywine, on September 11, 1777. He was promoted to captain on October 30 and exchanged some time in November. He was transferred to the 9th Pennsylvania on July 1, 1778, and although apparently never given command of a company, served with that organization until January 17, 1781.[44]

The men of the 9th Pennsylvania seem to have been fairly consistently uniformed, but in one of two different patterns. Six deserters, turning themselves over to the British between February, 1777, and August, 1778, are described as wearing brown uniform coats, faced with red in five cases and with buff in the sixth. Four others (between December, 1777, and August, 1778) were wearing "light-colored" coats. On the other hand, deserters of February, 1777, April, 1777, and August, 1778, had blue regimental coats with red facings, and one of these had a new cocked hat with white looping. Still another man, deserting in April, 1777, wore a yellow hunting shirt.[45]

The muster roll of Company H of this regiment, dated August 7, 1779, at West Point,[46] lists the ages of twenty-eight soldiers, the occupations of twenty-seven of them, the birthplaces of twenty-three, and the place of residence at the time of enlistment of twenty-six. The youngest, a fifteen-year-old, had no civilian occupation, and had been born "at sea"; he was, however, one of eight men on the list whose residence was given as Chester. The ages of the others were as follows: 19, 1; 20, 6; 21, 1; 23, 3; 24, 1; 27, 3; 28, 1; 29, 3; 34, 1; 35, 1; 36, 1; 39, 2; 40, 2; and 45, 1. There were thirteen farmers (although one of them styled himself a "planter"), three tailors, two shoemakers, two turners, two weavers, a carpenter, a miller, a butcher, a forgeman, and a coachman. Nine were American-born and fourteen had been born abroad. Of the native Americans, one was born in New Jersey, one in Maryland, and seven in Pennsylvania—one of these was from Germantown and three from Bucks County, while the other Pennsylvanians were not specific. Nine of the foreign-born were natives of Ireland, three of England, and one each of Scotland and Germany. As for places of residence at enlistment, one man came from Virginia and another (not the man who was born there) from New Jersey. Nine were from Philadelphia, eight (as noted) from Chester, two each from Berks, York, and Lancaster counties, and one from Cumberland County. There is no way of determining, of course, how typical these characteristics may have been of the regiment as a whole, but the pattern of a preponderance of foreign-born soldiers (and of Irishmen among them) is consistent with all available data on other Pennsylvania regiments.

Summary

Although the picture is not clear, such information as is available about both officers and enlisted men suggests that the 9th Pennsylvania Regiment drew a considerable proportion of its members from Philadelphia and nearby counties to the south and west. The situation is obscured, however, by the fact that so many of the company commanders were appointed on the basis of prior service, chiefly with the two State organizations, Miles's State Rifle Regiment and Atlee's State Battalion of Musketry, rather than on the basis of having recruited companies.

OPERATIONS

When the 9th Pennsylvania Regiment was organized, it was soon assigned to Washington's main army, becoming part of Brig. Gen. Thomas Conway's brigade. It must have seen some action in the patrol skirmishes of the spring and summer of 1777, for by July 17 of that year, a strength report listed one man as a prisoner of war, seven missing, and twenty-six dead (a number of whom, however, were probably victims of disease). The regiment had 247 officers and men available for duty, counting the three soldiers who were listed as prisoners under arrest. It also had seventeen men on detached duties, thirty-four men sick, and six men on furlough. It had lost eighty-four soldiers by desertion.[47]

The 9th Pennsylvania fought as part of Conway's brigade at the Battle of Brandywine, on September 11, 1777, when it was in the thick of the engagement around the Birmingham Meeting House on the American right flank and lost an ensign killed and a private wounded.[48] Although it was not part of the force surprised at Paoli on September 20, it was nearby, and was deployed to provide cover for the retreating troops of Wayne's two brigades. It also fought at the Battle of Germantown, on October 4, 1777, taking part in the frontal assault against the center of the British line. In that action, its only casualty was a second lieutenant who was wounded and taken prisoner.[49] In December, it was in the second line at Whitemarsh.[50] Apparently, a detachment was sent to join the outpost force, for two privates of the regiment were wounded in the action which took place between American and British skirmishers on December 7.[51]

During the winter which followed, the regiment was at Valley Forge. When the American army left its winter encampment to pursue the British from Philadelphia across New Jersey, the 9th Pennsylvania was in the brigade commanded by Brig. Gen. Charles Scott,[52] and therefore was pushed ahead with the leading elements of the army. When this advance force overtook the British rear guard, the 9th Pennsylvania was placed in a provisional task force under Anthony Wayne, who sent it to drive off a British cavalry detachment near Monmouth Court House. It thus became the first American unit to go into action in the Battle of

Monmouth, which took place on June 28, 1778. Later in the battle, it was attacked by the British 16th Light Dragoons, holding its fire until the last minute and then shattering the enemy charge with a volley.[53] After the entire advance force was ordered to withdraw to the main body of the army, the 9th Pennsylvania helped man the left flank of the American line, which withstood the British attempt to counterattack.[54] In this battle, the total casualties were extremely light, and despite its extensive contacts with enemy forces, the regiment lost only one man killed.[55] three wounded, and one missing.[56]

After spending the winter of 1778-1779 at Middlebrook, New Jersey, the 9th Pennsylvania became a major element of a temporarily formed "Light Infantry Corps" which was organized in June, 1779.[57] In the attack by this command upon Stony Point, New York, on July 16, 1779, most of the regiment was assigned to the left of the two columns which made the assault,[58] although twenty men of the 9th Pennsylvania comprised the forward element (the "forlorn hope," in eighteenth-century military parlance) of the right wing. Two sergeants of the 9th Pennsylvania were wounded in this action.[59] The leader of the "forlorn hope," 1st Lt. George Knox, of the 9th Pennsylvania Regiment, was awarded a brevet promotion to captain for his gallantry in the fight.[60]

On October 15, the regiment was in Brig. Gen. William Irvine's brigade at West Point. At that time, its strength was 255 officers and men.[61] It probably moved to Morristown for the winter. During the spring and summer of 1780, it fought scattered actions in New Jersey, losing a corporal and a private captured at Paramus on April 16[62] and a private wounded at Springfield on June 23.[63] It was also present at the fight at the Bergen Heights Blockhouse on July 21, when one private of the regiment was killed.[64] In addition, it was one of the regiments which marched from Tappan, New York, to West Point on September 25 to help strengthen that post when Benedict Arnold's treachery was exposed.

By December 1, the regiment was at Morristown.[65] When the mutiny broke out on January 1, 1781, the men of the 9th Pennsylvania at first did not join in. Like the 5th Pennsylvania Regiment, it was drawn up in line, apparently ready to resist the mutineers; but the rebellious men greatly outnumbered these two regiments, and when disaffected artillerymen brought up cannon, the men broke ranks and joined the mutiny.[66] The settlement of the men's complaints brought an end to the revolt, but was followed by a drastic reduction of strength of the Pennsylvania Line, and the 9th Pennsylvania was one of the regiments which were consequently disbanded. A considerable number of its personnel remained in the army, however, but as members of one of the three provisional battalions formed for service in the southern theater of operations.[67]

ORGANIZATION

A S ONE of the new units authorized by Congress on September 16, 1776,[1] the 10th Pennsylvania Regiment began organization on October 25, 1776.[2] However, it was initially plagued by controversies, extreme even for the times, over the relative seniority of its officers.

The man originally appointed as colonel was Joseph Penrose, who had been serving as major of the 5th Pennsylvania Battalion; but because he was granted less seniority than he claimed, he resigned on February 7, 1777.[3] To replace him, James Chambers was promoted from lieutenant colonel of the 1st Pennsylvania Regiment, but when after barely two months a chance came for him to be reassigned in his new rank to his old regiment, he accepted the transfer, becoming colonel of the 1st Pennsylvania Regiment on April 12, 1777.[4] His replacement was George Nagel, promoted from lieutenant colonel of the 9th Pennsylvania Regiment and assigned as commander of the 10th Pennsylvania, apparently with an adjusted date of rank of February 7, 1777.* Effective on July 1, 1778, as part of the general consolidation and reorganization of the Continental Line, the 10th Pennsylvania Regiment absorbed the existing 11th Pennsylvania (later identified as the "Old" 11th Pennsylvania—see Chapter XII). The colonel of the 11th Pennsylvania, Richard Humpton, was senior to Nagel and therefore succeeded to command of the amalgamated organization. Nagel, thus becoming supernumerary, left the army. Colonel Humpton remained in command of the 10th Pennsylvania until the regiment was disbanded on January 17, 1781.[5]

Initially, there was also a seniority problem with regard to the lieutenant colonelcy of the regiment. Lt. Col. James Dunlop, promoted from major, 6th Pennsylvania Battalion, became involved in a dispute over rank and resigned on January 23, 1777. On March 12, 1777, Adam Hubley was promoted to lieutenant colonel and transferred from his position as major of Hartley's "Additional" Continental Regiment.† He served with the 10th Pennsylvania until June 5, 1779, when he was appointed Lieutenant-Colonel Commandant of the "New" 11th Pennsylvania Regiment. Samuel Hay, major of the 7th Pennsylvania, was promoted to lieutenant colonel to replace him, continuing with the 10th Pennsylvania Regiment from that time until January 17, 1781.[6]

When the regiment was being formed, Major Henry Bicker was transferred in grade from the 3d Pennsylvania Battalion, but his promotion to lieutenant colonel, on December 6, 1776, brought his transfer to the 6th Pennsylvania Regiment. Adam Hubley replaced him briefly (see note below), but between January 12 and March 12, 1777, the regiment's majority remained vacant. On the latter date, Caleb North was promoted to the position from captain, 4th Pennsylvania Battalion. He served in this new capacity only until October 22, when he became lieutenant colonel of the "Old" 11th Pennsylvania Regiment. As a replacement, James Grier became major, being promoted from captain, 7th Pennsylvania Regiment. This appointment was challenged by a captain of the 5th · Pennsylvania Regiment, Michael Ryan; he was admittedly junior to Grier as a captain, but claimed precedence by virtue of his staff service as a brigade major. The dispute was finally settled by a board of officers, which on May 19, 1778, ruled in favor of Grier, who continued as major of the regiment until January 17, 1781.[7]

---

*See footnote, page 112.

†Hubley had been a captain in the 1st Pennsylvania Battalion until December 6, 1776, when he was promoted major of the 10th Pennsylvania Regiment. On January 12, 1777, he was transferred to Hartley's Regiment, only to be promoted and reassigned to the 10th Pennsylvania on March 12. See Heitman, pp. 305-306.

At one time or another, sixteen officers held rank as captain in the 10th Pennsylvania Regiment.

The senior captain, Thomas Herbert, who had been a captain in Atlee's State Battalion of Musketry, did not actually serve with the regiment, as he resigned on February 12, 1777. Of the others, Henry Shade (a former captain of Miles's State Rifle Regiment) was cashiered — for what reason is not known — on October 17, 1777; John Stoner (previously a first lieutenant in Miles's State Rifle Regiment) resigned on November 12, 1777; and William Cox, David Schrack, and William Wirtz became supernumerary on July 1, 1778.[8] As only one company muster roll for 1777 has survived (and that one is for the "Lieutenant Colonel's Company," which had no captain), it is not possible (with the probable exception of Captain Stoner) to determine which companies were originally commanded by which captains. Therefore, the description of the company organization of this regiment can begin only on September 10, 1778, after the absorption of the "Old" 11th Pennsylvania Regiment. The companies of that date and afterwards were:

- [Company A], the "Colonel's Company" of the regiment, nominally commanded by Col. Richard Humpton. The actual commander was John Steele, of Lancaster,[9] who had been appointed a first lieutenant in the regiment on December 4, 1776, and promoted to captain-lieutenant on May 27, 1778. On his promotion to captain on March 21, 1779,[10] filling a vacancy left by the death of Capt. George Calhoun (see below), he was given command of his own company. He was replaced as captain-lieutenant by Robert Patton, who on March 1, 1780, was himself promoted to captain[11] and transferred to command another company (see below). The actual command of Company A then passed to Jacob Giles Hicks, who was promoted from first lieutenant to captain-lieutenant. Hicks continued in this position throughout the rest of the war.[12]

- [Company B], the "Lieutenant Colonel's Company" of the regiment. The earliest muster roll of this unit shows men enlisted in 1776 and 1777.[13] Comparison of muster rolls shows that it served under Lt. Col. Adam Hubley during 1778,[14] but in 1779 its commander was listed as Capt. Robert Sample.[15] However, this would have been a paper arrangement, adopted, presumably, between the time of the departure of Lieutenant Colonel Hubley for his new assignment with the "New" 11th Pennsylvania and the arrival of his replacement, Lt. Col. Samuel Hay, as Captain Sample was actually a prisoner of war from March 7, 1778, until November 4, 1780, and did not return to duty following his exchange.[16] The company is again shown as the "Lieutenant Colonel's Company" (i.e., Lieutenant Colonel Hay's) in early 1780,[17] but from April through August of that year (the last muster roll on file) it was commanded by Capt. John Steele,[18] who, as previously noted, had been promoted to captain with a date of rank of March 21, 1779. He continued in command until January 17, 1781.[19]

- [Company C], the "Major's Company" of the regiment. The muster rolls show a preponderance of the same names in this unit from September 10, 1778, through August, 1780.[20] It was commanded throughout the period by Major James Grier.

- [Company D], commanded by Capt. George Calhoun, who may have been the George "Calhoon" who held land in Northumberland County in 1773 and 1774.[21] He was appointed a captain in the 10th Pennsylvania Regiment on December 4, 1776, and commanded this company until his death on March 21, 1779.[22] Substantial numbers of the men of this unit were assigned in 1779 to the company then nominally under Captain Sample[23] (see above), and after April, 1780, their names appear as members of Captain Steele's company (B). Evidently, this company and the "Lieutenant Colonel's Company" were consolidated under Steele's command.

- [Company E], commanded by Capt. Robert Sample, of Lancaster County.[24] As stated earlier, he was taken prisoner on March 7, 1778, but the company was still listed as being under his command in September and October, 1778,[25] and again in 1780.[26] Later in that year, however, the men of this company had been largely divided between Company D[27] and Company F, which by then was commanded by Capt. Robert Patton[28] (see below).

- [Company F], commanded by Capt. Harmon Stout, whose pre-war residence is not known. After serving as a second lieutenant in the 3d Pennsylvania Battalion (a predominantly Philadelphia-area unit—see Chapter V), he was appointed a first lieutenant in the 10th Pennsylvania Regiment on December 4, 1776, and promoted to captain on February 12, 1777, filling the vacancy created by the resignation of Capt. Thomas Herbert. He served as a company commander until his own resignation, which took place on March 1, 1780.[29] At that time, the men of this unit, together with a number of those from what had been Captain Sample's company (E), became Capt. Robert Patton's Company. Patton, who had been a second lieutenant in the "Old" 11th Pennsylvania Regiment and, from November 13, 1776, a first lieutenant in the 10th Pennsylvania, had been captain-lieutenant of the "Colonel's Company" of the regiment from April 1, 1779, until promoted to captain to fill the vacancy left by Captain Stout's resignation. Captain Patton commanded the company until Janaury 17, 1781.[30]

- [Company G], commanded by Capt. James Lang, of York County,[31] who had first served as an ensign and first lieutenant in Atlee's State Battalion of Musketry, and had been commissioned a captain, 10th Pennsylvania Regiment on December 4, 1776. He resigned his commission on April 1, 1779.[32] The bulk of his men then were transferred to what was nominally Captain Sample's company.[33]

• [Company H], commanded by Capt. Jacob Stake. He had been a third lieutenant in Miles's State Rifle Regiment, was commissioned a first lieutenant in the 10th Pennsylvania Regiment on December 4, 1776, and when Capt. John Stoner resigned on November 12, 1777, was promoted to replace him. Assuming that the company had originally been recruited by Stoner, it may have been drawn largely from Lancaster County, as Captain Stoner appears to be one of the men named John Stoner listed as living in Lancaster County in 1771,[34] 1772,[35] and 1773.[36] In any case, Captain Stake continued in command of this company from (presumably) November 12, 1777, until January 17, 1781.[37]

• [Company I], nominally commanded by Capt. Jacob Weaver. Actually, Captain Weaver could never have served with this unit at all. As an ensign in the 3d Pennsylvania Battalion, he had been taken prisoner at Fort Washington, New York, on November 16, 1776, and was not exchanged until December 12, 1780. This company was formed in his name, being mustered in as an independent company on January 13, 1777.[38] The fact that it was raised expressly to protect the town of Lancaster[39] strongly suggests that it was recruited largely in the immediately surrounding area. On November 7, 1777, it was relieved of that mission and assigned to the 10th Pennsylvania Regiment. Despite the fact that Captain Weaver could never have served with the regiment, he continued to be listed as a company commander through the last muster rolls of the 10th Pennsylvania (August, 1780),[40] and remained on the regiment's roster until January 17, 1781.[41]

Two other officers are carried as captains in the 10th Pennsylvania Regiment, but are not shown as company commanders. These are Ebenezer Carson and William McMurray. Carson, at the time a first lieutenant, was taken prisoner on September 3, 1777, near Iron Hill, in a preliminary engagement in the operations leading up to the Battle of Brandywine on September 11. Although he was promoted to captain on April 1, 1779, and remained on the roster until January 17, 1781, he continued to be a prisoner of war until his exchange on December 22, 1780.[42] McMurray, a first lieutenant in the "Old" 11th Pennsylvania, was transferred to the 10th Pennsylvania Regiment on July 1, 1778. Like Ebenezer Carson, he was promoted to captain on April 1, 1779, but at some time in 1780 was transferred to the Sappers and Miners (i.e., Engineers).[43] Quite possibly, the fact that he never commanded a company in the 10th Pennsylvania may mean that from the time of his transfer from the "Old" 11th Pennsylvania he was already serving with the Engineers on detached status, and that his transfer to the Sappers and Miners merely formalized a long-standing situation.

One report regarding the uniform of the 10th Pennsylvania Regiment relates to the officers. For them, the prescribed dress appears to have been a blue coat faced with red, red waistcoat and breeches, blue stockings, and a small "round" hat. Enlisted men from the unit who deserted in mid-1777, all from Company E, were described as variously dressed: one in striped trousers and a blue coat; another in a brown coat with red lapels; and a third all in white.[44]

Summary

Muster rolls indicate the pre-war residences of only four enlisted men of this regiment—one in Company A (Lancaster County), one in Company C (also Lancaster County), and two in Company D (one from Lancaster County and one from Germantown). On the basis of the origins of the company commanders or other circumstantial evidence, Companies E, H, and I would appear to have been recruited in and around Lancaster County, Company F possibly in the Philadelphia area, and Company G in York County. There is no indication of where Company B may have been raised. Capt. George Calhoun and his Company D may have been from Northumberland County. The presence of a Northumberland County company in a regiment in which most if not all of the other companies appear to have come from considerably farther east would not be impossible; it would, however, be something of an anomaly. Another point to bear in mind is that the influx of men from the "Old" 11th Pennsylvania when the two regiments were amalgamated on July 1, 1778, could have had some impact on such geographic homogeneity as may previously have existed. It seems fairly clear, however, that there was a substantial and perhaps preponderant Lancaster County identification within the 10th Pennsylvania Regiment.

OPERATIONS

According to one account,[45] elements of this regiment took part in the Battle of Princeton, on January 3, 1777. If so, they could only have been the few soldiers who had just been enlisted, as the 10th Pennsylvania was still in the process of its initial recruiting effort at that time. However, a sergeant of the regiment was wounded in that engagement.[46]

The regiment was organized and in the field with Washington's army in time to take part in the April 12 or 13, 1777 action at Bound Brook, New Jersey, where fifteen of its men were captured. In a skirmish near Princeton shortly afterward, it lost seven more.[47] By July 8, when it was at Morristown, its enlisted strength was down from the 233 who had been brought to the field to 189 present, and eleven of those were sick; twenty-eight others were sick in hospital, and the prisoner-of-war loss had risen to twenty-seven.[48]

The regiment fought in the Brandywine campaign, including participation by at least detachments in the preliminary action on September 3, 1777, at Iron Hill. The regiment as a whole was part of Anthony Wayne's division at the Battle of Brandywine itself, on September 11. There, it was with the force which unsuccessfully attempted to block General Knyphausen's assault across the Brandywine at Chadd's Ford. A first lieutenant and a private were wounded and a second lieutenant was killed.[49]

The 10th Pennsylvania lost another soldier wounded in the British surprise attack at Paoli on September 20.[50] It fought again at the Battle of Germantown, on October 4. In that action, it was part of Anthony Wayne's left-flank element of the force under Maj. Gen. John Sullivan which made the frontal attack on the British center. However, only one casualty—a private, wounded—was reported.[51] Some of the 10th Pennsylvania's men seem to have been detached to help defend Fort Mercer, near Red Bank, New Jersey, when the British forced their way up the Delaware, for a private of this regiment was wounded there on October 21.[52]

By November 1, the regiment's strength was down to 112 present for duty; nine others were present, but were marked sick; and forty-four were listed as absent, sick. The total remaining strength in enlisted men, therefore, was only 165.[53] There had been other losses as well. Aside from battle casualties, Capt. Henry Shade and Ensign Thomas Shanks had been cashiered.*

In December, with Wayne's division, the 10th Pennsylvania held a position near the center of the American line at Whitemarsh. However, it was not involved in any fighting.[54]

Following the winter of 1777-1778 at the Valley Forge encampment, the 10th Pennsylvania fought at the Battle of Monmouth, on June 28, 1778. It is not clear which part of the engagement involved this regiment. However, as it had one man wounded,[55] at least part of the unit must have got into combat.

Soon after this battle — on July 1 — the 10th Pennsylvania absorbed the "Old" 11th Pennsylvania Regiment. This augmentation brought the enlisted strength up to 366 as of October 10, although only 228 were present for duty; there were also twenty sick, two on furlough, and

---

*Shanks was convicted of stealing two pairs of shoes. Some months later, he volunteered to spy for the British, but was promptly caught, and on June 4, 1778, at Valley Forge, was hanged. See Fitzpatrick, XII, 14; John F. Reed, *Valley Forge, Crucible of Victory* (Monmouth Beach, New Jersey: Philip Freneau Press, 1969), p. 65.

ninety-one on detached service. Meanwhile, on September 13, 1778, the regiment had been at White Plains, New York,[56] moving to Fredericksburg, New York, by October 1.[57] Apparently, it spent the winter of 1778-1779 at Middlebrook, New Jersey.

During the following summer, on July 16, 1779, the 10th Pennsylvania was part of the force which attacked and captured Stony Point, New York, Lieutenant Colonel Hay being wounded in the assault.[58] It moved then to West Point, where it was serving in the garrison of that post, in Anthony Wayne's brigade, on October 15. Its strength at that time was 370 officers and men.[59] The winter of 1779-1780 it seems to have been stationed at Morristown, New Jersey, and in the summer of 1780 it was involved in a number of engagements in New Jersey. It lost one man captured by the British raiding force at Paramus, on April 16.[60] It was also present at the July 21 assault by forces under Anthony Wayne against the Blockhouse at Bergen Heights. In that action it helped in the initial action but did not break loose and join in the hopeless attempt to storm the stronghold. While the regiment was in action that day, however, one of its corporals was wounded and two privates were taken prisoner.[61]

The approach of winter brought the 10th Pennsylvania Regiment back to Morristown. There, on January 1, 1781, the men joined in the general mutiny by all the Pennsylvania troops who were present.[62] When the mutiny was settled, the 10th Pennsylvania was one of the five regiments which were disbanded, although some of its members may have served in one of the three provisional Pennsylvania battalions which were created for service in Virginia and, after the British surrender at Yorktown, in South Carolina.

Chapter XII
'Old' 11th Pennsylvania Regiment

ORGANIZATION

AT different times, the Pennsylvania Line had two organizations designated as the 11th Pennsylvania Regiment. The second of these (see Chapter XVI) was referred to as the "New" 11th Pennsylvania from the time of its formation; from about the same time, as a means of differentiation, the regiment which during its active existence had been merely the 11th Pennsylvania, came to be referred to as the "Old" 11th. It is that organization which will be discussed in this chapter.

The original 11th Pennsylvania was one of the five Pennsylvania regiments authorized for the Continental Army on October 25, 1776.[1] Some fourteen months later, it was absorbed into the 10th Pennsylvania Regiment in connection with the general restructuring which took effect on July 1, 1778.[2]

The commander of the 11th Pennsylvania throughout its service was Col. Richard Humpton, who, by virtue of his greater seniority, became commander of the 10th Pennsylvania when the two regiments were consolidated.[3]

The regiment had two lieutenant colonels. The first was Lt. Col. Francis Gurney. He was wounded at Iron Hill on September 3, 1777, in an action preceding the Battle of Brandywine, and on October 22, 1777, resigned his commission.[4] He was succeeded by Caleb North, who was promoted from major, 10th Pennsylvania. On July 1, 1778, he became lieutenant colonel of the 9th Pennsylvania Regiment.[5]

During the time that the "Old" 11th Pennsylvania existed, it had only one major. This was Francis Mentges, who had been a first lieutenant in Atlee's State Battalion of Musketry. When the 11th Pennsylvania ceased to exist, he was transferred to the 7th Pennsylvania.[6]

No company muster rolls for this regiment have been preserved. The companies and their commanders, however, were as follows:

• [Company A], commanded by Capt. Samuel Dawson, possibly the man of that name from Chester County.[7] He was commissioned directly from civilian life on November 13, 1776, continuing with the regiment until July 1, 1778, when he was transferred to the 8th Pennsylvania.[8]

• [Company B], commanded by Doctor* John Coates, who also appears to have been appointed a captain in this regiment without prior military service. His pre-war residence is not known. On May 8, 1777, at Piscataway, New Jersey, he was wounded in the right hand.[9] He resigned from the army on September 7, 1777,[10] being replaced by John Pearson, of Reading,[11] who was promoted from first lieutenant.[12] Pearson continued in command until July 1, 1778, when he was reassigned, in his case to the 9th Pennsylvania Regiment.[13]

• [Company C], commanded by Capt. Adolph William Hedrick, whose pre-war residence is unidentified. Although one source[14] says that Hedrick remained in the army until July 1, 1778, that assertion appears to be in error; he seems to have resigned his commission on October 30, 1777.[15] Reinforcing this probability is the fact that William Mackey was promoted from first lieutenant on that date to fill the vacancy.[16] At the time, Mackey was actually a prisoner of war, having been wounded and captured at the Battle of Brandywine, on September 11, 1777. However, he was promptly exchanged (in November, 1777), and served with the

---

*"Doctor" was his name, not a title, although in some accounts he is referred to as "John Coates." There was a Dr. John Coates in the Continental Army, but he was a different person, serving as Surgeon of a New York regiment during a period of time overlapping Capt. Doctor John Coates's service in the 11th Pennsylvania. See Heitman, pp. 161-162.

11th Pennsylvania from that time until his transfer to the 9th Pennsylvania on July 1, 1778.[17]

• [Company D], commanded by Capt. William Bradford, Jr., probably of Philadelphia.[18] After serving as a captain in the Flying Camp, Bradford was appointed as a captain in the 11th Pennsylvania on September 30, 1776. On April 10, 1777, he was appointed a lieutenant colonel in the Deputy Commissary General of Musters Department.[19] His place as a captain was taken by George Ross, Jr., who was promoted from first lieutenant.[20] Ross had been adjutant of the 2d Pennsylvania Battalion[21] prior to his appointment as a first lieutenant in the 11th Pennsylvania Regiment. On April 1, 1778, he resigned his captaincy,[22] which apparently remained unfilled during the remaining three months that the regiment continued to exist.

• [Company E], commanded by Capt. William Scull, probably the man of that name from Berks County.[23] Captain Scull served with the 11th Pennsylvania from the time of its organization until July 1, 1778, when he joined the Geographers' Department.[24]

• [Company F], commanded by Capt. William Henderson (not the Capt. William Henderson who served in the 4th Pennsylvania Regiment), who may have been from Philadelphia,[25] or may equally have been one of the men of that name from Chester County.[26] On February 22, 1777, he was transferred to the 4th Light Dragoons as Regimental Paymaster.[27] His replacement in the 11th Pennsylvania was Samuel Doan,[28] promoted from first lieutenant. The reorganization of July 1, 1778, made Doan supernumerary, and he left the army.[29]

• [Company G], commanded by Capt. John Douglass, possibly from Lancaster County.[30] Like many of the other captains of this regiment, he was appointed without prior service. He resigned his commission on December 7, 1777.[31] Apparently, no replacement was appointed.

• [Company H], nominally commanded by Capt. William McKissack. While serving as a captain of the Flying Camp, McKissack was taken prisoner at Fort Washington, New York, on November 16, 1776. Although he was appointed a captain in the 11th Pennsylvania on January 1, 1777, he never joined the regiment.[32] Presumably, the company was actually commanded by its first lieutenant.

The decision to add a ninth company to each Continental infantry regiment was not taken until May 27, 1778. By that time, the decision to consolidate the 11th Pennsylvania with the 10th Pennsylvania had also been taken, so no ninth company was added to this organization.

Uniforms seem to have varied by company. Of two men from Company G who deserted in November, 1776, one was wearing a green coat faced with white, and sky-blue breeches; and the other was dressed in a hunting shirt and leggings. Five months later, in April, 1777, a deserter from Company B had a light infantry cap, a blue coat with scarlet cape and cuffs, white waistcoat, and buckskin breeches. Just a month afterwards, a deserter from Company A appeared in a green coat with white facings; but a deserter from Company C in July, 1777, wore a blue coat. Two men from Company D who also deserted in July, 1777, were wearing brown coats, white waistcoats, and leather breeches.[33]

Summary

To the limited extent that information concerning the geographical origins of the company commanders is available, they appear to have come chiefly from the area of Philadelphia and of Chester, Berks, and possibly Lancaster counties. The short time that this organization was in existence, however, suggests that its original regional composition would have remained essentially unchanged.

OPERATIONS

Some of the officers of the 11th Pennsylvania are listed as having been serving in New York before the end of October, 1776. One of them, 2d Lt. Robert Patton, was taken prisoner at a skirmish near White Plains, New York, on October 27, 1776,* only two days after the regiment was officially authorized! Another, 2d Lt. Andrew Robinson, was captured at Fort Washington on November 16, barely three weeks later.[34] It seems clear, however, that these men were serving with other units when they were commissioned in the 11th Pennsylvania and were taken prisoner before they could enter upon their new appointments. Patton seems to have been exchanged promptly, for he served later in the 11th Pennsylvania until July 1, 1778, when he was transferred to the 10th Pennsylvania. Robinson, by contrast, was not exchanged until January 4, 1781.

Elements of the 11th Pennsylvania are also shown as part of the force at the Battle of Princeton, on January 3, 1777, where the command was one of five regiments making up a 500-man brigade.[35] Manifestly, only a fraction of the 11th Pennsylvania could have been involved. Later, at least some of the 11th Pennsylvania took part in the patrol actions in New Jersey which marked the spring and summer of 1777, for Captain Coates was wounded at Piscataway on May 8, and as of June 11, the regiment had lost thirty-four men dead and eight captured. At that time, it had 263 enlisted men present for duty.[36]

During that summer, the 11th Pennsylvania was assigned to the 2d Brigade of Anthony Wayne's division.[37] Some of its troops were de-

---

*Heitman, p. 430. He should not be confused—as he is in PA(5), III, 608—with another Pennsylvania officer, 1st Lt. Robert Patton of the Flying Camp, who was captured at Fort Washington, New York, on November 16, 1776.

tached to serve with the special task force (the "light infantry corps") under Brig. Gen. William Maxwell which was formed for the fall campaign opposing the British approach toward Philadelphia from the south. It was Maxwell's command which fought the delaying action at Iron Hill on September 3, 1777, when Lt. Col. Francis Gurney was wounded.

The regiment as a whole seems to have seen its first major action at the Battle of Brandywine, on September 11, 1777. As part of Wayne's division, it was deployed to cover Chadd's Ford across Brandywine Creek. When the British and Hessian element of the enemy force, under General Knyphausen, drove across the creek, the 11th Pennsylvania appears to have seen especially hard fighting. Although little information is available about enlisted casualties,* the regiment's losses in officers were relatively high: three second lieutenants were killed, another was wounded, and a third was captured; a first lieutenant was wounded and another wounded and captured.[38] The enlisted casualties were reported as four privates, wounded.[39]

The regiment was in combat again on September 20, when with the rest of Wayne's division it was surprised at Paoli. When the British struck the American camp, Wayne ordered Colonel Humpton, who commanded the division's right wing, to move left to high ground and take up a position to cover the withdrawal of the rest of the command. Instead, Humpton moved his troops to the right[40] — according to Wayne, this was "owing to some Neglect or Misapprehension in Colonel Humpton (which is not uncommon)."[41] Worse, Wayne charged, instead of moving his troops behind the campfires, Humpton moved them in front, silhouetting them for the attacking British.[42] The result was that the heaviest losses in the engagement were suffered by the units under Humpton's command,[43] which "completely dissolved" in the face of the enemy assault.[44] (However, the regiment's only casualty identified as occurring at Paoli was one private, wounded.[45]) Some historians have said that Wayne tried to make Humpton the scapegoat for the Paoli debacle,[46] while others have held that it was to divert blame from himself that Humpton later preferred charges of negligence against Wayne.[47] The court of inquiry which followed reached an ambiguous conclusion so Wayne demanded — and got — a court martial, which exonerated him. Whatever the facts of the case, the understandable coolness which developed between Wayne and Humpton eventually gave way to an amicable professional association.

In the meantime, the 11th Pennsylvania fought again at German-

---

*A statement in PA(5), III, 587, says that in this battle the 11th Pennsylvania Regiment lost "heavily."

town, on October 4, 1777. In this action, in which it helped assault the center of the British position, its only known casualties were its adjutant, 1st Lt. Thomas Lucas, who was killed,[48] and two privates wounded.[49] Its total losses during the campaign, however, must have been substantial, for by November 1, 1777, it had present for duty only eight officers and eighty enlisted men. Another sixty-six enlisted men were sick, and thirty-one were on detached service.[50]

The 11th Pennsylvania had no opportunity to do any fighting at Whitemarsh in early December, 1777. However, it was present, holding a portion of the first line, just to the right of the center.[51]

After spending the winter of 1777-1778 at Valley Forge with the other regiments of the Pennsylvania Line, the 11th Pennsylvania took part in the campaign across New Jersey which followed. At the Battle of Monmouth, on June 28, 1778, it was probably one of the three Pennsylvania regiments in the force which Aaron Burr led in a late-afternoon assault on the flank of a British counterattacking column.[52] Throughout the engagement, however, its only casualty was one enlisted man wounded.[53]

The amalgamation of the 11th Pennsylvania with the 10th Pennsylvania took place less than a week later, on July 1. As noted, some of the officers left the service and others were assigned to different regiments, but the remaining enlisted men would have gone with Colonel Humpton into the new organization.

Chapter XIII

12th Pennsylvania Regiment

ORGANIZATION

L IKE the "Old" 11th Pennsylvania, the 12th Pennsylvania Regiment came into being on October 25, 1776.[1] Also like the "Old" 11th, it was to have a short life, being absorbed by the 3d Pennsylvania Regiment in the reorganization which went into effect on July 1, 1778.[2]

The area from which the regiment was recruited comprised Northampton and Northumberland counties, but a preponderance of the men seem to have come from the West Branch of the Susquehanna, in what was then Northumberland County.[3]

The only colonel appointed to the 12th Pennsylvania was William Cooke. He was cashiered (for what offense has not been established) on March 4, 1778,* and was not replaced.

The lieutenant colonel of the regiment was Neigal Gray, of Northampton County.[4] While the regiment was at Valley Forge, he was tried by court martial and convicted of taking money from his troops to supplement their rations, and then defrauding them both of the extra food and the money they had paid.[5] He also was cashiered, effective June 2, 1778.[6]

James Crawford was major of the 12th Pennsylvania. He was wounded at the Battle of Brandywine, on September 11, 1777.[7] Becoming in-

*Heitman, p. 170. However, PA(5), III, 672 says that he resigned from the army on January 16, 1778.

volved in a dispute over seniority, he resigned his commission on October 12[8] or November 10, 1777[9] (the difference in dates presumably reflects the time when he submitted his resignation and the time when it was formally accepted). Again, no replacement was appointed.

The eight companies of the regiment and their commanders were as follows:

• [Company A], initially commanded by Capt. Peter Withington, apparently from Berks County. While the regiment was on its way to the combat zone in December, 1776, he became ill in Philadelphia and was sent "home" to Reading.[10] His illness proved mortal, and he died on May 11, 1777.[11] Although it cannot be stated with absolute assurance, it is probable that it was this vacancy which John Reily (or Reiley) was promoted to fill on May 20, 1777.[12] At the time of his promotion to captain, Reily was not available for duty, having been shot through the body in an engagement somewhere in the vicinity of Bonhamtown, New Jersey, on April 15, 1777. He recovered his health, however, and served with the regiment until July 1, 1778, when he was transferred to the 3d Pennsylvania when it absorbed the 12th Pennsylvania.[13] (See also Company H below.)

• [Company B], commanded by Capt. Nicholas Miller, who continued in command of this company throughout the life of the 12th Pennsylvania.[14] This unit was raised in Northumberland County.[15] Captain Miller was rendered supernumerary by the reorganization of July 1, 1778, and left the army.[16]

• [Company C], commanded by Capt. Hawkins Boone. It was this company, or at least a group of men from the 12th Pennsylvania under Captain Boone's command, which was attached to the task force under Col. Daniel Morgan which, in June, 1777, was sent to reinforce Maj. Gen. Horatio Gates in New York State.[17] Captain Boone and his men may have rejoined the 12th Pennsylvania when Morgan's task force was broken up after the Saratoga campaign (which ended on October 11, 1777); but in any case, Boone himself was transferred to the 6th Pennsylvania Regiment on July 1, 1778.[18] Like Company B, this unit was from Northumberland County.[19]

• [Company D], commanded by Capt. John Brady. Captain Brady was wounded at the Battle of Brandywine, on September 11, 1777.[20] He resigned from the army on March 9, 1778.[21] No record exists that anyone was promoted to replace him. Company D was also a Northumberland County unit.[22]

• [Company E], commanded by Capt. John Harris until March 1, 1777, when he resigned.[23] It seems clear that his replacement was Stephen Chambers, who was promoted from first lieutenant on March 1, 1777. Captain Chambers continued to serve with the regiment until he became supernumerary on July 1, 1778.[24] This company was another of the units raised in Northumberland County.[25]

• [Company F], commanded by Capt. Henry McKinley (or Makinley). He was a clergyman who taught at a classical academy at Carlisle.[26] He commanded this company from the formation of the regiment until the eve of its amalgamation with the 3d Pennsylvania Regiment, resigning his commission on June 18, 1778,[27] the day before the army left Valley Forge to pursue the British from Philadelphia across New Jersey.

• [Company G], commanded by Capt. Alexander Patterson, of Easton, in Northampton County.[28] He continued in the regiment until he became supernumerary on July 1, 1778.[29]

• [Company H], commanded by Capt. William Work. When Captain Work was cashiered on March 31, 1777[30] (for what offense is not known), the company then appears to have come under the command of Hana-niah Lincoln, promoted on May 20, 1777, from first lieutenant. Follow-ing his resignation on October 17, 1777,[31] the company may have come under its first lieutenant or had its men absorbed into other companies, for no one was promoted to fill Lincoln's vacancy. (It is possible, of course, that Lincoln became captain of Company A and that Captain Reily took command of Company H, as both men were promoted to captain on the same day.)

The 12th Pennsylvania never gained a ninth company.

The regiment seems to have had no identifiable uniform. Contem-porary records exist of deserters from the 12th Pennsylvania Regiment between January and June, 1777, but they were dressed in a motley varie-ty of what appears to have been civilian clothing.[32]

Summary

Neither company muster rolls nor strength reports for this organiza-tion have been found. However, the regiment was expressly formed of men primarily from Northumberland County, with considerable rep-resentation from Northampton County. Companies B, C, D, and E were definitely from Northumberland. Of the other four companies, Company G at least appears to have been from Northampton County, which may have supplied some of the regiment's other units as well.

OPERATIONS

The 12th Pennsylvania Regiment was recruited and equipped within little more than a month after it was authorized (a fact which possibly provides part of the explanation for the lack of a regimental uniform), for on December 18, 1776, the men left Sunbury, traveling by boat on the Susquehanna, on their way to join Washington's army in New Jersey.[33] It is doubtful that the regiment had reached anything approximating its full manning level, for it was one of five regiments making up a brigade (whose total strength was only five hundred men) which took part in the Battle of Princeton, on January 3, 1777.[34] From there, it moved with Washington into winter quarters at Morristown, New Jersey.

Because the members of this unit were frontiersmen, armed with rifles and experienced in scouting, the regiment was used extensively as a patrol force when the spring of 1777 brought an increase in operations. It was assigned to the brigade under Brig. Gen. Thomas Conway, and was based at Metuchen, New Jersey, between Quibbletown and Amboy. It seems, however, to have ranged over a considerable area, and it was involved in a succession of relatively minor but sometimes costly engagements. On April 12 or 13, 1777, it fought the British at Bound Brook, New Jersey.[35] On April 15, a detachment (presumably Company G) of the 12th Pennsylvania under Capt. Alexander Patterson attacked a British outpost near Bonhamtown, killing or capturing twenty-four enemy soldiers[36] but suffering one casualty when 1st Lt. Reily was shot[37] (see above). Less than a month later, on May 10, at Piscataway, the regiment was in a considerable fight as part of a Continental division engaged with three British regiments.[38] On this occasion, 1st Lt. Christopher Getley was wounded and taken prisoner, and his leg was amputated;[39] in addition, two privates were wounded, one of them losing his hand,[40] and 21 other men of the regiment were captured. One of these, however, escaped by running in among a flock of sheep and hiding.[41] There was still another sizable engagement on June 26, at Short Hills, involving division-size forces. Here, 2d Lt. Stewart Herbert was wounded.[42] Although records of the regiment's enlisted men are extremely sparse, they do list one soldier wounded at "Metuchen" (probably another name for the Short Hills engagement, although he may have been a casualty of a skirmish in that vicinity which had taken place on May 17)[43] as well as the others already mentioned.

As stated earlier, it was in June that Capt. Hawkins Boone and a detachment from the 12th Pennsylvania were placed in Col. Daniel Morgan's task force and sent to upstate New York to help oppose the advance from the north by the British force under Gen. John Burgoyne. The only specific reference to their experience in the Saratoga campaign states that two of the privates of the detachment were wounded at Bemis Heights in the action which occurred there (the "Second Battle of Freeman's Farm") on October 7, 1777.[44]

The rest of the regiment remained in Conway's brigade and marched south with Washington's army in August, 1777.

At the Battle of Brandywine, on September 11, the regiment was positioned on the American right flank, and it took part in the intensive combat around the Birmingham Meeting House. It "lost heavily" in this action.[45] However, the specifically reported casualties—presumably only a fraction of the total lost—were 2d Lt. William Boyd killed[46] and Major James Crawford and Capt. John Brady wounded.[47]

Not being part of Wayne's division, the 12th Pennsylvania was not involved at Paoli on September 20, but it fought again at the Battle of Germantown, on October 4, where 2d Lt. John Carothers was killed[48] and the regiment as a whole "again lost heavily,"[49] although once more, the only other casualties specifically recorded were light, being two privates wounded.[50] Although present at Whitemarsh, the regiment was with the rest of Conway's brigade in the second line, and was not engaged in the limited actions which occurred in early December.[51]

What with casualties and other forms of attrition, the 12th Pennsylvania was reduced to minimal strength before the end of the winter of 1777-1778, which it spent at Valley Forge. Apparently it continued its scouting and patrolling missions, however, for some of its members were involved in a skirmish near Bordentown, New Jersey, on May 8, 1778. In that engagement, 1st Lt. William McElhatton was wounded in the shoulder, losing the use of his arm.[52] By the time Washington's army moved out of camp to pursue the British into New Jersey, the 12th Pennsylvania had no field grade officers at all and it had, at most, five of its authorized eight captains. One of these, moreover, would have been acting as regimental commander. No doubt the enlisted strength was equally low.

The regiment had some role in the Battle of Monmouth, on June 28, 1778, for its fragmentary casualty reports show one man wounded in that action.[53] However, the statement that the "remnant" of the regiment was "nearly destroyed" at Monmouth[54] is certainly an exaggeration in view of the remarkably light losses that the American army experienced in that battle. The fact is that for all practical purposes, the 12th Pennsylvania already had virtually ceased to exist. Its absorption by the 3d Pennsylvania Regiment on July 1, 1778, merely formalized the situation.

Chapter XIV

Hartley's "Additional" Continental Regiment

Thomas Hartley

ORGANIZATION

HARTLEY'S Regiment was one of sixteen "additional" Continental regiments authorized by Congress on January 11, 1777.[1] The colonelcy was given to Thomas Hartley, of York,[2] previously lieutenant colonel of the 6th Pennsylvania Battalion, who commanded the regiment throughout the approximately two years it existed[3] before it was merged with Patton's Regiment (between December, 1778, and January, 1779) and redesignated as the "New" 11th Pennsylvania.[4]

The person originally appointed as lieutenant colonel of Hartley's Regiment was James Wilkinson, of Maryland.* He seems to have performed little if any service with the regiment, however, and soon va-

---

*This was the James Wilkinson, who, as a brigadier general in the early years of the nineteenth century, played a dubious role with the Spanish authorities in New Orleans and, later, was associated with Aaron Burr in the activities which have been labelled the "Burr Conspiracy."

cated his appointment to become Deputy Adjutant General of the Northern Department, on the staff of Maj. Gen. Horatio Gates.[5] He was replaced as lieutenant colonel of Hartley's Regiment by Morgan Conner, who was promoted from major, 1st Pennsylvania Regiment, on April 9, 1777. Lieutenant Colonel Conner continued in this position during the life of the regiment.[6]

The first major of Hartley's Regiment was Adam Hubley, who was transferred from the 10th Pennsylvania on January 12, 1777, but was promoted to lieutenant colonel and reassigned to the 10th Pennsylvania on March 12, 1777.[7] On that date, Lewis Bush was promoted from captain to become major of the regiment. After Bush was mortally wounded at the Battle of Brandywine (he died four days later, on September 15, 1777),[8] the majority remained vacant.

The records of this organization are not only scanty but extremely confusing. They indicate that instead of the eight captains authorized, the regiment began with no less than ten. On a speculative basis, it would seem that Hartley's Regiment was used to some extent as a "carrier" unit to provide justification for appointments of men actually serving in completely unrelated assignments. It may be assumed, therefore, that while James Wilkinson was nominally lieutenant colonel of the regiment, he actually continued as a member of General Gates's staff, where he was serving immediately before and immediately after his brief stint on the rolls of Hartley's Regiment. Similarly, the senior captain of the regiment was Evan Edwards, but in 1777 he is shown as aide-de-camp to Maj. Gen. Charles Lee,[9] although Lee was a prisoner of war from December 13, 1776, to May 6, 1778. Another officer, Barnet Eichelberger, was commissioned a captain in this regiment on January 12, 1777, but seems never to have accepted the appointment,[10] although he was still considered an officer of the regiment as late as December 10, 1777.[11]

Bearing the irregularities outlined above in mind, the companies of the regiment would seem to have been as follows:

• [Company A], initially commanded (at least nominally) by Capt. Lewis Bush. He had originally been commissioned in one of the Cumberland County companies of the 6th Pennsylvania Battalion.[12] Apparently, he became acting major of Hartley's Regiment almost from the time it was organized, and was formally promoted to that grade on March 12, 1777.[13] His replacement as company commander is not known, although it would seem likely that it was Isaac Sweeny. Although Sweeny was a second lieutenant until September 9, 1777, and was not promoted to captain until July 23, 1778,[14] he is mentioned as being a company commander in this regiment as early as May, 1777.[15] He continued with the regiment throughout its existence.

• [Company B], commanded by Capt. William Nicholls (or Nichols). He had previously been an ensign in one of the York County companies of the 6th Pennsylvania Battalion,[16] and was appointed as a captain in Hartley's Regiment on January 12, 1777. After over a year's service, he resigned his commission on March 11, 1778.[17] It is not apparent who became company commander in his place. The next promotion to captain in the regiment, which was awarded to Joseph Davis, did not take place until June 3, 1778. Davis had served as a first lieutenant in the 9th Pennsylvania Regiment, and was transferred in grade to Hartley's Regiment on January 15, 1777. He remained in the regiment until it was reorganized.[18]

• [Company C], commanded throughout its existence by Capt. Benjamin Stoddard,* of Maryland. He was appointed a captain directly from civilian life. On September 11, 1777, at the Battle of Brandywine, he was wounded,[19] but his wound did not prevent him from retaining command of the company. He was expressly commended in the warmest terms by Colonel Hartley for his role in combat against the Indians on September 29, 1778.[20]

• [Company D], like Company C, also had only one commander. This was Capt. George Boss (or Bush), of Delaware. He had been a lieutenant in the Delaware Battalion of the Flying Camp until his appointment as a captain of Hartley's Regiment on January 13, 1777.[21]

• [Company E], commanded by Capt. Robert Hopes. Like Captain Nicholls, he had been an ensign in one of the York County companies of the 6th Pennsylvania Battalion[22] prior to his appointment as a captain in Hartley's Regiment on January 13, 1777. He was killed at the Battle of Brandywine, on September 11, 1777,[23] and was replaced by Horatio Ross, who was promoted from first lieutenant. There is no record of when Captain Ross left the army,[24] but it appears that he gave up his commission before Hartley's Regiment was reorganized (see below).

• [Company F], commanded by Capt. Archibald McAllister, who may be one of the men of that name living in Chester County in 1771.[25] He was appointed a captain in Hartley's Regiment on January 13, 1777, without prior military service of record. He resigned his commission on November 19, 1777.[26] His replacement as company commander was James Forester (or Forrester),[27] who was promoted from first lieutenant on the date of McAllister's resignation. Captain Forester continued in this position for the rest of the regiment's life.[28]

• [Company G], commanded throughout its existence by Capt. James Kenny (or Kenney).[29] Several contemporaries of this name lived just before the outbreak of the Revolution in Chester[30] and Lancaster[31] coun-

---

*Later (from 1799 to 1801) he was the first Secretary of the Navy.

ties, and it is not possible to determine which of them, if any, might have been the James Kenny in question.

• [Company H], nominally commanded by Capt. William Kelly. Captain Kelly had been taken prisoner at Fort Washington on November 16, 1776, while serving as a second lieutenant in an independent company of Virginia riflemen. There is no record that he was exchanged, but he was appointed a captain in Hartley's Regiment on January 16, 1777, and was counted against its strength until his death, on September 9, 1777.[32] To fill this vacancy, Paul Parker was promoted from first lieutenant.[33] As in the case of Captain Ross, there is no record of the date when Parker's service with the regiment terminated,[34] and it is probable that he did not remain in the service for the full life of the regiment (see below).

Two other officers are listed as serving as captains in Hartley's Regiment. One of these was Andrew Walker, who was promoted from first lieutenant on January 23, 1778.[35] The other, Henry Carberry, of Maryland, was promoted from first lieutenant on November 30, 1778.[36] Presumably, one of these may have replaced Captain Ross and the other Captain Parker, although Walker may have been promoted when Barnet Eichelberger's name was finally dropped from the rolls, and Carberry may have been appointed to command the additional, ninth company, if in fact such a company was formed. Both remained in the regiment until it was reorganized and redesignated, and Carberry was particularly commended for his services during the action against the Indians on September 29, 1778.[37]

Some of the members of Hartley's Regiment appear to have been uniformed in a blue coat with white collar, and buckskin breeches, although one deserter from the organization in March, 1777 (very early in its service), was wearing a black hunting shirt.[38]

The regiment was sometimes referred to as "foot guards." The reason is obscure, for according to one authority, "there was nothing of distinction" about it.[39]

Summary

Of the original company commanders of Hartley's Regiment, two appear to have been from York County and one from Cumberland County. As they had all served with Colonel Hartley in the 6th Pennsylvania Battalion, it is possible that he merely brought them with him to his new command, and that they were not directly involved in recruiting their companies. It is also noteworthy that the regiment had three captains who were not Pennsylvanians—one from Maryland, a second from Delaware, and a third from Virginia. The other original captains who served with the regiment may have been from Chester and Lancaster counties.

Considering the date and circumstances of this organization's formation, it seems likely that its members were drawn from a variety of regions. Despite the fact that it was eventually chosen to be employed on the frontier, comments by Colonel Hartley concerning the lack of qualifications of his men for wilderness fighting (see below) suggest that the regiment probably did not include any substantial number of men from the outlying areas of the State.

OPERATIONS

The earliest reference to Hartley's Regiment after it was organized is as a part of Anthony Wayne's division at the Battle of Brandywine, on September 11, 1777. Presumably, Lieutenant Colonel Conner was actually acting in command of the regiment in this battle, as Colonel Hartley was in command of the 1st Brigade of the division throughout the regiment's service under Wayne.[40]

At Brandywine, Hartley's Regiment suffered considerable loss in its efforts to oppose the crossing of Chadd's Ford by Knyphausen's British and Hessian force. The only enlisted casualty reported specifically for this engagement was one man wounded.[41] However, even such sparse records of enlisted losses as have survived show ten men killed in unspecified actions, and some of these very possibly relate to Brandywine.[42] In addition, Major Lewis Bush,[43] Capt. Robert Hopes,[44] 1st Lt. James Lemon (or Lemmon),[45] and 2d Lt. James Dill[46] were killed and Capt. Benjamin Stoddard was wounded.[47]

The regiment was involved in action again at Paoli, on September 20. There, Colonel Hartley played a key role in hastily organizing a rear guard to hold off the British attackers. His men quickly rallied from the initial surprise and stood firm for long enough to permit the main body of the division to escape, then fell back in such good order that there was no substantial pursuit by the British.[48] One private was reported as being captured after being repeatedly stabbed by bayonets.[49]

The next engagement was at the Battle of Germantown, on October 4. Here, Hartley's Regiment was with Wayne's division as it carried out a frontal assault on the British center. The only records expressly pertaining to the regiment's casualties at Germantown show one soldier killed and another wounded.[50]

Hartley's Regiment was also present at Whitemarsh when the British tentatively attacked and then withdrew early in December. As part of Wayne's division, the regiment occupied a position just to the right of the center of the American first line; but like the other Continental units, it was not engaged.[51]

Shortly afterward, with the rest of the Pennsylvania Continentals, it went into winter quarters at Valley Forge, but in February, 1778, it was moved to York, to protect Congress, with which most of it moved to Philadelphia when the British evacuated that city in June. Thus, it was not involved in the Battle of Monmouth, on June 28.

About July 14, 1778, Hartley's Regiment was detached from its assignments and redeployed farther west. It was based on Sunbury, and its mission was to provide protection against Indian attacks in the frontier area.[52]

Indians and Tories were raiding freely throughout western and north-central Pennsylvania. Colonel Hartley soon decided that with so small a force, he could not provide any defense for the whole region, but that by taking the offensive, he might prevent or at least inhibit enemy attacks. Accordingly, he arranged for militia to be called out to augment his own regiment. On September 18, 1778, the force gathered at Muncy. The response by the militia was disappointing, for all told Hartley had only two hundred men when he had counted on twice that number. Nevertheless, early on September 21 he started out,[53] following the Sheshequin Path. The route proved extremely difficult,[54] but despite heavy rain and rough terrain, the force made steady progress. On September 26, the advance guard stumbled on a band of about twenty Indians. Both groups were surprised, but the troops fired first; the Indians' leader was killed, but the rest escaped. After scalping the dead Indian, Hartley's column moved on.[55]

Near Sheshequin, the soldiers liberated fifteen prisoners, from whom they learned that a deserter from one of the militia companies had brought warning of their approach. Hartley pressed on to the Indian town of Tioga. He found it abandoned, but captured another prisoner, who said that a force of five hundred Indians and Tories, reputedly under the Tory commander, Walter Butler, had gathered at Chemung, twelve miles away.[56]

Hartley would have liked to attack Chemung, which he said in his report to Congress "is now the recepticle of all villainous Indians &· Tories from the different Tribes and states," and the base from which "they make their Excursions against the Frontiers of N. York, Pennsylvania, Jersey & Wioming, & commit those horrid Murders and Devastations we have heard of." However, he was too badly outnumbered to take the risk. After burning Tioga, on September 28 he led his troops to Wyalusing, which they reached about 11 P.M. By that time, "our men [were] much worn down—our Whiskey & Flour was gone."[57] As he had started out barely a week before with supplies for twelve days, it would seem that the men had been reckless in what they consumed.

The column did not leave Wyalusing until noon on September 29. But seventy of the troops, "from real or pretended Lameness," Hartley said, "went into the Canoes, others rode on the empty Pack Horses, we had not more than 120 Rank & file to fall in the Line of March." The main body of the troops moving overland was organized into three detachments: Hartley's Continentals led, with the other two "divisions" being made up of militia. The rear guard of thirty men was commanded by Isaac Sweeny, "a valuable officer." The column ran into opposition almost immediately, but brushed it aside. Half an hour later the enemy struck again, and this time the troops had to deploy to drive off the attackers. Then, about 2 P.M., a heavy attack was launched against Sweeny's rear guard, which soon began to give way. Hartley sent one of the militia companies back to reinforce Sweeny, and some of the men in canoes, led by Captains Hawkins Boone (now on detached service from the 6th Pennsylvania Regiment) and John Brady (apparently serving as a volunteer or as a militia officer, as he had resigned his Continental commission in the 12th Pennsylvania the previous March), who had been attached to Hartley, landed and joined the fight. Meanwhile, Hartley hurried the rest of his troops undetected to high ground on the Indians' flank. From there he sent Captain Stoddard with the Continentals to swing around the enemy rear. "The War Hoop was given by our people," Hartley reported; "...we advanced on the Enemy on all sides, with great shouting & Noise, the Indians after a brave resistance of some minutes...fled with the utmost Haste..., & left ten dead on the ground."[58]

The total loss by Hartley's force was four killed and ten wounded. Colonel Hartley was disappointed that any of the enemy had escaped, but thought that his force had done well under the circumstances. "The men of my Reg¹," he explained, "were armed with Muskets & Bayonets, they were no great marksmen, and were awkward at wood Fighting." However, he observed, "the Bullet and three swan shot in each Piece made up, in some measure, for the want of skill." The rest of the march to Wyoming was untroubled. A detachment was left to help strengthen the garrison there. The remainder of the force returned to Sunbury, which they reached on October 5.[59]

During the two-week operation, Hartley's men had covered almost three hundred miles.[60] They had carried out the first important offensive against the Tory-Indian combination on the northern Pennsylvania frontier,[61] and had bought some degree of security for the settlements. In his report to the Supreme Executive Council of Pennsylvania, Colonel Hartley said that "Considering our numbers we pushed our good Fortune as far as we dare, we gave a present relief to the frontiers & turned back the Barbarians from Deluging our Country with the Blood of Helpless Mothers & Infants." He went on to say that "We are here on a Dangerous service, which gives us few opportunity's of gaining Laurels; we have a Vigilant & Dangerous Enemy, but it gives us pleasure to think we serve our Country & protect the helpless & innocent."[62]

But the expedition had brought only a respite from the raids. On November 9, Hartley reported to the Supreme Executive Council that a force of Tories and Indians was besieging Wyoming. He asked for reinforcements, but did not wait for them to arrive; by November 14, he was at Fort Jenkins, near Nescopeck.[63] From there he moved the following day toward Wyoming, driving off the Indians in the area.[64] Dispersing his few troops as garrisons for scattered forts throughout the region, he then waited for the promised reinforcements to arrive.

These consisted of what was left of another "additional" Continental unit, Col. John Patton's Regiment (see Chapter XV). According to a November 14 letter from the Supreme Executive Council to Colonel Hartley, Washington had dispatched this regiment on October 24.[65] It could not have been long after the arrival of Patton's men that, on December 16, Congress directed that Hartley's and Patton's organizations, along with four independent companies, be consolidated into one unit, to be designated as a new 11th Pennsylvania Continental Regiment (see Chapter XVI). Because of a minor error in phrasing, the decision was restated on January 13, 1779.[66] The effect was essentially the same, although some ambiguity was introduced in the records of the terminal dates of service of some officers of Hartley's Regiment who did not continue in the new organization.

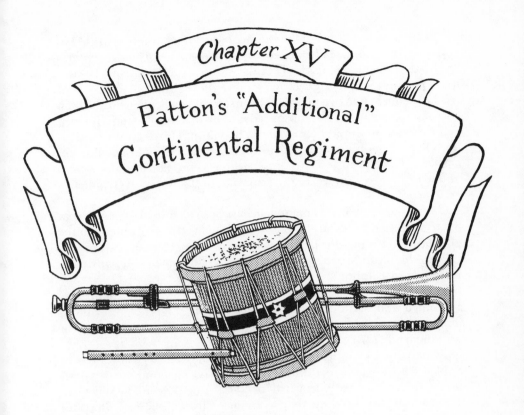

Chapter XV

Patton's "Additional" Continental Regiment

ORGANIZATION

THE second of the two "additional" Continental regiments raised primarily in Pennsylvania on authority of the resolution of Congress of December 27, 1776, was Patton's Regiment.[1] However, it also included a number of officers and enlisted men from New Jersey and Delaware.[2] Records of this organization are fragmentary, and it may never have been fully manned.

When the regiment was formed, command was given to Col. John Patton. He had been major of the second battalion of Miles's State Rifle Regiment[3] and had later been major of the 9th Pennsylvania. His appointment as colonel was dated January 11, 1777. He resigned his commission on February 3, 1778.[4] It would appear that he had not actually been functioning as regimental commander for some time, as another source dates his resignation in November, 1777.[5] Even though the regiment remained in existence for approximately another year, no one was promoted to be its colonel; however, it continued to be officially designated as "Patton's Regiment."

The lieutenant colonel of the regiment was John Parke (or Park).[6] His appointment also dated from January 11, 1777. After Colonel Patton's resignation, Lieutenant Colonel Parke was in actual command, but was never promoted. He resigned on October 29, 1778.[7]

The regiment had two majors. The first was Peter Scull, who had been a second lieutenant in Thompson's Battalion of Pennsylvania Riflemen and a captain in the 3d Pennsylvania Battalion. He resigned from Patton's Regiment on January 1, 1778,[8] and was replaced by Joseph Prowell (spelled "Powell" in some records[9]), who was promoted from captain. Major Prowell continued in this capacity for the rest of the regiment's existence.[10]

Only seven company commanders have been identified. It may be that the regiment never had its full complement of eight companies, but the possibility exists that the lack of mention of the eighth company merely reflects the incompleteness of the records. The known company commanders are as follows:

• [Company A], commanded by Capt. Joseph Prowell. He was directly appointed from civilian life on January 11, 1777.[11] It is not known who replaced him as company commander when he was promoted to major on January 1, 1778.

• [Company B], commanded by Capt. Lawrence Keene, whose pre-war residence has not been identified. After some sixteen months in this position, Captain Keene was detached to serve as aide-de-camp to Maj. Gen. Thomas Mifflin, holding that assignment from June 5, 1778, until shortly after Patton's Regiment was absorbed by Hartley's and redesignated as the 11th Pennsylvania.[12] During Keene's absence, the company would probably have been under the acting command of its first lieutenant.

• [Company C], commanded by Capt. Peter Grubb. Although he was from Lancaster County,[13] he had previously served as a third lieutenant in the Berks County company of Thompson's Pennsylvania Battalion of Riflemen,[14] then as a captain in the second battalion of Miles's State Rifle Regiment,[15] and later in the 10th Pennsylvania before being appointed to Patton's Regiment on January 13, 1777. He resigned on July 6, 1778.[16] No record has been found which identifies his replacement.

• [Company D], commanded by Capt. John Dennis, of New Jersey. He was taken prisoner at Red Bank, New Jersey—whether he was there on leave or, more probably, on duty, perhaps in connection with the defense of Fort Mercer and Fort Mifflin, is not recorded—on October 22, 1777. He did not survive to be exchanged, as he died in captivity on January 15, 1778.[17] Again, no information regarding a replacement has been found.

• [Company E], commanded by Capt. Abraham George Claypoole. He had prior service as an ensign in the Pennsylvania "Associators" (forerunners of the militia) before his appointment in Patton's Regiment as a captain-lieutenant on February 1, 1777. On June 10, 1778, he was promoted to captain, continuing in that rank while the regiment remained in existence.[18]

• [Company F], commanded by Capt. Allen McLane, of Delaware. He had been a lieutenant in the Delaware militia, and was appointed a captain in Patton's Regiment on January 13, 1777. This company was made up of Delaware men, and on December 16, 1778, when Patton's Regiment was merged with Hartley's Regiment, Captain McLane and his company were transferred to the Delaware Regiment.[19]

One other officer is mentioned in passing as a company commander.[20] This was 1st Lt. Edward Burke. He had been appointed a second lieutenant on January 15, 1777, and promoted to first lieutenant on October 4, 1777.[21] It is possible that he succeeded to a command vacated by the promotion, resignation, or absence of one of the captains. On the other hand, the implication of the reference to him is that he was already in command of a company at the time of the Battle of Germantown (whose date, it is worth noting, coincides with the date of his promotion to first lieutenant). Further, of the officers known to have been the original captains of Patton's Regiment, the first to vacate his captaincy was Joseph Prowell, promoted to major on January 1, 1778, and presumably in active command of his company up to that time.* It may be, therefore, that Lieutenant Burke should be listed as commander of a Company G. There is no information as to whether there was ever a Company H in this regiment; or, if so, of who commanded it.

Patton's Regiment would seem to have been in being before March, 1777, for at that time several deserters to the British were described as belonging to it. The regiment's uniform appears to have been a short brown jacket, buckskin breeches, and a round hat.[22]

As noted in Chapter XIV, on December 16, 1778, Congress directed that Hartley's Regiment absorb Patton's Regiment (less McLane's Company [F], which would be assigned to the Delaware Regiment) and four independent companies, to form the "New" 11th Pennsylvania.

Summary

Patton's Regiment, for the same reasons as Hartley's, would seem to have drawn its men from no one particular section, although there is

---

*Capt. Peter Grubb had been taken prisoner on October 22, 1777, but his capture did not create a vacant captaincy. Even though another officer would take over actual command of a company whose captain was taken prisoner, the captive captain continued to count against his regiment's authorized strength; and by common practice, the company continued to be identified by his name until such time as it was placed under the command of another captain.

some justification for believing that the Pennsylvanians in the regiment would have tended to come from the Philadelphia area and the counties surrounding it in the southeastern part of the State.

OPERATIONS

Little reference exists to this regiment's activities. However, the facts that one of its soldiers was wounded at Ash Swamp (near Plainfield), New Jersey, probably in early February, 1777,[23] and another was taken prisoner at Amboy on April 25 suggest that Patton's Regiment, or at least some of its elements, took part in the patrolling and skirmishing in New Jersey during the late winter and spring of 1777. It was also present at the Battle of Brandywine, where two privates are reported as having been wounded.[24] It is not listed among the units comprising Wayne's division or Conway's brigade, but as it is later shown as an element of the brigade commanded by Brig. Gen. Charles Scott,[25] it may have been under him during the campaign of the fall of 1777. If so, at Brandywine it would have been involved in the fighting around the Birmingham Meeting House, on the American right flank.

Similarly, at the Battle of Germantown, on October 4, 1777, if Patton's Regiment was part of Scott's brigade, it was in the flanking force led by Maj. Gen. Nathanael Greene, swinging in (late) from the north to roll up the British right. In this engagement, the regiment lost 2d Lt. William Patton killed[26] and one soldier wounded.[27]

Some personnel seem to have been sent to reinforce the Delaware River forts at this time. In any case, Captain Grubb was captured at Red Bank, New Jersey, on October 22, which coincides with the British operations against Fort Mercer, near Red Bank.[28]

At Whitemarsh, Scott's brigade (presumably including at least the bulk of Patton's Regiment) was deployed in the second line. It was not engaged in such action as took place when the British briefly attacked in early December, 1777.[29]

Patton's Regiment is expressly listed as a component of Scott's brigade at Valley Forge during the 1777-1778 winter encampment.[30] Before the winter was ended, the regiment seems to have been greatly reduced in strength, and certainly by the beginning of the campaign season in June it was more or less attached to the "additional" Continental regiment commanded by Col. William Grayson,[31] a preponderantly Virginia unit also in Scott's brigade.

At the Battle of Monmouth, on June 28, 1778, both Patton's and Grayson's regiments were detached from their brigade and placed under the tactical control of Anthony Wayne, in the army's advance element. Patton's Regiment took part in driving off an early British counterattack, and pursued the retreating enemy for a short distance, but was halted by artillery fire.[32] Wayne then formed a defensive line, with Patton's Regiment and the 9th Pennslyvania constituting its center, but this line was withdrawn without further involvement in combat.[33] During this battle, Patton's Regiment lost none of its members killed.[34] However, one private was wounded[35] and the regimental quartermaster, 1st Lt. James Bradford, was taken prisoner.[36]

Presumably, the regiment remained with Washington's army during the rest of the summer and part of the fall. It appears to be the organization which, on October 24, was sent west by Washington to reinforce Colonel Hartley on the frontier.[37] As already noted, on December 16, 1778, Congress directed the amalgamation of Hartley's and Patton's regiments and the designation of the new organization as the 11th Pennsylvania Regiment, reaffirming this decision on January 13, 1779.[38]

Chapter XVI
'New' 11th Pennsylvania Regiment

ORGANIZATION

THE "New" 11th Pennsylvania was formed as a result of two resolutions of Congress—one on December 16, 1778, and the other on January 13, 1779. It was to consist of Hartley's and Patton's "additional" Continental regiments (less Capt. Allen McLane's Company of Patton's Regiment) plus the four hitherto independent companies which had been raised by Captains James Calderwood, John Doyle, John Steele (or Steel), and John Wilkins.[1]

Actually, Captain Calderwood had been mortally wounded at Brandywine, dying on September 13, 1777.[2] Captain Doyle had been transferred to the 6th Pennsylvania Regiment on July 1, 1778.[3] Captain Steele had resigned on March 8, 1778.* Captain Wilkins had resigned a month later, on April 8, 1778.[4] Nevertheless, all these companies had continued to be known by the names of their original captains.

Calderwood's Company had been raised chiefly in Cumberland County, and for a time had been attached to Col. Daniel Morgan's 11th Virginia Regiment,[5] but when the 11th Virginia was absorbed by the 7th Virginia on September 14, 1778,[6] Calderwood's Company had become available for reassignment.

Captain Doyle would appear to be the John Doyle who was living in Philadelphia in 1774.[7]

As for Captain Steele, during the years immediately preceding the war, numerous men of that name and of appropriate age were residents of Philadelphia and of Chester and Lancaster counties,[8] but the one who seems to be the most likely candidate for a captaincy was the John Steel[e] who, in 1763, lived in Cumberland County.[9]

Captain Wilkins was from Carlisle, in Cumberland County.[10]

As noted in Chapters XIV and XV, Hartley's Regiment seems to have drawn its men from more settled areas of the State (that is, from Cumberland County east); and Patton's Regiment from Philadelphia and southeastern Pennsylvania. Other data tend to reinforce the likelihood that the "New" 11th Pennsylvania was manned largely by men from established communities rather than from frontier regions.

The muster rolls of the regiment are unique in the amount of information they provide about the individual enlisted men of the organization, listing for most personnel their occupations, heights, ages, and places of birth.

Of 176 men for whom civilian occupations are listed, 56 (31.8 per cent)

---

*Of four officers named John Steele, Heitman, p. 417, lists one from Virginia, two from Pennsylvania, and one from New York. The John Steele who commanded the independent company is said to have been assigned with his company to the 11th Pennsylvania on December 16, 1778, and to have remained with the regiment until January 17, 1781. The Capt. John Steele from New York is shown as serving with Malcolm's (Malcom's) "Additional" Continental Regiment until his resignation on March 8, 1778. Actually, it was the independent company of the *Pennsylvania* John Steele which was assigned to Malcom's Regiment and then *re*assigned to the "New" 11th Pennsylvania (see Berg, p. 120).

were farmers, and 7 (3.9 per cent) were laborers; the remaining 113 (over 64 per cent) claimed to be tradesmen or craftsmen. While some of the occupations—blacksmith, carpenter, butcher, and tinker, for example—were of a type required even in sparsely settled regions, others (such as silversmith, watchmaker, brass-founder, stocking weaver, vintner, and silk dyer) are more typical of urban and industrial-commercial areas.

In terms of height, the statistical average for the 213 men for whom this information was given was just under five feet six inches, but only three of the men were as tall as six feet, whereas forty-one (almost twenty per cent) stood only five feet three inches or less. Ages (218 men listed) ranged from a fifer of twelve to a private of sixty, but with the bulk of the soldiers (113, or 51.8 per cent) being in their twenties. However, there were thirty-three teen-agers (15 per cent) and ten men (4.6 per cent) aged fifty or older. Men in their thirties and forties had limited representation, at forty (18.4 per cent) and twenty-two (10.1 per cent), respectively, but these were ages at which family responsibilities could be expected to be particularly heavy.

Lacking comparably extensive data on other organizations, it is not possible to determine how typical this regiment's composition may have been. However, such information as has been found for other Pennsylvania Continental units is compatible in suggesting that a high proportion of the enlisted men were not native Americans. The muster rolls of the "New" 11th Pennsylvania list place of birth for 208 personnel. Of these, only fifty-nine (28.4 per cent) were native born. No less than ninety (43.3 per cent) were born in Ireland, forty-three (20.7 per cent) in England, eight (3.9 per cent) in Germany, six (2.9 per cent) in Scotland, and one each in Newfoundland and Wales. Of the native Americans, only forty (about two-thirds) gave Pennsylvania as their birthplace; another nine were not specific, but nine were natives of Maryland and one of North Carolina. One caveat which should be drawn from these figures, however, is that a significant number of the younger soldiers were among the foreign born, suggesting that in at least some instances they had been brought to America as infants or young children, and would therefore have grown up under essentially the same cultural influences as any native-born American.[11]

When the new regiment was formed, Col. Thomas Hartley was appointed as its commander. However, he resigned on February 13, 1779,[12] which appears to be the date on which the "New" 11th Pennsylvania effectively came into being. To replace him, Lt. Col. Adam Hubley became the commander. He was not advanced to colonel, as promotions to that grade had been discontinued. Instead, he was designated Lieutenant-Colonel Commandant, continuing in that position until January 17, 1781. He had previously served as a captain in the 1st

Pennsylvania Battalion, as major of the 10th Pennsylvania Regiment and briefly in Hartley's Regiment, and as lieutenant colonel of the 10th Pennsylvania.[13] His appointment was disputed by Morgan Conner, who had been lieutenant colonel of Hartley's Regiment, but this was settled by Conner's appointment on May 12, 1779, as Lieutenant-Colonel Commandant of the 7th Pennsylvania Regiment.[14]

There was also a controversy over the regiment's majority. Major Joseph Prowell, of Patton's Regiment, was initially appointed in the same grade to the "New" 11th Pennsylvania. However, the position was claimed by Evan Edwards, on the rolls of Hartley's Regiment but detached throughout much of the time to serve as aide-de-camp to Maj. Gen. Charles Lee. Apparently somewhat to the regret of Lieutenant Colonel Hubley, who considered Prowell "a worthy, good officer," a board of general officers ruled in favor of Edwards.[15] Prowell left the service on June 5, 1779,[16] and Edwards was promoted to major with a date of rank of December 10, 1778. He held that post throughout the regiment's existence.[17]

Capt. Joseph Davis, formerly of Hartley's Regiment, was assigned to the "New" 11th Pennsylvania, but he was killed by Indians near Wyoming on April 23, 1779,[18] and apparently never took command of one of the new companies.

The companies and their commanders were as follows:

• [Company A], the "Lieutenant Colonel's Company" of the regiment. Originally, it was actually commanded by Capt.-Lt. Jeremiah Jackson. According to one source,[19] he had been a lieutenant in Hartley's Regiment, but another[20] says that he had served in Patton's. In any event, he was promoted to captain on March 16, 1780, and assigned to replace Captain Forester[21] (see Company E, below). Taking Jackson's place as captain-lieutenant was Edward Burke, formerly of Patton's Regiment, who was promoted from first lieutenant; but he was promoted to captain on October 2, 1780,[22] replacing Captain Sweeny[23] (see Company H, below). The final captain-lieutenant, continuing with the company until January 17, 1781, was William McCurdy, previously of Hartley's Regiment, who was promoted from first lieutenant.[24] Only one company muster roll of Hartley's Regiment survived, and none of the names listed on it appears on the roster of this company.[25] From such records as do exist, however, Company A drew three men from Patton's Regiment[26] and one each from Doyle's[27] and Steele's[28] companies.

• [Company B], the "Major's Company" of the regiment. Throughout its existence it was commanded, at least nominally, by Major Evan Edwards.[29] Its muster roll[30] shows five men from Patton's Regiment,[31] one from Calderwood's Company,[32] and one from Steele's Company.[33]

• [Company C], commanded by Capt. George Bush, of Delaware,

formerly a captain in Hartley's Regiment, who apparently was carried as captain of this company throughout the life of the "New" 11th Pennsylvania.[34] According to some records, in May, 1779, he became Regimental Paymaster in addition to his duties as company commander,[35] and resigned from the army on March 11, 1780.[36] If he did vacate command of his company, no one appears to have been promoted to replace him. The company roster[37] shows four men from Hartley's Regiment[38] and six from Patton's.[39]

• [Company D] was commanded from its formation until January 17, 1781, by Capt. Lawrence Keene. He had previously been carried as a captain of Patton's Regiment, but had actually served as aide-de-camp to Maj. Gen. Thomas Mifflin until shortly before the "New" 11th Pennsylvania was activated.[40] Names on the muster roll[41] indicate that one man had previously served in Patton's Regiment,[42] four in Calderwood's Company,[43] and seven in Steele's Company.[44]

• [Company E], initially commanded by Capt. James Forester, formerly of Hartley's Regiment. Forester died on March 16, 1780,[45] and was replaced by Jeremiah Jackson, who was promoted from captain-lieutenant. Captain Jackson retained command of the company until January 17, 1781.[46] This company's muster roll[47] lists thirteen men previously in Hartley's Regiment,[48] one in Patton's Regiment,[49] and one in Steele's Company.[50]

• [Company F], commanded for its whole service by Capt. Andrew Walker, transferred to the "New" 11th Pennsylvania from Hartley's Regiment.[51] The records of this company[52] show only one man from one of the older units, a soldier formerly in Doyle's Company.[53]

• [Company G], commanded by Capt. Abraham George Claypoole, who had earlier served in Patton's Regiment. He commanded this company until January 17, 1781.[54] Listed on the company's rolls[55] were one former member of Hartley's Regiment,[56] six of Patton's,[57] and two of Steele's Company.[58]

• [Company H], whose first commander was Capt. Isaac Sweeny, originally of Hartley's Regiment. Captain Sweeny died on October 2, 1780,[59] and was replaced by Edward Burke,[60] who was promoted from captain-lieutenant and remained as captain of this company until January 17, 1781.[61] This company's muster roll[62] contains no names on the existing rosters of the organizations from which the "New" 11th Pennsylvania was formed. The muster roll is incomplete, but almost all of the dates of enlistment of the men listed on it antedate the formation of the regiment, so it is obvious that it contained a large proportion of prior-service men, presumably drawn from the "New" 11th Pennsylvania's parent units.

- [Company I], commanded continuously by Capt. Henry Carberry, of Maryland, who originally had been a lieutenant and captain in Hartley's Regiment.[63] His company's roster[64] includes one man from Hartley's Regiment,[65] two from Calderwood's Company,[66] and one from Steele's Company.[67]

The "New" 11th Pennsylvania apparently was well equipped, considering the stage of the war when it was formed. Six deserters in May, 1779, were uniformly clad in round hats and long blue coats with buff facings. In August, 1780, some deserters were wearing round hats, white breeches, and blue coats with red facings, indicating that they had been issued the uniform prescribed for infantry regiments of the Middle Atlantic States in October, 1779.[68]

Summary

Because of the limited information about some of the component elements from which the "New" 11th Pennsylvania Regiment was formed, it can be described in terms of its regional origins only in a relatively general way. Further, those component elements did not remain intact, but were broken up and their members scattered throughout the regiment. Whereas in other regiments, each company often had its own geographic character, each company of the "New" 11th Pennsylvania tended to be essentially a cross-section of the units from which the regiment was formed.

The regiment as a whole must have had considerable representation from Cumberland County, since Calderwood's Company was raised there, Wilkins' Company was probably from the same county, and Steele's Company may well have been. Also, some of the men of Hartley's Regiment seem to have been drawn from Cumberland and York counties. The other areas of Pennsylvania chiefly represented in the "New" 11th Pennsylvania would seem almost certainly to have been Lancaster, Berks, and Chester counties, and the city and county of Philadelphia. One thing that is evident, however, is that contrary to some assertions that have been made,[69] the "New" 11th Pennsylvania Regiment was emphatically not made up of men recruited in any significant numbers from the western counties of the State.

OPERATIONS

The chief references to the operations of the "New" 11th Pennsylvania Regiment pertain to its service as part of the Sullivan Expedition, which took place between late July and early October, 1779, beginning shortly after the regiment was formed.

Just prior to that time, on June 25, the "New" 11th Pennsylvania was at Sunbury. Present for duty were the lieutenant colonel, the major, four captains, the captain-lieutenant, eleven subalterns, the regimental staff, and 291 enlisted men.[70] By July 20, the regiment had moved to Wyoming,[71] where it waited until Maj. Gen. John Sullivan arrived with the bulk of the rest of his force. For the purpose of the expedition, the "New" 11th Pennsylvania was assigned to the brigade commanded by Brig. Gen. Edward Hand. This organization was designated as the "Light Infantry Corps," and formed the advance element of the army.[72]

The junction was made by July 30, and the combined force left Wyoming on July 31, moving west and north. The area through which the troops passed had been the object of extensive British and Indian raiding, and the men came to think of themselves as a force for retribution. Lieutenant Colonel Hubley commented on the frequent evidences of destruction and atrocity. The region had been occupied "by an industrious sett of Inhabitants tho' Poor, yet happy with their situation, untill that envied [invidious?] moment when the British Tyrant, let loose upon them, his Emissaries, the Savages of the Wood, who not only destroy'd & laid waist those Cotages, but in cool blood masacred, and cut of[f] the Inhabitants, not even sparing the gray locks or helpless Infant."[73]

The terrain was rough, and progress was made even slower by the necessity to wait for the army's baggage, which was being transported in boats. On August 3, near the Tunkhannock, two Indians were found on the flanks, but they fled.[74] On August 5, the army passed the site where Hartley's Regiment had defeated the Indians on September 29, 1778, and moved on to camp in the Wyalusing Valley. Although the possibility of encountering hostile Indians was considered to be increasing, the troops found no sign of the enemy. By August 8, scouts began to find Indian camps which seemed to have been recently abandoned.[75] Then, early on August 11, the army crossed the "Tioga Branch" (the Chemung River) of the North Branch of the Susquehanna. The crossing was made under tactical conditions—the Light Infantry Corps covered the opposite bank while the artillery blasted away at thickets and wooded areas to flush out any possible ambushers; then the Light Infantry Corps crossed, the men clasping hands to get through the strong current, and pushed beyond the river bank for about a hundred yards to establish an outpost line; finally, the main body of the army followed. The crossing, however, was unopposed, and the troops advanced beyond the ruins of Queen Esther's village (destroyed by Hartley's force a year before) and camped on the peninsula formed by the Chemung and the Susquehanna. An eight-man scouting party was sent on to reconnoiter the Indian town of Chemung, twelve miles away.[76]

Two regiments were assigned the task of fortifying the campsite as a base, and the rest of the force, including the "New" 11th Pennsylvania, marched at 8 P.M. on August 12 to attack Chemung, which the scouts reported as being still occupied. Because of the rough ground and the lack of knowledgeable guides, it was after daylight on August 13 before the assault force reached Chemung, which had just been evacuated. Captain Bush's company of the "New" 11th Pennsylvania was sent ahead to try to locate the Indians. On returning, Bush reported an occupied Indian village, called Newtown (now Elmira, New York), a few miles to the north, and the whole force moved forward. After advancing several miles, the troops in front were fired on from a hill to their right. The "New" 11th Pennsylvania deployed and "pushed up the Hill with a degree of interpidity seldom to be met with, and under a very severe fire from the savages." Bush and his company tried to circle around to the rear of the Indians, but the savages retreated before they could be cut off. This ended the combat for the day. During the action, six enlisted men had been killed and Captain Walker, Captain Carberry, and Adjutant William Huston, along with eight privates and a guide, had been wounded. Except for the guide and one of the enlisted men, all the casualties were from the "New" 11th Pennsylvania.[77] According to the enemy commander, the Tory Col. John Butler, the force attacked by the Americans consisted of about twenty Delaware Indians led by Capt. Rowland Montour, and had only one man killed.[78]

When the rest of the army came up, men were put to work burning the village and destroying the crops in the surrounding fields. While this was going on, Indian snipers killed one man and wounded several others. When the area had been laid waste, the army turned back to its base camp, which it reached, "considerably fatigued," about 8 P.M.[79]

The bulk of the army remained at the base camp, waiting for the arrival of troops under Brig. Gen. James Clinton from New York. This force reached the camp on August 22. It included Major James Parr and a company of men from the 1st Pennsylvania, and the entire 4th Pennsylvania Regiment. One of the officers of the latter unit, 1st Lt. Erkuries Beatty, wrote that "On our coming in to Camp we was saluted by 13 Pieces of Cannon which was Returned by our two little pieces, on the River we found Genl. Hands Brigade under arms with a Band of Musick which played Beautiful as we passed by them."[80] During the next day or two, the fortifications (named Fort Sullivan) at the camp were completed. On August 26 the army, less troops left to man Fort Sullivan, resumed its march northward.[81]

The advance force met its first opposition on August 28, when a scouting party was fired on, but no one was hit. However, scouts reported finding a considerable body of Indians at Newtown, beyond the point where the engagement had taken place some two weeks earlier. Accordingly, the army marched toward Newtown on the morning of

August 29, the Light Infantry Corps comprising the leading element, with a small force under Major Parr forming the point. There was a brief action at Newtown, where an Indian outpost fired on Parr's detachment and then fell back. Parr cautiously sent a man up a tree to see what might lie ahead. It was a wise precaution, for the soldier detected a group of Indians in position behind a long breastwork which stretched all the way from the river to the mountains.[82]

Parr reported this discovery to General Hand. The General moved the Light Infantry Corps forward, deploying it about three hundred yards in front of the Indian entrenchment. Parr and his men crept even farther forward, to within a hundred yards of the enemy position. Although there was a heated exchange of fire between Parr's force and the Indians, neither side suffered much damage. While this was going on, General Sullivan swung part of the main body around the Indians' left flank, trying to cut off their escape route. About mid-afternoon, the guns of the 4th Continental Artillery, under Col. Thomas Procter, opened a bombardment of the Indians' position, and Hand's men were about to charge. Before they could launch their attack, however, the Indians fled. Meanwhile, some of the Indians had moved off to their left and now attacked the flanking force, which drove through at the cost of several wounded but was unable to block the Indians' withdrawal. This ended the engagement. Hubley noted that "In the course of the day we took nine scalps (all savages) and two prisoners," who reported that the enemy force had consisted of five hundred Indians, two hundred Tories, and about twenty British troops.[83] One of the prisoners was a Tory and the other was a Negro.[84]

Colonel Butler's version of the fight from the Indian side stated that the total forces which he and Joseph Brant had available numbered no more than six hundred. He said that the Indians were terrified by the artillery fire, which caused them to abandon their breastwork and scatter to their villages. He admitted to losing five of his rangers (Tories) killed or captured, and three wounded; and said that the Indians had five killed and nine wounded.[85] However, an American who was present at the battle reported having seen nine Indian scalps, and said that he had heard that the bodies of fourteen other Indians had been found.[86]

By this time, the expedition found that it had been inadequately supplied with provisions. Sullivan asked the men if they were willing to continue the operation on half rations, promising that when they had to subsist on vegetables instead of meat they would receive a cash commutation in lieu of rations. Lieutenant Colonel Hubley said that the troops "cheerfully agreed to the request of the General." Accordingly, the army resumed its advance on August 31.[87]

It drove on into New York, burning Indian towns and destroying crops. The route lay along Seneca Lake, then on September 14 to the main Indian town of Genesee, some miles west of and across the Genesee River from the modern town of Geneseo.[88] In addition to enduring shortages of provisions, negotiating rugged terrain, and suffering from bad weather, the troops met other hazards. On September 3, for example, Lieutenant Beatty noted that a "great many large rattlesnakes was killed to day."[89] There were no more large-scale battles, but the troops were subjected to occasional sniping, and once a scouting party of twenty-four men was cut off: nine escaped but six were killed and nine others were taken prisoner. (At Genesee the bodies of two of the prisoners were found; they had been tortured to death, and their bodies mutilated.) However, Hubley took satisfaction from the army's accomplishment of its mission which, he said, was "the total ruin of the Indian settlements and distruction of their crops."[90] And one of the scouts who escaped was the redoubtable Private Timothy Murphy[91] (see Chapter II).

The army then turned back, retracing its route and "laying waist" to such cultivated fields as it had missed on its way north. There was no more combat. However, Lieutenant Beatty observed that all were suffering "Hungry bellies and hard Duty now which I think we may call hard times."[92] But on September 24, the force reached an advance base which had been established, and found a stock of badly needed supplies waiting for it.[93] The troops camped and, Beatty reported, "drew each officer & soldier one Jill of Whiskey after a fatigue of near one Month without a drop."[94] The safe return, combined with news that Spain had joined the alliance against Britain, provided justification for a celebration, which was held on September 25. The troops were formed and fired what Lieutenant Colonel Hubley called a "few de joy."[95] According to Lieutenant Beatty, however, the feu de joie "did not please the General [Hand] and he made the musquitry fire again afterwards."[96] The officers of each brigade were issued five gallons of spirits; bullocks were roasted; and while the officers sat on the ground under a "bowery" circled by thirteen pine-knot torches the drums and fifes of the 4th Artillery provided music.[97] Beatty said that "We suped very hearty and then went to drinking our spirits."[98] No less than thirteen toasts were drunk—the last of which was "May the Enemies of America be metimorphos'd into pack-horses, and sent on a Western Expedition against the Indians." It is easy to believe Hubley's statement that "the Officers being very jovial and the evening was spent in great Mirth and jolity."[99] And "Afterwards," Beatty reported, "there was two or three Indian Dances led down by Genl. Hand and performed by the rest middling well."[100] Lieutenant Colonel Hubley noted that the army did not march the following day, which is understandable, but his explanation that it stayed in camp because of rain is not completely convincing.[101] Lieutenant Beatty was more forthright, entering in his journal the admission that "Did not feel very well this morning after my frolick."[102]

The return to Fort Sullivan, which was reached on September 30, was uneventful. The garrison commander entertained the general and field officers that night at "an elegant Dinner," and "we regal'd ourselves and great joy & good humour was visible in every Countenance. Colo¹ Proctors Band & Drums & fifes played in Concert the whole time." On October 2, there was another banquet, this time hosted by General Sullivan. "In the evening to conclude the mirth of the day, we had an Indian dance."[103] On the following day, Fort Sullivan was demolished, and on October 4, the army marched to Weusakin. Next morning the troops boarded boats and started down the North Branch of the Susquehanna, reaching Wyoming during the middle of the afternoon of October 7,[104] when the expedition was officially ended and the various units scattered to other stations.

The "New" 11th Pennsylvania Regiment remained assigned to Hand's brigade, which returned to duty with Washington's main army. As of March 25, 1780, the regiment's present-for-duty strength was 189.[105] Its total enlisted strength as of April 30, 1780, was 349.[106] By the end of 1780, the "New" 11th Pennsylvania was stationed at Morristown, New Jersey. It was the men of this regiment who started the unruly shouting and protesting on January 1, 1781, which rapidly spread to become the mutiny of all the Pennsylvania regiments which were present.[107] The "New" 11th was one of the organizations inactivated following the settlement of the mutiny, when the infantry strength of the Pennsylvania Line was reduced to six regiments. There are no records to indicate how many of its members may have joined one of the three provisional battalions formed at that time for service in the southern campaign.

Chapter XVII

Pennsylvania State Rifle Regiment
Penna. State Battalion of Musketry
Penna. State Regiment
13th Penna. Regiment

Walter Stewart

ORGANIZATION

THE 13th Pennsylvania Regiment of the Continental Army evolved from the Pennsylvania State Regiment, which itself was an amalgamation of two older units, the Pennsylvania State Rifle Regiment and the Pennsylvania State Battalion of Musketry. To trace the organizational history of the Continental unit, each of the parent units will first be treated individually, then the organizations formed from their consolidation will be described.

Pennsylvania State Rifle Regiment

This organization, usually known (from its commander's name) as Miles's Regiment, was one of several formed for the purpose of providing for the defense of Pennsylvania proper. Under the terms of the resolution of the Pennsylvania House of Representatives passed on March 5, 1776, it was to consist of 1,000 men, enlisted until January 1, 1778. They were to be armed with rifles, and would be organized in two battalions of six seventy-eight-man companies each.[1] In concept, therefore, this unit more closely approximated post-Revolutionary regimental organizations than did the other regiments/battalions formed at that time.

The colonel of the regiment was Samuel Miles, who was appointed on March 13, 1776. He commanded the regiment until he was taken prisoner at the Battle of Long Island, on August 27, 1776. Although he was eventually exchanged—on December 28, 1776—reorganizations had by that time eliminated his former command as an independent entity.[2] On his exchange, he was appointed a brigadier general in the State forces of Pennsylvania.[3]

One of the regiment's two battalions was commanded by Lt. Col. James Piper, of Bedford County.[4] He also was captured at the Battle of Long Island, after having been wounded. He died at an unspecified date in September, 1776, while still a prisoner.[5]

The other battalion commander was Lt. Col. Daniel Brodhead, of Berks County.[6] After the Battle of Long Island he became acting commander of the remnants of Miles's Regiment and the Pennsylvania State Battalion of Musketry, which were consolidated into a single provisional battalion.[7] On October 25, 1776, however, he was transferred to the 4th Pennsylvania Regiment.[8]

The major of the 1st Battalion of the regiment was Ennion Williams. He resigned from the army on February 4, 1777,[9] when Lewis Farmer, although junior to him, was promoted to lieutenant colonel over his head.[10]

In the 2d Battalion, the major was John Patton. On October 25, 1776, he was transferred to the 9th Pennsylvania Regiment.[11]

The Fifth Series of *Pennsylvania Archives* lists the companies of the regiment as pertaining to the 1st Battalion or the 2d Battalion. However, only four companies are shown as belonging to the 1st Battalion, while the 2d Battalion is shown as having eight companies. As the resolution authorizing the regiment's formation prescribed two battalions of six companies each, the breakdown in the *Archives* would appear to be incorrect. In the absence of any clear record which allocates companies to battalions in equal numbers, no attempt is made here to speculate on which company belonged to which battalion.

The companies and their commanders were as follows:

• [Company A], commanded by Capt. Henry Shade, who was appointed from Northampton County.[12] On December 5, 1776, he was transferred to the 10th Pennsylvania,[13] being succeeded as company commander by Capt. John McGowan.[14] McGowan had entered the army as a third lieutenant in the 1st Pennsylvania Battalion, and had become adjutant of Miles's Regiment, being promoted to captain on October 24, 1776. On January 3, 1777, he was transferred to the 4th Pennsylvania Regiment.[15]

• [Company B], commanded by Capt. Casper Weitzel, appointed from Sunbury, in Northumberland County.[16] He left the army in January, 1777.[17]

• [Company C], commanded by Capt. Richard Brown, who was appointed from Bedford County.[18] He had been a third lieutenant in Thompson's Rifle Battalion. On August 27, 1776, at the Battle of Long Island, he was taken prisoner.[19] There is no record that he was ever exchanged. His successor as company commander was James Francis Moore, also of Bedford County,[20] who was promoted from first lieutenant on October 25, 1776. He continued with the regiment throughout its various reorganizations as long as it existed as a distinct unit.[21]

• [Company D], commanded by Capt. Philip Albright, who was appointed from York County.[22] He resigned his commission on January 23, 1777.[23]

• [Company E], commanded by Capt. John Murray, appointed on March 7, 1776, from Paxtang Township in what was then Lancaster County but is now Dauphin County.[24] Prior to his appointment, he had held a commission (since January 9, 1776) as an ensign in the 6th Pennsylvania Battalion. He was promoted to major in the Pennsylvania State Regiment (see below) on March 18, 1777.[25]

• [Company F], commanded by Capt. John Marshall. This company was raised in Hanover Township, in what is now Dauphin County.* Marshall later became a captain in the Pennsylvania State Regiment.[26]

• [Company G], commanded by Capt. William Peebles, who was appointed from Cumberland County.[27] He was captured at the Battle of Long Island and died in October, 1776, while still a prisoner.[28]

• [Company H], commanded by Capt. Henry Christ, Jr., who was appointed from Berks County.[29] He resigned his commission on March 19, 1777.[30]

• [Company I], commanded by Capt. Joseph Erwin. This company was recruited in Westmoreland County.[31] Captain Erwin was transferred on November 15, 1776, to the 9th Pennsylvania Regiment.[32]

• [Company K†], commanded by Capt. Peter Grubb, Jr., appointed

---

*PA(5), II, 332. Heitman, p. 380, says that John Marshall's captaincy was in the Pennsylvania State Battalion of Musketry, but manifestly is confusing him with Capt. *Abraham* Marshall of that organization.

†As American Army units traditionally are not lettered as "J," that designation has been omitted in this listing.

from Lancaster County. He had prior military service as a third lieutenant in Thompson's Rifle Battalion. He was transferred to the 10th Pennsylvania on November 27, 1776.

• [Company L], commanded by Capt. Lewis Farmer, who was appointed from Philadelphia.[35] He was wounded at the Battle of Long Island but remained in command of his company until promoted major in the Pennsylvania State Regiment on March 14, 1777.[36]

• [Company M], commanded by Capt. Andrew Long, appointed from Bucks County. He resigned from the army on October 14, 1776, due to ill health.[37]

The only information concerning the uniform of this regiment relates to descriptions of the clothing worn by deserters from the organization. Of six men who deserted in June and July, 1776, all were wearing hunting shirts and trousers. Two of the hunting shirts were black, one was described as "a lead color," and the others were "light colored."[38]

Pennsylvania State Battalion of Musketry

This organization was authorized by the same resolution of the Pennsylvania House of Representatives which, on March 5, 1776, created Miles's State Rifle Regiment. Like that unit, it was originally intended solely for the defense of the State. However, it was to consist of "regular" troops (that is, armed with muskets rather than rifles) and was to total 500 men organized in eight companies of fifty-eight enlisted men and three officers each.[39]

Samuel John Atlee, of Lancaster County, was appointed colonel to command the battalion on March 21, 1776. He was taken prisoner at the Battle of Long Island, on August 27, 1776, and was not exchanged until August 6, 1778.[40] Upon his exchange, he did not reenter the army.[41] However, the organization was known throughout its existence as "Atlee's Battalion."

The battalion's lieutenant colonel was Caleb Parry. He was killed at the Battle of Long Island.[42]

James Potts was the battalion's major, but he resigned his commission on July 11, 1776,[43] and no one was promoted to replace him.

The companies and their captains were as follows:

• [Company A], commanded by Capt. Patrick Anderson, appointed from Chester County.[44] He continued as commander of this company when the organization was merged into the Pennsylvania State Regiment.[45]

• [Company B], commanded by Capt. Peter Z. Lloyd.[46] He appears to be the Peter Lloyd who was living in Philadelphia in 1774.[47] On August 11, 1776, he was detached to serve as aide-de-camp[48] or as brigade-major[49] to Brig. Gen. James Ewing of the Pennsylvania "Associators." He continued in that position until November, 1776.[50] Apparently he did not return to the battalion, but no one was promoted to replace him.

• [Company C], initially commanded by Capt. Francis Murray, who was appointed from Bucks County.[51] He was captured at the Battle of Long Island and was exchanged on December 9, 1776. On returning to duty he was promoted to major in the Pennsylvania State Regiment, effective May 2, 1777.[52] In the meantime, he had been succeeded as company commander by Morton Garrett (or Garret), who was promoted from first lieutenant on October 25, 1776.[53] Captain Garrett resigned on February 12, 1777.[54]

• [Company D], whose original commander was Capt. Abraham Marshall.[55] Captain Marshall's pre-war residence is not certainly known, although it seems probable that he was the man of that name living in Philadelphia County from 1779 on.[56] He resigned on July 12, 1776,[57] when he was replaced by Joseph McClellan,[58] who was promoted from first lieutenant on July 15, 1776. On January 1, 1777, Captain McClellan was transferred to the 9th Pennsylvania.[59]

• [Company E], commanded by Capt. Thomas Herbert. This company was recruited in Lancaster County.[60] Captain Herbert was taken prisoner at the Battle of Long Island, on August 27, 1776. He was exchanged the following November, and almost immediately (on December 4, 1776) was transferred to the 10th Pennsylvania.[61]

• [Company F], commanded by Capt. Abraham DeHuff. This company was also recruited in Lancaster County.[62] Apparently it was assigned, after the Battle of Long Island, to the garrison of Fort Washington, New York, for Captain DeHuff was taken prisoner there on November 16, 1776. He was not exchanged until April 20, 1778, and apparently did not return to duty.[63]

• [Company G], commanded by Capt. John Nice.[64] It would seem that this was the John Nice who in 1774 lived in Philadelphia County or the city of Philadelphia.[65] He was still another of the members of the battalion taken prisoner at the Battle of Long Island. Upon his exchange, on December 9, 1776, he was assigned to the Pennsylvania State Regiment.[66]

• [Company H], commanded by Capt. Joseph Howell, Jr., probably of Philadelphia.[67] He also was captured at the Battle of Long Island. He did not return to duty with this organization following his exchange on December 9, 1776, but later served in the 2d Pennsylvania Regiment.[68]

With regard to the uniform of this battalion, three deserters during the period April-May, 1776, were dressed in a variety of civilian clothing. However, a deserter in late May was wearing a blue coat lined with blue, and three who deserted in July were all wearing blue coats with red facings, buckskin breeches, and white stockings, and one had a hat bound with yellow.[69]

Pennsylvania State Regiment

On October 5, 1776, the Pennsylvania Council of Safety took the first step toward consolidating the remnants of Miles's Regiment and Atlee's Battalion by asking Lieutenant Colonel Brodhead to supply lists of those of his officers who desired to join the Continental Army and those who wanted to remain in the service of the State.[70] About three weeks later, on October 25, the Council of Safety specified which companies of the regiment and the battalion were to be consolidated to form the new organization. The Council also prescribed that what was to be the Pennsylvania State Regiment would have ten companies, eight of them armed with muskets and the other two with "Riffles."[71] The new regiment began to take shape early in 1777, and was officially activated (on paper) in its new configuration on March 1.[72]

The man initially appointed to command the regiment was Col. John Bull, who had briefly been colonel of the 1st Pennsylvania Battalion until his officers threatened to resign rather than serve under him (see Chapter III). Once again, the officers objected to Bull. On June 3, 1777, they protested formally to the Pennsylvania House of Representatives. Their complaint was that since Colonel Bull had served neither in the State Rifle Regiment nor in the State Battalion of Musketry, his appointment as commander of the Pennsylvania State Regiment completely violated their seniority rights; and they accompanied their protest with a thinly veiled threat to resign in a body.[73] The situation was saved when Colonel Bull was appointed adjutant general of Pennsylvania militia effective June 17, 1777,[74] thus vacating his position as regimental commander. He was replaced by Col. Walter Stewart. While eighteenth-century officers were extremely sensitive to matters of rank and seniority, it seems likely that the officers of the Pennsylvania State Regiment must have objected to Colonel Bull on other, unspecified grounds. In any case, no objection was raised to Colonel Stewart's appointment, even though he had had no more connection with the State Rifle Regiment or the State Battalion of Musketry than Colonel Bull.

Meanwhile, on June 6, 1777, the Pennsylvania authorities had offered the Pennsylvania State Regiment to Congress for incorporation into the Continental Army, and added to it, as an eleventh company, a unit commanded by Capt. John Pugh, which had been raised as an independent company to guard powder mills.[75] The transfer of the regiment to the Continental service was formalized on June 10, 1777.[76]

Col. Walter Stewart, who was to command the regiment throughout its existence, had begun his military service as a captain in the 3d Pennsylvania Battalion, but on June 7, 1776, had been appointed aide-de-camp in grade to Maj. Gen. Horatio Gates, being promoted to lieutenant colonel on November 19, 1776.[77]

The lieutenant colonel of the regiment was Lewis Farmer. He had been a captain in Miles's Regiment and was appointed major of the Pennsylvania State Regiment, then promoted to lieutenant colonel on May 2, 1777.[78]

Because of its size, the Pennsylvania State Regiment had two majors. Initially, these were Lewis Farmer and John Murray (like Farmer, Murray had been a captain in Miles's Regiment, and was appointed major in the Pennsylvania State Regiment on March 18, 1777). When Farmer was promoted to lieutenant colonel, Francis Murray (formerly a captain in Atlee's Battalion) was promoted to fill the second majority,[79] giving the regiment two Majors Murray.

Upon the formation of the companies of the Pennsylvania State Regiment, only four were commanded by officers who had been captains either in Miles's Regiment or Atlee's Battalion. The companies of the new regiment and their commanders were as follows:

• [Company A], commanded by Capt. Patrick Anderson, who had commanded Company A of Atlee's Battalion. Only ten of the men of the new company appear to be veterans of Atlee's Battalion, and only six of these had been in Captain Anderson's former company (raised in Chester County). The bulk of the prior-service men in this unit (twenty-five) had been in Capt. Henry Christ's Berks County company (H) of Miles's Regiment. Seven others had been in Capt. Lewis Farmer's Company L of that regiment, which had been raised in the Philadelphia area.[80]

• [Company B], commanded by Capt. James Carnaghan. He had been a second lieutenant in Miles's Regiment. Captured at the Battle of Long Island, on August 27, 1776, he had been exchanged on December 10 of that year. While he was still a prisoner, he had been promoted to first lieutenant (on October 24, 1776). He was appointed a captain in the Pennsylvania State Regiment on January 15, 1777.[81] Thirty of the members of his company had served in Miles's Regiment and four in Atlee's Battalion. The largest number (19) from any one of the older companies had been in Capt. Joseph Erwin's Company I, recruited in Westmoreland County, of Miles's Regiment.[82] This was the same unit in which Carnaghan had served as a second lieutenant.[83]

• [Company C], commanded by Capt. John Robb. He also had been a second lieutenant in Miles's Regiment. He was appointed a captain in the Pennsylvania State Regiment on April 18, 1777.[84] Of the men of this company, thirty-one were veterans of Miles's Regiment and fifteen of Atlee's Battalion. Sixteen of these men were from Capt. Casper Weitzel's Northumberland County company (B) of Miles's Regiment (the same company in which Captain Robb had been a lieutenant[85]), ten from Capt. Philip Albright's York County company (D) of the same organization, and ten from Capt. Patrick Anderson's Chester County company (A) of Atlee's Battalion.[86]

• [Company D], commanded by Capt. Matthew Scott. As a first lieutenant in Miles's Regiment, he had been taken prisoner at the Battle of Long Island and exchanged on December 8, 1776. His appointment as a captain in the Pennsylvania State Regiment was dated April 18, 1777.[87] His company included thirty-six men from Miles's Regiment and six from Atlee's Battalion. Of these veterans, thirty-three had belonged to Capt. William Peebles' Cumberland County company (G) of Miles's Regiment.[88] It was in that company, also, that Captain Scott had served as a first lieutenant.[89]

• [Company E], commanded by Capt. James Francis Moore, who had been a lieutenant in Miles's Regiment until he was promoted to captain on October 25, 1776.[90] All but two of the forty-two veterans in this company were from Miles's Regiment, sixteen of them from Capt. Richard Brown's Bedford County company (C)—the company in which Moore had served[91]—and thirteen from the Northampton County company (A) first commanded by Capt. Henry Shade and then by Capt. John McGowan.[92]

• [Company F], commanded by Capt. John Marshall, who had commanded Company F, raised in the present Dauphin County, in Miles's Regiment. He had fifty-one veterans of that regiment and three veterans of Atlee's Battalion in his new company, twenty-two of the men having served under him in Miles's Regiment. Among the other prior-service men, there was considerable representation (nine men) from Capt. Philip Albright's York County company (D) of Miles's Regiment. Also, there were five men each from Capt. Richard Brown's Company C (raised in Bedford County) and Capt. John Murray's Company E (like Captain Marshall's first company, raised in modern Dauphin County), likewise of Miles's Regiment.[93]

• [Company G], commanded by Capt. John Nice, who had commanded Company G (probably raised in Philadelphia) of Atlee's Battalion. In his new company, he had twenty-four men from Miles's Regiment and eleven from Atlee's Battalion, only five of whom were from his old company. The largest representation among these veterans was provided by fourteen men from Capt. Lewis Farmer's Philadelphia company (L) of Miles's Regiment.[94]

• [Company H], commanded by Capt. John Spear (or Speer), who had been first lieutenant of Company M (commanded by Capt. Andrew Long and apparently raised in Bucks County) of Miles's Regiment.[95] Spear had been wounded and taken prisoner at the Battle of Long Island. The date of his exchange is not known, but he was appointed a captain in the Pennsylvania State Regiment on February 6, 1777.[96] This company had eighteen men who had been in Miles's Regiment (twelve of them with Spear in Company M) and nine from various companies of Atlee's Battalion, most of them from Philadelphia-area units.[97]

• [Company I], commanded by Capt. John Clark. He also had been a first lieutenant in Miles's Regiment, serving in Capt. John Marshall's Company F, from modern Dauphin County.[98] On January 14, 1777, he was assigned as aide-de-camp to Maj. Gen. Nathanael Greene, but was appointed a captain in the Pennsylvania State Regiment barely a month later, on February 20.[99] This company had forty-seven veterans, two of them from Atlee's Battalion and the other forty-five from Miles's Regiment. Of the latter, twenty-one had been in Capt. John Murray's company (E), from the present Dauphin County; twelve were from Capt. Peter Grubb's Lancaster County company (K); four each were from Capt. John Marshall's Dauphin County company (F) and the Northampton County company (A) commanded successively by Capt. Henry Shade and Capt. John McGowan; and three were from Capt. Lewis Farmer's Philadelphia-area company (L).[100]

• [Company K], commanded by Capt. Robert Gray. He had been battalion quartermaster of Atlee's Battalion, and was appointed a captain in the Pennsylvania State Regiment on February 28, 1777.[101] His prior-service men totalled 32. Of the seventeen veterans of Atlee's Battalion, eight had been in Capt. Francis Murray's Bucks County company (C). Five other men had come from Capt. Peter Grubb's Lancaster County company (K) of Miles's Regiment. The rest of the veterans were drawn in ones and twos from six companies of Atlee's Battalion and seven companies of Miles's Regiment.[102]

• [Company L], commanded by Capt. John Pugh. This unit had been raised as an independent company to guard powder mills, and was added to the Pennsylvania State Regiment on June 6, 1777.[103] It is likely that Captain Pugh was one of the men named John Pugh living in Chester County in 1774.[104] No muster rolls of this company have survived. In any case, after August 12, 1777, this company ceased to exist as a separate unit (see below).

The Pennsylvania State Regiment appears to have been uniformed in a standard pattern by mid-June of 1777. The coat was blue, with red lining and facing—similar to the uniform of Atlee's Battalion. The coat, however, had white buttons inscribed P$_R$S.[105]

13th Pennsylvania Regiment

Within less than a month after being taken into the Continental service, the Pennsylvania State Regiment was unofficially called the 13th Pennsylvania Regiment, being so designated in a strength return of July 6, 1777,[106] although it was not officially assigned a number until November 12, 1777.[107] Initially, the 13th Pennsylvania Regiment was the same organization as the Pennsylvania State Regiment, merely having a new name. However, the enlistments of many of the men who had originally joined Miles's Regiment or Atlee's Battalion expired on January 1, 1778, and those of most of the rest from those two organizations expired in April and May of the same year. With the discharge of a large proportion of these men, the regiment was drastically reduced in strength. The decision was made, therefore, to incorporate what was left into the 2d Pennsylvania Regiment, this reorganization to take effect on July 1, 1778.[108]

The colonel of the 13th Pennsylvania throughout its existence was Walter Stewart. When the 13th Pennsylvania was absorbed by the 2d Pennsylvania on July 1, 1778, he became the commander of the consolidated regiment.[109]

The lieutenant colonelcy continued to be held by Lewis Farmer. However, the reorganization of July 1, 1778, made him supernumerary and he left the army.[110]

During most of its existence, the 13th Pennsylvania had two majors. The senior of the two (the "first major"), John Murray, held this position until July 1, 1778, when he became the major of the 2d Pennsylvania Regiment. The "second major," Francis Murray, served with the 13th Pennsylvania until February 21, 1778, when he and several men of the command were captured at Newtown, in Bucks County,[111] while he was on his way to his home. He was not exchanged until December 25, 1780, and never returned to duty.[112]

The 13th Pennsylvania continued briefly to consist of eleven companies. On August 12, 1777, however, Capt. John Pugh resigned his commission[113] and Colonel Stewart redistributed the men of Pugh's company (L of the Pennsylvania State Regiment) among the other units of the regiment, reducing the total number of companies to ten[114]—still two companies larger than what was at that time the normal regimental size.

Only two company muster rolls (for Companies C and D) have been found, but they are very similar in composition to the corresponding companies in the Pennsylvania State Regiment. Since the 13th Pennsylvania retained the same company commanders as the Pennsylvania State Regiment (except for Captain Pugh, of Company L), and since the 13th

Pennsylvania had such a short existence, it seems virtually certain that no significant changes in personnel distribution occurred.

The companies and their commanders were as follows:

• [Company A], commanded by Capt. Patrick Anderson. On October 20, 1777, he was "superseded" and left the army.[115] There is no record that anyone was promoted to take his place.

• [Company B], commanded by Capt. James Carnaghan. On July 1, 1778, he was transferred to the 8th Pennsylvania.[116]

• [Company C], commanded by Capt. John Robb, who became supernumerary and left the army when the regiment was incorporated into the 2d Pennsylvania on July 1, 1778.[117]

• [Company D], commanded by Capt. Matthew Scott. He also became supernumerary on July 1, 1778.[118]

• [Company E], commanded by Capt. James Francis Moore. Like Captain Carnaghan, he was transferred to the 8th Pennsylvania on July 1, 1778.[119]

• [Company F], commanded by Capt. John Marshall. On September 25, 1778, after the reorganization, he resigned from the army.[120]

• [Company G], commanded by Capt. John Nice. When the reorganization took place on July 1, 1778, he was transferred to the 6th Pennsylvania Regiment.[121]

• [Company H], commanded by Capt. John Spear. He died at Valley Forge on February 8, 1778,[122] of intermittent fever after an illness of two weeks.[123] By that time the regiment was already at greatly reduced strength. In all probability, the remaining men in this company were reassigned to other units within the regiment.

• [Company I], commanded by Capt. John Clark, who was transferred to the 8th Pennsylvania on July 1, 1778.[124]

• [Company K], commanded by Capt. Robert Gray. He became supernumerary on July 1, 1778, and left the service.[125]

Probably, most of the men of the 13th Pennsylvania continued to wear the uniform of the Pennsylvania State Regiment. However, deserters from the 13th Pennsylvania during the winter of 1777-1778 were variously clad, one wearing a hunting shirt, another wearing a blue uniform coat with white facings, and a third wearing a brown uniform coat with buff facings.[126]

Summary

Pennsylvania State Rifle Regiment

Of the twelve companies of this regiment, no less than four were from frontier areas of the State—that is, Northampton, Northumberland, Bedford, and Westmoreland counties. Four others were raised in counties which, at least in some sections, were on the fringes of the frontier; specifically, these were companies from Lancaster County (including two companies raised in what is now Dauphin County) and Cumberland County. The remaining four companies were from the more settled areas of York, Berks, and Bucks counties and the city and county of Philadelphia.

Pennsylvania State Battalion of Musketry

By contrast, all but two of the companies of Atlee's Battalion were from areas of Pennsylvania which had been settled for some time. One company was from Chester County, at least one and probably three others were from the Philadelphia area, and one was from Bucks County. The other two companies of the battalion were from Lancaster County. Part of that county was well settled, but other parts verged on the frontier. In general, however, the Pennsylvania State Battalion of Musketry appears to have had a distinctly eastern flavor.

Pennsylvania State Regiment

To the extent that records exist, it appears that the Pennsylvania State Regiment drew 322 men from Miles's Regiment and 81 from Atlee's Battalion. On the probably incorrect assumption that the muster rolls are complete, this would mean that almost a third (31.3 per cent) of Miles's men and over a fifth (21.2 per cent) of Atlee's men also served in the Pennsylvania State Regiment.

To a degree, the companies of this regiment seem to have retained distinct regional flavors. One company had mostly Westmoreland County men, another mostly Cumberland County men, a third was made up chiefly of men from Chester County, and three others primarily of men from Philadelphia and surrounding counties. The other companies were mixtures; but to a considerable extent, men from similar regional environments tended to join the same companies: for example, one company drew its troops from Bedford and Northumberland counties—widely separated, but both located on frontiers. The Lancaster County men (including those from modern Dauphin County) made up the bulk of three companies, but one of these had considerable representation also from Bedford and York counties, another included sizable numbers from Northumberland County, and the other had a Bucks County contingent.

In general, the Pennsylvania State Regiment was drawn from the entire area of the State; but in view of the distribution of the population, the frontier areas had a disproportionately heavy representation.

13th Pennsylvania Regiment

Retaining as it did a virtually unchanged structure, the 13th

Pennsylvania perpetuated the character of the Pennsylvania State Regiment, being merely the same organization under a new designation.

OPERATIONS

Pennsylvania State Rifle Regiment-Pennsylvania State Battalion of Musketry

As these two organizations spent all their service in close association, their operations will be described in a single section.

Although both organizations were formed for the defense of the State,[127] both were soon committed to service with (but not as part of) the Continental Army.

Miles's Regiment was recruited almost completely to its authorized strength within six weeks, and toward the end of June, 1776, the companies assembled at Marcus Hook, just above the Delaware boundary.[128] The men, of course, were generally untrained and undisciplined. Sgt. James McMichael was surprised to note that on the first Sunday after his company had arrived, "This day the soldiers appeared much intoxicated."[129]

During a period of a week or so, detachments were used to assist in a joint land and naval attack against British naval vessels in the river and in suppressing Tory activities in Delaware and New Jersey. However, the attack on the ships was unsuccessful and the Tories had been dealt with by local militia before the Pennsylvanians arrived.[130]

In July, both Miles's Regiment and Atlee's Battalion were ordered to Amboy, New Jersey, to join the Pennsylvania contingent at the Flying Camp, Miles's Regiment arriving on July 16 and Atlee's Battalion on July 21. On July 24, 1776, Miles had 867 officers and men present for duty. The corresponding figure for Atlee's Battalion was 406.[131]

Relations with the Associator officer designated to command the Flying Camp, Brig. Gen. Daniel Roberdeau, soon became strained. He had been elected to this position; but as Miles's and Atlee's men had not taken part in the vote, they refused to serve under him;[132] and soon afterwards (on August 10 for Miles's Regiment and August 11 for Atlee's Battalion) the two commands were ordered to move to New York City. On arrival, they were assigned to the brigade commanded by Gen. William Alexander, more commonly referred to as Lord Stirling.[133]

On August 25, 1776, Gen. William Howe's British and Hessian army moved from Staten Island to the western end of Long Island. Both of the Pennsylvania State organizations were promptly sent to Long Island to reinforce the American units occupying defenses north of the British landing areas. The Pennsylvanians were stationed on the left flank of the American line, near Flatbush. Their own left flank was not anchored on any defensible terrain feature. To cover this vulnerability, patrols were sent out to the west. Lieutenant Colonel Brodhead wrote on September 5 that "we constantly scouted by Day, which beside mounting a Guard of one hundred men & an advance party of subaltern and thirty [men] to the left of us, was hard Duty for our Reg't...."[134]

The battle began before dawn on August 27, with a British advance northward against the right-flank units of the American line, near Gowanus Bay. This was in fact a secondary attack. Unknown to the Americans, the main British force was swinging to the northeast on the road from Gravesend to Jamaica so that it could veer westward and fall unexpectedly upon the American left.

Part of Atlee's Battalion was ordered to reinforce the troops on the right. Then the whole battalion was ordered forward, its mission being to delay the British long enough for Lord Stirling to complete deploying the rest of his brigade on high ground a little to the rear. When Stirling's troops were in position, Atlee moved his men back and took position on the left of Stirling's force.[135]

In the meantime, Colonel Miles had warned Gen. John Sullivan of the danger that the British might attempt an enveloping attack, using the Jamaica road to advance into striking position, but Sullivan ignored him. Then, about 7 A.M., Miles saw enemy forces in motion to his front, and started forward, in the direction of Flatbush, to intercept them. He had gone only a short distance, however, when he was stopped by Col. Samuel Wyllys, whose Connecticut regiment (the 22d Continentals) was guarding the approach from Flatbush. Wyllys, as a Continental officer, outranked Miles, who held only a State commission; and Wyllys refused to allow the Pennsylvanians to go farther, arguing that they should stay and reinforce his men. Miles insisted, however, that the main danger lay on the Gravesend-Jamaica road, and finally persuaded Wyllys to let him go to block the point where he was sure that the threat would develop. Striking off across country to the east, Miles led his men in a rapid, two-mile march. But to his chagrin he found not only that he was too late, but that the British had now moved between him and the American lines.[136]

During this march, the troops got badly strung out. The 1st Battalion was with Colonel Miles; but he had lost contact with the 2d Battalion of the Rifle Regiment, under Lieutenant Colonel Brodhead. Miles had sent Major Ennion Williams with orders to Brodhead to join the 1st Battalion, but by the time Williams found Brodhead he had no way of knowing where Miles and the 1st Battalion might have gone. Brodhead, however, started off to the east, in the general direction he knew Miles had taken. Anticipating contact with enemy troops, he tried to deploy his men from Indian file into line of battle. This plunged the unit into confusion, compounded by the fact that Major John Patton misunderstood the orders and moved off to the right with half the battalion. Before Patton could be recalled, Brodhead caught sight of what he estimated to be four to five thousand enemy troops to his immediate front. In the face of such numbers, he moved the men with him into a wooded area to the left. Seeing some American artillerymen with a fieldpiece and a howitzer trying to unlimber in a wood still farther to the left, he sent a number of his men to support them. As these men were taking position, however, the 22d Continentals raced through in disorder. Their panic spread to Brodhead's men, most of whom joined the retreat. Brodhead wrote that "I did all in my power to rally the musquetry [the 22d Continentals] & Riflemen [his own men], but to no purpose, so that when we came to engage the Enemy, I had not fifty men, notwithstanding which we after about three Rounds, caused the Enemy to retire, and as the Enemy's main body was then nearly between us and the lines, I retreated to the lines, having lost out of the whole [2d] Battalion, about one hundred men, officers included, which, as they were much scattered, must be chiefly prisoners...."[137]

Atlee's Battalion, a little to the west of Miles and Brodhead, had not been idle. It had been ordered to move to the left from its position beside Stirling, to try to block a large British force approaching that flank. Atlee's men raced the British for a tactically significant hill, but the British got to it first and, at a range of fifty yards, opened fire. The Pennsylvanians broke, but soon rallied and stormed the hill, driving the British off, but only as far as a stone wall about sixty yards away, where the Redcoats took cover. The weather, Colonel Atlee wrote, was "intencely hott," and the battalion had taken some losses, including Lieutenant Colonel Parry, killed in this engagement. Before long, the British launched another attack, which was also driven off. By this time Atlee's ammunition was exhausted, but fortunately his men were able to intercept an ammunition cart on its way to another unit and appropriate its contents. This, with what the troops could find on dead and wounded enemy soldiers, enabled them to drive off still another attack about half an hour later. By then, however, other enemy forces had got well to their rear and they were almost completely encircled. Unable to get any answer to his request for instructions from Lord Stirling, Atlee said that "I judged it most prudent to join the Brigade." On arriving at the brigade's position, however, he found the lines empty; at a distance he caught sight of the rear of Stirling's force, retreating toward Brooklyn, but in danger of being cut off by a British force angling in from the flank. Atlee then hurled his battalion toward these troops, delaying them for a quarter of an hour, which gave Stirling's men time to escape. But Atlee was now cut off from the rear and blocked by enemy troops to his front and his left. Worse, his men were out of ammunition. There were enemy forces to the right as well, but they were somewhat scattered, so he led his men in that direction, hoping to move by infiltration back to the American lines protecting Brooklyn. The Pennsylvanians narrowly escaped several parties of enemy troops, which took them under fire, but finally Atlee realized that his battalion was completely hemmed in. "... Nearly fatigued to death," he wrote, "not having eat or drank since the day before...,no alternative presenting, I was obliged to surrender..., having with me about 40...." He was taken to General Howe, "receiving as we passed thro' the right wing of the British Army the most opprobrious and scurrulous Language."[138]

Miles, with the 1st Battalion of the Rifle Regiment, had decided to try to cut his way through the British troops between him and American-held ground to the north. Half a mile after he started his withdrawal he stumbled on a large force of enemy light infantry. The Pennsylvanians opened fire but the British counterattacked with the bayonet. Unable to reload before the British were on top of them, and neither trained nor equipped for bayonet fighting (the rifles, being individually manufactured, would not accommodate any standard bayonet), the riflemen broke for the rear. When Miles was able to get them together, he told them to make their way to the American lines as best they could. Miles himself remained behind with part of the men, hidden in a wood. When the area seemed clear, he and his detachment started out, but quickly ran into more British. The Americans fired, then charged; they lost some men but succeeded in capturing the major commanding the British force. Then they resumed their escape attempt, moving as they could and hiding when they had to. Everywhere they turned, however, they found themselves cut off. Finally, about mid-afternoon, some Hessians found them where they were taking cover and made them prisoners.[139]

Of the three Pennsylvania commanders, only Lieutenant Colonel Brodhead had succeeded in reaching the American lines. Some of the men of the other two battalions joined him there, and with a composite force he helped drive off an enemy attack. As the British retreated, Brodhead was sent farther to the right to cover the withdrawal of other American units. He observed resentfully that "Here I remained 'till almost night before I was relieved, notwithstanding the Generals there had a number of Reg'ts who were not engaged, and had had little or no fatigue." With justice, he went on to say that "Upon the whole, less Generalship never was shown in any Army since the Art of War was understood...." This was in contrast to the performance of his soldiers, of whom he said, "No troops could behave better..., for though they seldom engaged less than five to one, they frequently repulsed the Enemy with great Slaughter, and I am confident that the number killed and wounded on their side, is much greater than on ours, notwith-standing we had to fight them front & rear under every disadvantage."[140]

Whatever casualties they inflicted, the three Pennsylvania battalions had suffered heavily. The muster rolls of Miles's Regiment show five officers and men known killed, another five wounded, and 185 missing, some of whom were killed but most were captured. The corresponding totals for Atlee's Battalion were four killed, four wounded, and 98 captured. In the regiment, Colonel Miles and Lieutenant Colonel Piper were among the prisoners. The regiment's other losses included two captains (Brown and Peebles) captured and one (Farmer) wounded, three lieutenants killed, and ten lieutenants captured. In Atlee's Battalion, two companies (C and H) had had all their officers captured. The battalion's losses in officers amounted to four captains, two lieutenants, and four ensigns captured, as well as the battalion commander (Colonel Atlee) captured and the second-in-command (Lieutenant Colonel Parry) killed.

The army as a whole had suffered heavily. Writing on September 6, ten days after the battle, Capt. Casper Weitzel said that "The number of English and Hessians killed is surprising great, and of ours very tri-fling; but they have taken about seven hundred of our people prisoners, and amongst them more officers than perhaps ever was known in the like number of men." He also reported that there had been some atrocities. One of Weitzel's men had been wounded in the thigh and was unable to walk; "the d- - - -d savage Hessians and English Light Infantry, run their bayonets thro' him, and two of Captain Albright's men, who were also badly wounded, and murdered by them."[141]

What was left of the three Pennsylvania State battalions, consolidated under Lieutenant Colonel Brodhead's command, was withdrawn from Long Island to Manhattan about 9 P.M. on August 29.[142] Washington directed that the remnants of these battalions would continue for the time being as a provisional regiment under Brodhead.

Morale in this organization was not good. On September 19, the men lodged a formal complaint about inadequate rations, clothing, and blankets. They also charged that they had not been paid, although Lieutenant Colonel Brodhead insisted that they had been paid all that was due up to August 1, and that some had been paid to September 1. Nevertheless, the men began deserting in groups, taking their arms with them. One group of about thirty, led by a corporal of Atlee's Battalion, was prevented from leaving only by force. The corporal, who had failed to shoot a lieutenant only because his musket misfired, now tried to bayonet an ensign, but was restrained and put under guard. Some fifty-eight of the men who had gone back to Pennsylvania then drew up a petition which they sent to the Pennsylvania Countil of Safety. In it they stated that they had been told that they would be out of the State only for six weeks, but had actually been away for two months. "We never had half of our Provisions Given us that was allowed to us…, nor never received any pay for the time we were out of the Province." They concluded with the assurance that "Your Petitioners did not leave New York for Cowardice but for bad usage, and we are willing to fight to Defend the Province where we were Inlisted."[143]

What with casualties and desertions, on September 27, 1776, the three battalions combined mustered a total of only 48 officers and 529 enlisted men. At this time, the command was at Mount Washington, not far from Kingsbridge, New York.[144]

Part of the organization fought at the Battle of White Plains on October 28.[145] This component kept the Hessians on the enemy's right wing under fire for an hour, but had to fall back when British cavalry began to work its way into position to cut the Pennsylvanians off from the American lines. That night, they marched about four miles and camped on a hill near the Hudson. Sergeant McMichael said that "Being without our baggage and cooking utensils,…we were very uncomfortable."[146]

The rest of the composite force, consisting of parts of Atlee's Battalion, had been assigned to the garrison of Fort Washington. These men were captured there on November 16, 1776.[147]

In the meantime, the troops who had been at White Plains had crossed the Hudson on November 9 and, with the rest of Washington's army, reached New Brunswick, New Jersey, on the afternoon of November 17. They were still, quite evidently, a rowdy lot. Sergeant McMichael reported that "Here our soldiers drank freely of spirituous liquors. They have chiefly got a disorder, which at camp is called Barrel Fever, which differs in its effects from any other fever—its concomitants are black eyes and bloody noses." A day or so later, the British were reported approaching from Newark, and Lord Stirling's brigade (from which the Pennsylvanians were now detached) marched to meet them.[148] The men of the Pennsylvania State battalions, remaining at New Brunswick, were assigned temporarily to Col. Edward Hand's command[149] (the 1st Pennsylvania Regiment, also consisting at that time of riflemen) as the garrison of the town. On November 27, word came that British attacking forces were on the way, "causing us to prepare to meet them," Sergeant McMichael noted in his journal, "but we are reduced to so small a number we have little hopes of victory." In fact, British forces came into view at about 1 o'clock in the afternoon of December 1. "We were all under arms on the parade," said McMichael. "After a heavy cannonade of an hour, in which we had two killed, we received orders to evacuate the town…."[150]

Having been reassigned to Stirling's brigade,[151] what remained of the Pennsylvania State units moved through Princeton, ferrying across the Delaware into Pennsylvania at dawn on December 8, and on the following day moving to the vicinity of Coryell's Ferry where, Sergeant McMichael noted, "we encamped in the woods. Weather very cold."[152]

In the attack on the Hessian garrison of Trenton on December 26, they were a part of the left wing, under Gen. Nathanael Greene, which swept down upon the unsuspecting enemy.[153] McMichael exulted that "We drove them furiously.... Our loss was but trifling." The fighting was all over in two hours. Later in the day, the Pennsylvania State troops crossed back over the river, escorting prisoners to Newtown, and "after suffering much fatigue we reached our camp." Not until December 30 did they return to Trenton, remaining there to help drive off the British assault on the bridge across Assunpink Creek which took place during the late afternoon of January 2, 1777.[154]

Shortly after midnight on January 3, the army stealthily left Trenton and marched toward Princeton, hoping to surprise the garrison there, depleted as it was by the force which had gone to strike Trenton. By now, the Pennsylvania State troops, reduced in numbers to about two hundred, were under Major Ennion Williams and were assigned to the brigade commanded by Brig. Gen. Hugh Mercer. Nearing Princeton, General Mercer saw what he thought was an isolated detachment of British dragoons, and threw forward his leading skirmish line, consisting of half of the Pennsylvania riflemen and twenty Virginians armed with muskets, to attack the horsemen. But when the Americans pursued the dragoons through an orchard they suddenly found themselves facing a deployed line of about 250 British infantry with two fieldpieces. The British fired first, but their volley passed over the Americans' heads. Mercer's men then dashed forward. The British fell back in good order, halting forty or fifty yards away and forming again. For a few minutes there was a furious exchange of fire. Then the British fixed bayonets and charged. None of the riflemen had bayonets. Some fled, a number of them were cut down where they stood, and General Mercer was mortally wounded.[155] Sergeant McMichael claimed that "Having retreated a short distance, we were reinforced, when we immediately rallied, and with the utmost precipitation put our foes to retreat."[156]

The Americans occupied Princeton only briefly, moving northward on the same day. By January 24, the Pennsylvania State troops were part of a 350-man force under Col. Mordecai Buckner, of the 6th Virginia. They reached the vicinity of Quibbletown (New Market) where, McMichael reported, they were attacked by six hundred enemy troops supported by three cannon, "but at the commencement of the attack the Colonel rode off with precipitation, which was to us a great disadvantage. However, the ground was advantageous, and we killed and wounded seventy of the enemy, with a loss of only four men slightly wounded."*

This appears to be the last combat action in which the remnants of Miles's Regiment and Atlee's Battalion took part, although they remained in New Jersey until about the middle of February.[157] Before the winter was out, they had been brought to Philadelphia and then moved to Billingsport, New Jersey, a few miles down the Delaware, to begin the process of reorganization as the Pennsylvania State Regiment.[158]

Pennsylvania State Regiment

On April 17, 1777, the organization beginning to take shape as the Pennsylvania State Regiment moved from Billingsport to Red Bank, New Jersey. James McMichael (who had been commissioned a second lieutenant) said that there, "Our regiment was properly arranged [that is, organized in companies]"; and three of the companies, including Company I, to which McMichael was assigned, moved into camp at Liberty Island (also called Gibbitt Island), "where we were entertained by a harmonious band of music, and passed the day in jolity."[159] As of June 2, the Pennsylvania State Regiment stationed in and around Red Bank numbered 524 enlisted men,[160] having been brought up to this strength by former prisoners of war who had rejoined after being exchanged and by new recruits.

On June 15, the regiment moved to Philadelphia. Rumors that Colonel Bull was going to be kept in command despite the officers' protest were causing considerable discontent, and on June 17, Lieutenant McMichael and sixteen other officers wrote out their resignations and in a body started toward the State House to deliver them. On the way they were stopped by Lieutenant Colonel Farmer (their own preference for regimental commander). He told them that Colonel Bull was being replaced by Colonel Walter Stewart, who requested that all the regiment's officers meet him at 4 P.M. at the City Tavern. When they gathered as requested and were spoken to by Colonel Stewart, they evidently were soon won over, and McMichael says that following the Colonel's assurances, "After drinking some gallons of Madeira, we returned to our Lodgings much satisfied."[161]

On June 19, the regiment's enlisted strength had grown to 562. Only 199 of these, however, had enlisted for the duration of the war. The remaining 363 would be due for discharge on January 1, 1778. Moreover, only 556 of the men were present for duty as of a strength report dated June 20.[162]

---

*PA(2), XV, 204. Col. Buckner was cashiered on February 9, 1777 (see Heitman, p. 130).

Two days later, on June 22, the regiment left Philadelphia, marching to join Washington's army in the vicinity of Middlebrook, New Jersey. By the end of July it was back in Pennsylvania. It took part in the army's march through Philadelphia on August 24 and then moved to the vicinity of Wilmington, Delaware. Some of its members, including Capt. John Marshall, were detached to serve in the "light infantry" task force under Brig. Gen. William Maxwell, but the regiment as a whole was assigned to the brigade of Brig. Gen. George Weedon, in Nathanael Greene's division. As such, the Pennsylvania State Regiment took part in the marching and counter-marching which marked Washington's slow withdrawal of his army toward Chadd's Ford on Brandywine Creek. During this time, Lieutenant McMichael described the regiment as "being extremely fatigued for want of rest and severe marching." Finally, on September 10, Weedon's brigade took position on high ground on the east bank of the Brandywine, overlooking Chadd's Ford.[163]

The British attack began on the morning of September 11, when the Hessian General Knyphausen led a part of the enemy force due east against Maxwell's outpost line. During this engagement, Captain Marshall was wounded. In a short time Maxwell's men had fallen back across the Brandywine and the British occupied the west bank of the creek. Lieutenant McMichael wrote that "We all paraded near Chadd's Ford, and had a heavy cannonade followed by small arms on both sides, but not much execution done owing to the distance." Late in the day, however, when the British main attack began to crush the American right flank to the north, at the Birmingham Meeting House, the Pennsylvania State Regiment was with the rest of Weedon's brigade as it led Greene's division, racing northeastward to hold off the enemy pursuit and cover the retreat of the hard-hit Americans. "We took the front and attacked the enemy at 5.30 P.M.," McMichael wrote, "and being engaged with their grand army [main attack force], we at first were obliged to retreat a few yards and formed in an open field, when we fought without giving way on either side until dark." By then their ammunition was almost exhausted, and they were ordered to Chester, which they reached after marching all night. McMichael considered that "This day for a severe and successive engagement exceeded all I ever saw. Our regiment fought at one stand about an hour under incessant fire, and yet the loss was less than at Long Island; neither were we so near each other as at Princeton, our common distance being about 50 yards."[164] Indeed, so far as reported casualties are a guide, the regiment's loss was substantially "less than at Long Island," totalling only one ensign killed[165] and two sergeants[166] and a private[167] wounded.

The Pennsylvania State Regiment moved with the main army as

Washington tried to block the enemy's successive advances toward Philadelphia. It saw no fighting, but endured exhausting marches. But Washington was outmaneuvered and Philadelphia was lost. Then, on October 3, the regiment received orders which the men knew presaged an attack.[168]

At the Battle of Germantown, on October 4, 1777, the Pennsylvania State Regiment appears to have been still part of Weedon's brigade, and certainly was with the left wing, under Nathanael Greene, which had the mission of hitting the right flank of the British line and rolling it up toward the center. In a letter of October 12, 1777, to Maj. Gen. Horatio Gates, Colonel Stewart wrote that "When I first engaged we were a mile and a half from Germantown, and before we ended I got to the Market house at Germantown." Apparently, the Pennsylvania State Regiment became separated from its parent organization but drove ahead independently. Colonel Stewart said that his men engaged two British regiments and "they both ran lustily and I took a little flush redoubt with three pieces of Cannon from them[;] I had cursed hot Work for it before they left them...."[169] But Maj. Gen. Adam Stephen (later cashiered for having been drunk on this occasion) ordered Stewart to withdraw, and the regiment fell back with the rest of the army to Perkiomen Creek. Lieutenant McMichael reported that

> I had previously undergone many fatigues, but never any that so much overdone me as this. Had it not been for the fear of being taken prisoner, I should have remained on the road all night. I had marched in twenty-four hours 45 miles, and in that time fought four hours, during which we advanced so furiously through buckwheat fields, that it was almost an unspeakable fatigue.[170]

Nevertheless, at Germantown no more than at Brandywine had the regiment suffered severe losses. Colonel Stewart reported on October 27, 1777, that in the two actions together, twenty-two of his men had been wounded and only sixteen were either missing or known killed, although he thought that most of the missing had been either killed or badly wounded.[171] The reports of casualties by name indicate the regiment's losses at Germantown as being a first lieutenant,[172] a drummer,[173] and two privates[174] wounded. However, both this list and the casualty list for the Battle of Brandywine are clearly incomplete. Present for duty at the end of October were 42 officers and 409 enlisted men; another 118 men were sick, 69 were on detached service, four were on furlough, and four had deserted.[175]

The regiment moved with the army as Washington tried to make up his mind whether to attack the British in Philadelphia or to wait for spring. Then, on November 12, 1777, the Pennsylvania State Regiment was formally redesignated as the 13th Pennsylvania Regiment of the Continental Line.

13th Pennsylvania Regiment

By November 28, the 13th Pennsylvania was with the main army at Whitemarsh. It was present there when the British made their hesitant advance and withdrawal during the first week or so of December, but did not take part in such action as occurred. On December 12, the regiment as well as Washington's other troops marched to Gulph Mills, and a week later moved on to Valley Forge to go into winter quarters.[176]

The regiment's strength rapidly declined during the winter, due to the expiration of a large number of enlistments on January 1, 1778, and of still others within the next few months. Although the number of his troops was dwindling, Colonel Stewart took positive action to improve the effectiveness of his officers. To develop esprit and mutual good feeling, he instituted a program whereby officers of various grades took turns in hosting a succession of dinners for each other. To develop or enhance their military competence, he carried out a series of what in more modern terminology would be called "tactical walks," in which he took his officers around the camp, discussing the best uses of the terrain against the various avenues of approach which an attacking enemy might use.[177]

To a degree, these turned out to be wasted efforts, for in the spring, when the reorganization of the army was directed, one of the provisions was that the 13th Pennsylvania was to be absorbed by the 2d Pennsylvania Regiment. As this was not scheduled to take place until July 1, 1778, however, what was left of the regiment was to serve through one more campaign.

That was the campaign ending with the Battle of Monmouth, on June 28, 1778. In that engagement, the 13th Pennsylvania was part of the advance element commanded by Major General Lafayette. The regiment helped form the right flank of the defensive line adopted by the Americans when the British launched their first counterattack.[178] Then the left flank of this line, misunderstanding the situation, withdrew without orders and left Lafayette's troops alone and exposed until word reached them to fall back to the village of Freehold. There, the 13th Pennsylvania was attached to Anthony Wayne's task force and occupied a position to defend the village.[179] It was also with Wayne in the advance he led over a narrow causeway through swampland, and helped beat off the attack by a picked British force which sought to crush the Americans while they were pinned in front of the swamp. In this part of the action, Colonel Stewart was wounded[180]—apparently becoming the only casualty which, despite its participation in some of the hottest action of the battle, the regiment sustained that day.[181]

In essence, the Battle of Monmouth marked the end of the 13th Pennsylvania. Many of its personnel continued in uniform, most of them in the 2d Pennsylvania Regiment, although a number of the officers served in a variety of different organizations treated in other chapters of this book. For a description of the further service of the bulk of the veterans of the 13th Pennsylvania, see Chapter III.

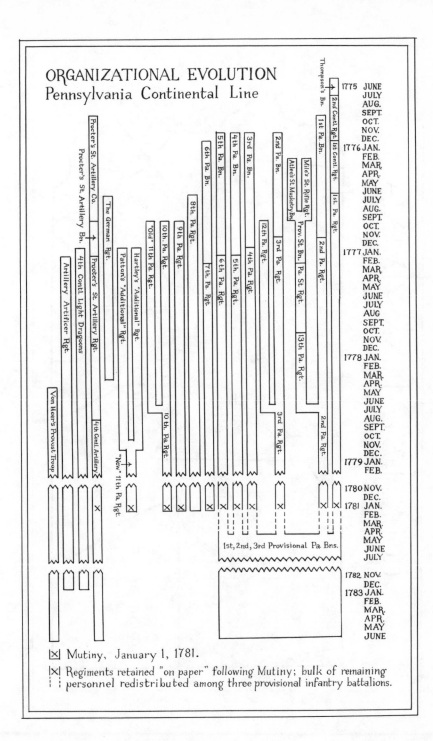

ORGANIZATIONAL EVOLUTION
Pennsylvania Continental Line

Thompson's Bn.

2nd Cont'l Rgt. | 1st Cont'l Rgt.

Procter's St. Artillery Co.

Procter's St. Artillery Bn.

1st Pa. Bn.

Miles' St. Rifle Rgt.

Atlee's St. Musketry Bn.

Prov. St. Bn. Pa. St. Rgt.

1st. Pa. Rgt.

The German Rgt.

2nd Pa. Bn.

3rd Pa. Bn.

4th Pa. Bn.

5th Pa. Bn.

6th Pa. Bn.

8th Pa. Rgt.

"Old" 11th Pa. Rgt.

10th Pa. Rgt.

9th Pa. Rgt.

7th Pa. Rgt.

6th Pa. Rgt.

5th Pa. Rgt.

4th Pa. Rgt.

12th Pa. Rgt.

3rd Pa. Rgt.

13th Pa. Rgt.

2nd Pa. Rgt.

4th Cont'l Light Dragoons

Procter's St. Artillery Rgt.

Patton's "Additional" Rgt.

Hartley's "Additional" Rgt.

Artillery Artificer Rgt.

Von Heer's Provost Troop

4th Cont'l Artillery

"New" 11th Pa. Rgt.

10th Pa. Rgt.

3rd Pa. Rgt.

2nd Pa. Rgt.

1st, 2nd, 3rd Provisional Pa. Bns.

1775 JUNE
JULY
AUG.
SEPT.
OCT.
NOV.
DEC.
1776 JAN.
FEB.
MAR.
APR.
MAY
JUNE
JULY
AUG.
SEPT.
OCT.
NOV.
DEC.
1777 JAN.
FEB.
MAR.
APR.
MAY
JUNE
JULY
AUG
SEPT.
OCT.
NOV.
DEC.
1778 JAN.
FEB.
MAR.
APR.
MAY
JUNE
JULY
AUG.
SEPT.
OCT.
NOV.
DEC.
1779 JAN.
FEB.
1780 NOV.
DEC.
1781 JAN.
FEB.
MAR.
APR.
MAY
JUNE
JULY
1782 NOV.
DEC.
1783 JAN.
FEB.
MAR.
APR.
MAY
JUNE

⊠ Mutiny, January 1, 1781.

⊠ Regiments retained "on paper" following Mutiny; bulk of remaining
ⅈⅈ personnel redistributed among three provisional infantry battalions.

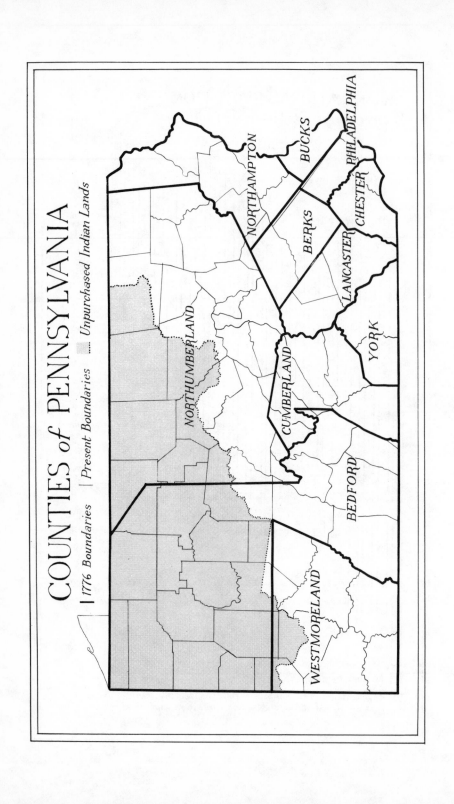

COUNTIES of PENNSYLVANIA

| 1776 Boundaries | Present Boundaries ⣿⣿ Unpurchased Indian Lands

NORTHAMPTON

BUCKS

PHILADELPHIA

CHESTER

BERKS

LANCASTER

YORK

NORTHUMBERLAND

CUMBERLAND

BEDFORD

WESTMORELAND

Chapter XVIII
4th Continental Artillery

ORGANIZATION

THE organizational history of the 4th Continental Artillery follows a somewhat different pattern from that of the other Pennsylvania Continental regiments. Partly, this is because it remained under State control for considerably longer than the other Pennsylvania organizations. Part of the difference, also, stems from the inherent organizational and tactical differences between infantry and artillery regiments of the period.

There were, further, differences in prescribed structures. Artillery regiments, in theory, were larger units than infantry regiments. An infantry regiment as authorized on May 27, 1778, had nine companies, six of them commanded by captains, one by the major, one by the lieutenant colonel, and one nominally by the colonel but actually by the regiment's one captain-lieutenant; and each company also had a first lieutenant and an ensign (or second lieutenant). An artillery regiment of the same date was supposed to have twelve companies, each with a captain, a captain-lieutenant, a first lieutenant, and three second lieutenants.

The reason for this large strength in officers was that artillery companies were never employed tactically as a whole; rather, they were broken up into detachments which, with their guns, were put in direct support of infantry regiments or brigades. While the number of guns per company varied according to caliber, mission, and availability, the theoretical armament of a company in a field artillery role was on the order of four to six pieces. These would be employed, however, in pairs or even singly, manned by semi-autonomous detachments under the command of one or two officers from the company.

On January 1, 1781, the authorized company strength of an artillery regiment was reduced from twelve to nine. There was no change, however, in the number or grades of officers authorized per company.

Procter's Pennsylvania Artillery Company and Battalion; Pennsylvania State Artillery Regiment

The 4th Continental Artillery Regiment had its beginning as a single company, formed for the defense of Pennsylvania, which was authorized by the Pennsylvania Council of Safety on October 16, 1775. It was to be stationed at Fort Island,* in the Delaware River, just below the mouth of the Schuylkill, manning six eighteen-pounder cannon. Its prescribed strength was one captain, one lieutenant, and twenty-seven enlisted men (including a fifer and a drummer), all committed to twelve months' service.[1] Thomas Procter (or Proctor), a native of County Longford, Ireland, who had lived in Philadelphia working as a carpenter for more than a decade,[2] was appointed captain of the company on October 27, 1775. Commissioned on the same day as lieutenant of the company was Francis Procter, Sr.,[3] father of Thomas.[4]

On November 1, the Council of Safety directed the Barracks Master of the barracks "near this City" to put the barracks into proper repair; and on November 3, instructed him to admit Capt. Procter and his company to quarters there, issuing them "the Bedding late belonging to the Royal Artillery Company, and with what other necessarys belonging to the Province, for their accommodation, that you may have in your power to

---

*Better known as Mud Island, it was the site of an uncompleted defensive work later named Fort Mifflin.

supply him with." On November 6, however, the Council of Safety noted that the barracks could not be ready to receive troops for "about 10 days."[5]

Other difficulties soon developed. Captain Procter was both stubborn and hot-tempered. In a dispute of an unspecified nature with Capt. William Williams and 1st Lt. Samuel Watson of the 1st Pennsylvania (infantry) Battalion, then in process of organization, both Thomas and Francis Procter acted in a manner which, on December 6, the Council of Safety unanimously agreed was "unbecoming officers." After the Council "recommended" that the two Procters "make a suitable acknowledgement to the parties injured, which they have peremptorily refused to comply with," a resolution was passed that both of them be dismissed the service, and on December 8, the resolution was put into effect.[6]

The company functioned without a commissioned officer for almost three weeks. Then Lt. Jeremiah Simmons of the armed boat *Warren*[7] was directed by the Council of Safety to take command and move the unit "with all possible dispatch" to Liberty (also called Gibbitt) Island.[8] But on the following day, Captain Procter was restored to command—he had requested reinstatement; he promised to make the directed "acknowledgements" to Captain Williams; and Lt. Watson said that he did not expect or require such acknowledgements on his part.[9] Captain Procter's "dismissal," therefore, was in essence merely a suspension from command. But no mention was made of Lt. Francis Procter, Sr., who apparently did not return to service at that time; and Lieutenant Simmons, transferred now from the *Warren,* was commissioned first lieutenant of the company on February 24, 1776.[10]

By early April, the company was back at Fort Island. At that time, authorization was granted to increase its strength to 120 men.[11] Apparently, this also involved an increase in officers. On May 28, Lieutenant Simmons was promoted to captain-lieutenant;[12] on June 19, Francis Procter, Jr.* was listed[13] as "Lieutenant and Fire-worker"† (he had been a "matross," equivalent to private, in the original company, enlisting on October 30, 1775[14]); and on June 28, John Martin Strobagh (who had been a lieutenant of marines on board the *Hornet*[15]) was appointed a second lieutenant, but with an antedated date of rank of May 13.[16] A muster roll covering the period June 30-July 31, 1776, shows Thomas Procter as captain of the "First Company of Pennsylvania Artillery," Jeremiah Simmons as captain-lieutenant, Hercules Courteney (or Cour-

---

*He was a younger brother of Thomas Procter. See Newman Dorland, p. 168, Note 185.

†A "fireworker" supervised the preparation and loading of the proper explosive charge. Considering the relative crudity of the science of metallurgy at that time, this was a vitally important responsibility if breech bursts were to be prevented. Later in the war this function was assigned to an enlisted specialist called a "bombardier."

tenay) as first lieutenant, John Martin Strobagh as second lieutenant, and Francis Procter, Jr. as lieutenant and fireworker (or third lieutenant). The company included 121 enlisted men—a quartermaster sergeant, three sergeants, a corporal-clerk, three corporals, seven bombardiers, 24 gunners,* 73 matrosses,† 6 musicians, one fifer, and two drummers.[17]

Then, on August 14, 1776, the Council of Safety directed that Procter's artillery unit be increased to a strength of 200 men, organized in two companies. Each company was to have a captain-lieutenant and three lieutenants. The whole force was to continue under Thomas Procter, who was promoted to major as of that date.[18]

This organization did not formally take effect until October 5, 1776. At that time, the companies were organized with John Martin Strobagh as commander of the First Company and Thomas Forrest as commander of the Second Company.[19] Evidently, the provision that the company commanders would hold the rank of captain-lieutenant had been amended, for both Strobagh[20] and Forrest[21] were appointed as captains effective October 5. Captain Strobagh's previous service has been noted. Captain Forrest, a Philadelphian, had been a captain of marines (in the Pennsylvania service) since March 13, 1776, serving with a "floating battery" in the Delaware River.[22]

On the same day that the new structure came into being, Captain Strobagh and fifty men were moved to Fort Montgomery, part of the Philadelphia defenses.[23] But the arrangement was already showing signs of dissolution, as the enlistments of the original members of the company were beginning to expire on October 30, 1776. On that date, the Council of Safety directed Major Procter to reenlist as many as he could, this time for the duration of the war. All who did reenlist were to be paid a bounty of ten dollars.[24]

The organization remained based at Fort Island during December, 1776, when Captain Forrest, with 3d Lt. Patrick Duffy (or Duffey) of his own company and 1st Lt. Worley Emes of Captain Strobagh's company were ordered to report to General Washington. With his force, they took part in the attack on Trenton on December 26. Immediately afterward, Major Procter went to New Jersey, arriving in time to be present at the Battle of Princeton on January 3, 1777. The bulk of the command was assembled at Morristown on January 16. The following day, when Brig. Gen. Henry Knox (the commander of the Continental artillery) left for

---

*The "gunner" was in charge of laying and aiming the piece.

†"Matross" was the term used for a basic artillery crewman. He helped ram the ammunition home, swab the bores, serve as ammunition handler, and manipulate the cannon.

New England, Procter was put in temporary charge of all the artillery of Washington's army.[25]

At this point, something of a tug-of-war appears to have developed between the State and the Continental authorities. Washington wanted the Pennsylvania artillery transferred to the Continental Army, but the Pennsylvania authorities wanted to keep it under State control. Although the Council of Safety acted on February 6, 1777, to expand the Pennsylvania artillery to a regiment of eight companies,* promoting Procter to colonel, the regiment remained a State organization and the resolution was explicit in stating that it was "for the defence of this State."[26] On February 28, however, the Council passed a resolution that authorized the regiment to serve in any part of the United States, and provided an enlistment bounty of twenty dollars for new recruits. Men currently in the organization would be paid the difference between the new bounty and the ten-dollar bounty they had received earlier.[27]

Although the Pennsylvania State Artillery Regiment was not offered to Congress to be part of the Continental Army until June 6, 1777,[28] and was not technically accepted by Congress as part of the quota of Continental units which Pennsylvania was to furnish until September 3, *1778*,[29] it was considered, it was at least informally designated, and for all practical purposes (except for dependence for pay and equipment) it was in fact the 4th Continental Artillery Regiment from February 6, 1777.

Independent Pennsylvania Artillery Company

Before taking up the organizational development of the artillery regiment which evolved from Procter's unit, the Independent Pennsylvania Artillery Company will be briefly described.

This unit had its genesis in a resolution by the Pennsylvania Council of Safety on January 29, 1776, to appoint officers for an artillery company to serve in Canada.[30] On February 8, Bernard Romans was approved for appointment as captain of the company.[31] The only records of this unit's service that have been found are a statement in a letter of January 2, 1777, from Anthony Wayne that Romans' organization (numbering only twelve officers and enlisted men) had refused to stay at Fort Ticonderoga and had left for Pennsylvania;[32] the report of two men wounded at the Battle of Brandywine; and another report of a sergeant wounded at the Battle of Monmouth.[33] According to the army

---

*The regiment's strength was fixed at one colonel, one lieutenant colonel, one major, eight captains, eight first lieutenants, eight second lieutenants, eight lieutenant fireworkers, the usual array of staff officers, and 575 enlisted men—twelve of whom were to comprise a band.

reorganization plan, this company was supposed to be absorbed by the 4th Continental Artillery on January 8, 1778.[34] Apparently, this plan was abandoned, for while Captain Romans was not transferred to that regiment, he retained command of his company until June 1, 1778, when he resigned,[35] and was succeeded by Gibbs Jones, who was promoted from captain-lieutenant on that date and continued to serve until his own resignation, which did not take place until April 14, 1780.[36] By that time, the company appears to have virtually ceased to exist due to officer resignations and to desertions and discharges of enlisted men.[37]

4th Continental Artillery

Although his promotion was not authorized until February 6 and his new regiment did not begin to be organized until March 3, Thomas Procter was by some administrative legerdemain assigned a Continental date of rank of February 5, 1777. He was to serve as colonel of the regiment until his resignation on April 18, 1781.[38]

The original lieutenant colonel of the regiment, promoted from captain of Procter's Pennsylvania artillery battalion on March 3, 1777, was John Martin Strobagh. Following his death on December 2, 1778,[39] he was replaced by Thomas Forrest, who was promoted from major. Forrest resigned from the army on October 7, 1781.[40] He was not replaced for more than a year. On December 24, 1782, Andrew Porter was promoted to the lieutenant colonelcy from major, but was assigned a date of rank of January 1, 1782.[41] As the senior officer remaining in the regiment, he was eventually designated as Lieutenant-Colonel Commandant,[42] continuing in command until June 17, 1783, by which time the organization was disbanded.[43]

The first major of the regiment was Thomas Forrest, who was appointed on February 5, 1777, having been a captain in Procter's Pennsylvania artillery battalion.[44] When he was promoted to lieutenant colonel on December 2, 1778, he was replaced as major by Benjamin Eustis, of Massachusetts, who was promoted from captain and transferred from the 3d Continental Artillery on that date. Major Eustis died on October 6, 1781,[45] and Isaac Craig was promoted from captain, effective on December 7, 1781, serving to June 17, 1783.[46] However, the 4th Continental Artillery (presumably due to the fact that its elements were now widely scattered) was eventually authorized a second major. That promotion went to Capt. Francis Procter, Jr. on December 24, 1782, although it was antedated to January 1, 1782. Procter retired from the army on January 1, 1783,[47] at which time the regiment began to be sharply reduced in size.

Although the 4th Continental Artillery was authorized eight companies,* it originally consisted of only seven, with an eighth being added in mid-July, 1777. From the resignation of captains without replacement, it would seem to have been reduced to seven in the early part of June, 1779. On January 1, 1781, two companies (both raised in Pennsylvania) were transferred to the 4th Continental Artillery from the 2d Continental Artillery.[48]

The companies and their commanders were as follows:

• [Company A], commanded by Capt. Gerard Jacob Dircks (also listed as Jacob Gerhard Derick), a native of the Netherlands. On November 15, 1776, he had been appointed as a captain in the 9th Pennsylvania (infantry) Regiment, but on March 3, 1777, was transferred to the 4th Continental Artillery. He served only four months, resigning on July 6, 1777; but despite his brief time in uniform, he was awarded a brevet promotion to lieutenant colonel on November 5, 1778, "as a testimony of his merit and services in the army."[49] His replacement as captain was Charles Turnbull. Turnbull had been an enlisted man in Procter's Pennsylvania artillery company, which he joined on October 30, 1775, and in which he was listed as a corporal on November 27, 1775,[50] and as a sergeant on the muster roll for the period June 30-July 31, 1776.[51] On October 5, 1776, he was commissioned a second lieutenant in Procter's Pennsylvania artillery battalion, assigned to Captain Strobagh's company.[52] He was appointed captain-lieutenant in the 4th Continental Artillery on March 3, 1777. Some six weeks later, on April 13, he was taken prisoner at Bound Brook, New Jersey. Although he was still a prisoner of war, his seniority brought his promotion to captain on July 16, 1777. He was not exchanged until April 3, 1780. On returning to American control, he rejoined the regiment, remaining on duty with it until the army was demobilized in June, 1783.[53]

• [Company B], commanded by Capt. Hercules Courteney. His initial commission had been as first lieutenant of Procter's Pennsylvania artillery company, in which he was serving by the period June 30-July 31, 1776.[54] As of October 5, 1776, he was assigned in the same grade to Capt. Thomas Forrest's company of Procter's Pennsylvania artillery battalion.[55] By January 1, 1777, he had been promoted to captain-lieutenant, and on March 3, 1777, he was appointed captain, 4th Continental Artillery.[56] At Valley Forge, on December 28, 1777, he was

---

*The term "battery" was not used at that time to designate a specific organization. Instead, it was used on an *ad hoc* basis to describe a tactical combination of guns and personnel, usually in a fixed position.

tried by court martial, the charge being "leaving his howitzer in the field in the action at Brandywine [on September 11, 1777] in a cowardly, unofficerlike manner." The court found him guilty, but "as he has ever supported the character of a brave man" he was sentenced only to be reprimanded by the artillery brigade commander (Brig. Gen. Henry Knox) "in the presence of all the Artillery officers." Due to what Washington called "the state of the evidence," however, the sentence was disapproved, with the direction that Courteney be "discharged from arrest without censure."[57] But Courteney proved unable to stay out of trouble. On February 27, 1778, he was again tried by court martial, this time for neglect of duty, leaving camp while Officer of the Day, and lodging out of camp without permission.[58] On this occasion there was no question of clemency, and he was dismissed the service effective March 3.[59] His replacement as captain was Patrick Duffy. Like Turnbull, Duffy had been an enlisted member of Procter's Pennsylvania artillery company, which he joined on October 30, 1775, as a bombardier.[60] By the period June 30-July 31, 1776, he was listed as a corporal and company clerk.[61] He was commissioned a third lieutenant on October 5, 1776, when the company was expanded to battalion strength, and assigned to Capt. Thomas Forrest's company.[62] He was promoted to first lieutenant on January 1, 1777,[63] captain-lieutenant of the 4th Continental Artillery on March 3, 1777,[64] and to captain on February 29, 1778, following Courteney's court-martial conviction. Duffy himself was dismissed the service on October 11, 1781,[65] for what reason does not appear to be recorded. Jonathan Douglass, a native of New Jersey who had entered the 4th Continental Artillery as a first lieutenant on April 1, 1777, was promoted from captain-lieutenant on October 12, 1781, to replace Duffy, continuing with the regiment until January 1, 1783.[66]

• [Company C], commanded by Capt. Francis Procter, Sr. Although he does not appear to have returned to State service after his dismissal on December 8, 1775 (see above), at some time during 1776 he was a prisoner of war (when and where he was captured and when he was exchanged are not recorded). He was appointed a captain in the 4th Continental Artillery on March 3, 1777.[67] On May 14, 1778, at Valley Forge, he was tried by a brigade court martial (of which his son, Col. Thomas Procter, was president) for "scandelous and infamous behaviour unbecoming the character of an officer and a gentleman; also for breaking his arrest & threatening Capt. Rice's life [presumably, this was Capt. Joseph Rice of the 4th Continental Artillery] in an ungentleman like manner in different companies." He was acquitted of the charge of breaking his arrest, but was found guilty of "scandelous behavior unbecomming the character of a gentleman and an officer" and was dismissed the service.[68] The vacancy thus created was filled by William Ferguson.

However, Ferguson was a prisoner of war at the time, and thus could not take over actual command until he was exchanged, which occurred only on December 1, 1780. From that time until January 1, 1783, however, he served with the regiment.[69] He had begun his service on October 30, 1775, as a bombardier in Procter's Pennsylvania artillery company,[70] and by December 11, 1775, was a corporal.[71] On October 5, 1776, he was commissioned a third lieutenant and assigned to Captain Strobagh's company of the Pennsylvania artillery battalion,[72] becoming a captain-lieutenant in the 4th Continental Artillery on March 14, 1777. A month later, on April 13, at Bound Brook, New Jersey, he was taken prisoner* and, as noted above, was held until late 1780, when he returned to duty.

• [Company D], commanded by Capt. Bartholomew von Heer. Von Heer had served briefly as adjutant of a special, independent battalion formed under a Saxon volunteer, the Baron von Ottendorff, but within less than a month, on April 14, 1777, was commissioned a captain in the 4th Continental Artillery, with a date of rank of March 3. On July 1, 1778, he resigned to accept appointment as captain of a separate company of light dragoons formed to serve as provost guards.[73] John Brice (or Bryce) was promoted from captain-lieutenant to fill this vacancy. He had originally been an ensign in the 1st Pennsylvania (infantry) Battalion, but had been promoted to captain-lieutenant and transferred to the 4th Continental Artillery on March 14, 1777. He did not remain for long as a captain in this regiment, however, for later in the summer he was assigned as aide-de-camp to Major General Lafayette, being promoted to major at an unspecified date thereafter.[74] His promotion removed him from the total number of captains charged against the regiment's authorized strength, thereby permitting the promotion to captain, on March 3, 1779, of Robert Coultman, who had entered the 4th Continental Artillery as a captain-lieutenant on May 8, 1777, but ranking from March 14.[75] Captain Coultman continued as a company commander until June, 1783.[76]

• [Company E], commanded by Capt. Isaac Craig. During 1776, Craig held a State commission as a captain of marines. On March 3, 1777, he was appointed a captain in the 4th Continental Artillery, serving as such until his promotion to major on October 7, 1781.[77] The vacant captaincy was filled by the promotion from captain-lieutenant, on October 17,

---

*Heitman, p. 225. The fact that Ferguson's promotion to captain was dated April 14, 1778, a full month before the dismissal of Capt. Francis Procter, Sr., probably has an administrative explanation—e.g., the vacancy could be considered retroactively to have existed since the date when charges were preferred against Captain Procter, which (especially considering the vast number of courts martial at Valley Forge) could well have been a month before the trial; or it may be that Ferguson had some claim to added seniority, provided by an adjusted date of rank.

1781, of William Power. Although a Pennsylvanian, he had been commissioned a captain-lieutenant in the 2d Continental Artillery, on January 1, 1777, serving in one of the two companies of that regiment which were reassigned to the 4th Continental Artillery on January 1, 1781 (see below). He remained in the 4th Continental Artillery until January 1, 1783.[78]

• [Company F], commanded by Capt. Francis Procter, Jr. This company appears to have been the last of the regiment's original eight to be formed. Captain Procter, who as noted above had been a matross and a third lieutenant in his brother's State company in early 1776 and had been promoted to second lieutenant when that company was expanded to a battalion, had been appointed a captain-lieutenant in the 4th Continental Artillery on March 3, 1777, and was promoted to captain on July 16, 1777. He held this rank until December 24, 1782, when he was promoted to be "second" major, although with a retroactive date of rank of January 1, 1782.[79] His promotion permitted the advancement to captain, also effective on January 1, 1782, of William Martin. Martin had been appointed a first lieutenant in the 4th Continental Artillery on April 1, 1777. A year later, on March 21, 1778, he was captured by a British raiding party at Hancock's Bridge, New Jersey. His promotion to captain-lieutenant took effect on June 1, 1778, but he remained a prisoner until December 4, 1780. Returning to the regiment, he continued in the service until January 1, 1783.[80]

• [Company G], commanded by Capt. Joseph Rice. His original commission had been as a captain in the State service, assigned to the "floating battery" which made up part of the Delaware River defenses of Philadelphia.[81] He was appointed captain in the 4th Continental Artillery on March 3, 1777, continuing to serve in that grade until he resigned from the army on September 26, 1780.[82] The vacancy created by this resignation was filled by the promotion of Worley Emes. He had entered the Pennsylvania artillery battalion on October 5, 1776, as first lieutenant of Captain Strobagh's company,[83] and was appointed to the same rank in the 4th Continental Artillery in March, 1777, being promoted to captain-lieutenant on July 16, 1777. He remained in the regiment until January 1, 1783.[84]

General Washington stated explicitly on May 5, 1781, that by the autumn of 1780, the 4th Continental Artillery was two companies short of its full complement.[85] The theoretical strength of an artillery regiment, as established on January 1, 1781, was nine companies, a reduction from the total of twelve prescribed on May 27, 1778;[86] but the maximum strength of the 4th Continental Artillery seems never to have exceeded eight (if it is assumed that there was one company for each officer serving in the grade of captain). As one company (see Company

H, below) seems to have been absorbed into other units in June, 1779, the total would have dropped to the seven implied by Washington's statement. To correct this situation, two companies of the 2d Continental Artillery were transferred to the 4th Continental Artillery on January 1, 1781. This actually brought the 4th Continental Artillery's strength in companies (if not in personnel) to a peak it had never previously reached. The sequence of events appears to have been as follows:

• [Company H], commanded by Capt. Amos Wilkinson. Initially, Wilkinson had been a second and first lieutenant in the 1st Pennsylvania (infantry) Battalion, becoming a captain in the 4th Continental Artillery on March 14, 1777. Some two years later, on June 7, 1779, he resigned his commission.[87] It appears that this company then ceased to exist as a separate unit, its personnel presumably being absorbed by other companies of the regiment. As noted above, however, on January 1, 1781, two companies of the 2d Continental Artillery were transferred to the 4th Continental Artillery. One of these was Capt. Andrew Porter's company. It was made up of Pennsylvanians, and in effect replaced Wilkinson's company. Porter, a native of the modern Montgomery County, had operated a school of mathematics in Philadelphia until June 19, 1776, when he was granted a State commission as captain of marines, assigned to the frigate *Effingham*.[88] He had become a captain in the 2d Continental Artillery on January 1, 1777. As mentioned earlier, some four months after his transfer to the 4th Continental Artillery, he was promoted (on April 19, 1781) to major.[89] The captaincy he vacated was filled on the same date by the promotion from captain-lieutenant of James McClure, of New Hampshire, who also had been transferred from the 2d Continental Artillery. Captain McClure continued to serve with his new organization until January 1, 1783.[90]

The second of the 2d Continental Artillery companies transferred to the 4th Continental Artillery was:

• [Company I], commanded by Capt. James Simonds. Although Captain Simonds himself was from Massachusetts, the company was made up of Pennsylvanians, having been recruited specifically in Philadelphia.[91] It continued under Captain Simonds until January 1, 1783,[92] when the regiment began the process of demobilization.

So few company muster rolls of the 4th Continental Artillery have been preserved that it is impossible to determine with any assurance the composition of any given company. However, a roster of 22 officers and 183 enlisted men, dated April 3, 1779, and showing place of birth for each individual, does exist.[93]

Only ten of the officers were native Americans, although nine of these were Pennsylvanians (three of them from Philadelphia or Philadelphia County). Of the remaining twelve, seven (including Col. Thomas

Procter) were born in Ireland, three in England, one in Scotland, and one (Francis Procter, Jr., whose parents were Irish) in Nova Scotia.

A similar pattern exists for enlisted men, although with a somewhat greater diversity of nationalities.

Native Americans accounted for eighty-seven, sixty of whom (about two-thirds) were Pennsylvanians. Twelve of the other American-born troops came from New Jersey, six from Virginia, four from Maryland, two from New York, and one each from Delaware, Georgia, and New England. Of the Pennsylvanians, the specific native areas of only fourteen are listed: ten from Philadelphia County and one each from Lancaster, Bucks, Chester, and Cumberland counties. With regard to the ninety-six men born abroad, sixty (almost two-thirds) were Irishmen, twenty-three were Germans, nine were Englishmen, three were Scots, and one was a Welshman.

The preponderance of foreign-born members of the 4th Continental Artillery is consistent with such information as is available on the national make-up of other Pennsylvania Continental regiments. This cannot be interpreted, however, as necessarily reinforcing that information, which is too limited to justify general application. Furthermore, an artillery regiment required skills that were by no means as commonly available as those required for infantry or cavalry. Two important sources of trained artillerymen were seamen and prior-service men, which would help to explain a high proportion of men with more cosmopolitan backgrounds than those of the farmers and tradesmen who readily found places in the Pennsylvania infantry organizations.

In this connection, it would appear to be significant that fifteen of the eighteen men rated as gunners were foreign-born, although it is also true that of the six bombardiers, half were native Americans. If all the non-commissioned officers and technical specialists are combined, it can be seen that only twenty-six were native Americans, while thirty-nine were foreign-born; whereas the less technically skilled positions (matrosses, fifers, and drummers) were filled by fifty-seven foreigners and sixty-one Americans. Put another way, while foreign-born soldiers accounted for 52.5 per cent of the total, they held 60 per cent of the positions requiring technical skills but only about 48 per cent of the relatively unskilled assignments.

As to the extent to which these men may have been deserters from the enemy, it is impossible to say how many of the British-born or German-born members of the unit might have been living in America before the Revolution. But it may be significant that of the five German-born enlisted men of this regiment whose native provinces are listed, three were from Hesse. General Washington strongly opposed the enlistment of British and Hessian deserters, but Procter's organization was technically a State unit until September 3, 1778. Apart from the likelihood that the lack of men qualified for badly needed technical assignments would tend to make the authorities willing to compromise, Colonel Procter—who in any case was evidently a man of independent and autocratic personality—was, as a State officer, in a position for many months to be able to ignore constraints placed on Continental organizations.

The members of the two companies of the 2d Continental Artillery which were transferred on January 1, 1781, to the 4th Continental Artillery were shown as being predominantly residents of the Philadelphia area at the time of their enlistments. Of nine officers and fifty enlisted men, forty-six were from Philadelphia or Philadelphia County and four from Chester County. Eight, however, were from York County, and one man enlisted in the company in New York City.[94]

The uniform of Procter's Pennsylvania artillery organizations appears to have featured a short blue coat faced with white or buff, white breeches, and a round hat bounded with worsted.[95] On October 2, 1779, however, the uniform for all Continental artillerymen was prescribed by General Order. The coat was to be blue, faced and lined with scarlet, with yellow buttons,[96] the officers' buttonholes to be edged with narrow gilt lace and the enlisted men's with yellow tape, and the buttons to bear the raised letters, USA.[97] However, one of Colonel Procter's frequent clashes with his superiors came as a result of his insistence that his officers continue to wear their Pennsylvania uniforms rather than those prescribed for Continental artillery.[98]

Summary

The men who made up Procter's artillery company, the two-company battalion to which it was expanded, and the Pennsylvania Artillery Regiment (later the 4th Continental Artillery Regiment) which it became, seem to have been recruited largely in the area around Philadelphia. A few came from more inland parts of Pennsylvania, but only two are known to have been from as far west as Cumberland County. One of these, John Hays, was a Carlisle barber (known to tradition chiefly as the husband of Molly Ludwig Hays, who as "Molly Pitcher" became the heroine of the Battle of Monmouth) who served one twelve-month enlistment in Procter's company, later joining the 7th Pennsylvania (infantry) Regiment. The other, Hermanus Thornton, was a matross in the 4th Continental Artillery in 1777 and was still on the regiment's rolls in 1779. For reasons that have been suggested, a large proportion of the members of the regiment were not natives of America, although a number of these may well have been established in Pennsylvania for varying periods of time before the Revolution.

OPERATIONS

With regard to artillery operations in the field, it should be borne in mind that cannoneers marched on foot. The guns were towed by horses, but these were often obtained by commercial contract, in which cases they were driven by civilian drivers. In action, the horses would be unharnessed and taken to safer ground, and the guns would then be manhandled by the sheer brute strength of the matrosses.

Before the young General Buonaparte made his revolutionary innovations in artillery tactical doctrine, the eighteenth-century practice for a given action was to distribute the guns and their crews among the infantry brigades which were being supported. A theoretical ratio was four fieldpieces per infantry brigade, but the actual ratio varied considerably. Beyond this, while some elements of a single artillery regiment could be serving with one major force, other elements could be stationed at geographically distant locations. For example, at one stage of the war, part of the 4th Continental Artillery was at Fort Pitt, another part at Carlisle, still another at Lancaster, and the rest with Maj. Gen. Nathanael Greene's army in South Carolina.[99]

Procter's State Artillery Company and Battalion; Pennsylvania State Artillery Regiment

Procter's company of Pennsylvania artillery, formed basically to defend the river approaches to Philadelphia, never saw combat. After the formation of the Pennsylvania artillery battalion, however, one element did get into action. That was a detachment, made available to the Flying Camp, which was stationed at Fort Washington during the fall of 1776. Records have not been found which indicate what members of the battalion were involved. All that is known for certain is that on November 16, 1776, one of the matrosses who was on the company muster roll for June 30-July 31, 1776,[100] John Corbin, of Virginia, was a member of a gun crew stationed at Laurel Hill, on the heights above the Harlem River north of Fort Washington itself. As the British attack began, the American battery withstood a heavy bombardment from the frigate, H. M. S. *Pearl*, and from Hessian cannon across the Harlem.[101] When British troops began crossing the Harlem River, the American guns could not be depressed sufficiently to be brought to bear, but as the assault force moved upward it lost the protection of the defilade and the advance was slowed.[102] The guns then were able to shift attention to the *Pearl*, damaging the frigate's rigging and putting roundshot through her hull. During this phase of the engagement, Corbin was killed.[103] At that point, his wife, Molly, who had accompanied him to war, stepped in and "filled with distinguished Bravery the post of her Husband, . . . serving a piece of Artillery" until she was wounded "and utterly disabled by three Grape shott."[104] For this service, she eventually was awarded a private's half pay for life.[105]

The next action involving the Pennsylvania artillery battalion was the Trenton-Princeton campaign toward the end of 1776 and extending into the first few days of 1777.

For the Pennsylvania artillerymen, activity began when, on December 1, 1776, Major Procter was directed to send part of his battalion to join the main army under Washington. This detachment was drawn from Capt. Thomas Forrest's company, and consisted of two brass six-pounders and fifty men, Forrest himself being in charge. With him were Third Lieutenant Duffy of his own company and First Lieutenant Emes, attached from Strobagh's company.

Forrest's force took part in the December 26 attack on the Hessian garrison at Trenton.[106] On December 28, Lieutenant Duffy wrote to Procter that the artillerymen had returned to McKonkey's Ferry the day before, "after a very fataguing (though successfull) engagement, in which [I] can assure you, the Artillery got applause." He went on to say that "I had the Honour of being detach'd up the Main Street in front of the Savages [Hessians, so known for their brutality at the Battle of Long Island], without any other piece, and sustained the fire of Several gunns from the Houses on each side, without the least loss. . . ." However, Duffy continued, serious shortages had developed. "The men are very much Nonplus'd for Shoes and Watch Coats," he said, and hoped that Procter could forward these articles.[107]

On the next day, Captain Forrest reported in much the same vein, saying that "...We have return'd from Trenton after defeating the Brass Caps and Crous coups." What made his situation urgent, Forrest noted, was that "Am now under marching orders on an other Expedition over the river," but "The men are not able to move for want of Shoes and Watch Coats, which I expect you'll forward [by] bearer immediately, with Gunn Screws, and the Regimental Coats. . . ."[108] Whether or not the requested equipment was sent, Procter arrived himself, bringing more men and two or three additional guns of the battalion but leaving a considerable number of his men still manning the defenses at Fort Island.[109]

Forrest's men were soon back in New Jersey, attached to the outpost force under Col. Edward Hand which, on January 2, 1777, carried out a delaying action against the advancing enemy troops led by Lord Cornwallis. With two of Forrest's fieldpieces in support, Hand's men held off the British while the bulk of the American army dug itself in on the other side of Assunpink Creek.[110]

For the Princeton operation the next day, Captain Forrest's force was put in support of Col. James Potter, of the Pennsylvania Associators, with Brig. Gen. Thomas Mifflin's brigade,[111] part of Maj. Gen. John Sullivan's division.[112] Procter himself was with Brig. Gen. John Cadwalader's brigade of Pennsylvania Associators,[113] part of Maj. Gen. Nathanael Greene's division. Included in Cadwalader's brigade was a Pennsylvania Associators artillery unit, not part of Procter's command, under Capt. Joseph Moulder.[114]

During the battle, on January 3, 1777, Procter was engaged when Cadwalader's brigade tried briefly to halt the British who drove back the first American attacking force to make contact (Brig. Gen. Hugh Mercer's brigade), and then fell back also, leaving one of Captain Moulder's guns behind in the retreat. Soon after, Washington took personal command of these troops and led a counterattack which recovered the piece. This advance also caused the British to break for the rear.[115]

Not long after this, Colonel Potter's force was sent to block a bridge where the Princeton-Trenton road crossed Stony Brook, sealing off the British in Princeton from a line of retreat and from reinforcement from the direction of Trenton. Soon after reaching this point, however, the Americans under Potter were confronted by a numerically superior British force—this was a column which had started from Princeton to join Cornwallis in Trenton before the Americans attacked, but had turned back upon hearing the sound of firing to the rear. The British drove off the Americans and crossed the brook. Colonel Potter was slightly wounded and captured, but Forrest managed to get his guns away safely.[116]

The force to which Procter was attached was more fortunate. Driving ahead into Princeton itself, the Americans found three brass six-pounders abandoned by the British. Procter did not have enough horses to tow them away, but he was able to unharness the horses from one of his own guns, an inferior iron three-pounder, and substitute one of the British cannon. The second captured gun was thrown down a well, but there was not time enough to dispose of the third (which the British later recovered) before the Americans had to leave to avoid the possibility of being trapped by Cornwallis, now certainly on the way from Trenton.[117]

Washington then moved his army north, eventually going into winter quarters at Morristown, New Jersey. Procter and Forrest went with the army, and on January 16, 1777, were joined at Morristown by Captain Strobagh's company. However, part of the command, under Captain-Lieutenant Courteney, remained in the Delaware River defenses. On the following day, with the departure on leave of Brig. Gen. Henry Knox, Procter assumed temporary command of all the artillery with Washington's army.* A month later, on February 20, word reached him that the artillery battalion was to be increased to regimental size and that he had been promoted to colonel to command it.[118]

Although this organization was to exist for another year and a half as the Pennsylvania Artillery Regiment, it was considered to be a Continental regiment, and functioned as such. Therefore, in this book it will be referred to as the 4th Continental Artillery from this date onward, although it did not technically become a Continental unit until September 3, 1778.

4th Continental Artillery

There is no record of combat involving any part of the regiment until April 13, 1777, when Captain-Lieutenants Turnbull and Ferguson, with twenty cannoneers and two guns,[119] were serving with a five hundred-man outpost force under Maj. Gen. Benjamin Lincoln at Bound Brook, New Jersey. On that date, Lord Cornwallis led a surprise attack from New Brunswick, approaching to within two hundred yards of Lincoln's headquarters before being seen. Lincoln and his staff managed to escape; but the artillerymen and their fieldpieces were captured—the only loss sustained by the American force.[120]

The next reference to the 4th Continental Artillery consists of orders issued by Washington to Colonel Procter on July 16, 1777. The regiment was to move to Trenton, waiting there until the British intentions were clearer. Procter reached Trenton on July 24, and sent orders that same day to Courteney (now a captain), who was still at Fort Island, to join the rest of the command. Courteney's arrival on August 22 brought the whole regiment together in one place for the first time in its existence.[121] From Trenton, the regiment moved by flatboat down the Delaware River to Chester, then marched to Wilmington, Delaware, where it joined Wayne's division and moved northward to Chadd's Ford, on Brandywine Creek.[122]

Procter's guns were sited on the high ground above Chadd's Ford, and from that position engaged on the morning of September 11, 1777, in a duel with Knyphausen's cannon on the other side of the stream. When the American right flank crumbled, however, British troops came driving down from the north and got to within thirty yards of the gun positions before they were seen. No infantry had been deployed to cover the American cannon, and the crews on the extreme right of the artillery position had to flee, abandoning three of their guns. The rest of Procter's force took up a position about two hundred yards to the rear; but before

---

*Actually, the only artillery forces remaining with the army from then until April, 1777, were Procter's men and two companies of New Jersey artillery. See Berg, p. 26.

long, General Wayne ordered the artillery to retreat, sending orders at the same time to Col. James Chambers, commanding the 1st Pennsylvania Regiment, to cover the artillery's withdrawal. "But to my surprise," Colonel Chambers wrote, "the artillerymen had run and left the howitzer behind." Two fieldpieces were brought off, escorted by about sixty men of the 1st Pennsylvania. Chambers then sent a party to bring off the howitzer while the rest of his regiment laid down covering fire. "But before this could be done, the main body of the foe came within thirty yards, and kept up the most terrible fire. . . ." Nevertheless, Chambers reported, "I brought all the brigade artillery safely off. . . ."[123]

In all this chaos, someone remembered to order the drivers to abandon their ammunition wagons and flee. However, one of the drivers belonging to Captain Courteney's company, a Negro named Edward Hector,[124] refused to obey. Instead, he moved out with his wagon and team and, as he passed abandoned muskets discarded by retreating infantrymen, gathered them up, eventually making his way safely to the army's rendezvous point at Chester.[125]

Despite Hector's achievement and the efforts of Colonel Chambers' men, the 4th Continental Artillery lost a number of its guns and the bulk of its available ammunition at the Battle of Brandywine.[126]

Elements of the 4th Continental Artillery were again in action at the Battle of Germantown, on October 4, 1777. The detachments were under the over-all control of Capt.-Lt. Jonathan Brewer, and apparently consisted of only two guns, under 2d Lt. Joseph Barker and 1st Lt. William Ritter, respectively. Lieutenant Barker's gun, a six-pounder, was put in position on the Germantown Road, almost directly opposite the Chew House.[127] The blast of its firing was so sharp that it caused blood to run from the ears of William McMullen, an Irish-born matross.[128] Corporal Nicholas Copple was blinded during the action,[129] and Hermanus Thornton, the matross from Cumberland County, was seriously injured when he was run over by a "cannon wagon."[130] There is no other record of the part played by the 4th Continental Artillery in this battle except that Captain-Lieutenant Brewer was captured—he was exchanged in August, 1778, but resigned his commission on February 10, 1779.[131]

If any part of the regiment was at Whitemarsh, it was not engaged when the British attacked in early December. There was a "parke" of artillery (which units comprised it are not specified) deployed in two "wings" behind the forward line of the defenses,[132] and quite possibly one or both of these "wings" included elements of the 4th Continental Artillery, but cannon do not appear to have been brought into action during the engagement.

Substantial portions of the regiment, however, were at Valley Forge, although manning levels had seriously deteriorated. On February 27, 1778, General Washington stated that "Our loss of matrosses in the last campaign in killed and wounded was considerable, and it has not been a little increased this winter by desertions from Col. Proctor's corps."[133]

There were other losses as well. Aside from the dismissals of Capt. Hercules Courteney and Capt. Francis Procter, Sr., 1st Lt. William Martin and 2d Lt. James Smith were taken prisoner on March 21, 1778, at Hancock's Bridge, New Jersey, while attending a meeting which was surprised by a British and Tory raiding force.[134] Possibly because of its reduced strength, the regiment did not accompany the main army into New Jersey when Washington left Valley Forge in June to pursue the British who had evacuated Philadelphia. Instead, the artillerymen were assigned to guard and provost duty in the newly liberated capital city.[135]

On August 4, 1778, little more than a month after the Battle of Monmouth, the regiment's strength was down to only 220, and on August 28, Colonel Procter formally requested permission from Pennsylvania's Supreme Executive Council to recruit men from other states. Apparently, the situation which had developed finally precipitated action on the part of Congress to agree, on September 3, 1778, that the artillery regiment should count as part of the quota of Continental units which Pennsylvania was charged with furnishing.[136] However, the new status, which merely formalized what had existed in fact for more than eighteen months, brought little improvement. As of December 21, the regiment's total strength was down to 208, and only 144 of these were available for duty—41 were sick, 16 were on detached service, and 7 were on furlough. As of March 19, 1779, the present-for-duty strength had dropped to 142.[137]

At this stage, at least part of the organization was manning the fortifications at Billingsport, New Jersey, on the Delaware below Philadelphia. But on May 18, 1779, Colonel Procter was ordered to take his regiment and join the force assembling under Maj. Gen. John Sullivan to attack the Iroquois in northern Pennsylvania and New York State. Procter joined General Sullivan at Easton on May 20. While the infantry proceeded on foot up the North Branch of the Susquehanna, the guns and baggage were loaded on a fleet of 214 boats. Colonel Procter was put in charge of this part of the force.[138]

When Sullivan's command reached the Chemung River, on August 11, 1779, several six-pounders under Lieutenant Colonel Forrest were brought into play to bombard the area on the other side of the ford before the infantry attempted to cross.[139] At the engagement at Newtown (Elmira, New York) on August 29, the artillery was deployed directly in front of a long breastwork held by the enemy. An infantry flanking force was sent around the enemy left to try to cut off any line of retreat. Firing began at about 3 P.M. Before the flanking force could get into the enemy's rear, however, the Indians and Tories "retreated from their works with the greatest precipitation."[140]

Col. John Butler, the Tory officer in command at Newtown, said that the Americans had "six pieces of Cannon & Cohorns [light mortars]," which began "discharging shells, round & grape shot, Iron Spikes &c. incessantly which soon obliged us to leave. . . ." As they fell back, "The shells bursting beyond us, made the Indians imagine the Enemy had got their Artillery all round us, & so startled & confounded them that [a] great part of them run off," adding that "Many of the Indians made no halt, but proceeded immediately to their respective Villages. . . ."[141]

The only artillery casualty reported for this action was a cannoneer named Thomas Tweedy, who was shot through the right leg.[142]

The Sullivan Expedition experienced no further engagements of any magnitude. The only other rounds the artillery fired appear to have been blanks, used for signals and, on occasions of ceremony such as the arrival of reinforcements and the return of the expeditionary force to its base camp, for the firing of salutes. Repeated references exist, however, to the 4th Continental Artillery's band, whose playing added a touch of festivity and pomp which seems to have been greatly appreciated (see Chapter XVI).

Following the campaign with Sullivan, the erosion of the 4th Continental Artillery's strength continued. Some of the men were with Washington's main army, but at least some others were at the ordnance depot at Carlisle. As of March 29, 1780, the regiment mustered only 189 officers and men.[143] On May 20, Captain Craig started with an understrength company for Fort Pitt, which he reached on June 25,[144] thereby dispersing the organization even farther. During the summer, part of the unit was with General Wayne, as four fieldpieces of the regiment were in support of the two brigades with which he attacked the Blockhouse at Bergen Heights, New Jersey, on July 21. The log walls, however, proved to be too strong for such light projectiles to penetrate.[145] In this action, Thomas Tweedy was wounded again, this time through the *left* leg.[146]

The part of the regiment which was with the main army went into winter quarters at Morristown late in 1780, and its enlisted members joined with the other Pennsylvania troops there in the mutiny which broke out on January 1, 1781. Indeed, with their cannon the artillerymen threatened the soldiers who at first were reluctant to take part in the mutiny until they too broke ranks and sided with the mutineers.[147]

When the mutiny was settled, a good number of the artillerymen reenlisted. Not long afterwards, on April 18, Colonel Procter resigned from the army. His resignation had nothing to do with the mutiny, but arose from a dispute with President Joseph Reed, of the Pennsylvania Supreme Executive Council, over which junior officers should be promoted in the reorganized regiment. Procter and Reed had long been at loggerheads, and while General Washington wrote Procter a courtly letter thanking him for the many services he had rendered, Reed was less gracious, writing to Washington that "We cannot consider Colonel Procter's resignation in the light of a public misfortune...."[148]

Craig's company of the regiment, uninvolved in the mutiny, remained at Fort Pitt; but in the latter part of May, 1781, the rest of the regiment, on completing the furloughs the men had been granted, gathered at York with the other re-enlisted Pennsylvania Continentals. There, a new complaint broke out, this time over whether the men were to get their arrears of pay in specie or in depreciated paper money. Fearing another mutiny, General Wayne took harsh measures. Accounts of what happened vary extensively, but it appears that six men—two of them artillerymen—were tried by what amounted to drumhead courts martial and three of them were executed. One of the latter was John Fortescue, of the 4th Continental Artillery. The other artilleryman, William Crofts, escaped being shot. His offense had been appearing drunk on parade and making impertinent threats to Major Eustis.[149]

In the west, Craig's force was directed to join an expedition under Brig. Gen. George Rogers Clark, of the Virginia militia, which was being formed to attack Detroit. Craig and his men left Fort Pitt on July 29, 1781, and reported to Clark at the Falls of the Ohio, but the project was eventually abandoned and the artillerymen returned to Fort Pitt, where they arrived on December 26.[150]

Meanwhile, the members of the regiment who were at York, amounting to one company with six fieldpieces, started for Virginia on May 26. Crossing the Potomac at Georgetown, however, the boat carrying the cannon capsized and all six guns went into the water. The cannon were retrieved but the ammunition was ruined.[151]

In Virginia, the artillerymen served through the summer in Wayne's provisional brigade, under Lafayette's over-all command.[152] As June progressed, Cornwallis withdrew his troops from the vicinity of Charlottesville southeastward, to Williamsburg and beyond, the Americans following close behind.

But Cornwallis was a dangerous opponent. Early in July, he deceived Wayne into believing that the main part of the British force had crossed the James River to Portsmouth, and on July 6, at Green Spring, near Jamestown, Wayne led his five hundred men in an attack on what he thought was only the rear guard of the enemy army. Lafayette was to move up in support as soon as he could reach the field.

Wayne advanced into a carefully prepared ambush. The British outposts let themselves be driven back across marshy ground into dense woods, luring the Americans into range of the muskets of the concealed main body of Cornwallis' force. Lafayette, approaching from a different angle, was able to see these troops, but could not reach the field before the trap was sprung and the enemy dashed forward to encircle an advance element of Wayne's brigade. But instead of retreating, Wayne charged with the rest of his men, disrupting the momentum of the enemy attack; and in the confusion which followed, safely brought off his troops. In the action, however, he had to abandon the two cannon which were supporting his brigade.[153] Most of their crews had been killed and all the horses were killed or disabled. At least, though, the surviving cannoneers had been able to spike the two guns before having to retreat.[154] The only artillery casualty in this action who is identified by name was Capt.-Lt. Jesse Crosley, who was shot in the hip.[155]

Although the siege of Yorktown which soon followed was principally an affair for artillerymen and engineers, it required heavy cannon, and the Pennsylvania artillery, armed only with light fieldpieces, took little part. There is a record, however, of one Pennsylvania artilleryman, Henry Love, losing his left leg during the battle.[156]

After Cornwallis surrendered on October 19, 1781, elements of the 4th Continental Artillery, amounting to three understrength companies, were ordered south to join Maj. Gen. Nathanael Greene's army in South Carolina. As of November 10, their strength in officers and enlisted men was reported as being 129. The remainder of the regiment totalled only 106 men, including those based on Fort Pitt and others stationed in other parts of Pennsylvania.[157]

The elements in the south saw still more action. Some of the artillerymen were with the force with which General Wayne cleared the British troops out of all of Georgia except Savannah, finally compelling them, on July 12, 1782, to evacuate that city. During this campaign, one cannoneer was wounded.[158] Other detachments were with the forces opposing the British at Charleston, South Carolina, and in these operations still another of the Pennsylvania artillerymen was wounded.[159]

The regiment's strength remained relatively constant, for a report of March 21, 1782, shows 70 members of the regiment at Philadelphia, Lancaster, and Carlisle; 34 at Fort Pitt; and 131 with Greene, for a total strength of 29 officers and 206 enlisted men.[160] On January 1, 1783, however, the 4th Continental Artillery was reduced to four companies;[161] and at the end of that month, the three companies in the south, stationed at that time at James Island, South Carolina, had only sixty officers and men among them.[162] With the accelerating demobilization of the Continental Army, the entire artillery of the army was reduced, on June 17, 1783, to only two companies, neither of them from the 4th Continental Artillery.[163] The remaining men of that regiment had begun to be furloughed on June 11, and the last of them were mustered out of the service on November 15.[164]

Chapter XIX
4th Continental Light Dragoons

ORGANIZATION

THE Continental Army had four regiments of cavalry, formally designated as "light dragoons." They were used for scouting, patrolling, and covering missions and for courier service. Except for surprise encounters with enemy patrols, they were intended to fight on foot. As originally conceived, and as prescribed on March 14, 1777, a dragoon regiment was to have six troops, each consisting of a captain, a lieutenant, a cornet (the cavalry equivalent of infantry ensign or artillery second lieutenant), and forty-one enlisted men. With the field-grade officers and regimental staff, the regiment would total 280 personnel. The reorganization of May 27, 1778, retained the six-troop structure, but added a lieutenant and twenty-three enlisted men to each troop, bringing the theoretical total to 416 officers and enlisted men. January 1, 1781, brought still another reorganization, this one reflecting a conceptual change imposed by necessity. Six more privates were added to each troop and minor changes were made to the staff, bringing the regimental total to 455 officers and men; but only four of the troops were mounted, the remaining two consisting of infantry. This new type of unit was called a "legionary corps,"[1] and provided a more versatile organization, roughly equivalent in an embryonic way to a regimental combat team.

But cavalry was an expensive branch of the service. Mounts had to be purchased, and, due to hard usage and perennial shortages, required frequent replacement. Saddles and other "horse furniture" had to be procured. Weapons suitable for mounted men were also in short supply: sabers could be manufactured, but pistols and carbines had to be imported. Due to this combination of limiting factors, no Continental cavalry regiment ever had much more than three hundred men, and only about half of these could be mounted. More often, the regiments mustered no more than 150 men.[2]

The 4th Continental Light Dragoon regiment was authorized by Congress on January 1, 1777,[3] and on January 5, Stephen Moylan was appointed its colonel. He had previously been the Continental Army's Quartermaster General (in grade of colonel), and at the time of his appointment to the new regiment, was serving as an aide on Washington's staff. He continued as commander of the regiment until it was disbanded.[4]

Of the key officers (captain through colonel) of the original regiment, only Moylan himself and one captain were from Pennsylvania. One captain was from Maryland, and the rest of the captains, the lieutenant colonel, and the major were Virginians.[5] The enlisted men, however, were largely from Pennsylvania,[6] chiefly from Philadelphia and its vicinity.[7]

For more than two years after its formation, the 4th Dragoons had no field-grade officer except for Colonel Moylan. Not until December 10, 1779, was Lt. Col. Benjamin Temple, of the 1st Continental Light Dragoons (a Virginian), transferred to fill the vacancy. He continued with the 4th Light Dragoons during the rest of the regiment's existence.[8]

Similarly, the 4th Dragoons had no major until another Virginian, Moore Fauntleroy, was promoted from captain on August 1, 1779.[9] He remained on the regiment's roster from that time on, although on February 10, 1783, Maj. Gen. Arthur St. Clair complained that Fauntleroy had been absent from duty for many months.[10]

The 4th Dragoon regiment was authorized six troops, and actually had that number on July 3, 1781,[11] but the names of only five original captains have been found. The troops and their commanders appear to have been as follows:

• [Troop A], commanded by Capt. Moore Fauntleroy. After serving in 1776 as an ensign and second lieutenant in the 5th Virginia (infantry) Regiment, he was appointed a captain in the 4th Continental Light Dragoons on January 21, 1777. He was taken prisoner at the Battle of Germantown, on October 4, 1777. The date of his escape or exchange is not known; but as noted above, he was promoted to major on August 1, 1779.[12] Records do not indicate the promotion or appointment of any officer to fill the captaincy he vacated. The regiment's first appointment to captain after Fauntleroy's promotion was that of Larkin Smith, but that did not take place until April 1, 1780, eight months later. Smith, still another Virginian, had been commissioned a cornet in the 4th Dragoons on August 1, 1777, promoted to lieutenant on September 4, 1778, and after becoming a captain continued with the regiment as long as it remained in existence.[13]

• [Troop B], commanded by Capt. David Hopkins, of Virginia. He had been a volunteer with Benedict Arnold's Quebec expedition in 1775, and was appointed a captain in the 4th Continental Dragoons on January 21, 1777. At an unknown date in 1780, he was promoted to major of the 1st Continental Dragoons.[14] It is possible that his replacement was Capt. Henry Willis, of Pennsylvania, concerning whom the records are contradictory. He was appointed a cornet in the 4th Dragoons in June, 1777, and according to one version,[15] was promoted to second lieutenant on June 25, 1781, and to captain on an unspecified subsequent date, serving to the end of the war. Another version,[16] however, says that he was promoted to captain on December 22, 1780, and resigned his commission on April 24, 1781, at which time he was replaced by Capt. Thomas Overton, a Virginian, who had been a lieutenant in the 9th Virginia (infantry) Regiment until July 1, 1779, when he had been appointed a first lieutenant in the 4th Dragoons. He served with that regiment through the rest of the war.[17]

• [Troop C], commanded by Capt. Thomas Dorsey, of Pennsylvania. He began his service as a captain of infantry, initially in the 1st Pennsylvania Battalion and then in its successor unit, the 2d Pennsylvania Regiment. He became a captain in the 4th Dragoons on January 10, 1777, but is listed as "omitted" in August of the same year.[18] No promotion occurred which can be associated with the departure from the service (whatever the circumstances may have been) of Captain Dorsey. The first such promotion after he left the regiment, which took place on February 8, 1778, was that of John Heard, of New Jersey. After having been a second lieutenant of New Jersey artillery in 1776, Heard had become a first lieutenant of the 4th Dragoons on January 20, 1777. He served as a captain in that regiment from the date of his promotion to the end of the war.[19]

• [Troop D], commanded by Capt. David Plunkett, of Maryland. His prior service had been as a second lieutenant in Smallwood's Maryland Regiment. Appointed a captain in the 4th Continental Light Dragoons on January 10, 1777, he was taken prisoner on October 20 of that year (location and circumstances unknown, although possibly in conjunction with the defense of Fort Mercer, near Red Bank, New Jersey), and resigned from the army on March 13, 1779.[20] Possibly to fill this vacancy, Peter Manifold was promoted to captain from first lieutenant on April 14, 1779. One of the comparatively few Pennsylvania officers, he had originally joined the regiment as a cornet, on April 14, 1778, being promoted barely two weeks later (on May 1) to lieutenant. He resigned on October 30, 1780.[21] Apparently the vacancy remained unfilled for some time.

• [Troop E], commanded by Capt. Vashel D. Howard, of Virginia. He was commissioned a captain in the 4th Dragoons on January 24, 1777, but died on March 15, 1778.[22] There was no promotion to captain in the regiment from that time until December 22, 1778, when John Craig, a Pennsylvanian, was promoted from first lieutenant. He had been a second lieutenant in the 2d Pennsylvania (infantry) Battalion and a first lieutenant in the 3d Pennsylvania (infantry) Regiment before transferring to the 4th Dragoons on March 22, 1977. He stayed with the organization to the end of the war.[23]

Other officers who at one time or another served as captains in the 4th Continental Light Dragoons were:

• Capt. Zebulon Pike,* of New Jersey. Appointed a cornet in the 4th Dragoons on March 1, 1777, he became the regimental adjutant on November 20, 1777, was promoted lieutenant on March 15, 1778, and captain on December 25, 1778. On June 1, 1780, he was appointed regimental paymaster, holding that position until the end of the war.[24]

• Capt. Erasmus Gill, of Virginia. He was appointed a captain in the 4th Dragoons in February, 1779, but with a retroactive date of rank of December 25, 1778. He had prior service as a sergeant, ensign, and second lieutenant in the 2d Virginia (infantry) Regiment. On October 3,

---

*Father of the Brig. Gen. Zebulon Pike who discovered Pike's Peak and who was killed at Toronto during the War of 1812.

1779, he was taken prisoner at Savannah, Georgia, and after his exchange (on October 22, 1780), served to the end of the war.[25]

• Capt. Lawrence Frank, of Pennsylvania. Having been commissioned a first lieutenant, 4th Continental Light Dragoons on October 1, 1779, he was promoted to captain some time in 1782 and served in that grade throughout what remained of the war.[26]

Whatever the regiment's pattern of promotions or company strength may have been, it is clear that some time prior to its demobilization the 4th Dragoons had reached a total of six companies, commanded at the end by Captains Smith, Heard, Craig, Gill, Overton, and Frank.

The uniform originally adopted for the 4th Dragoons featured coats captured from the British. These were red, with blue facings. However, the first detachment of the regiment to join Washington at Morristown, New Jersey, in the spring of 1777, was mistaken for British soldiers, to the consternation of the American civilians the troops met along the way. On May 12, General Washington wrote to Colonel Moylan, directing him to change the color, "which may be done by dipping into what kind of dye that is most proper to put upon *Red*. I care not what it is, so that the present colour be changed."[27] Apparently, some of the men wore linen hunting shirts for a time,[28] but before long the regiment was uniformed in green coats trimmed with red, green cloaks with red capes, red waistcoats, buckskin breeches, and leather caps trimmed with bear skin.[29] By the terms of the General Order of October 2, 1779, however, all dragoon regiments were thenceforth to wear blue coats, faced and lined with white, with white buttons.[30]

For recruiting, the 4th Dragoon Regiment had been assigned to the area between the North (Hudson) River and the Susquehanna;[31] but, as noted above, it appears to have drawn the bulk of its men from the Philadelphia region. The original enlistments expired in the latter part of September, 1780. The regiment had never been filled, and only eleven of the old members re-enlisted at that time for the duration of the war.[32] With new recruits, it totalled only eighty men (with fifteen officers!) by the spring of 1781.[33] The nearest thing to a complete roster, purportedly showing all the enlisted men who ever served with the regiment, lists only 213 names.[34]

Summary

In comparison with infantry and artillery organizations, the term "regiment" is misleading as applied to Continental cavalry units. The 4th Light Dragoon regiment, raised chiefly in and around Philadelphia, seems seldom to have exceeded a hundred troopers by very much, and frequently to have fallen to much lower manning levels. As numerical weakness limited the uses which it could serve, it operated in small detachments or with men functioning independently as individuals.

OPERATIONS

Even more markedly than was the case for artillery, American Continental cavalry was employed in small, widely dispersed detachments. It performed valuable services in observing and reporting enemy movements, screening its own infantry's movements, covering exposed flanks, and providing messengers for dissemination of tactical orders. Except for brief skirmishes, however, it almost never saw extensive combat.

As already noted, the first elements of the 4th Continental Light Dragoons arrived at Morristown on May 12, 1777. For the next two months they were carrying out patrolling activities in the vicinity of Middlebrook, New Jersey. A return dated July 16, 1777, indicates that three troops (under Captains Dorsey, Hopkins, and Plunkett) were in the field. They drew a total of 172 rations, but upwards of twenty of these appear to have been for the authorized regimental laundresses.[35]

Four days later, at Elizabeth, New Jersey, nineteen men of Captain Craig's troop, disgruntled because they had not been paid, left for Philadelphia in defiance of orders, to demand the money due them. Two troops of the 1st Dragoons brought them back, but the horses were too stiff to permit further movements until they could be rested.[36] The deserters were tried by court martial in early August, by which time the regiment was at Neshaminy, in Bucks County, Pennsylvania. All nineteen were sentenced to be hanged, but General Washington commuted the sentence and, on August 19, transferred the men to infantry regiments.[37]

The 4th Dragoons took part with the rest of the army in the march through Philadelphia on August 24, moving on south toward Wilmington, Delaware. From there, the regiment formed part of the escort for General Washington when he reconnoitered toward the British army's landing place at Head of Elk, Maryland, and helped drive off an enemy scouting force attempting a probe northward.[38]

During the Battle of Brandywine, on September 11, the dragoons operated chiefly as scouts and couriers, under the over-all direction of Count Casimir Pulaski, soon to be named commander of all the Continental cavalry. Some of the 4th Dragoon regiment may have taken part in Pulaski's successful attempt to block the British forces trying to cut off the American line of retreat to Chester, but no specific documentation to this effect has been found. On September 13, however, a detachment of the 4th Dragoons was sent to retrieve military stores being held at French Creek, in Chester County, and the rest of the troopers were used to provide cover for the fords across the Schuylkill River.[39]

As at Brandywine, the role of the regiment at the Battle of Germantown was to provide covering and scouting forces and messenger service. Presumably, some or all of the regiment may have been with Pulaski's force delaying the British pursuit. It does not appear to have been heavily engaged, although it may have seen some action, for Captain Fauntleroy was captured during this battle.

Scouting and patrolling continued to occupy the 4th Dragoons. On November 9, 1777, Captain Craig and a detachment were officially commended for capturing a number of enemy soldiers.[40] When Washington took up a defensive position at Whitemarsh, the regiment helped cover the left flank of the position, but was not engaged during the tentative British advance.[41]

The 4th Dragoons moved with the rest of the army to Valley Forge on December 19, 1777. Although the bulk of the army's cavalry was sent to Trenton in order to ease the demands on the Valley Forge locality for fodder, the 4th Dragoons appear to have stayed at Valley Forge until March 20, 1778. On that date, Colonel Moylan was ordered to move his command to Trenton. Over the next several weeks, there was frequent patrolling, which gave rise to several skirmishes, but the lack of fit horses and suitable equipment limited the action which could be taken.[42] Then, on May 28, Washington sent orders for all the cavalry regiments to join the army at Valley Forge. Before the troopers could arrive, however, the orders were countermanded and the cavalrymen were directed to keep close watch over British movements in the vicinity of Philadelphia.[43]

When the British evacuated Philadelphia and started across New Jersey on June 18, the cavalry stayed close on their heels, keeping Washington informed of their direction of march.[44] In fact, the 4th Dragoons clung so close that on June 25 they overran the camp followers marching in the rear of the British columns.[45] On June 27, the day before the Battle of Monmouth, the regiment captured a number of prisoners and sent them back for interrogation.[46]

Like most Revolutionary War battles, Monmouth was an infantry and artillery fight, with cavalry playing its part chiefly before and after the actual clash. The 4th Dragoons seem to have had no part in the engagement itself, and there is no record that the regiment suffered any casualties on that day. On the other hand, Moylan's men did follow up the British withdrawal on June 29, but they were too weak in numbers and the horses were too exhausted to do anything except maintain a watch over enemy movements.[47]

After the Battle of Monmouth, the 4th Continental Light Dragoons remained in New Jersey through the summer. The regiment's base was at Hackensack, but its assignment was to patrol the area toward the Hudson and to keep the British forces under observation.[48] By early October, the regiment had moved to Lancaster, Pennsylvania. From there it was ordered to Durham, Connecticut, for the winter of 1778-1779. It operated along the New York-Connecticut border during the summer of 1779.[49] On July 11, it saw its next sizeable action when it accompanied a militia force to try to prevent a British amphibious raid on the town of Norwalk. By the time the Americans arrived, the enemy troops had made their landing and had set the town on fire. Colonel Moylan led an attack, during which, he reported, "a vast deal of ammunition [was] wasted, to very little purpose, as in general our militia kept at awfull distance." Although the raiding force, concealed by the smoke from the burning town, withdrew successfully to its ships, the cavalry took four prisoners.[50]

During the rest of that summer, the bulk of the regiment continued to operate in the same general area, serving as part of the force under Brig. Gen. John Glover.[51] Some of the regiment appears to have gone to the Southern theater about this time, as Captain Gill (who was mentioned by name as capturing the four prisoners at Norwalk on July 11) was himself taken prisoner at Savannah, Georgia, on October 3.[52]

The regiment as a whole spent the winter of 1779-1780 in Connecticut. Quarters for men and horses were inadequate, and the 4th Dragoons had to be scattered over a distance of five miles, an impossible situation for any organization which might be called upon to react quickly. Colonel Moylan claimed that "No Regiment could be more orderly than the 4th since they have come into this State," but the troopers were unpopular with the local civilians. Shortages of supplies and equipment were acute. "We have an exceeding cold day," Moylan noted on January 22, 1780, "and the Regiment so badly off for undercloaths that they are much to be pitied."[53] He reported on February 15 that there were 130 Pennsylvanians in the organization—probably the bulk of its enlisted strength—but a week later he stated that even this small number was not effective "for want of breeches, boots, shirts and stockings."[54] The shortages were still acute as late as April 14.[55]

Apparently, spring brought more supplies, and the summer definitely brought more action. On July 21, 1780, the 4th Dragoon regiment was part of the force under Brig. Gen. Anthony Wayne which attacked the Blockhouse at Bergen Heights, New Jersey. It carried out the only part of the operation which was completely successful, driving off the considerable collection of Tory-owned cattle and horses at Bergen Neck while

Wayne's infantry and artillery tried vainly to reduce the garrison which was holding the Blockhouse.[56]

According to one authority,[57] parts of the regiment were sent to the Southern theater during 1780, sustaining heavy losses at the Battle of Camden, South Carolina, on August 16, the survivors being absorbed into a composite dragoon unit commanded by Lt. Col. William Washington, originally of the 3d Continental Dragoons. This claim seems to be unlikely. No other reference to 4th Dragoon participation in that battle has been found. Moreover, it is clear that the greater part of the regiment spent the winter of 1780-1781 at Lancaster,[58] and there was a detachment at West Point.[59]

Because of these dispositions, the 4th Dragoons did not take part in the January 1 mutiny of the Pennsylvania Line at Morristown, New Jersey.[60] Nevertheless, they staged a minor revolt of their own. On May 21, 1781, a number of the dragoons, with their weapons, marched on the Lancaster jail, determined to release one of the members of the regiment who was confined there. The jail was guarded by a militia sentry, who ordered the cavalrymen to halt. One of the troopers continued to move forward, threatening the sentry with a cocked and loaded pistol. When he tried to wrest away the sentry's musket, the sentry shot and killed him. As the dragoon fell, his pistol dropped out of his hand and fired when it hit the ground, with the result that a militiaman standing nearby was wounded in the thigh.[61]

The regiment had become greatly reduced in effectiveness. As of April 6, Major General St. Clair reported that the 4th Dragoons had only eighty men, and only fifty of those were mounted,[62] and there was no improvement by mid-July. Even so, by the end of June, part of the regiment had joined Wayne's provisional brigade in Virginia.[63] As of July 3, the regiment's total enlisted strength is shown as being only 101 men. They were organized in six troops, but were very unevenly distributed, the largest troop numbering forty-two men and the smallest only three.[64]

By October 1, 1781, what was left of the 4th Dragoons (now officially the 4th Legionary Corps) was all assembled at Williamsburg, in Virginia. From there, it went on to the siege of Yorktown, where it was assigned to the "right division."[65] By November 1, still at Yorktown, it had fourteen officers and ninety-four enlisted men, and another forty men and four officers had already marched south to join Major General Greene. The mounts of the men in Virginia were in very poor condition, and Colonel Moylan predicted that they would not be capable of marching for at least four months.[66]

The only part of the regiment which saw any further action during the war was the detachment in the south, which by the end of 1781 numbered approximately one hundred officers and men. This force was assigned to the command which Anthony Wayne led into Georgia,[67] leaving South Carolina on January 4, 1782. During the course of the campaign, which ended with the occupation of Savannah on July 12, 1782, what was left of the 4th Dragoons was absorbed into a mixed command (including elements of the 1st and 3d Dragoon regiments) under Col. George Baylor, 3d Continental Light Dragoons.* As for the elements of the regiment which had not gone south from Virginia, by December 15, 1782, their strength had dropped to one mounted troop and one troop of foot soldiers. The foot troop was transferred to the Pennsylvania infantry (although the men continued to be paid at the higher rate prescribed for cavalry),[68] and the mounted troop was mustered out.[69]

*Griffin, p. 126. It seems likely that Berg's statement that in 1780 remnants of the 4th Dragoons were absorbed into a mixed command under Lt. Col. Washington, 3d Dragoons, reflects a confusion with what actually happened in 1782.

Chapter XX
Miscellaneous Organizations

I N ADDITION to the regiments which have been described in previous chapters, Pennsylvania furnished several other units to the Continental Army. Beyond that, individual Pennsylvania soldiers served, sometimes in considerable strength, in a number of organizations not associated with Pennsylvania. An example of the latter case is the so-called 2d "Canadian" Regiment, commanded by Col. Moses Hazen. It was known as "Congress' Own" because it was raised from the colonies at large, although it drew 153 of its officers and men from Pennsylvania.[1] Reference has been made in an earlier chapter to entire companies of Pennsylvanians in the 2d Continental Artillery, which was largely a New York regiment. Pennsylvanians also served in Armand's "Partisan Legion,"[2] Pulaski's Legion,[3] and Von Ottendorff's Battalion,[4] among others.

However, because the subject of this book is the Pennsylvania Line organizations of the Continental Army, such units as Hazen's Regiment will not be examined. The miscellaneous organizations which will be treated in this chapter are those consisting exclusively or substantially of Pennsylvanians, which were credited to Pennsylvania's assigned unit quota.

For the sake of clarity, the format of the chapter departs somewhat from that of previous chapters, with the organization and operations of each unit being treated individually before the next unit is taken up.

The organizations which are discussed below are the German Regiment, the Regiment of Artillery Artificers, and Von Heer's Troop of Light Dragoons (provost guards).

The German Regiment

ORGANIZATION

On June 27, 1776, Congress authorized formation of an eight-company regiment to consist of soldiers of German extraction, enlisted for three years. Although it was assigned as part of the Pennsylvania Line, four of its companies were to be raised in Maryland. Later, the four Pennsylvania companies were increased to five.[5] On February 26, 1778, however, the unit was transferred from the Pennsylvania Line to the Maryland Line, and was designated (although seldom called) the 8th Maryland Regiment.[6] On January 1, 1781, it was inactivated,[7] with most of its enlisted men being transferred to Hazen's Regiment.[8]

The original commander of the German Regiment was Col. Nicholas Hausegger, of Lebanon, in what was then Lancaster County,[9] who was promoted on July 17, 1776, from major of the 4th Pennsylvania Battalion. At the Battle of Princeton in early January, 1777, he was captured, and never returned to duty. According to one account, he was "superseded" on March 19, 1777, "having joined the enemy."[10] Another version says that he returned to his farm, where he died in July, 1786.[11] The two statements are not incompatible, and accounts exist stating that, in 1778, Hausegger circulated among American prisoners of war in New York and tried to persuade them to defect.[12] There is ambiguity of information about his replacement.*

The first lieutenant colonel of the German Regiment was George Strickler, of Maryland, who had previously served as a captain in Smallwood's Maryland Regiment, and who was appointed to his new organization on July 17, 1776. On April 29, 1777, he resigned his commission.[13] To replace him, Ludwig Weltner (also from Maryland) was promoted from major. Lieutenant Colonel Weltner held the command until the regiment was disbanded on January 1, 1781.[14]

---

*According to Heitman (page 73), Baron Henry Leonard Philip d'Arendt was appointed colonel of the German Regiment on March 19, 1777, but left on a twelve-month leave, from which he never returned, on August 18, 1778. The *Pennsylvania Archives*, however, omit any reference to D'Arendt and state—PA(5), III, 785—that after Hausegger's capture, Lt. Col. Ludwig Weltner succeeded to the command.

Weltner had been directly appointed as major on July 17, 1776. Upon his promotion to lieutenant colonel, Capt. Daniel Burchardt, of Philadelphia,[15] was promoted to major, his date of rank being given as April 7, 1777. He resigned on July 2, 1779.[16] At one stage, there appear to have been two majors in the regiment (possibly on the basis that a regiment was authorized three field-grade officers), for on April 9, 1777, George Hubley, of Lancaster,[17] was also promoted from captain to major. On February 7, 1779, however, he died.[18] After Major Burchardt's resignation on July 2, 1779, the German Regiment seems to have spent the rest of its existence without any major at all.

The records do not indicate which of the companies were considered Pennsylvania units rather than Maryland units. Although five of the regiment's nine companies were credited to Pennsylvania, six of the original company commanders were Pennsylvanians. Furthermore, a comparison of the names on the seven available company muster rolls with the list of Pennsylvania troops in the German Regiment shows Pennsylvanians in all companies, although in varying numbers ranging from three in each of two companies to thirty-two in one company.

Two points concerning the enlisted men of this regiment are worth particular note.

One is that the regiment was by no means made up of troops who were all of German background. Judging by the apparent nationality of the names, at least, only 388 of the 462 enlisted—less than eighty-four per cent—are definitely or even apparently German. Even granting the vagaries of eighteenth-century spelling and the near illiteracy of many company clerks, names such as John Armstrong, John Bennet, Timothy Cahill, James Calhoun, Philip Fitzpatrick, Thomas Hazlewood, Patrick Kelley, William Lewis, Hugh McKay, Jacob McLain, Thomas Mahoney, James Murphy, Richard O'Quin, and Cornelius Quinlan (all of which appear on the roster) could hardly be anglicized versions of German names.

The other particular point is that the Pennsylvania members of the regiment were largely recruited from the eastern part of the State. Of the two rosters showing place of enlistment, one (of sixty-nine men) shows fifty-five men from Philadelphia or Philadelphia County, six from Lancaster County, five from Berks County, two from Northampton County, and one from Chester County.[19] Another roster, consisting of 106 names, shows eighty-three from Philadelphia, ten from Lancaster, six from Berks, four from Northumberland, two from Northampton, and one from Bucks.[20]

The company commanders were:

- Capt. Daniel Burchardt, appointed captain on July 8, 1776, and promoted to major on April 7, 1777.[21] The next promotion to captain which is recorded took effect on May 9, 1777, when Peter Boyer (or Bowyer), of Philadelphia,[22] was advanced from first lieutenant, having served in that grade since July 12, 1776. He remained as a captain in the German Regiment until January 1, 1781.[23] Presumably, Captain Boyer was promoted to fill the vacancy created when Captain Burchardt was advanced in rank.

• Capt. George Hubley, of Lancaster.[24] He also had been commissioned on July 8, 1776. As noted earlier, he was promoted to major on April 9, 1777.[25] It seems likely that it was to fill this vacant captaincy that Charles Baltzell, of Maryland, was promoted on May 10, 1777, from the first lieutenancy he had been filling since July 12, 1776. He continued with the regiment until January 1, 1781.[26]

• Capt. Joseph Bunner, of Pennsylvania. He served as a captain in the German Regiment from July 8, 1776, to January 1, 1781.[27]

• Capt. Benjamin Weiser, of Pennsylvania. Appointed a captain on July 8, 1776, he was cashiered the following October 31 "for misconduct at Montressor's Island."[28] Frederick William Rice, a Pennsylvanian, who had been a first lieutenant since July 12, 1776, was promoted to captain on January 4, 1777, possibly as Weiser's replacement. He served as a captain until January 1, 1781.[29]

• Capt. John David Woelpper, of Pennsylvania. After serving as a first lieutenant in the 3d Pennsylvania Battalion, he was appointed a captain in the German Regiment on July 17, 1776. Not quite two years later, on June 11, 1778, he was transferred to the Invalid Corps.[30] No one appears to have been promoted to replace him.

• Capt. William Heyser, of Pennsylvania. He served with the German Regiment from July 12, 1776, until he resigned on May 21, 1778.[31] Again, records have not been found to show who if anyone was promoted to take his place.

• Capt. Philip Graybill (or Graybell), of Maryland. He was commissioned in the regiment as a captain on July 8, 1776, and resigned on March 12, 1778.[32] Although there is a slight overlap in dates, it may be that it was his resignation which brought the promotion of Bernard Hubley, of Pennsylvania, with a date of rank of February 24, 1778. Hubley had been a first lieutenant in the regiment since August 12, 1776, and remained as a captain until January 1, 1781.[33]

After February 8, 1778, the German Regiment also had a captain-lieutenant, who would have been the actual commander of the "Lieutenant Colonel's Company" of the regiment. This was Philip Shrawder (or Schrader), of Philadelphia.[34] He had been commissioned as a second lieutenant on July 12, 1776, and was promoted to first lieutenant on May 13, 1777, and to captain-lieutenant on February 8, 1778. He remained in that position until January 1, 1781.[35]

No description of any special uniform for the German Regiment has been found. The only reference to the dress of this regiment relates to two deserters (one in 1777 and the other in 1778), one of whom was wearing an "old green coat over his regimentals" and the other a white hunting shirt and breeches.[36]

Summary

The German Regiment, which contained a statistically significant number of non-Germans, was raised in Pennsylvania and Maryland. Although five of its nine companies were theoretically made up of Pennsylvanians and the other four companies of men from Maryland, Pennsylvanians in varying numbers were in fact scattered through all seven of the companies for which muster rolls survive. The bulk of these Pennsylvania troops were enlisted in eastern Pennsylvania, overwhelmingly from Philadelphia and its near vicinity.

OPERATIONS

The German Regiment did not reach the theater of active operations until after the Battle of Long Island (on August 27, 1776). However, it joined Washington's army soon afterward, as at least part of it seems to have been present at the action at Randall's Island (then called Montresor's Island), New York, on September 10, 1776, when a British landing party seized the island by surprise. Judging from the fact that Captain Weiser was cashiered for misconduct on this occasion, there was some official displeasure at the German Regiment's performance. Some of its members may have been attached to the garrison of Fort Washington, for one of its officers, 1st Lt. Robert Caldwell, was wounded and captured there on November 16, 1776.[37] The regiment as a whole was present at New Brunswick, New Jersey, on December 1, as part of Lord Stirling's brigade.[38] The Americans were subjected to an artillery bombardment but no contact was made.

The first sustained action in which the German Regiment participated was the Battle of Trenton, on December 26, 1776. In that engagement, it was part of the brigade of Brig. Gen. Roche de Fermoy, fighting alongside the 1st Pennsylvania Regiment.[39] It also served with the 1st Pennsylvania in the delaying action against Lord Cornwallis' attack on January 2, 1777, helping to buy time for Washington to organize his defenses behind Assunpink Creek.[40] During this operation, it had one private wounded.[41] On the following day, still with the 1st Pennsylvania (but with the brigade now under the acting command of Col. Edward Hand), it took part in the Battle of Princeton,[42] during which Colonel Hausegger was captured (or defected).

The German Regiment probably saw some action in the spring of 1777, as one private was reported missing in action after the engagement at Piscataway on May 10 or 11.[43] At some time during those months, it was assigned with Maryland troops to the brigade of Brig. Gen. Prud'-homme de Borre, of Maj. Gen. John Sullivan's division.

In that assignment, it was present at the Battle of Brandywine, on September 11, 1777. De Borre's brigade was on the right flank of the right, or northern, wing of the American army. When Gen. William Howe launched his surprise flank attack against the American right, De Borre panicked and led his men in a precipitate flight,* seriously eroding the strength of the American position and contributing to the defeat which occurred. The German Regiment's only reported loss was 1st Lt. John Weidman, who was captured.[44]

The regiment was also present at the Battle of Germantown, on October 4, still in Sullivan's division.[45] As such, it took part in the frontal attack against the center of the British line. According to one account,[46] it sustained casualties in its Pennsylvania contingent of four privates wounded. However, the regiment's rolls of Pennsylvania members list a sergeant and four privates as having been wounded in this action.[47]

In all probability, the German Regiment was at Whitemarsh, but it was not involved in combat on that occasion. It moved with the rest of the army to Valley Forge,[48] and there, on February 26, 1778, was transferred to the Maryland Line.[49] Consequently, it ceases to be relevant to this study and will not be treated further except to mention that it took part in the Battle of Monmouth, on June 28, 1778; it was one of the elements of Sullivan's expedition against the Indians in the summer and fall of 1779; and by the spring of 1780 was stationed on the frontiers of Northumberland County.[50]

The Regiment of Artillery Artificers

ORGANIZATION

The Regiment (or "Corps") of Artillery Artificers was roughly analogous to a modern depot ordnance organization. It was concerned with the manufacture and repair of weapons (particularly cannon), vehicles, and ammunition.

---

*As a foreign volunteer, he was allowed to resign rather than face a court martial for cowardice.

The unit had its beginnings when Col. Benjamin Flower, who had been Commissary of Military Stores of the Flying Camp, was directed on January 16, 1777, to form an artillery artificer regiment. Colonel Flower commanded the unit from that time until his death, on April 28, 1781.[51] No colonel was appointed to take his place.

The only other field-grade officer of the regiment was its major, Charles Lukens, who was appointed to that position on March 8, 1777, and left the army on August 30, 1780.[52]

The companies and their commanders were as follows:

• [Company A], commanded by Capt. Jesse Roe. This unit was intended to serve as a "field company," providing ordnance direct support to combat units.[53] Captain Roe was commissioned on February 3, 1777, but resigned on January 23, 1778.[54] A comparison of muster rolls shows that the company then came under the command of Capt. Noah Nicholas (or Nichols), of Massachusetts, who was apparently detached (not transferred) from the 2d Continental Artillery, and who resigned on April 3, 1780.[55] There is no record of whether another officer was put in command or the members of the company were distributed among other elements of the regiment.

• [Company B], commanded by Capt. Nathaniel Irish. This was one of two "depot companies," functioning in a fixed location and engaged in manufacture and major repair of weapons and equipment.[56] Captain Irish was commissioned on February 7, 1777. In December, 1780, he was "omitted."[57] Even before that time, as of April, 1780, the men of this company appear to have been added to the company commanded by Capt. Thomas Wylie (see below).[58]

• [Company C], commanded by Capt. David Pancoast. This was a second "depot company."[59] Captain Pancoast, appointed on February 10, 1777, resigned in April, 1778.[60] No conclusive information is available to show who replaced him, although it is likely that this company was the same as the one eventually commanded by Capt. John Jordan (see below).

• [Company D], commanded by Capt. Isaac Coren. Originally, his had been an independent company of artillery, but it was promptly attached to the Regiment of Artillery Artificers[61] as the "laboratory" company,[62] for fabricating ammunition. Coren was cashiered on June 30, 1780.[63] Again, his replacement (if there was one) is not known.

• [Company E], commanded by Capt. Thomas Wylie. This unit was raised as additional company, authorized on February 11, 1778.[64] As noted above, the members of what formerly had been the company of Capt. Nathaniel Irish were eventually added to Wylie's command. Wylie had initially been appointed as a captain-lieutenant (on February 17,

1777). He was promoted to captain on February 1, 1778, and served to the end of the war.[65]

References exist to three other company commanders: John Jordan, Theophilus Parke, and James Gibson. It seems probable that these officers took over company commands vacated by other officers, although the absence of muster rolls makes it impossible to document such an assumption. On the other hand, it seems unlikely that they would have commanded newly-raised companies, as no authority suggests that the Regiment of Artillery Artificers had more than five companies.

In any case, Captain Jordan, who had been commissioned a captain-lieutenant on February 17, 1777, was promoted to captain on May 7, 1778—in the month following Captain Pancoast's resignation. Such information as is available about Jordan's command suggests that, like Pancoast's company, it functioned as a depot company. Jordan remained in the service until January 1, 1783.[66]

Theophilus Parke was appointed first lieutenant on May 7, 1778, and promoted to captain-lieutenant in August, 1779.[67] Although he is listed as a captain,[68] there is no record of his promotion to that grade. Further, there is a record that he was cashiered on March 25, 1780[69]—prior to the time that any of the regiment's captains except Captain Pancoast (who seems to have been replaced by Captain Jordan) had left the service.

Capt. James Gibson is listed with the regiment's captains,[70] but was probably attached rather than assigned to Colonel Flower's command, as his commission was actually in Col. Jedutham Baldwin's regiment of quartermaster artificers.[71]

Information on places of residence is available only for Companies A and D. Of twenty-eight men listed in Company A on February 14, 1780, twenty-four were from Philadelphia, two from Lancaster County, and one each from Berks and Chester counties.[72] As of June 1, 1782, the same company again listed twenty-eight men—twenty-four from Philadelphia, three from Lancaster County, and one from Chester County.[73] As for Company D, on April 2, 1779, it mustered seventy-two men. Of these, thirty-two were from Cumberland County, twenty-one from Philadelphia, thirteen from Northampton County, three from Lancaster County, one each from Bucks and York counties, one from Maryland, and one from New York.[74]

Because the mission of this regiment required the services of skilled craftsmen, it seems likely—despite the thirteen men from Northampton County in Company D—that most of its men would necessarily have been recruited in areas of commercial and industrial activity. Consequently, it is probable that the other companies were also raised in the more economically developed portions of eastern Pennsylvania.

Available information suggests that members of this regiment were not uniformly clothed. Those men who did have uniforms appear to have worn the standard artillery coat—blue or black faced with red.[75]

Summary

This regiment, operating as an agency of the staff rather than as a tactical unit, had an irregular and erratic organization. Consisting largely of technicians, it seems to have drawn its members from the eastern part of the State.

OPERATIONS

Records of the Artillery Artificer Regiment and its component elements are sparse. As of April, 1780, Company E, including what was left of Company B, was stationed at Carlisle, under Capt. Thomas Wylie, performing depot and laboratory duties.[76] With that organization at the same time was part of Company C;[77] the remainder of that company was stationed at Philadelphia, working at the United States Armory or at the "ordnance yard."[78] Also at Philadelphia was a company of the regiment designated as "late Capt. Parkes" (Parke having just been dismissed the service). The specialties of most of its members are given as "Sadler," "Shoemaker," or "Sower," indicating that this unit was performing quartermaster rather than ordnance duties.[79]

By November 1, 1782, considerable change in locale if not in function had taken place. Most of the men of Companies E and C had moved south, with the bulk of them stationed at what apparently was a base depot at New London, Virginia, although some small detachments remained at Philadelphia and others were at Fort Pitt and with the "Southern Army" in South Carolina and Georgia.[80] Judging by the dates on which their captains left the army, these companies would have been mustered out by the end of 1782.

Von Heer's Troop

ORGANIZATION

The army reorganization of May 27, 1778, provided for the establishment of one company, or troop, of provost guards, to be organized and equipped as light dragoons.[81] The functions of this unit were those of military police: it provided local security, conducted searches for deserters, stood ready to suppress any disorders by troops, and during active campaigns it established straggler lines to the rear of the army to halt and turn back men who got lost from their organizations or who were trying to avoid combat. In addition, it had the responsibility of providing hangmen for military executions.

The commander of this troop was Bartholomew von Heer, who resigned his captaincy in the 4th Continental Artillery to accept the new appointment on June 1, 1778. He retained the command for the remainder of the war, and was awarded a brevet promotion to major for his services.[82]

Captain von Heer was a resident of Reading, in Berks County,[83] but was a native of Germany. Indeed, although the troop was raised in Pennsylvania, only one of its three officers and thirteen of its fifty-three enlisted members were Pennsylvanians. One trooper was from New Jersey, one was from Massachusetts, and one was a Mohawk Indian. Except for a lieutenant and a trooper who were Swiss, all the remainder were natives of Germany. The men were recruited from widely scattered sections of the State. Twenty were enlisted in Philadelphia, but fifteen were from Bucks County. There were nine men from Lancaster County and eight from Berks. One man was enlisted in New Jersey.[84]

Originally, Von Heer's Troop was not assigned as part of the Pennsylvania quota,[85] but it was so designated by July 9, 1781. By that time, many of the enlistments were about to expire, and the organization had to be recruited up to strength again during the early part of 1782. The newly enlisted men served for only a few months, as almost all were furloughed during the summer of 1783. Two non-commissioned officers and eight troopers remained on duty until at least October 3, 1783, serving with Washington as couriers, and a few may have continued until November.[86]

There is no record of any uniform or insignia peculiar to this organization. Presumably, its members wore the blue coat faced and lined with white which, after October 2, 1779, was prescribed for all Continental light dragoons.[87]

Summary

This troop was initially raised in widely separated parts of Pennsylvania. In its original configuration, at least, it was made up of men who overwhelmingly were foreign born, all but one of the foreign born being Germans. Seven of them were Hessians by birth, but by the nature of the organization's duties it is extremely unlikely that they would have been deserters from Hessian regiments.

OPERATIONS

Because of its inherent character, a provost troop would not take part in combat operations in the same sense as a conventional cavalry unit.

Indeed, no record of specific activities of Von Heer's Troop has been found, except that on September 16, 1780, it was stationed at Tappan, New York.[88] The nature of its duties would keep it at or near the army's headquarters, and in fact it was attached to (but not made a part of) Washington's Life Guard.[89] It may reasonably be assumed, therefore, that from the time of its activation until it was effectually disbanded, it accompanied General Washington in his movements through New Jersey, New York, and eventually Virginia.

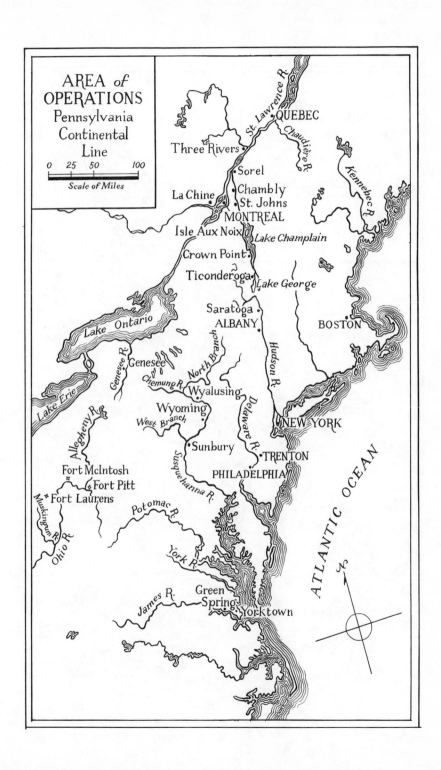

AREA *of*
OPERATIONS
Pennsylvania
Continental
Line

0   25   50   100

Scale of Miles

Three Rivers
Sorel
La Chine
Chambly
St. Johns
MONTREAL
Isle Aux Noix
Crown Point
Ticonderoga
St. Lawrence R.
QUEBEC
Chaudière R.
Kennebec R.
Lake Champlain
Lake George

Saratoga
ALBANY
BOSTON

Lake Ontario
Genesee R.
Genesee
North Branch
Chemung R.
Wyalusing
Hudson R.

Lake Erie
Allegheny R.
Wyoming
West Branch
Delaware R.
NEW YORK

Fort McIntosh
Fort Pitt
Fort Laurens
Muskingum R.
Ohio R.
Sunbury
Susquehanna R.
TRENTON
PHILADELPHIA

Potomac R.

York R.

James R.
Green
Spring
Yorktown

ATLANTIC OCEAN

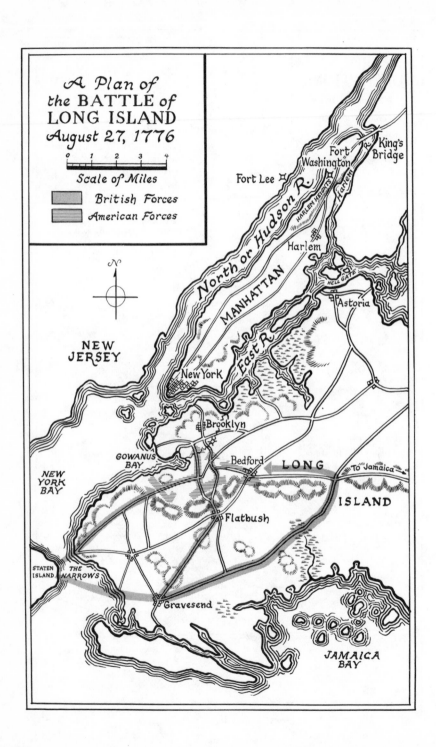

A Plan of
the BATTLE of
LONG ISLAND
August 27, 1776

Scale of Miles
0 1 2 3 4

British Forces
American Forces

N

Fort Lee

Fort Washington

King's Bridge

North or Hudson R.

Harlem

HARLEM HEIGHTS

Harlem

HELL GATE

Astoria

MANHATTAN

East R.

NEW JERSEY

New York

Brooklyn

GOWANUS BAY

Bedford

LONG

To Jamaica

NEW YORK BAY

ISLAND

Flatbush

STATEN ISLAND

THE NARROWS

Gravesend

JAMAICA BAY

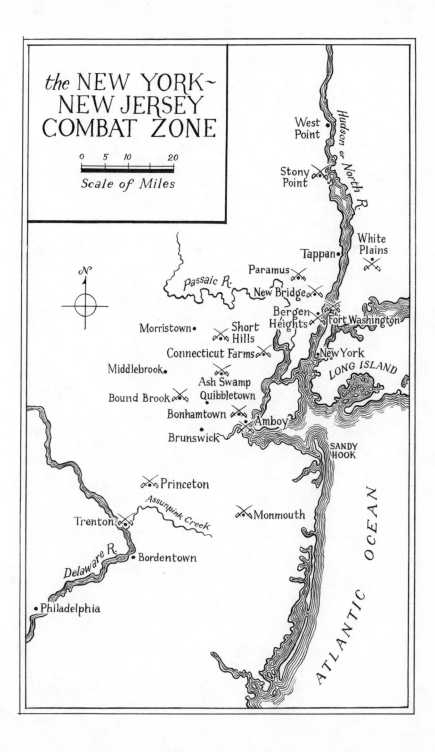

the NEW YORK~
NEW JERSEY
COMBAT ZONE

0   5   10   20
Scale of Miles

N

West
Point

Hudson or North R.

Stony
Point

White
Plains

Tappan

Passaic R.

Paramus

New Bridge

Bergen
Heights

Fort Washington

Morristown

Short
Hills

Connecticut Farms

New York

LONG ISLAND

Middlebrook

Ash Swamp

Bound Brook

Quibbletown

Bonhamtown

Brunswick

Amboy

SANDY
HOOK

Princeton

Assunpink Creek

Monmouth

Trenton

Delaware R.

Bordentown

Philadelphia

ATLANTIC OCEAN

APPENDIX A

Regional Origins Of Organizations

ALLOWING for the various mergers, redesignations, and permutations which took place, and making every effort to avoid counting any unit twice, the total number of Pennsylvania Continental infantry companies (of battalions and regiments treated in this book) which has been arrived at is 155, based on the following reasoning:

	Total
Thompson's Rifle Battalion, organized with 9 companies, lost 2 at Quebec; when the organization became the 1st Pennsylvania Regiment, therefore, it had to form 2 new companies, for a total of	11
The 2d, 4th, and 6th Battalions originally had 8 companies each; after these battalions became the 3d, 5th, and 7th Regiments, each added a ninth company, for a total of	27
The 3d and 5th Battalions had 8 companies each, for a total of	16
The 4th and 6th Regiments, although theoretically based on the 3d and 5th Battalions, were in essence formed from newly recruited men (the men of the battalions having been captured at Fort Washington), and therefore are considered as complete additions, thus representing a total in new companies of	18
The 8th through the 10th Regiments each had 9 companies, for a total of	27
The "Old" 11th and the 12th Regiments had 8 companies each, and Hartley's Regiment probably had only 8, for a total of	24
Patton's Regiment appears to have been understrength, with a total of	7
The German Regiment had 5 of its 9 companies raised in Pennsylvania, for a total of	5
Miles's State Rifle Regiment had a total of	12
Atlee's State Musketry Battalion had a total of	8
Total	155

The "New" 11th Regiment and the 13th Regiment, representing consolidations of existing regiments, have not been counted.

With varying degrees of certainty, the regional origins of 132 of these companies have been identified, plus two additional companies which came primarily from one of two specific counties, although which of the two cannot be established.

As might be expected, the largest number of companies came from Philadelphia City and County (thirty, plus possibly one of the two companies whose exact origin is unclear). Chester County (then including Delaware County) furnished the next largest number (eighteen, plus both of the two uncertain companies). Lancaster County furnished fourteen (three of which came from modern Dauphin County), plus the second of the uncertain companies. Cumberland County also supplied fourteen companies (one of them from what is now Franklin County). Berks County furnished eleven companies; Northumberland, Westmoreland, and York counties each furnished nine companies; Northampton County furnished eight; and Bedford and Bucks counties each supplied five.

Considering Philadelphia City and County, Chester County, Lancaster County (less Dauphin), Berks County, and Bucks County to be in the "eastern" region of the State; Cumberland, York, and modern Dauphin to be in the "central" region; and Northumberland, Northampton, Bedford, and Westmoreland counties to be in the "frontier" region, the following distribution emerges:

Region	Companies
Eastern	77 (including the two whose exact county origin is uncertain)
Central	26
Frontier	31

In view of the distribution of population in the State, the representation from the "frontier" region is particularly noteworthy, and becomes even more so in view of the existence, at least in the Northumberland-Northampton-Westmoreland portions of the frontier, of a persistent threat of Indian attack. It should be emphasized, however, that impressive as it is, the figure for the "frontier" region represents only about one-fourth of the total of Pennsylvania companies whose regional origins have been identified. Further, of the twenty-one companies for which no regional identity has been found, the bulk were in regiments primarily from the central and eastern regions.

A detailed breakdown of the origins of the Pennsylvania units, by county, showing the battalion and/or regiment to which they belonged and the letter designation assigned to them in this book, follows below (references indicated by footnotes are located at the end of the tabulation).

	Assigned To	Companies	
BEDFORD COUNTY	Thompson's Rifle Battalion/		
	1st Pennsylvania Regiment	1	(A)
	3d Pennsylvania Regiment	1	(H)
	4th Pennsylvania Regiment	1	
	8th Pennsylvania Regiment	1[1]	(E)
	Miles's State Rifle Regiment[2]	1	(C)
	Total infantry companies	5	
BERKS COUNTY	Thompson's Rifle Battalion/1st		
	Pennsylvania Regiment	1	(G)
	1st Pennsylvania Battalion	1[1]	(B)

Assigned To	Companies	
1st Pennsylvania Battalion/2d		
Pennsylvania Regiment	1[1]	(C)
2d Pennsylvania Battalion	1[1]	(F)
3d Pennsylvania Regiment	1	(C)
4th Pennsylvania Regiment	1[1]	(A)
5th Pennsylvania Battalion[3]	2	(E, G)
"Old" 11th Pennsylvania Regiment[4]	1[1]	(E)
12th Pennsylvania Regiment[5]	1[1]	(A)
Miles's State Rifle Regiment[2]	1	(H)
Total infantry companies	11	

Berks County also furnished substantial numbers of Von Heer's Troop of Light Dragoons (Provost Guards).

BUCKS COUNTY	1st Pennsylvania Battalion	1[1]	(G)
	4th Pennsylvania Battalion/5th		
	Pennsylvania Regiment	1	(C)
	5th Pennsylvania Battalion[3]	1	(A)
	Miles's State Rifle Regiment[2]	1	(M)
	Atlee's State Musketry Battalion[2]	1	(C)
	Total infantry companies	5	
CHESTER COUNTY	4th Pennsylvania Battalion/5th		
	Pennsylvania Regiment	6	(A, B, D, E, F, G)
	5th Pennsylvania Battalion[3]	½[6]	(H)
	6th Pennsylvania Regiment	3[1]	(A, B, C)
	9th Pennsylvania Regiment	4	(E, F,[1] G,[1] I[1])
	9th Pennsylvania Regiment	½[6]	(H)
	"Old" 11th Pennsylvania Regiment[4]	1[1]	(A)
	"Old" 11th Pennsylvania Regiment[4]	[1[1]	(F)[7]]
	Hartley's Regiment[8]	1[1]	(F)
	Hartley's Regiment[8]	[1[1]	(G)[9]]/
	Atlee's State Musketry Battalion[2]	1	(A)
	Pennsylvania State Regiment[2]	1	(L)
	Total infantry companies	18 certain, plus 2 possible	
CUMBERLAND COUNTY	Thompson's Rifle Battalion	1[10]	(D)
(less modern	6th Pennsylvania Battalion/7th		
Franklin County)	Pennsylvania Regiment	6	(A, B, C, D, E, F)
	9th Pennsylvania Regiment	1[1]	(C)
	12th Pennsylvania Regiment[5]	1[1]	(F)
	Hartley's Regiment[8]	1[1]	(A)
	Calderwood's Independent Company	1	
	Steele's Independent Company[8]	1[1]	
	Miles's State Rifle Regiment[2]	1	(G)
	Total infantry companies	13	

Cumberland County also furnished a major proportion of at least one company of the Regiment of Artillery Artificers.

DAUPHIN COUNTY	Thompson's Rifle Battalion	1[10]	(I)
(then part of	Miles's State Rifle Regiment[2]	2	(E, F)
Lancaster County)	Total infantry companies	3	
FRANKLIN COUNTY	Thompson's Rifle Battalion/1st		
(then part of	Pennsylvania Regiment	1	(A)
Cumberland County)	Total infantry companies	1	

	Assigned To	Companies
LANCASTER COUNTY	Thompson's Rifle Battalion/1st Pennsylvania Regiment	1 (H)
(less modern	4th Pennsylvania Battalion/5th Pennsylvania Regiment	1[1] (H)
Dauphin County)	6th Pennsylvania Regiment	1 (D)
	10th Pennsylvania Regiment	3 (E,[1] H,[1] I)
	"Old" 11th Pennsylvania Regiment[4]	1[1] (G)
	Hartley's Regiment[8]	[1[1] (G)[9]]
	Patton's Regiment[8]	1[1] (C)
	Miles's State Rifle Regiment[2]	1 (K)
	Atlee's State Musketry Battalion[2]	2 (E, F)
	Total infantry companies	11 certain, plus 1 possible

Lancaster County also furnished substantial numbers of Von Heer's Troop of Light Dragoons (Provost Guards).

	Assigned To	Companies
NORTHAMPTON COUNTY	Thompson's Rifle Battalion/1st Pennsylvania Regiment	1 (F)
	2d Pennsylvania Regiment	1[1] (I)
	2d Pennsylvania Battalion	2 (A, C)
	4th Pennsylvania Regiment	1[1] (D)
	6th Pennsylvania Regiment	1[1] (H)
	12th Pennsylvania Regiment[5]	1[1] (G)
	Miles's State Rifle Regiment[2]	1 (A)
	Total infantry companies	8

	Assigned To	Companies
NORTHUMBERLAND COUNTY	Thompson's Rifle Battalion/1st Pennsylvania Regiment	1 (E)
	4th Pennsylvania Regiment	2[1] (B, G)
	10th Pennsylvania Regiment	1[1] (D)
	12th Pennsylvania Regiment[5]	4 (B, C, D, E)
	Miles's State Rifle Regiment[2]	1 (B)
	Total infantry companies	9

	Assigned To	Companies
PHILADELPHIA CITY AND COUNTY	1st Pennsylvania Battalion/2d Pennsylvania Regiment	4[1] (A, D, E, F)
	1st Pennsylvania Battalion	1[1] (H)
	2d Pennsylvania Regiment	1[1] (B)
	2d Pennsylvania Battalion/3d Pennsylvania Regiment	1[1] (D)
	5th Pennsylvania Battalion[3]	4 (B, C, D, F)
	5th Pennsylvania Battalion[3]	½[6] (H)
	6th Pennsylvania Regiment	1[1] (I)
	9th Pennsylvania Regiment	2[1] (B, D)
	9th Pennsylvania Regiment	½[6] (H)
	10th Pennsylvania Regiment	1 (F)
	"Old" 11th Pennsylvania Regiment[4]	1 (D)
	"Old" 11th Pennsylvania Regiment[4]	[1[1] (F)[7]]
	Miles's State Rifle Regiment[2]	1 (L)
	Atlee's State Musketry Battalion[2]	4[1] (B, D, G, H)
	Doyle's Independent Company[11]	1
	The German Regiment	5
	Total infantry companies	30 certain, plus 1 possible

Philadelphia City and County also provided most of the members of the ultimately nine companies of the 4th Continental Artillery, the six troops of the 4th Continental Light Dragoons, the largest single contingent of Von Heer's Troop of Light Dragoons (Provost Guards), and the bulk of at least one company of the Regiment of Artillery Artificers.

	Assigned To	Companies	
WESTMORELAND COUNTY	2d Pennsylvania Battalion	1	(B)
	Miles's State Rifle Regiment[2]	1	(I)
	8th Pennsylvania Regiment	7	
	Total infantry companies	9	
YORK COUNTY	Thompson's Rifle Battalion/1st Pennsylvania Regiment	1	(C)
	4th Pennsylvania Regiment	1[1]	(F)
	6th Pennsylvania Regiment	1[1]	(E)
	6th Pennsylvania Battalion/7th Pennsylvania Regiment	2	(G, H)
	10th Pennsylvania Regiment	1[1]	(G)
	Hartley's Regiment[8]	2[1]	(B, E)
	Miles's State Rifle Regiment[2]	1	(D)
	Total infantry companies	9	

NOTES

[1]Based on known or probable pre-war residence of the original company commander.

[2]Consolidated into the Pennsylvania State Regiment, which was redesignated as the 13th Pennsylvania Regiment, and then (on July 1, 1778) absorbed by the 2d Pennsylvania Regiment.

[3]Captured at Fort Washington, New York, November 16, 1776.

[4]Absorbed by the 10th Pennsylvania Regiment on July 1, 1778.

[5]Absorbed by the 3d Pennsylvania Regiment on July 1, 1778.

[6]This company was raised jointly in Chester County and Philadelphia.

[7]This company may have been from either Chester County or Philadelphia.

[8]Consolidated into the "New" 11th Pennsylvania, January 13, 1779.

[9]This company may have been from either Chester County or Lancaster County.

[10]Largely wiped out at Quebec, December 31, 1775.

[11]Split up in November, 1776, and distributed between the 8th and "Old" 11th Pennsylvania Regiments.

APPENDIX B

The Individual Soldier

Introduction

ACCORDING to a carefully qualified estimate,[1] Pennsylvania is
said to have provided 25,678 members of the Continental Army.
This figure, however, explicitly relates to the number of appointments
and enlistments, not to the number of men who served, since it would
include as two men a soldier who completed an enlistment in a twelve-
month battalion and then re-enlisted in a three-year regiment. Using
the same source's rule of thumb correction factor, this would mean that
the Pennsylvania contingent of the Continental Army consisted of
some seventeen thousand officers and men.

In theory, the ratio of officers to enlisted men was one officer to
seventeen enlisted men according to the 1776 battalion structure, and
one officer to fifteen enlisted men according to the 1778 regiment.[2] Actually, as the strength in officers was usually complete, or approximately so, whereas all units were, for most of the war, substantially understrength in enlisted men, a ratio of one officer to ten enlisted
men is probably much closer to the reality.

If that ratio is accepted, the number of individual enlisted men
supplied by Pennsylvania to the Continental Army would have been
somewhere between fifteen and sixteen thousand. Allowing for the fact
that Pennsylvanians served in several Continental organizations not assigned to the Pennsylvania quota (see Chapter XX), the total figure for
the number of enlisted men serving in Pennsylvania *units* would
appear to be about fifteen thousand.

Against the background of even that reduced total, the information
concerning the individual Continental soldiers from Pennsylvania is
extremely sparse. For what it is worth, however, such information as is
available will be presented in this appendix. In the absence of a larger
sampling, it is impossible to say how representative of the Pennsylvania Line as a whole the following figures may be. However, it is
worth noting that to the extent that corresponding data have been
found for more than one regiment, they tend to be consistent from regiment to regiment.

The four categories in which information is available, and which
will be discussed in turn, are age at time of enlistment, place of birth,
height, and pre-war occupation.

AGE AT TIME OF ENLISTMENT

Available records show the ages at time of enlistment for 1,068 members of the organizations which made up the Pennsylvania Continental Line. In varying degrees, such information has been found for all Pennsylvania Continental units except for the 3d and 5th Pennsylvania battalions and Patton's Regiment. In the case of nine of the battalions or regiments, the total for each amounts to ten men or less. On the other hand, data are available for fairly substantial proportions of thirteen battalions or regiments as well as for Von Heer's Troop. Further, for the 6th Pennsylvania Battalion and the 1st, 2d, 3d, and "New" 11th Pennsylvania regiments, the totals range from 92 to 215 names per organization. It seems justifiable to conclude, therefore, that the age distribution indicated by these figures is reasonably representative of what actually prevailed throughout the Pennsylvania Line.

These records reveal that four boys as young as ten and one man as old as seventy-three enlisted in the Pennsylvania Line. Indeed, there were thirty-six soldiers listed who were between the ages of ten and fourteen (inclusive) when they joined the Army. While a number of these would have served as fifers or drummers, the bulk are listed as ordinary private soldiers. At the other extreme, seven of the fourteen men enlisting at age fifty-four or older (and all but one of the men aged fifty-seven or older) entered the Army in 1780,[3] probably reflecting a lowering of standards due to increasing shortages of available recruits.

Certainly, by eighteenth-century criteria, men were considered mature at an earlier age than today, and life expectancy was substantially less. Also, following the British Army practice, drummers' and fifers' positions tended (as noted above) to be reserved for boys. Thus, the presence in the Continental Army of young boys is probably less remarkable than that of men in their sixties and seventies. At the same time, if the terms of reference laid down by the Pennsylvania Militia Act of 1777 can be used as a guide, eighteenth-century concepts of what constituted the normal age brackets of military service (eighteen to fifty-three, inclusive) were not markedly different—especially at the younger levels—from those of the present time. Yet, no less than 122 Pennsylvania Continental soldiers (over eleven per cent of the known total) are shown as having joined at ages seventeen or under, and ten (about one per cent of the total) at age fifty-four or older. It is worth noting that there were almost one and a half as many enlistees in the ten- to seventeen-year age group (covering eight years) as in the thirty-eight- to fifty-three-year age group (covering sixteen years).

For understandable reasons, it was a young man's army. The average of the known enlistment ages of Pennsylvania Continental soldiers is twenty-five years and five months. There was, moreover, a marked modal preponderance in the younger age brackets. Men aged from eighteen to thirty-two account for 774 (over seventy-two per cent) of the 1,068 enlistees whose ages are known. Of these, 586 (nearly fifty-five per cent of the total) were in their twenties. These would have been the men who not only were physically equal to the rigors of field service but also were less likely to have commitments to families and to established occupations.

The following table lists, by total and by organization, the known figures for enlistment ages of soldiers of the Pennsylvania Line:

Age	Pa. Infantry Battalions						Pa. Infantry Regiments										Old New 11th			Miles's	Hartley's	German	4th Artillery	4th Dragoons	Artificers	Von Heer's Troop	Total
	Thompson's	1st	2d	4th	6th	Atlee's	1st	2d	3d	4th	5th	6th	7th	8th	9th	10th	11th	12th	13th								
10								1	1											1						2	4
11								3	1																		3
12							1	2	5		3			1													10
13							1		1	1	3			2			1										7
14							2	1	4		1						3										12
15							2	3	8	2	4	1		2	1		1									1	14
16					1		3	5	1	1				3		3	3					3	1	1			29
17					9		5	7	4		7	1	1		1	3	1					1		1			43
18					6		4	6	2	2	6	1		2		1	4					1	3	1			41
19					14		11	9	6	2	5	4	2		2	5	11		3			3		1		1	65
20					18		5	6	5	1	8	6		3	6	2	8		2			3	1	2			72
21					7		9	9	5	3		1	1	4	2	2	6					3	1	2		2	92
22					10		15	6	6	3		5		2			19			1			1		1	1	68
23					5		2	10	4	3	3	4	2	2	5	1	16		1			1			1		63
24	1			1	8		7	5	8	4	2	1	1		2	2	13		1			3	2	2		2	71
25					5	1	3	6	4	4	1	3		2		2	8				1	3	2	1		1	58
26					1		7	7	1	3	1	2		3	2		18	1				2		2			55
27					2		3	2	1	2	1		3		4	3	16			1		1					44
28			1	2			4	3	2	6	1	1		2	1		6	1	1			1		1		1	33
29			1		1		1	6	3	4			1	2	4		6					1					30
30		1			1		3	4	4	6			2	2		2	5										35
31			1					7	4	7					2	1	5					1					22
32								1		3			2	1			11	1									25
33					2		1	3		6	3	3		1	1		4					1	1				25
34							3		1	1	1	2	2	1	1		6										19
35					1			1	1			3		1			3		1								14
36					1		2	2		2		3					3		1			1					11

	37	38	39	40	41	42	43	44	45	46	47	48	49	50	51	52	53	54	55	56	57	58	59	60	61	62	63	64	65	66	67	68	69	70	71	72	73	TOTAL
	9	7	1	1	8	4	7	5	3	5	4	6	1	5	2		1	4		1	2	1		1	1			1									1	1,068
	1																																					12
				1																																		3
	1																																					14
																																						13
																																						29
																																						1
																																						3
				1																																		13
																																						3
	1	2	1	7	1	4		1	4	1		1	2	1		1	3		1	1																		215
																																						10
	1		1													1																						37
		2	2					1																														41
	1							1																														38
																																						19
			1													1																						48
	1	1			1			1	1																													55
		2	1		1			1		2																												75
	2	1	3	1					1	1																												92
	1	2	1	4	1	2	3	1		1	1		1				1	1		1		1		1				1										139
		1	1	2	1		1			1																												104
																																						1
		1																																				94
																																						4
																																						3
																																						1
																																						1

Place of Birth

Generally speaking, the soldiers of the Pennsylvania Line appear to have been predominantly of British extraction, although with a considerable admixture of men of German background. However, a small number of notable exceptions are matters of record.

Two men are explicitly identified in the muster rolls as Indians. These are Shawnee John, called "a Shawanese Indian," who served originally in Captain Lowdon's Northumberland County company of Thompson's Rifle Battalion[4] and later in the 6th Pennsylvania Regiment;[5] and Isaac Woolsy, of Von Heer's Troop, who is listed as "Mohac" and "Mohack" under the heading, "Provinces."[6]

The muster rolls of the Pennsylvania Continental organizations show two other soldiers as Negroes. These are Drummer Polydore Redman, who served in the 5th Pennsylvania Battalion[7] (but is not on the rolls of the members of that unit—almost the entire command—who were captured at Fort Washington, New York); and Private Stacey Williams, of Humphrey's Company of the 6th Pennsylvania Regiment, who was wounded at the Battle of Brandywine and who lived after the war in Philadelphia until his death at age seventy-six in 1820.[8] Still a third Negro who served in the Pennsylvania Line was Edward Hector, a driver in Courteney's Company of the 4th Continental Artillery. The muster roll which lists his name does not show him as a Negro,[9] which suggests that very possibly there were other black soldiers, unidentified as such, fighting in Pennsylvania regiments; however, the obituary notice of his death on January 3, 1834, at Norristown, at "about 90 years of age," describes him as "a colored man."[10] Finally, a pension application from John Francis identifies him as a Negro: he had served in Epple's Company of the 3d Pennsylvania Regiment until both his legs were "much shattered" by grapeshot at the Battle of Brandywine on September 11, 1777.[11]

A strength return of Negroes in the Continental Army, dated August 24, 1778,[12] shows 755 Negroes in fourteen infantry brigades. Of the Pennsylvania brigades, Anthony Wayne's (consisting at that time of the 1st, 2d, 7th, and 10th Pennsylvania regiments with a combined enlisted strength of 1,363) had only two Negroes; the 2d Pennsylvania Brigade (made up of the 3d, 5th, 6th, and 9th Pennsylvania regiments, with a total of 1,117 enlisted men)[13] had thirty-five Negro soldiers. Omitted from this return are any Negroes who might have been members of the 4th and 8th Pennsylvania regiments, Hartley's Regiment, and Patton's Regiment. Also, the thirty-seven Negro soldiers in the two Pennsylvania brigades reported on August 24, 1778, would not have included Edward Hector who as an artilleryman would not have been assigned to an infantry brigade, and John Francis, who had been incapacitated for service almost a year prior to the date of this return.

By inference, at least, it seems that non-Caucasians were rare among the Pennsylvania Continental forces (and they were expressly excluded from the militia), in any case during the earlier part of the Revolution. Pennsylvania's population on the eve of the Revolution has been estimated at 300,000 whites and 2,000 blacks, which itself indicates that black participation, even on a strictly proportional basis, would predictably be quite small in absolute numerical terms. An indication of the rarity of black soldiers in Pennsylvania units is found in a letter from Capt. Persifor Frazer, of the 4th Pennsylvania Battalion, who wrote to his wife on July 25, 1776, from Ticonderoga, expressing astonishment at the composition of some of the New England units of the garrison. "Among them," he said, "there is the strangest mixture of Negroes, Indians, and Whites, with old men and mere children, which together with a nasty, lousy appearance make a most shocking spectacle."[14]

Limited representation of other groups was also found in the Pennsylvania ranks. Private John Otney, a 1778 recruit in the 13th Pennsylvania Regiment, was born in France.[15] Private Nicholas McCoy, of Andrew Walker's Company of the "New" 11th Pennsylvania Regiment, was born in Newfoundland[16]—possibly while his parents were en route to Pennsylvania, presumably, in view of his name, from Ireland. Similar circumstances may explain the birth "at sea" of Private John Hamilton, who in 1778 enlisted (aged fifteen) in Capt. John Davis' Company of the 9th Pennsylvania Regiment.[17] Anthony Spinkhouse, listed on June 6, 1781, as a deserter from the 4th Pennsylvania Regiment and described as aged twenty-eight, a tailor, and having "a great turn for dealing," was born in Spain.* Private Casper Hauser of Von Heer's Troop was born in Switzerland.[18]

The striking feature about the 582 soldiers for whom places of birth are given is that only 195 of them (barely over one-third) were native-born Americans. Of these, 135 were born in Pennsylvania. The remainder either gave other colonies as their birthplaces or (in sixteen cases) did not specify the location.

The remaining two-thirds (387) of the troops with identified birthplaces were foreign born. No less than 217 (over fifty-six per cent of the foreign born and over thirty-seven per cent of the known total) were born in Ireland. In other words, so far as available records in-

*PA(5), II, 1071. Spinkhouse certainly is not a recognizably Spanish name, although Otney (see above) could be an anglicized version of a French name. It is possible that either or both names had been changed, or that the place of birth was an accident of travel rather than a reflection of nationality.

dicate, the Irish-born alone outnumbered the troops in the Pennsylvania Line who were identified as native born. The next largest foreign-born contingent consisted of men from various provinces of what is now Germany, totalling eighty-seven (just under fifteen per cent of the total). Following them were the English born, of whom there were sixty-four (not quite eleven per cent of the total). There were also twelve Scots and two Welshmen.

In drawing any conclusions from these figures, three caveats should be observed.

One is that a fairly significant number of the foreign-born soldiers also fell among the younger age groups. It is likely, therefore, that they had spent most of their lives in America and, while European by background, were American by conditioning.

A second qualification stems from the very small size of the sampling which is available. By itself, a total of 582 out of an estimated enrollment of fifteen thousand is manifestly inadequate as a basis for firm conclusions. It is quite possible that in many instances, listing places of birth may have been considered pertinent only for men who were not native Americans, so that the mere absence of any notation of birthplace may indicate that a soldier was American born. On the other hand, the one consideration which suggests a degree of validity to a broad application of these figures to the Pennsylvania Line as a whole is the fact that the general pattern recurs fairly consistently in each organization for which more than minimal data are provided.

Finally, the ratio of native to foreign born in the Pennsylvania population at large at the time of the Revolution is not known. Quite possibly, therefore, the composition of the Pennsylvania Line, in terms of national origin, may have been a reasonably accurate reflection of the national origins of the people of the Commonwealth as a whole.

The following table shows place of birth, by regiment, of the members of the Pennsylvania Line, as listed in the published *Pennsylvania Archives:*

PLACE OF BIRTH	2d Pa. Bn.	6th Pa. Bn.	1st Pa. Rgt.	2d Pa. Rgt.	4th Pa. Rgt.	6th Pa. Rgt.	9th Pa. Rgt.	"New" 11th Pa. Rgt.	13th Pa. Rgt.	4th Artillery	4th Dragoons	Von Heer's Troop	TOTAL
America													195
Unspecified				8				8					(16)
Delaware				1						1			(2)
Georgia										1			(1)
Maryland								9		4		1	(14)
Massachusetts							1						(1)
New England							1						(1)
New Jersey				1			1			12		1	(15)
New York										2			(2)
North Carolina								1					(1)
Pennsylvania													(135)
Unspecified				3	5		3	21		46		13	(91)
Berks Co.				1									(1)
Bucks Co.							3			1			(4)
Chester Co.				2			1	1		1			(5)
Cumberland Co.		1						1					(2)
Lancaster Co.				5				5					(10)
Northampton Co.				1									(1)
Northumberland Co.				2									(2)
Philadelphia City & Co.				2			1	3		10			(16)
York Co.				1				2					(3)
Virginia							1			6			(7)
England	1			6	2	3	1	41	1	9			64
France						1							1
Germany				15	1			9	2	23	1	36	87
Ireland		21	1	15	14		9	90	4	60			217
Newfoundland							1						1
Scotland				2	1			6		3			12
At Sea										1			1
Spain												1	1
Switzerland							1						1
Wales								1		1			2
TOTALS	1	22	1	65	23	4	26	198	7	182	1	52	582

HEIGHT

Statistics on individual height are recorded for only 275 Pennsylvania Continental soldiers. They show that these troops ranged from four feet, three and one-half inches for a ten-year-old fifer to six feet, two inches for one soldier. The average is five feet, five and three-fourths inches, almost identical with the mode, which is five feet, six inches.

Considering the fact that eighteenth-century Americans tended to be considerably shorter than their present-day counterparts, the average height of the Pennsylvania Continental may seem surprising, as the average American draftee of World War I was also five feet, six inches tall, although the average for American draftees of World War II was two inches greater. On the other hand, to the extent that the available figures can be considered applicable across the board, the average for the Continental soldier could be misleading, for the *median* height of the Pennsylvania troops was just under five feet, four inches. The over-all impression given by a body of typical Pennsylvania soldiers, therefore, would be of men noticeably shorter than a comparable group of modern American soldiers, accentuated by a comparatively small number of men standing much taller than the bulk of their fellows.

There seems to be little positive correlation between height and either age or place of birth. While the individuals at the lower end of the scale tended to include a considerable number of the younger soldiers, they did not account for all of them, and among the shorter soldiers were substantial numbers of older men. Also, both American-born and foreign-born soldiers are found throughout the entire range of recorded heights.

The available data on this characteristic of the Pennsylvania Continental enlisted men are tabulated below:

Height	Number	Height	Number
4′ 3½″	1	5′ 5 ″	27 ·
4′ 4 ″	1	5′ 5½″	4
4′ 7 ″	1	5′ 6 ″	43
4′ 9 ″	1	5′ 6½″	9
4′ 10 ″	1	5′ 7 ″	29
4′ 11″	1	5′ 7½″	5
5′	3	5′ 8 ″	34
5′ 1 ″	4	5′ 8½″	2
5′ 1½″	1	5′ 9 ″	14
5′ 2 ″	14	5′ 9½″	3
5′ 2½″	2	5′ 10 ″	12
5′ 3 ″	20	5′ 11″	8
5′ 3½″	3	6′	2
5′ 4 ″	27	6′ 2 ″	1
5′ 4½″	2	Total	275

Prewar Occupations

For 273 enlisted men of the Pennsylvania Line, representing nine different organizations, records exist showing prewar occupations. These men had been employed in fifty-one different activities.

As might be expected, the most common calling was that of farmer, listed for ninety-two (33.7 per cent) of the men. The next most frequently listed occupation was shoemaker, with twenty-three, followed closely by weaver (nineteen), tailor (eighteen), blacksmith (twelve), and carpenter (also twelve). (Two other men styled themselves as cabinetmakers, and a third man as a chairmaker.) Only seven were classed merely as laborers. The remaining forty-two trades were represented by anything from one to nine men each. Despite the fact that farming was the greatest *single* occupation, it is worth noting that almost sixty-four per cent of these soldiers claimed to be tradesmen or craftsmen of one sort or another.

Grouping the various related activities into broad categories, 107 of the men (39.2 per cent) had been employed in food production and processing, seventy-two (36.4 per cent) in one or another aspect of clothing manufacture, thirty (10.9 per cent) in woodworking and construction, twenty-one (7.7 per cent) in metal work, twelve (4.4 per cent) in transportation, and seven (2.6 per cent) in providing personal services. The rest of the occupations were so disparate that they can only be grouped as "miscellaneous."

Overwhelmingly, these were men who worked with their hands—the sole exceptions being one clerk and one schoolmaster—but they included members of skilled crafts, among them being a watchmaker, a clockmaker, and a silversmith. While many of the trades were those required in any community, a number reflected life-styles in which luxuries played a normal part. Apart from those already mentioned, these included a vintner, a coachman, a silk dyer, a staymaker, and a bookbinder.

Although the unit representation is limited, the numbers of men in each occupation in the following table is shown by organization, as the types of tradesmen in a given regiment or battalion may suggest some clues as to its regional background.

OCCUPATION	4th Pa. Bn.	6th Pa. Bn.	2d Pa. Rgt.	4th Pa. Rgt.	6th Pa. Rgt.	9th Pa. Rgt.	"New" 11th Pa. Rgt.	German Rgt.	Hartley's Rgt.	TOTAL
Baker			1				1			2
Barber							6			6
Blacksmith	1		2				8	1		12
Bookbinder							1			1
Brass box fitter		1								1
Brass founder										
Brickworker/Mason			1	1		1	6			9
Brushmaker							1			1
Butcher						1	1			2
Cabinetmaker							2			2
Carpenter			1				11			12
Chairmaker			1							1
Chandler							1			1
Clerk							1			1
Clock/Watchmaker		1				1				2
Coachman		1								1
Cooper		1	1				5			7
Currier		1								1
Cutler		1								1
Distiller			1				1			2
Farmer			24			12	56			92
Forgeman						1	1			2
Glazier							1			1
Hatter							6			6
Hosier/Stocking Weaver			1				2			3
Laborer							7			7
Mariner							1			1
Miller						1	3			4
Millwright							1			1
Pinmaker							1			1

Occupation										Total
Plasterer							1			1
Potter								1		1
Ropemaker							1			1
Saddlemaker		5								5
Schoolmaster	1									1
Shoemaker		2		5		3	13			23
Silkdyer							1			1
Silversmith							1			1
Soapboiler							1			1
Staymaker							1			1
Stonecutter			1							1
Tailor		1		5		3	9			18
Tanner							2			2
Tinker							2			2
Tobacconist						2	1			3
Turner		1				1	1			3
Vintner		1								1
Wagonmaker							1			1
Waiter			2		1					3
Weaver			2	2		2	12		1	19
Wheelwright							3			3
TOTAL	2	12	40	12	1	27	177	1	1	273

SUMMARY

It is important to repeat that the figures given in this appendix are grossly incomplete as a reflection of the estimated fifteen thousand enlisted men who served at one time or another in the Pennsylvania units of the Continental Army during the Revolutionary War. Nevertheless, they constitute the only specific data which are available. Furthermore, despite their inadequacy, they do at least suggest some insights.

To the extent that they can be relied upon, they tell us that the typical Pennsylvania soldier was a young man, about halfway between his twenty-fifth and twenty-sixth birthdays when he joined the Army. He was more likely than not to have been born outside America, most probably in Ireland; and (if names on the muster rolls are a valid indication), he was slightly more prone to be a Scotch-Irish Protestant than a Catholic from the southern counties. In the words of some of the muster rolls of recruits, in many cases "he had the brogue on his tongue." If he was German instead of Irish, he often spoke with an accent, and sometimes did not speak English at all—a situation which, except perhaps in the German Regiment, must have been a cause of consternation to his sergeant. He stood about five feet, six inches. He was frequently a farmer, but more probably had been engaged in a skilled or semi-skilled trade before becoming a soldier.

We do not know how likely he was to be married (although logic would indicate that he had not yet taken on the responsibilities of a wife and family), or how much schooling he had been given — or, indeed, to what extent he was literate at all.

We do know, however, that although the desertion rate was appalling, our typical soldier of the Pennsylvania Continental Line was, by and large, long-suffering, enduring, and steadfast in his devotion to the cause which he had embraced.

Battles and Engagements

THE following table lists the actions involving units of the Pennsylvania Line, together with the Pennsylvania organizations which are known or believed to have taken part in them:

Engagement	Participating Units
July 29, 1775, Charlestown Neck, Mass.	Doudle's Company (C), Thompson's Rifle Battalion
August 27, 1775, Ploughed Hill, Mass.	Thompson's Rifle Battalion
November 9, 1775, Lechmere's Point, Mass.	Thompson's Rifle Battalion (less Hendricks' and Smith's companies—D and I)
December 31, 1775, Quebec, Canada	Hendricks' and Smith's companies (D and I), Thompson's Rifle Battalion
May 27, 1776, La Chine, Canada	Harmar's and Lamar's companies (D and H), 1st Pennsylvania Battalion
June 9, 1776, Three Rivers, Canada	Jones's and Jenkins' companies (B and F), 1st Pennsylvania Battalion 2d Pennsylvania Battalion Robinson's, Lacey's, and Church's companies (B, C, and E), 4th Pennsylvania Battalion 6th Pennsylvania Battalion
August 27, 1776, Battle of Long Island, N. Y.	1st Pennsylvania Regiment Miles's State Rifle Regiment Atlee's State Musketry Battalion
August 29-30, Covering Force, Retreat from Long Island	1st Pennsylvania Regiment 3d Pennsylvania Battalion 5th Pennsylvania Battalion
Montresor's (Randall's) Island, N.Y.*	Detachment, German Regiment
Lake Champlain, October 11-13, 1776	Elements, 2d Pennsylvania Battalion 4th Pennsylvania Battalion 6th Pennsylvania Battalion
Throgg's Neck, N. Y., October 12, 1776	Detachment, 1st Pennsylvania Regiment
Battle of White Plains, N. Y., October 28, 1776	1st Pennsylvania Regiment Miles's Regiment/Atlee's Battalion (consolidated)
Fort Washington, N. Y., November 16, 1776	Detachment, 1st Pennsylvania Regiment 3d Pennsylvania Battalion 5th Pennsylvania Battalion Detachment, Miles's Regiment/Atlee's Battalion (consolidated) Detachment, German Regiment Detachment, Procter's Artillery Battalion

*Actions occurred here on September 10 and again on September 23, 1776. It is not clear which of these two engagements involved the Pennsylvania troops in question.

New Brunswick, N. J., December 1, 1776	1st Pennsylvania Regiment Miles's Regiment/Atlee's Battalion (consolidated) German Regiment
"First" Battle of Trenton, December 26, 1776	1st Pennsylvania Regiment Miles's Regiment/Atlee's Battalion (consolidated) German Regiment Detachment, Procter's Artillery Battalion
"Second" Battle of Trenton, January 2, 1777	1st Pennsylvania Regiment German Regiment Detachment, Procter's Artillery Battalion
Battle of Princeton, January 3, 1777	1st Pennsylvania Regiment Elements of: 2d Pennsylvania Regiment 4th Pennsylvania Regiment 10th Pennsylvania Regiment "Old" 11th Pennsylvania Regiment 12th Pennsylvania Regiment Miles's Regiment/Atlee's Battalion (consolidated) German Regiment 2 Detachments, Procter's Artillery Batalion
Quibbletown (New Market), N. J., January 24, 1777	Miles's Regiment/Atlee's Battalion (consolidated)
Ash Swamp (Plainfield), N. J., early February, 1777	Patton's Regiment
Bound Brook, N. J., April 12/13, 1777	2d Pennsylvania Regiment 3d Pennsylvania Regiment 4th Pennsylvania Regiment 8th Pennsylvania Regiment 10th Pennsylvania Regiment 12th Pennsylvania Regiment Detachment, 4th Artillery
Bonhamtown, N. J., April 15, 1777	Patterson's Company (G), 12th Pennsylvania Regiment
Piscataway, N. J., April 20, 1777	1st Pennsylvania Regiment
Amboy, N. J., April 25, 1777	2d Pennsylvania Regiment Patton's Regiment
Piscataway, N. J., May 8, 1777	"Old" 11th Pennsylvania Regiment
Piscataway, N. J., May 10, 1777	12th Pennsylvania Regiment German Regiment
Metuchen, N. J., May 17, 1777	12th Pennsylvania Regiment
Middletown, N. J., May 26/27, 1777	6th Pennsylvania Regiment
Somerset Court House, N. J., June 14, 1777	1st Pennsylvania Regiment
New Brunswick, N. J., June 22, 1777	1st Pennsylvania Regiment 5th Pennsylvania Regiment
Short Hills, N. J., June 26, 1777	3d Pennsylvania Regiment 12th Pennsylvania Regiment

Iron Hill (Cooch's Bridge), Del.,
    September 3, 1777

Detachment, 2d Pennsylvania Regiment
Detachment, 10th Pennsylvania Regiment
Detachment, "Old" 11th Pennsylvania
    Regiment
Detachment, Pennsylvania State Regiment

Battle of Brandywine,
    September 11, 1777

1st Pennsylvania Regiment (less
    Parr's Company—E)
2d Pennsylvania Regiment
3d Pennsylvania Regiment
4th Pennsylvania Regiment
5th Pennsylvania Regiment
6th Pennsylvania Regiment
7th Pennsylvania Regiment
8th Pennsylvania Regiment (less
    3 Detachments)
9th Pennsylvania Regiment
10th Pennsylvania Regiment
"Old" 11th Pennsylvania Regiment
12th Pennsylvania Regiment (less
    Detachment)
Pennsylvania State Regiment
German Regiment
Hartley's Regiment
Patton's Regiment
4th Artillery
4th Dragoons

First Battle of Freeman's Farm, N. Y.,
    September 19, 1777

Parr's Company (E), 1st Pennsylvania
    Regiment
3 Detachments, 8th Pennsylvania
    Regiment
Detachment, 12th Pennsylvania
    Regiment

Paoli "Massacre," September 20, 1777

1st Pennsylvania Regiment (less
    Parr's Company—E)
2d Pennsylvania Regiment
4th Pennsylvania Regiment
5th Pennsylvania Regiment
7th Pennsylvania Regiment
8th Pennsylvania Regiment (less
    3 Detachments)
10th Pennsylvania Regiment
"Old" 11th Pennsylvania Regiment
Hartley's Regiment

Battle of Germantown, October 4, 1777

1st Pennsylvania Regiment (less
    Parr's Company—E)
2d Pennsylvania Regiment
3d Pennsylvania Regiment
4th Pennsylvania Regiment
5th Pennsylvania Regiment
6th Pennsylvania Regiment
7th Pennsylvania Regiment
8th Pennsylvania Regiment (less
    3 Detachments)
9th Pennsylvania Regiment

10th Pennsylvania Regiment
"Old" 11th Pennsylvania Regiment
12th Pennsylvania Regiment (less Detachment)
Pennsylvania State Regiment
German Regiment
Hartley's Regiment
Patton's Regiment
Detachments, 4th Artillery
4th Dragoons

Second Battle of Freeman's Farm, N. Y., October 7, 1777

Parr's Company (E), 1st Pennsylvania Regiment
3 Detachments, 8th Pennsylvania Regiment
Detachment, 12th Pennsylvania Regiment

Fort Mercer/Red Bank, N. J., October 21, 1777

Detachment, 10th Pennsylvania Regiment
Detachment, Patton's Regiment

Whitemarsh, December 6-10, 1777

1st Pennsylvania Regiment
2d Pennsylvania Regiment
3d Pennsylvania Regiment
4th Pennsylvania Regiment
5th Pennsylvania Regiment
6th Pennsylvania Regiment
7th Pennsylvania Regiment
8th Pennsylvania Regiment
9th Pennsylvania Regiment
10th Pennsylvania Regiment
"Old" 11th Pennsylvania Regiment
12th Pennsylvania Regiment
13th Pennsylvania Regiment
German Regiment
Hartley's Regiment
Patton's Regiment
4th Artillery
4th Dragoons

Bordentown, N. J., May 8, 1778

Detachment, 12th Pennsylvania Regiment

Battle of Monmouth, June 28, 1778

1st Pennsylvania Regiment
2d Pennsylvania Regiment
3d Pennsylvania Regiment
4th Pennsylvania Regiment
5th Pennsylvania Regiment
6th Pennsylvania Regiment
7th Pennsylvania Regiment
9th Pennsylvania Regiment
10th Pennsylvania Regiment
"Old" 11th Pennsylvania Regiment
12th Pennsylvania Regiment
13th Pennsylvania Regiment
Patton's Regiment
4th Dragoons

Wyalusing, Pa., September 29, 1778

Hartley's Regiment

Indian Expedition from Schoharie, N. Y., October, 1778

Simpson's Company (E), 1st Pennsylvania Regiment
4th Pennsylvania Regiment

McIntosh's Ohio River Expedition, December, 1778-January, 1779	8th Pennsylvania Regiment
Norwalk, Conn., July 11, 1779	4th Dragoons
Stony Point, N. Y., July 16, 1779	1st Pennsylvania Regiment (less Simpson's Company—E) 3d Pennsylvania Regiment 5th Pennsylvania Regiment 6th Pennsylvania Regiment 7th Pennsylvania Regiment 9th Pennsylvania Regiment 10th Pennsylvania Regiment
Brodhead's Expedition, August 11-September 14, 1779	8th Pennsylvania Regiment
Newtown (Elmira), N. Y., August 13, 1779	Simpson's Company (E), 1st Pennsylvania Regiment "New" 11th Pennsylvania Regiment
Newtown (Elmira), N. Y., August 29, 1779	Simpson's Company (E), 1st Pennsylvania Regiment 4th Pennsylvania Regiment "New" 11th Pennsylvania Regiment 4th Artillery
Savannah, Ga., October 3, 1779	Detachment, 4th Dragoons
Newbridge/Paramus, N. J., April 16, 1780	Detachment, 3d Pennsylvania Regiment Detachment, 6th Pennsylvania Regiment Detachment, 7th Pennsylvania Regiment Detachment, 9th Pennsylvania Regiment Detachment, 10th Pennsylvania Regiment
Paramus, N. J., May 18, 1780	2d Pennsylvania Regiment
Connecticut Farms, N. J., June 7, 1780	2d Pennsylvania Regiment
Springfield, N. J., June 23, 1780	9th Pennsylvania Regiment
The Blockhouse, Bergen Heights, N. J., July 21, 1780	1st Pennsylvania Regiment 2d Pennsylvania Regiment 3d Pennsylvania Regiment 5th Pennsylvania Regiment 6th Pennsylvania Regiment 7th Pennsylvania Regiment 9th Pennsylvania Regiment 10th Pennsylvania Regiment Detachment, 4th Artillery 4th Dragoons
Brown's Ferry, N. J., October 6, 1780	Elements, 6th Pennsylvania Regiment
Green Spring, Va., July 6, 1781*	Detachments, 4th Artillery
Yorktown, Va., October, 1781*	Detachments, 4th Artillery Detachments, 4th Dragoons
Georgia Campaign, January-July, 1782	Detachments, 4th Artillery Detachments, 4th Dragoons
Charleston Campaign, January-November, 1782†	Detachments, 4th Artillery

*Elements of the old regiments of the Pennsylvania Line, grouped now into the 1st and 2d [Provisional] Pennsylvania infantry battalions, also took part in these operations.

†Elements of the old regiments of the Pennsylvania Line, grouped now into the 1st, 2d, and 3d [Provisional] Pennsylvania infantry battalions, also took part in this campaign.

APPENDIX D

Casualties

T HE surviving records which list by name the individual casualties
in Pennsylvania Continental organizations indicate a total of
1,476* killed, wounded, captured, missing, and died of non-combat
causes. This represents almost nine per cent of the estimated seventeen
thousand total enrollment (officers and enlisted men) of the Pennsylvania Line (see Appendix B). Of these, 178 were killed or mortally
wounded, 290 were wounded, 572 were captured, 240 were listed as
missing in action,** and 196 died from other than combat causes. In
addition, one lieutenant colonel, two captains, a first lieutenant, and
twenty-two privates are shown as having died while being held as
prisoners of war.†

Although a nine per cent casualty rate is not insignificant, it is
obvious that the actual losses—certainly in the enlisted ranks—were
somewhat higher than the available figures reveal.

For example, almost the entire 3d Pennsylvania Battalion was taken
prisoner at Fort Washington, New York, on November 16, 1776, yet only
twelve enlisted men (as contrasted with twenty-six officers) are listed by
name as having been captured; none is listed as having been killed; and
only five are listed as having been wounded. On the other hand, for the
5th Pennsylvania Battalion, also captured at Fort Washington, the
records list 254 enlisted men captured, 6 as killed, and 5 wounded. In all
probability, the battalions were approximately equal in size, and each
must have lost something on the order of four hundred men captured.
Similarly, although the 7th Pennsylvania Regiment was unofficially
reported at the time to have lost sixty-one enlisted men killed or
wounded at Paoli on September 20, 1777, only two soldiers of that
regiment are identified by name as having been wounded in that action,
and none is listed as killed. Again, the attack on the Blockhouse at
Bergen Heights, New Jersey, on July 21, 1780, was reported as costing
the 1st and 2d Pennsylvania Regiments, together, a total of fifteen killed

---

*A single individual wounded on two separate occasions is listed as two casualties. By
the same token, an individual wounded and taken prisoner in a given engagement is listed
both as wounded and captured.

**Many of these, no doubt, were captured; but some undoubtedly rejoined their units,
some were probably killed, and others may have deserted.

†The figures on non-combat deaths do not include a lieutenant colonel, a major, a
surgeon, and a corporal who at various times were drowned; two soldiers killed in brawls
with other soldiers; a sergeant shot accidentally; an ensign killed in a duel; or five privates
who were hanged.

and forty-nine wounded, but the losses of these organizations in that engagement who have been specifically identified total only three officers and enlisted men killed, one officer and three enlisted men wounded, and one enlisted man captured. Even when the casualties from other units which participated are added, the total loss (seven killed, nine wounded, and three captured) which can be derived from casualty records represents substantially less than a third of the total reported at the time.

The records do show eighty-two personnel killed in action and thirty-four wounded without any identification of the date or place where the casualty was sustained. While these losses may well help to fill the gaps between the numbers of casualties reported for an engagement and the numbers of individuals listed by name as being killed, wounded, or captured in that engagement, it seems improbable that they account for all the differences. For enlisted men, complete records were manifestly not kept, and it is likely that not all the records that were kept have survived.

Because of the record-keeping that was necessary concerning officer appointments, however, data on officer casualties can be viewed with considerably more confidence. Even for officers, there are undoubtedly some omissions, but they are insignificant in comparison with those involving enlisted men.

With these considerations in mind, the data presented in this appendix are offered not as conclusive information, but as representing the best information which it has been possible to assemble.

Table I, at the end of the appendix, provides a comprehensive listing of casualty information. It shows the killed, wounded, captured, and missing of each grade in each organization in each action.

Table II presents a comparison of the losses of each Pennsylvania Continental organization, broken down into officer and enlisted categories, and gives both total losses and losses per month during which the organization existed.††

According to these figures, the heaviest loss was sustained by the 5th Pennsylvania Battalion. However, 277 of the 290 casualties which that battalion lost were men captured. A somewhat more meaningful comparison can perhaps be found by considering only casualties who were killed or wounded. The resulting figures are shown in Table III. These indicate that in terms of gross totals, with sixty-seven personnel killed or wounded, the 1st Pennsylvania Regiment lost more than twice as many of its members as its four closest competitors, the 2d, 3d, 4th, and 5th Pennsylvania regiments, each with thirty losses.

††It must be recognized that differences in the totals for different organizations may be a reflection less of variations in exposure to combat than of the degree of conscientiousness with which the records of a unit were maintained.

Because the 1st Pennsylvania Regiment was in the field at least six months before almost all the other Pennsylvania Continental regiments, the fact that its total killed and wounded outnumber those of all other units of the Pennsylvania Line is to be expected. If the totals are compared with the months of the respective units' operational existence, however, it will be seen that the heaviest *rate* of loss was sustained by the 5th Pennsylvania Battalion, followed by Thompson's Rifle Battalion (the forerunner of the 1st Pennsylvania Regiment) and then by the "Old" 11th Pennsylvania Regiment.

Table IV presents the totals for killed, wounded, captured, missing, and non-combat deaths by grade.

Because information is so sparse, there is little point in attempting any analysis of the available enlisted casualty figures. The case for officers, however, is quite different.

As can be seen, no officers were reported as missing in action—undoubtedly another example of the importance that was attached to the administration of officers' records.

The fact that the total for killed (forty-one) is so close to the total for wounded (fifty-eight) suggests that any wound which was other than slight was very likely to prove fatal. This could be a consequence of the types of weapons used (in particular, the heavy lead slug fired by muskets) or the lack of medical knowledge, and probably reflects both.

For purposes of comparing the losses sustained by different officer grades, certain additional computations have been considered necessary.

Specifically, examination has been limited to "line" officers, excluding staff personnel—adjutants, quartermasters, chaplains, surgeons, and surgeon's mates. Beyond this, due to the similarity of their duties, the grades of ensign through captain-lieutenant have been consolidated under the heading of "subalterns." Finally, in order to establish a basis of comparison, a figure has been developed which represents the numerical strength of each grade.

If the number of Pennsylvania Continental units had been constant throughout the war, and if their prescribed complement of officers had been consistent, it might be possible to use the officer make-up of such a "standard" regiment or battalion as a criterion. Neither of these conditions, of course, prevailed. Therefore, the approach which has been taken has been to determine by actual count the number of officers who served in each grade at any time during the Revolution, holding positions in any Pennsylvania Continental organization. Admittedly, this leads to inflation of totals, since many officers served in more than one grade. On the other hand, the losses which are listed cover the experience of the Pennsylvania Line during the whole war, and relate to the grade in which the officer was serving at the time he became a casualty. In any case, the intention is to give only general comparisons between the vulnerabilities of the various grades.

To this end, Table V examines loss rates for subalterns as a group and for the grades of captain through colonel.

In terms of gross totals, it is predictable that subalterns, who account for 144 casualties, had the highest number of losses. Nor is it surprising that, as rank increased, the total number of losses decreased, with the minor exception that ten colonels became casualties in contrast to nine lieutenant colonels.

Looked at on a comparative basis, however, a somewhat different picture is seen.

First, when the total losses suffered by a specific grade is related to the total number of individuals who served in that grade, subalterns emerge as the least vulnerable of all officer categories, since they lost only one out of every 5.6 of their number; and colonels, losing one out of three of *their* number, are found to have been the most vulnerable of all. It should be emphasized, however, that except for colonels, the loss rate in each grade is a very close approximation of one out of five, with captains and majors being lost at slightly greater than that rate and lieutenant colonels and subalterns at slightly less.

Looked at another way, the percentage of the total casualties which a given grade sustained can be compared with the percentage of the total incumbencies which is represented by the number of people who served in that grade. Thus, while subalterns accounted for 63.4 per cent of the total number of people who served in all grades, they suffered only 58.3 per cent of the total officer casualties. By contrast, colonels, who amount to only 2.6 per cent of the total strength, account for 4.1 per cent of the casualties. This approach reveals that, to a slight degree, captains and majors suffered losses that were disproportionately larger than their share of the total strength, while lieutenant colonels suffered very slightly less than their proportional share of the losses.

While the similarity in proportions of loss might seem to reflect the approximately equal involvement of all ranks in close combat, it should be noted that the nature of the loss has a significant statistical impact. The bulk of colonels, for example, were lost as prisoners of war. To obtain some idea of what could be considered battlefield losses, Table VI addresses the same factors as Table V, but shows totals only for killed and wounded. Under these criteria, majors and lieutenant colonels emerge as the most vulnerable grades, in comparison with their numbers, sustaining losses at a rate of almost one and a half times that of captains and subalterns, and nearly twice that of colonels. Comparing the grade percentages of total casualties with grade percentages of total strength reveals a parallel pattern.

It is understandable that the nature of their duties would make colonels less vulnerable than other officers to being killed or wounded. They were most likely to become casualties in situations of total disintegration such as Three Rivers or Long Island; this fact suggests why most of the colonels who were lost were lost as prisoners. It is not clear, however, why majors in particular suffered so much more heavily than the other commissioned grades.

One further aspect of the available casualty figures for the Pennsylvania Continental units which offers material for analysis concerns the subject of wounds in general. In 150 cases, data exist specifying the part of the body in which the wound was suffered. These data are shown in Table VII.

Of course, the total of 290 recorded wounds cannot be considered to be at all complete, and it may well be that the information which pertains to slightly over half of them is misleading.

For what it may be worth, however, the record shows that sixty of the wounds—forty per cent of those known—were in the hips or legs, and only thirty-three (twenty-two per cent) in the torso, with another thirty-nine (twenty-six per cent) in the arms and hands, and eighteen (twelve per cent) in the head.

It appears likely, however, that at least some of the wounds to the head, hands, and possibly the shoulder may not have been the results of enemy fire but of the explosion of the soldier's own weapon, caused by improper loading, defective manufacture, or fouled bores.

Apart from that possibility, the total of the wounds to the torso and the arms and hands (which includes the bulk of bayonet wounds) only slightly exceeds the total wounds in the legs and feet. This is somewhat surprising, considering the fact that the upper part of the body offered a larger target. It may be a reflection of the close quarters at which actions were fought, or of the low velocity of musket balls, whose trajectory would tend to begin dropping at relatively short ranges. It also suggests that body wounds more often proved fatal.

Table VIII lists the total casualties sustained by engagement. These figures indicate that Fort Washington, Long Island, and Quebec accounted for the greatest number of Pennsylvania Continental losses. All these, however, were disasters in which large numbers of men were captured or missing. Considering only killed or wounded, the figures for these actions drop to twenty-one for Fort Washington, twenty-five for Long Island, and nineteen for Quebec. These compare with twenty-six men killed or wounded in the series of skirmishes in New Jersey in the spring and summer of 1777. To the extent that figures are available, they indicate that the Pennsylvania Line's bloodiest engagements were the

Battle of Brandywine, with seventy-four reported casualties, and the Battle of Germantown, with fifty-one.

The final tabulation (Table IX) shows the total number of casualties by year (omitting, of course, the 116 losses unidentified by place or date). The available figures indicate that over ninety per cent of all the losses of the Pennsylvania Line were sustained during the three years 1775-1777, with less than ten per cent occurring during the remaining five years of the war. Primarily, this heavy concentration of casualties reflects the losses of men captured or missing at Quebec, Three Rivers, Long Island, and Fort Washington. Considering only killed or wounded, the total for the years 1775-1777 drops to 260, or just over fifty per cent of a total of 512 for the war as a whole. The fact is that after the Battle of Monmouth, on July 27, 1778, in which casualties were extremely light for so large an engagement, the Pennsylvania Line was employed almost entirely in patrol actions until the provisional battalions were formed after the 1781 mutiny and, with the elements of the 4th Continental Artillery and the 4th Continental Dragoons, marched south to fight at Green Spring and to take part in the siege of Yorktown.

TABLE I

Casualties by Unit, Type, and Engagement

Organization	Killed	Wounded	Cap-tured	Missing	Died	Total
Thompson's Rifle Bn.						
Ploughed Hill, Mass.,						
Aug. 27, 1775						1
Private	1					
Boston, Sept., 1775						2
Corporal			1			
Private			1			
Lechmere's Point, Mass.,						
Nov. 9, 1775						3
Private	1	1	1			
Quebec, Dec. 31, 1775						112
Captain	1					
1st Lieutenant		1	1			
2d Lieutenant			1			
Sergeant	1		6			
Corporal			2			
Drummer			1			
Private	7	9	82			
Non-combat						4
1st Lieutenant					1	
Private					3	
Total	11	11	96	0	4	122

Organization	Killed	Wounded	Cap-tured	Missing	Died	Total
1st Pennsylvania Bn.						
La Chine, May 27, 1776						1
Private		1				
Three Rivers, June 9, 1776						1
Private			1			
Non-combat						1
Ensign					1	
Total	0	1	1	0	1	3
2d Pennsylvania Bn.						
Three Rivers, June 9, 1776						23
Captain		1				
1st Lieutenant		1	2			
Chaplain			1			
Surgeon			1			
Sergeant				1		
Private	1	4	3	8		
Lake Champlain, Oct. 11-13, 1776						
Colonel		1				1
Non-combat						21
Captain					1	
Ensign					2	
Sergeant					1	
Corporal					1	
Private					16	
Total	1	7	7	9	21	45
3d Pennsylvania Bn.						
Skirmish, Nov. 8, 1776						1
Sergeant		1				
Ft. Washington, Nov. 16, 1776						44
Colonel			1			
Major			1			
Captain			7			
1st Lieutenant			5			
2d Lieutenant		1	7			
Ensign			4			
Surgeon			1			
Drummer		1	1			
Private		4	11			
Total	0	7	38	0	0	45
4th Pennsylvania Bn.						
Three Rivers, June 9, 1776						5
Sergeant				1		
Private		4				
Long Island, Aug. 27, 1776						1
Private		1*				

*Obviously, this man was a casual who for some reason had not yet joined or was absent from his parent unit, which during August, 1776, was located at Fort Ticonderoga.

Organization	Killed	Wounded	Cap-tured	Missing	Died	Total
Non-combat						8
2d Lieutenant					1	
Drummer					2	
Private					5	
Total	0	5	0	1	8	14
5th Pennsylvania Bn.						
Ft. Washington, Nov. 16, 1776						289
Colonel			1			
Major			1			
Captain	1		6			
1st Lieutenant			3			
2d Lieutenant			7			
Ensign			4			
Surgeon			1			
Sergeant			22			
Corporal			14			
Drummer			2			
Fifer			1			
Private	6	5	215			
Non-combat						1
Private					1	
Total	7	5	277	0	1	290
6th Pennsylvania Bn.						
Three Rivers, June 9, 1776						53
Colonel			1			
Captain			1			
1st Lieutenant			1			
2d Lieutenant			2			
Sergeant			2			
Corporal			1			
Private	3	1	41			
Isle aux Noix, June 24, 1776						10
Captain	1		2			
1st Lieutenant			1			
2d Lieutenant			1			
Ensign	1					
Private	1		3			
Lake Champlain, Oct. 11-13, 1776						3
Private		1	2			
Non-combat						13
Sergeant					1	
Corporal					2	
Private					10	
Total	6	2	58	0	13	79
1st Pennsylvania Rgt.						
Long Island, Aug. 27, 1776						10
Adjutant		1				

Organization	Killed	Wounded	Cap-tured	Missing	Died	Total
Sergeant		1				
Private		4	4			
White Plains, Oct. 27, 1776						1
Private		1				
Ft. Washington, Nov. 16, 1776						1
Captain			1			
New Brunswick, Dec. 1, 1776						1
Private		1				
Trenton, Jan. 2, 1777						1
Private						
Princeton, Jan. 3, 1777						1
Private	1					
Piscataway, Apr. 20, 1777						1
Sergeant		1				
New Brunswick, June 15, 1777						1
Private		1				
Short Hills, June 26, 1777						1
Private		1				
Brandywine, Sept. 11, 1777						12
Colonel			1			
Captain		1				
3d Lieutenant	2					
Sergeant		3				
Corporal		1				
Private		3				
Paoli, Sept. 20, 1777						7
Quartermaster		1				
Surgeon's Mate	1					
Sergeant		1				
Private		3	1			
Germantown, Oct. 4, 1777						4
2d Lieutenant			1			
3d Lieutenant			1			
Private			2			
Freeman's Farm, Oct. 6, 1777						2
Private		2				
New Brunswick, Dec. 24, 1777						1
Captain			1			
Monmouth, June 28, 1778						3
Quartermaster		1				
Sergeant		1				
Drummer		1				
Miles Square, Aug. 31, 1778						1
Corporal		1				
Stony Point, July 16, 1779						1
Sergeant		1				
Genesee, Sept. 13, 1779						2
1st Lieutenant	1					
Private	1					

Organization	Killed	Wounded	Cap- tured	Missing	Died	Total
Paramus, Mar. 23, 1780						2
Sergeant		1	1			
Blockhouse, July 21, 1780						7
1st Lieutenant		1				
Sergeant	1					
Private	2	2	1			
Place & Date Unknown						14
Private	8	6				
Non-combat						9
2d Lieutenant					1	
Private					8	
Total	16	45	13	0	9	83

Former members of the 1st Pennsylvania Regiment serving in the 1st or 2d [Provisional] Pennsylvania Battalion sustained the following losses:

Green Spring, July 6, 1781						5
Sergeant	1					
Corporal	1					
Private		3				
Yorktown, Oct., 1781						1
Private		1				

2d Pennsylvania Regt.						
Bound Brook, Apr. 12/13, 1777						1
Private		1				
Iron Hill, Sept. 3, 1777						1
2d Lieutenant		1				
Brandywine, Sept. 11, 1777						3
Private		2	1			
Paoli, Sept. 20, 1777						4
Captain		1				
1st Lieutenant	1	1				
Private		1				
Philadelphia, Sept. 26, 1777						1
Captain			1			
Germantown, Oct. 4, 1777						3
Major		1	1			
Private		1				
Monmouth, June 28, 1778						2
Private		2				
Paramus, Apr. 16, 1780						1
1st Lieutenant	1					
Connecticut Farms, N. J., June 7, 1780						1
Private	1					
Blockhouse, July 21, 1780						5
1st Lieutenant	2					
Private	2	1				
Place & Date Unknown						8
Corporal		1				
Private	4	3				

Organization	Killed	Wounded	Cap-tured	Missing	Died	Total
Non-combat						5
Sergeant					2	
Private					3	
Total	13	20	3	0	5	41

Former members of the 2d Pennsylvania Regiment serving in the 1st or 2d [Provisional] Pennsylvania Battalion sustained the following losses:

Organization	Killed	Wounded	Cap-tured	Missing	Died	Total
Green Spring, July 6, 1781						2
Corporal		1				
Private˙		1				
Yorktown, Oct., 1781						1
Private		1				

3d Pennsylvania Rgt.

Organization	Killed	Wounded	Cap-tured	Missing	Died	Total
Bound Brook, Apr. 12/13, 1777						1
Private		1				
Short Hills, June 26, 1777						1
Ensign	1					
Brandywine, Sept. 11, 1777						1
Ensign		1				
Germantown, Oct. 4, 1777						2
2d Lieutenant	1					
Private		1				
Monmouth, June 28, 1778						2
Lt. Colonel	1					
Private		1				
Stony Point, July 16, 1779						1
Private		1				
Paramus, Apr. 16, 1780						2
Major	1					
Private			1			
Blockhouse, July 21, 1780						1
Private		1				
Place & Date Unknown						18
Sergeant	1					
Corporal	2					
Private	5	10				
Non-combat						7
2d Lieutenant					1	
Sergeant					1	
Private					5	
Total	12	19	1	0	7	39

Former members of the 3d Pennsylvania Regiment serving in the 1st or 2d [Provisional] Pennsylvania Battalion sustained the following losses:

Organization	Killed	Wounded	Cap-tured	Missing	Died	Total
Green Spring, July 6, 1781						1
Sergeant	1					
Yorktown, Oct., 1781						1
Private		1				

Organization	Killed	Wounded	Cap-tured	Missing	Died	Total
4th Pennsylvania Rgt.						
Bound Brook, Apr. 12/13, 1777						1
Private		1				
Brandywine, Sept. 11, 1777						4
Captain		1				
Private	2	1				
Paoli, Sept. 20, 1777						2
Major	1					
Private		1				
Germantown, Oct. 4, 1777						7
1st Lieutenant		1	3			
2d Lieutenant		1				
Private		2				
Monmouth, June 28, 1778						1
Private		1				
Stony Point, July 16, 1779						1
Private		1*				
Genesee, Sept. 13, 1779						6
Corporal	2					
Private	4					
"Western Expedition," Dec. 13, 1779						1
Sergeant	1					
Place & Date Unknown						7
Sergeant	1					
Corporal	1					
Private	4	1				
Non-combat						8
Sergeant					1	
Private					7	
Total	17	12	3	0	8	40

Former members of the 4th Pennsylvania Regiment serving in the 1st or 2d [Provisional] Pennsylvania Battalion sustained the following losses:

Green Spring, July 6, 1781						2
Private	2					
Yorktown, Oct., 1781						1
Private	1					
5th Pennsylvania Rgt.						
Brandywine, Sept. 11, 1777						14
Lt. Colonel			1			
Major		1				
Captain		2	1			
1st Lieutenant	1		1			
Ensign		1				
Corporal		2				
Private		3	1			
Paoli, Sept. 20, 1777						3
Ensign	1					
Private		2				

*This soldier must have been on detached service, as the 4th Pennsylvania Regiment was serving in upstate New York at the time of the Stony Point action.

Organization	Killed	Wounded	Cap-tured	Missing	Died	Total
Germantown, Oct. 4, 1777						1
Private		1				
Stony Point, July 16, 1779						2
Private		2				
Paramus, Apr. 16, 1780						1
Captain			1			
Place & Date Unknown						11
Sergeant	1					
Corporal	1					
Private	6	3				
Non-combat						3
1st Lieutenant					1	
Private					2	
Total	10	17	5	0	3	35

Former members of the 5th Pennsylvania Regiment serving in the 1st or 2d [Provisional] Pennsylvania Battalion sustained the following losses:

	Killed	Wounded	Cap-tured	Missing	Died	Total
Green Spring, July 6, 1781						3
Private		3				

6th Pennsylvania Rgt.	Killed	Wounded	Cap-tured	Missing	Died	Total
Northern New Jersey, May 27, 1777						1
2d Lieutenant	1					
Brandywine, Sept. 11, 1777						2
Sergeant		1				
Private		1				
Paoli, Sept. 20, 1777						1
Private		1				
Germantown, Oct. 4, 1777						4
Ensign		1				
Sergeant		1				
Private	1	1				
Monmouth, June 28, 1778						2
1st Lieutenant			1			
Private		1				
Fort Freeland, July 29, 1779						1
Captain	1*					
Paramus, Apr. 16, 1780						3
1st Lieutenant			1			
Private	1	1				
Blockhouse, July 21, 1780						1
Private		1				
Brown's Ferry, Oct. 6, 1780						1
Private		1				
Place & Date Unknown						2
Sergeant	1					
Private		1				
Non-combat						1
1st Lieutenant					1	
Total	5	10	3	0	1	22

*On detached service from the regiment.

Organization	Killed	Wounded	Cap-tured	Missing	Died	Total

Former members of the 6th Pennsylvania Regiment serving in the 1st or 2d [Provisional] Pennsylvania Battalion sustained the following loss:

Organization	Killed	Wounded	Cap-tured	Missing	Died	Total
Green Spring, July 6, 1781						1
1st Lieutenant			1			

Organization	Killed	Wounded	Cap-tured	Missing	Died	Total
7th Pennsylvania Rgt.						
Brandywine, Sept. 11, 1777						1
Private	1					
Paoli, Sept. 20, 1777						5
Lt. Colonel		1				
Captain		2				
Sergeant		1				
Private		1				
Germantown, Oct. 4, 1777						4
1st Lieutenant		1				
Sergeant		1				
Corporal		1				
Private		1				
Monmouth, June 28, 1778						1
Sergeant		1				
Stony Point, July 16, 1779						1
Private		1				
Paramus, Apr. 16, 1780						3
1st Lieutenant		1	2			
Brown's Ferry, Oct. 6, 1780						1
Private		1				
Place & Date Unknown						5
Private	4	1				
Non-combat						0
Total	5	14	2	0	0	21

Former members of the 7th Pennsylvania Regiment serving in the 1st or 2d [Provisional] Pennsylvania Battalion sustained the following loss:

Organization	Killed	Wounded	Cap-tured	Missing	Died	Total
Green Spring, July 6, 1781						1
Captain		1				

Organization	Killed	Wounded	Cap-tured	Missing	Died	Total
8th Pennsylvania Rgt.						
Bound Brook, Apr. 12/13, 1777						6
1st Lieutenant		1				
2d Lieutenant		1				
Private		3	1			
Brandywine, Sept. 11, 1777						2
Major		1				
Sergeant		1				
Freeman's Farm, Sept. 19, 1777						2
Captain		1	1			
Paoli, Sept. 20, 1777						1
Private		1				
Germantown, Oct. 4, 1777						3
2d Lieutenant	1					
Private		1	1			

Organization	Killed	Wounded	Cap-tured	Missing	Died	Total
Potter's Fort, July 27, 1778						2
Private	2					
Ohio River Expedition, Jan., 1779						1
Private		1				
New Jersey Border, Apr., 1779						1
Private	1*					
Brodhead's Expedition, Aug., 1779						1
Private	1					
Date & Place Unknown						4
Drummer	1					
Private	3					
Non-combat						57
Colonel					1	
Lt. Colonel					1	
Captain					4	
Enlisted Men (grade unknown)					51	
Total	9	11	3	0	57	80
9th Pennsylvania Rgt.						
Brandywine, Sept. 11, 1777						2
Ensign	1					
Private		1				
Germantown, Oct. 4, 1777						2
2d Lieutenant		1	1			
Whitemarsh, Dec. 6, 1777						2
Private		2				
Monmouth, June 28, 1778						1
Sergeant		1				
Stony Point, July 16, 1779						2
Sergeant		2				
Paramus, Apr. 16, 1780						2
Corporal			1			
Private			1			
Springfield, N. J., June 23, 1780						1
Private		1				
Blockhouse, July 21, 1780						1
Private		1				
Date & Place Unknown						5
Private	5					
Non-combat						5
Captain					1	
Private					4	
Total	6	9	3	0	5	23

*On detached service from the regiment.

Organization	Killed	Wounded	Captured	Missing	Died	Total
10th Pennsylvania Rgt.						
Princeton, Jan. 3, 1777						1
Sergeant		1				
Iron Hill, Sept. 3, 1777						1
2d Lieutenant			1			
Brandywine, Sept. 11, 1777						3
1st Lieutenant		1				
2d Lieutenant	1					
Private		1				
Paoli, Sept. 20, 1777						1
Private		1				
Germantown, Oct. 4, 1777						1
Private		1				
Red Bank (Ft. Mercer), Oct. 21, 1777						1
Private		1				
Monmouth, June 28, 1778						1
Private		1				
Stony Point, July 16, 1779						1
Lt. Colonel		1				
Paramus, Apr. 16, 1780						1
Private			1			
Blockhouse, July 21, 1780						3
Corporal		1				
Private			2			
Place & Date Unknown						3
Private	2	1				
Non-combat						9
Captain					2	
Sergeant					1	
Corporal					1	
Private					5	
Total	3	10	4	0	9	26
"Old" 11th Pennsylvania Rgt.						
Piscataway, May 8, 1777						1
Captain		1				
Iron Hill, Sept. 3, 1777						1
Lt. Colonel		1				
Brandywine, Sept. 11, 1777						10
1st Lieutenant		1	1			
2d Lieutenant	3		1			
Private		4				
Paoli, Sept. 20, 1777						1
Private		1				
Germantown, Oct. 4, 1777						3
2d Lieutenant	1					
Private		2				
Patrolling, Feb. 14, 1778						1
1st Lieutenant			1			

Organization	Killed	Wounded	Cap-tured	Missing	Died	Total
Patrolling, Feb. 20, 1778						1
2d Lieutenant	1					
Place & Date Unknown						6
Sergeant Major		1				
Drum Major			1			
Private	4					
Non-combat						0
Total	10	11	3	0	0	24

12th Pennsylvania Rgt.						
Bonhamtown, Apr. 15, 1777						2
Captain		1				
1st Lieutenant		1				
Piscataway, May 8, 1777						6
1st Lieutenant		1				
Sergeant			2			
Private		2	1			
Short Hills, June 26, 1777						1
2d Lieutenant		1				
Brandywine, Sept. 11, 1777						3
Major		1				
Captain		1				
2d Lieutenant	1					
Germantown, Oct. 4, 1777						2
Private		2				
Freeman's Farm, Oct. 6, 1777						2
Private		2				
Monmouth, June 28, 1778						1
Private		1				
Place & Date Unknown						2
Private	1	1				
Non-combat						1
Captain					1	
Total	2	14	3	0	1	20

Former members of the 12th Pennsylvania Regiment serving in the 1st or 2d [Provisional] Pennsylvania Battalion sustained the following loss:

Green Spring, July 6, 1781						1
1st Lieutenant		1				

Miles's State Rifle Rgt.						
Staten Island, July 26, 1776						1
Private	1					
Long Island, Aug. 27, 1776						185
Colonel			1			
Lt. Colonel			1			

Organization	Killed	Wounded	Cap-tured	Missing	Died	Total
Captain		1	2			
1st Lieutenant		1	5			
2d Lieutenant	1		1			
3d Lieutenant	1	1	1			
Surgeon			1			
Surgeon's Mate			1			
Sergeant Major				1		
Sergeant			1	8		
Drummer/Fifer				6		
Private		5	4	142		
Ft. Washington, Nov. 16, 1776						1
2d Lieutenant			1			
Princeton, Jan. 3, 1777						1
Sergeant		1				
Northern New Jersey, March, 1777						1
Sergeant	1					
Place & Date Unknown						1
Private	1					
Non-combat						4
Sergeant					1	
Private					3	
Total	5	9	19	157	4	194
Atlee's State Musketry Bn.						
Long Island, Aug. 27, 1776						92
Colonel			1			
Lt. Colonel	1					
Captain			4			
1st Lieutenant			2			
Ensign			4			
Sergeant		3		1		
Corporal	1					
Private	1	2	1	71		
Ft. Washington, Nov. 16, 1776						4
Captain			1			
1st Lieutenant			1			
Private		1	1			
Place & Date Unknown						0
Non-combat						4
Sergeant					1	
Private					3	
Total	3	6	15	72	4	100
Pennsylvania State Rgt.						
Brandywine, Sept. 11, 1777						3
Ensign	1					
Sergeant		1				
Private		1				

Organization	Killed	Wounded	Cap-tured	Missing	Died	Total
Germantown, Oct. 4, 1777						4
1st Lieutenant		1				
Drummer		1				
Private		2				
Total	1	6	0	0	0	7
13th Pennsylvania Rgt.						
Newtown, Pa., Feb. 21, 1778						1
Major			1			
Place & Date Unknown						7
Adjutant		1				
Private	5	1				
Non-combat						2
Captain					1	
Private					1	
Total	5	2	1	0	2	10
The German Rgt.						
Ft. Washington, Nov. 16, 1776						2
1st Lieutenant		1	1			
Princeton, Jan. 3, 1777						2
Colonel			1			
Private		1				
Piscataway, May 8, 1777						1
Private				1		
Brandywine, Sept. 11, 1777						1
1st Lieutenant		1				
Germantown, Oct. 4, 1777						5
Private		5				
Place & Date Unknown						2
Private		2				
Non-combat						7
Major					1	
Private					6	
Total	0	9	3	1	7	20
Hartley's Rgt.						
Brandywine, Sept. 11, 1777						6
Major	1					
Captain	1	1				
1st Lieutenant	1					
2d Lieutenant	1					
Private		1				
Paoli, Sept. 20, 1777						1
Private		1				
Germantown, Oct. 4, 1777						2
Private	1	1				
Place & Date Unknown						9
Sergeant	1					
Corporal	1					

Organization	Killed	Wounded	Cap- tured	Missing	Died	Total
Private	7					
Non-combat						2
Captain					1	
Private					1	
Total	14	4	0	0	2	20
Patton's Rgt.						
Ash Swamp (Plainfield), Feb., 1777						1
Private		1				
Amboy, Apr. 25, 1777						1
Private			1			
Brandywine, Sept. 11, 1777						2
Private		2				
Germantown, Oct. 4, 1777						2
2d Lieutenant	1					
Private		1				
Red Bank (Ft. Mercer), Oct. 22, 1777						1
Captain			1			
Monmouth, June 28, 1778						1
Private		1				
Place & Date Unknown						11
Sergeant	2					
Private	9					
Non-combat						1
Major					1	
Total	12	5	2	0	1	20
"New" 11th Pennsylvania Rgt.						
Wyoming, Apr. 23, 1779						1
Captain	1					
Newtown (Elmira), Aug. 13, 1779						3
Captain		1				
Adjutant		1				
Private		1				
Place & Date Unknown						0
Non-combat						4
Captain					2	
Sergeant					1	
Private					1	
Total	1	3	0	0	4	8
4th Continental Artillery						
Ft. Washington, Nov. 16, 1776						1
Private	1					
Bound Brook, Apr. 12/13, 1777						2
Captain-Lieutenant			2			
Brandywine, Sept. 11, 1777						5
2d Lieutenant	1					
Private		3	1			

Organization	Killed	Wounded	Cap- tured	Missing	Died	Total
Germantown, Oct. 4, 1777						1
Corporal		1				
Hancock's Bridge,						
Mar. 21, 1778						2
1st Lieutenant			1			
2d Lieutenant			1			
Monmouth, June 28, 1778						1
Sergeant		1*				
Newtown (Elmira), Aug. 29,						
1779						1
Private		1				
Blockhouse, July 21,						
1780						1
Private		1				
Green Spring, July 6,						
1781						1
Captain-Lieutenant		1				
Savannah, *ca.* June 24,						
1782						1
Private		1				
Charleston Campaign,						
ca. Nov. 14, 1782						1
Private		1				
Place & Date Unknown						1
Private		1				
Non-combat						15
Lt. Colonel					1	
Major					1	
Captain-Lieutenant					1	
1st Lieutenant					1	
3d Lieutenant					1	
Sergeant					1	
Private					9	
Total	2	11	5	0	15	33
4th Continental Light Dragoons						
Germantown, Oct. 4,						
1777						1
Captain			1			
Red Bank (Ft. Mercer),						
Oct. 20, 1777						1
Captain			1			
Savannah, Oct. 3, 1779						1
Captain			1			
Non-combat						2
Captain					1	
Private					1	
Total	0	0	3	0	2	5
Artillery Artificers Rgt.						
Non-combat						2
Colonel					1	
Private					1	
Total	0	0	0	0	2	2

*On detached service from the regiment.

TABLE II

Unit Total Loss Rates

Organization	Officers	Enlisted Men	Total	Operational Months*	Losses per Operational Month
Thompson's Rifle Bn.	5	117	122	11	11.1
1st Pennsylvania Bn.	1	2	3	10	.3
2d Pennsylvania Bn.	10	35	45	11	4.1
3d Pennsylvania Bn.	27	18	45	5	9.0
4th Pennsylvania Bn.	1	13	14	10	1.4
5th Pennsylvania Bn.	24	266	290	5	58.0
6th Pennsylvania Bn.	11	68	79	10	7.9
1st Pennsylvania Rgt.	16	73	89	54	1.6
2d Pennsylvania Rgt.	10	28	38	48	.58
3d Pennsylvania Rgt.	6	32	38	46	.83
4th Pennsylvania Rgt.	7	34	41	48	.85
5th Pennsylvania Rgt.	11	27	38	43	.88
6th Pennsylvania Rgt.	7	13	20	43	.47
7th Pennsylvania Rgt.	8	14	22	43	.51
8th Pennsylvania Rgt.	12	67	79	48	1.65
9th Pennsylvania Rgt.	4	19	23	43	.53
10th Pennsylvania Rgt.	6	20	26	48	.54
"Old" 11th Pennsylvania Rgt.	11	13	24	12	2.0
12th Pennsylvania Rgt.	9	12	21	18	1.2
Miles's State Rifle Rgt.**	19	175	194	10	19.4
Atlee's State Musketry Bn.	14	86	100	10	10.0
Pennsylvania State Rgt.†	2	5	7	6	1.2
13th Pennsylvania Rgt.	3	7	10	7	1.4
The German Rgt.††	5	15	20	19	1.1
Hartley's Rgt.	6	14	20	18	1.1
Patton's Rgt.	3	17	20	18	1.1
"New" 11th Pennsylvania Rgt.	5	3	8	24	.33
4th Continental Artillery	11	22	33	74	.45
4th Continental Light Dragoons	4	1	5	70	.07
Artificers Rgt.	1	1	2	71	.03
Von Heer's Troop	0	0	0	63	—

*These figures represent an estimate of the time during which the organization was actually in the field.

**With 12 companies, this regiment was half again as large as the standard regiment/battalion of the time. For comparison, therefore, its loss rate should be considered equivalent to 12.9.

†This unit had 10 companies, compared with the standard unit's 8. Comparatively, therefore, its loss rate equivalent could be said to be .96 rather than 1.2.

††All figures pertain only to the months during which this regiment was assigned to the Pennsylvania Line.

TABLE III

Unit Loss Rates, Killed and Wounded

Organization	Officers	Enlisted Men	Total	Operational Months*	Loss per Operational Month
Thompson's Rifle Bn.	2	20	22	11	2.0
1st Pennsylvania Bn.	—	1	1	10	.1
2d Pennsylvania Bn.	3	5	8	11	.73
3d Pennsylvania Bn.	1	6	7	5	1.4
4th Pennsylvania Bn.	—	5	5	10	.5
5th Pennsylvania Bn.	1	11	12	5	2.4
6th Pennsylvania Bn.	2	6	8	10	.8
1st Pennsylvania Rgt.	11	56	67	54	1.24
2d Pennsylvania Rgt.	8	22	30	48	.63
3d Pennsylvania Rgt.	5	25	30	46	.65
4th Pennsylvania Rgt.	4	26	30	48	.63
5th Pennsylvania Rgt.	6	24	30	43	.7
6th Pennsylvania Rgt.	3	12	15	43	.35
7th Pennsylvania Rgt.	6	14	20	43	.47
8th Pennsylvania Rgt.	5	14	19	48	.4
9th Pennsylvania Rgt.	2	13	15	43	.35
10th Pennsylvania Rgt.	3	10	13	48	.27
"Old" 11th Pennsylvania Rgt.	8	13	21	12	1.75
12th Pennsylvania Rgt.	8	9	17	18	.94
Miles's State Rifle Rgt.**	5	9	14	10	1.4
Atlee's State Musketry Bn.	1	8	9	10	.9
Pennsylvania State Rgt.†	2	5	7	6	1.2
13th Pennsylvania Rgt.	1	6	7	7	1.0
The German Rgt.††	1	8	9	19	.47
Hartley's Rgt.	5	13	18	18	1.0
Patton's Rgt.	1	16	17	18	.94
"New" 11th Pennsylvania Rgt.	3	1	4	24	.17
4th Continental Artillery	2	11	13	74	.18
4th Continental Light Dragoons	0	0	0	70	0
Artificers Rgt.	0	0	0	71	0
Von Heer's Troop	0	0	0	63	0

*These figures represent an estimate of the time during which the organization was actually in the field.

**As this regiment was one and a half times the size of the standard regiment/battalion of the time, for purposes of comparison its loss rate should be reduced to .93.

†As this regiment had 10 companies, compared with 8 for a standard organization, for purposes of comparison its loss rate should be reduced to .96.

††All figures pertain only to the months during which this regiment was assigned to the Pennsylvania Line.

TABLE IV
Losses by Grade

Grade	Killed	Wounded	Cap-tured	Missing	Died	Total
Colonel	—	2	6	—	2	10
Lieutenant Colonel	2	3	2	—	2	9
Major	3	4	4	—	3	14
Captain	6	17	33	—	14	70
Captain-Lieutenant	—	1	2	—	1	4
1st Lieutenant	7	16	35	—	4	62
2d Lieutenant	14	6	25	—	3	48
3d Lieutenant	3	1	2	—	1	7
Ensign	5	3	12	—	3	23
Adjutant	—	3	—	—	—	3
Quartermaster	—	2	—	—	—	2
Chaplain	—	—	1	—	—	1
Surgeon	—	—	4	—	—	4
Surgeon's Mate	1	—	1	—	—	2
Total officer losses	41	58	127	0	33	259
Sergeant Major	1	—	—	1	—	2
Drum Major	—	1	—	—	—	1
Sergeant	13	26	34	11	11	95
Corporal	9	9	19	—	4	41
Drummer/Fifer	—	3	5	6	2	17
Private	114	193	387	222	146	1,062
Total enlisted losses	137	232	445	240	163	1,217
Total, all grades	178	290	572	240	196	1,476

TABLE V
Line Officer Loss Rates

Grade	Total Serving in Grade	% of Total Officers Serving	Losses	Loss/Total Serving in Grade	% of Total Officer Loss
Colonel	33	2.6	10	1:3.3	4.1
Lt. Colonel	48	3.8	9	1:5.3	3.6
Major	64	5.1	14	1:4.6	5.7
Captain	317	25.1	70	1:4.5	28.3
Subalterns	802	63.4	144	1:5.6	58.3
Total	1,264		247		

TABLE VI
Line Officer Loss Rates, Killed and Wounded

Grade	Total Serving in Grade	% of Total Officers Serving	Losses	Loss/Total Serving in Grade	% of Total Officer Loss
Colonel	33	2.6	2	1:16.5	2.2
Lt. Colonel	48	3.8	5	1:9.6	5.4
Major	64	5.1	7	1:9.1	7.5
Captain	317	25.1	23	1:13.8	24.7
Subalterns	802	63.4	56	1:14.3	60.2
Total	1,264		93		

TABLE VII
Nature of Wounds

Head	11	Arm	19
Face	1	Wrist	5
Chin	1	Hand	15
Eyes	3	Total	39
Jaw	1		
Neck	1	Hip	2
Total	18	Thigh	11
		Leg	30
Shoulder	12	Knee	10
Breast	1	Ankle	3
Ribs	2	Foot	3
Body	6	Heel	1
Side	6	Total	60
Groin	6		
Total	33		

Grand total   150

TABLE VIII
Losses by Engagement

Engagement	Killed	Wounded	Captured	Missing	Total
Ploughed Hill, Aug. 27, 1775	1	—	—	—	1
Boston, Sept., 1775	—	—	2	—	2
Lechmere's Point, Nov. 9, 1775	1	1	1	—	3
Quebec, Dec. 31, 1775	9	10	93	—	112
La Chine, May 27, 1776	—	1	—	—	1
Three Rivers, June 9, 1776	4	11	57	10	82
Isle aux Noix, June 24, 1776	3	—	7	—	10
Staten Island, July 26, 1776	1	—	—	—	1
Long Island, Aug. 27, 1776	5	20	34	229	288
Lake Champlain, Oct. 11-13, 1776	—	2	2	—	4
White Plains, Oct. 27, 1776	—	1	—	—	1
Skirmish, Nov. 8, 1776	—	1	—	—	1
Fort Washington, Nov. 16, 1776	8	13	321	—	342
New Brunswick, Dec. 1, 1776	—	1	—	—	1
Trenton, Jan. 2, 1777	—	1	—	—	1
Princeton, Jan. 3, 1777	—	4	1	—	5
Ash Swamp (Plainfield), Feb., 1777	—	1	—	—	1
Northern New Jersey, Mar., 1777	1	—	—	—	1
Bound Brook, Apr. 12/13, 1777	—	8	3	—	11
Bonhamtown, Apr. 15, 1777	—	2	—	—	2
Piscataway, Apr. 20, 1777	—	1	—	—	1
Amboy, Apr. 25, 1777	—	—	1	—	1
Piscataway, May 8, 1777	—	4	3	1	8
Northern New Jersey, May 27, 1777	1	—	—	—	1
New Brunswick, June 15, 1777	—	1	—	—	1

Engagement	Killed	Wounded	Cap-tured	Missing	Total
Short Hills, June 26, 1777	1	2	—	—	3
Iron Hill, Sept. 3, 1777	—	2	1	—	3
Brandywine, Sept. 11, 1777	18	47	9	—	74
1st Freeman's Farm, Sept. 19, 1777	—	1	1	—	2
Paoli, Sept. 20, 1777	4	21	1	—	26
Philadelphia, Sept. 26, 1777	—	—	1	—	1
Germantown, Oct. 4, 1777	6	34	11	—	51
2d Freeman's Farm, Oct. 7, 1777	—	4	—	—	4
Fort Mercer (Red Bank), Oct. 21, 1777	—	1	2	—	3
Whitemarsh, Dec. 6, 1777	—	2	—	—	2
New Brunswick, Dec. 24, 1777	—	—	1	—	1
Patrolling in Pennsylvania, Feb. 14, 1778	—	—	1	—	1
Patrolling in Pennsylvania, Feb. 20, 1778	1	—	—	—	1
Newtown, Pa., Feb. 21, 1778	—	—	1	—	1
Hancock's Bridge, Mar. 21, 1778	—	—	2	—	2
Monmouth, June 28, 1778	1	14	1	—	16
Potter's Fort, July 27, 1778	2	—	—	—	2
Miles Square, Aug. 31, 1778	—	1	—	—	1
Ohio River Expedition, Jan., 1779	—	1	—	—	1
New Jersey Border, Apr., 1779	1	—	—	—	1
Wyoming, Apr. 23, 1779	1	—	—	—	1
Stony Point, July 16, 1779	—	9	—	—	9
Fort Freeland, July 29, 1779	1	—	—	—	1
Brodhead's Expedition, Aug., 1779	1	—	—	—	1
1st Newtown (Elmira), Aug. 13, 1779	—	3	—	—	3
2d Newtown (Elmira), Aug. 29, 1779	—	1	—	—	1
Genesee, Sept. 13, 1779	8	—	—	—	8
Savannah, Oct. 3, 1779	—	—	1	—	1
"Western Expedition," Dec. 13, 1779	1	—	—	—	1
Paramus, Mar. 23, 1780	—	1	1	—	2
Paramus, Apr. 16, 1780	3	1	9	—	13
Connecticut Farms, N. J., June 7, 1780	1	—	—	—	1
Springfield, N. J., June 23, 1780	—	1	—	—	1
The Blockhouse, July 21, 1780	7	9	3	—	18
Brown's Ferry, Oct. 6, 1780	—	2	—	—	2
Green Spring, July 6, 1781	5	11	1	—	17
Yorktown, Oct., 1781	1	3	—	—	4
Savannah, *c.* June 24, 1782	—	1	—	—	1
Charleston, *c.* Nov. 14, 1782	—	1	—	—	1
Place and Date Unknown	82	34	—	—	116
Total	178	290	572	240	1,280

TABLE IX

Losses by Year

Year	Total Losses	Killed and Wounded
1775	118	22
1776	731	71
1777	203	167
1778	24	19
1779	28	27
1780	37	24
1781	21	20
1782	2	2
Unknown	116	116

APPENDIX E

Personnel Data

A LTHOUGH certainly less than complete, the official strength returns of the Continental Army—see Charles H. Lesser, *ed.*, *The Sinews of Independence* (Chicago: University of Chicago Press, 1976)—provide considerable information, by month, on such details of individual units as assigned strengths, number of sick, and total desertions. Despite the incomplete nature of these returns, the figures which do exist provide a basis for at least tentative comparisons between Pennsylvania organizations at various stages of the war, between the several Pennsylvania organizations, and between the Pennsylvania organizations as a whole and the rest of the Continental Army serving in the same zone of operations.

Data exist for artillery and cavalry as well as infantry, but the figures often were shown for artillery and cavalry by branches rather than by specific regiments, thus preventing the determination of valid regimental totals. Therefore, this appendix addresses infantry units only.

A further limitation is that consideration is restricted to rank and file (privates, drummers, fifers, and corporals). They will be examined in terms of assigned strengths, sick rates (distinguishing between sick, present; sick, absent; and total sick), and desertion rates. These rates reflect the percentage of assigned rank and file reported as sick or listed as deserters during a given month.

Because the nature of the organizations varied as the war progressed, the personnel data will be examined in terms of two chronological phases: the period from the time the first Pennsylvania Continental unit reached the field in August, 1775, to the end of December, 1776; and the period from the beginning of 1777, when most of the twelve-month battalions were mustered out and replaced by three-year regiments, to the last strength report submitted (for November, 1780) prior to the mutiny of the Pennsylvania Line at Morristown, New Jersey, on January 1, 1781. Within each phase, subdivisions will be made, as appropriate, to distinguish between units serving in differing circumstances.

ASSIGNED STRENGTHS, RANK AND FILE

Phase I—August, 1775-December, 1776

Until May, 1776, the only Pennsylvania unit actually in the field as part of the Continental Army was the organization known successively as Thompson's Pennsylvania Battalion, 2d Continental Regiment, and 1st Continental Regiment. Table I below presents strength figures for this unit and average strengths of all other (non-Pennsylvania) battalions or regiments taking part in the siege of Boston.

TABLE I

Rank and File Strengths, August, 1775-February, 1776

Unit	Aug.	Sept.	Oct.	Nov.	Dec.	Jan.	Feb.	Av.
Thompson's Bn.	849	535	535	438	445	686	750	605
Av. Non-Pa. Units	490	479	471	459	406	495	452	465
Pa./Non-Pa. Av.	1.73	1.17	1.14	.95	1.10	1.39	1.66	1.30

The marked discrepancy between the totals for August is due to the unorthodox organization of Thompson's Battalion—nine companies instead of the normal eight per battalion, together with exceptionally large companies. The substantial reduction in the size of Thompson's Battalion between August and September results from the departure of two companies on the Quebec expedition, although even reduced to seven companies, the battalion was still larger than the average non-Pennsylvania organization. No explanation has been found for the reduction in Thompson's Battalion's strength between October and November. However, the sharp rise in personnel in January and February probably reflects the attachment to the Pennsylvania unit, for the duration of the siege, of the independent Virginia and Maryland rifle companies (previously listed separately, these disappear from the strength returns at the same time that Thompson's Battalion is redesignated as the 1st Continental Regiment) and, in February, the return of the Quebec expedition survivors. It should also be noted that in all months except November, Thompson's Battalion was consistently larger than the non-Pennsylvania average by significant margins, and that even in November, it was below that average by only five per cent.

With much of the Army moving from Boston to the New York City area during March, 1776, no strength returns for that month were submitted. Throughout the next few months, additional Pennsylvania battalions reached the field. On July 1, 1776, the enlistments of Thompson's Battalion expired, and the unit was reconstituted as the 1st Pennsylvania Regiment. The two State units, Miles's Regiment and Atlee's Battalion, joined Washington's Command in August, but the earliest information concerning their strengths after doing so relates to the period after they had been consolidated into a provisional organization, treated here as a single unit. Table II displays strengths in terms both of totals and of percentages of the Command's non-Pennsylvania averages, for the period ending in December, 1776. Here, as later, averages have been adjusted as appropriate to allow for variations in the number of months for which figures are available.

TABLE II
Rank and File Strengths, Washington's Command, April-December, 1776

Unit	Apr.	May	June	July	Aug.	Sept.	Oct.	Nov.	Dec.	Av.
A. Expressed as Totals										
Thompson's Bn.	511	507	577	(A)	(A)	(A)	(A)	(A)	(A)	532
1st Pa. Rgt.	(B)	(B)	(B)	305	(C)	317	387	364	520	379
3d Pa. Bn.	(D)	(D)	517	500	(C)	484	(C)	(E)	(E)	500
5th Pa. Bn.	(D)	(D)	494	495	(C)	474	(C)	(E)	(E)	488
Prov'l State Bn.	(D)	(D)	(D)	(D)	(C)	574	496	(C)	369	480
Pa. Av.	511	507	529	433	(C)	462	442	364	445	464
Non-Pa. Av.	433	490	502	495	(C)	469	459	388	306	443
B. Expressed as Percentage of Corresponding Month's Non-Pennsylvania Average										
Thompson's Bn.	1.18	1.03	1.15	(A)	(A)	(A)	(A)	(A)	(A)	1.12
1st Pa. Rgt.	(B)	(B)	(B)	.62	(C)	.68	.84	.94	1.70	.90
3d Pa. Bn.	(D)	(D)	1.03	1.01	(C)	1.03	(C)	(E)	(E)	1.02
5th Pa. Bn.	(D)	(D)	.98	1.00	(C)	1.01	(C)	(E)	(E)	.99
Prov'l State Bn.	(D)	(D)	(D)	(D)	(C)	1.22	1.08	(C)	1.21	1.17
Pa. Av/Non-Pa. Av.	1.18	1.03	1.05	.87	(C)	.99	.96	.94	1.45	1.05

(A) Inactivated; (B) Not organized; (C) No record; (D) Not joined; (E) Captured

The average strength of Pennsylvania units varied considerably from unit to unit and, for individual units, from month to month. Considering the Pennsylvania contingent as an entity and taking the period as a whole, however, the average monthly unit strength of Pennsylvania units approximated that of non-Pennsylvania units.

On a month-by-month basis, the average strength of the Pennsylvania units as a whole also coincided closely with the non-Pennsylvania average except for July and December. The drop in the Pennsylvania average for July is due to the drastic reduction which occurred when Thompson's Battalion was mustered out and less than fifty-three per cent of its members re-enlisted in the newly formed 1st Pennsylvania Regiment which replaced it. As for December, no explanation has been found for the significant rise in the strength of what was left of the Pennsylvania contingent, which raised its average unit strength forty-five per cent above that of the command's non-Pennsylvania unit average. Possibly the imminent threat to Pennsylvania itself brought the temporary accession of volunteers or the attachment (to the 1st Pennsylvania Regiment) of Associator detachments.

Considering individual Pennsylvania units, the average monthly strengths conformed closely to the pattern of the non-Pennsylvania average for most months. The 1st Pennsylvania Regiment was significantly below the non-Pennsylvania average only in July, September, and (to a considerably lesser extent) October, and it was significantly above that average, for reasons that have been suggested, in December; the Provisional State Battalion—which, after all, was a combination of remnants of two organizations—was well above the non-Pennsylvania average during all months for which records are available.

During part of the same period, four Pennsylvania battalions were serving in the Northern Department—during May and June in Canada, and from July through November (no returns are available after that month) at or in the vicinity of Fort Ticonderoga. Table III consists of strength figures and percentages for that Department.

TABLE III
Rank and File Strength, Northern Department, May-November, 1776

Unit	May	June	July	Aug.	Sept.	Oct.	Nov.	Av.
A. Expressed as Totals								
1st Pa. Bn.	585	456	(C)	455	432	472	(A)	480
2d Pa. Bn.	415	407	(C)	429	414	388	413	411
4th Pa. Bn.	156(F)	319(F)	(C)	522	503	480	508	398
6th Pa. Bn.	648	620	(C)	502	486	470	465	532
Pa. Av.	451	426	(C)	477	459	453	462	454
Non-Pa. Av.	460	445	(C)	360	341	316	351	379
B. Expressed as Percentage of Corresponding Month's Non-Pennsylvania Average								
1st Pa. Bn.	1.27	1.02	(C)	1.26	1.27	1.49	(A)	1.18
2d Pa. Bn.	.90	.91	(C)	1.19	1.21	1.23	1.18	1.08
4th Pa. Bn.	.34(F)	.72(F)	(C)	1.45	1.48	1.52	1.45	1.05
6th Pa. Bn.	1.41	1.39	(C)	1.39	1.43	1.49	1.32	1.40
Pa. Av/Non-Pa. Av.	.98	.96	(C)	1.33	1.35	1.43	1.32	1.20

 (F) Only part of the organization was in the field

No records exist for July because the force was retreating.

Over the entire period, the average monthly strength of the Pennsylvania contingent exceeded the average monthly strength of non-Pennsylvania units by twenty per cent. This was due, however, to the sharper decline in non-Pennsylvania units' average strength after the retreat from Canada than in the average Pennsylvania unit. Prior to that time, the Pennsylvania average had been slightly below (two to four per cent) the non-Pennsylvania average; afterwards, however, the Pennsylvania average exceeded the non-Pennsylvania average by thirty-two to forty-three per cent.

As for individual Pennsylvania units, the 2d Pennsylvania Battalion experienced the smallest net loss, mustering a strength in November which was less than one-half of one per cent below its May level, although this loss was minimized to a degree by an increase in strength between October and November. The 4th Pennsylvania Battalion lost comparatively little strength once all its companies had arrived, and from August onward was consistently the largest of the Pennsylvania organizations—a situation attributable in large part to the fact that substantial elements of this battalion did not reach the field until all units had returned to Fort Ticonderoga.

The greatest proportional loss among the Pennsylvania forces was in the 6th Battalion, whose November strength was twenty-eight per cent below its strength in May. The 1st Pennsylvania Battalion also lost heavily, dropping almost twenty per cent between May and October. The timing of these losses differs, as the 6th Battalion's reduction largely occurred, for readily conceivable reasons, between June and August, whereas there is no apparent explanation for the fact that the 1st Battalion sustained its chief loss between May and June.

As a basis for comparison, the average non-Pennsylvania unit's strength declined approximately twenty-four per cent during the period, whereas the average strength of the Pennsylvania contingent actually increased marginally—although this is misleading, being due to the fact that in May only a fraction of the 4th Pennsylvania Battalion was on hand to be counted.

Table IV compares the average strengths for Pennsylvania units and non-Pennsylvania units by major command.

TABLE IV
Average Rank and File Strengths, Pennsylvania and Non-Pennsylvania Units, by Major Command

	Apr.	May	June	July	Aug.	Sept.	Oct.	Nov.	Dec.	Av.
A.　Expressed as Totals										
Pa. Units										
a.　Washington's Command	511	507	529	433	(C)	462	442	364	445	462
b.　Northern Department	(C)	549(G)	494(G)	(C)	477	459	453	462	(C)	482
c.　Relative Strength(a/b)	n/a	.92	1.07	n/a	n/a	1.01	.98	.79	n/a	.96
Non-Pa. Units										
a.　Washington's Command	433	490	502	495	(C)	469	459	388	306	443
b.　Northern Department	(C)	460	445	(C)	360	341	316	351	(C)	379
c.　Relative Strength(a/b)	n/a	1.07	1.13	n/a	n/a	1.38	1.45	1.11	n/a	1.17
B.　Expressed as Percentage of Corresponding Month's Non-Pennsylvania Average										
Washington's Command	1.18	1.03	1.05	.87	(C)	.99	.96	.94	1.45	1.05
Northern Department	(C)	1.19(G)	1.11(G)	(C)	1.33	1.35	1.43	1.32	(C)	1.27

(G) Adjusted to disregard incomplete battalion

The figures above show that the Pennsylvania units in Washington's Command maintained essentially the same average size as the Pennsylvania units in the Northern Department until November, 1776, when the figure for Washington's Command dropped to a level twenty-one per cent below that for the Northern Department. With regard to the non-Pennsylvania units, however, the average strength was consistently greater in Washington's Command, and by an order of magnitude ranging from a low of seven per cent in May to a peak forty-five per cent in October, and averaging seventeen per cent.

The figures also show that the Pennsylvania average was more consistently at or significantly above the non-Pennsylvania average in the Northern Department than in Washington's Command.

In terms of organizations, Pennsylvania during this period furnished to the two major commands, combined, a total of eight battalions (counting the provisional battalion made up of the survivors of Miles's Regiment and Atlee's Battalion as a single unit, and excluding the German Regiment, for which figures covering this time-frame are not available). The corresponding maximum figures for other states are: Massachusetts, 27; Connecticut, 13; Virginia, 5½; New Hampshire, 5; New York, 4; Rhode Island, 3; New Jersey, 3; Maryland, 2½; and Delaware, 1. Prescribed manning levels per company and the number of companies per regiment, however, varied somewhat from state to state.

Phase II—April, 1777-November, 1780

For this phase, average monthly strengths are examined in terms of somewhat arbitrarily defined six-month periods designated as "Winter Encampments" (December through May) and "Campaign Seasons" (June through November). Although some variations occurred in the months actually spent in these two environments from one year to another, they are not significant. A further qualification which should be noted is that figures for 1777 are available for a "Winter Encampment" consisting only of April and May, and for a "Campaign Season" only of October and November.

Because a major reorganization occurred on July 1, 1778, when the thirteen existing Pennsylvania regiments were consolidated into ten, Table V is restricted to the first three seasons.

TABLE V
Rank and File Strengths (Monthly Averages),
Washington's Command, April, 1777-May, 1778

Regiment	April-May, 1777		Oct.-Nov., 1777		Dec., 1777-May, 1778	
	Pa. Rgtl. Strength	Pa. Rgt./ Non-Pa. Av.	Pa. Rgtl. Strength	Pa. Rgt./ Non-Pa. Av.	Pa. Rgtl. Strength	Pa. Rgt./ Non-Pa. Av.
1st Pa.	335	1.83	323	1.30	333	1.21
2d Pa.	33(H)	.18	135	.54	109	.39
3d Pa.	137	.75	159	.64	162	.59
4th Pa.	130	.71	145	.58	157	.57
5th Pa.	246	1.34	281	1.13	270	.98
6th Pa.	(D)	(D)	158	.64	152	.55
7th Pa.	(D)	(D)	191	.77	169	.61
8th Pa.	379	2.07	367	1.48	351	1.27
9th Pa.	193	1.05	178	.72	193	.70
10th Pa.	96(H)	.52	183	.74	202	.73
"Old" 11th Pa.	138	.75	164	.66	137	.50
12th Pa.	231	1.26	198	.80	186	.67
13th Pa.	(D)	(D)	573	2.31	305	1.11
German Rgt	365	1.99	344	1.39	301(J)	n/a
Patton's Additional	124	.68	188	.76	100	.36
Hartley's Additional	155	.85	234	.94	228(K)	n/a
Pa. Av (L)	182	.99	239	.96	195	.71
Non-Pa. Av.	183	—	248	—	276	—

(H) In process of organization; (J) December, 1777-January, 1778 only; (K) December, 1777 only; (L) Adjusted to compensate for variations in months for which figures are available.

The preceding table shows that the Pennsylvania regiments *as a whole,* while averaging marginally smaller monthly strengths than the average non-Pennsylvania regiment until the end of the 1777 campaign season, coincided very closely with that average. Once Washington's Command entered the winter encampment at Valley Forge, however, the average strength of Pennsylvania regiments dropped drastically in relation to the average for all non-Pennsylvania units. This was a reflection of significantly higher Pennsylvania rates for desertion, as will be discussed in a later section of this appendix. It is especially noteworthy that the drop in the relative strength of the Pennsylvania contingent during that period is attributable primarily to a minority of the regiments—the 2d and "Old" 11th Pennsylvania regiments, whose monthly average strengths, respectively, dropped approximately nineteen per cent and seventeen per cent during the December, 1777-May, 1778 period; and Patton's Regiment, which dropped almost seventeen per cent during the same period. (The German Regiment is excluded from consideration because of its transfer in February to the Maryland Line, and Hartley's Regiment is excluded because of its redeployment to York, Pennsylvania, in January, 1778. The 13th Pennsylvania experienced a drop of almost forty-seven per cent from its monthly average during the previous period, but even so was still substantially above the average strength of non-Pennsylvania regiments.)

Considering individual units, in the April-May, 1777, period, thirteen Pennsylvania regiments were in the field. Six of these (the 1st, 5th, 8th, 9th, 12th, and German regiments) were above the non-Pennsylvania average by amounts ranging from five to 107 per cent. Of the remaining seven, however, the largest (Hartley's) mustered only eighty-five per cent of the non-Pennsylvania average. The next three largest (the 3d, 4th, and "Old" 11th) ranged between seventy-one and seventy-five per cent of that average; and the remaining three (Patton's, the 10th, and the 2d) were at sixty-eight, fifty-two, and eighteen per cent of the non-Pennsylvania average.

For the October-November period, sixteen Pennsylvania regiments were with the command. Only five (the 1st, 5th, 8th, 13th, and German) were above the non-Pennsylvania average. Hartley's Regiment was only marginally below that average, at ninety-four per cent, but all other Pennsylvania regiments were between twenty per cent and forty-six per cent below the non-Pennsylvania avarage.

During the Valley Forge encampment, the Pennsylvania regiments became relatively even more understrength. Once Hartley's Regiment and the German Regiment were reassigned (early in the period), fourteen Pennsylvania regiments remained. Only the 1st, 8th, and 13th continued to be above the non-Pennsylvania average strength; the 5th Pennsylvania, however, was almost at that average, but Patton's Regiment and the 2d Pennsylvania were both more than sixty per cent below the average; the 3d, 4th, 6th, and "Old" 11th were all between forty and fifty per cent below; and the 7th, 9th, and 10th had shortfalls from the average amounting to thirty to thirty-nine per cent.

During the period covered by Table V, the seven Pennsylvania regiments organized on the foundations of the original twelve-month battalions averaged a monthly strength which was only about forty-two per cent of the average monthly strengths of their predecessor units during 1776. Even allowing for losses during the later period, it is clear that the re-enlistment rate in the regiments when the battalions were mustered out had been relatively low.

Apart from the April-May, 1777, period, when several regiments were only partly organized, the Pennsylvania regiments varied greatly in average monthly strengths. During the Valley Forge encampment, for example, eight mustered fewer than two hundred men each, three had between two and three hundred, and only four totaled over three hundred apiece.

The summer of 1778 not only brought the previously mentioned reorganization, it also saw the 4th and 8th Pennsylvania regiments detached from Washington's Command for service in other areas. Table VI lists strength figures for each of the Pennsylvania regiments and for all of the non-Pennsylvania regiments combined which were serving immediately under Washington in New Jersey and the Hudson Highlands from June, 1778, through November, 1779.

TABLE VI
Rank and File Strengths (Monthly Averages), Washington's Command, June, 1778-November, 1779

	June-Nov., 1778		Dec., 1778-May, 1779		June-Nov., 1779	
Regiment	Pa. Rgtl. Strength	Pa. Rgt./ Non-Pa. Av	Pa. Rgtl. Strength	Pa. Rgt./ Non-Pa. Av	Pa. Rgtl. Strength	Pa. Rgt./ Non-Pa. Av
1st Pa.	281	.77	271	.88	231	.75
2d Pa.	368	1.01	415	1.34	392	1.27
3d Pa.	322	.89	349	1.13	317	1.03
5th Pa.	277	.76	293	.95	280	.91
6th Pa.	200	.55	224	.72	196	.64
7th Pa.	191	.53	210	.68	196	.64
9th Pa.	191	.53	210	.68	187	.61
10th Pa.	290	.80	324	1.05	307	.99
Pa. Av.	265	.73	287	.93	263	.83
Non-Pa. Av.	363	—	309	—	308	—

Despite the reduction in the number of the Pennsylvania regiments and the redistribution of personnel from the three inactivated regiments, the increase in manning levels of the Pennsylvania units was less than the increase in the average non-Pennsylvania unit, so that the disparity between the Pennsylvania and non-Pennsylvania averages remained almost as great in the June-November, 1778, period as it had been during the winter encampment at Valley Forge. The next winter encampment (December, 1778-May, 1779) brought these averages almost into line, but during the June-November, 1779, period, while the non-Pennsylvania average total strength remained almost constant, the Pennsylvania units averaged some seventeen per cent less.

Regarding specific Pennsylvania regiments, the July 1, 1778, reorganization brought major increases in the strengths of the 2d, 3d, and 10th regiments. The 6th and 7th regiments also increased in size, but the 1st Pennsylvania dropped nearly sixteen per cent. Except for the 1st Pennsylvania, the average monthly strength of all Pennsylvania regiments of the command rose during the December, 1778-May, 1779, period, only to drop again during the 1779 campaign season to about the same levels that had prevailed during the campaign season of 1778—that is to say, about eight per cent, on the average, below the 1778-1779 winter encampment average.

So far as distribution of strength is concerned, the reorganization brought initial improvement—two regiments averaged three hundred men or over, four averaged between two and three hundred, and only two (with 191 each) fell below two hundred. The increases during the December, 1778-May, 1779, period altered the distribution so that three regiments averaged over three hundred men each (one of them having over four hundred), all the rest averaging between two and three hundred. June-November, 1779, found three of the Pennsylvania regiments with over three hundred men, but only two in the two-to three-hundred range, the other three numbering between 187 and 196.

Despite the increases, most of the Pennsylvania regiments were relatively smaller, by substantial amounts, than the average non-Pennsylvania regiment. Only the 2d Pennsylvania was consistently above that average. The 3d and 10th Pennsylvania regiments rose somewhat above the average in the 1778-1779 winter encampment, but the 10th dropped slightly below the average in the succeeding campaign season. During these two latter periods, the 5th Pennsylvania's strength was sustained at less than ten per cent below the average, but the other Pennsylvania regiments experienced shortfalls ranging from twenty to almost fifty per cent below the non-Pennsylvania average.

During these same periods, the 4th Pennsylvania was serving on the New York frontier and with the Sullivan Expedition; the "New" 11th was formed of Patton's and Hartley's regiments and sent to Wyoming, and then took part in the Sullivan Expedition; and the 8th Pennsylvania was operating at and out of Fort Pitt. Records for all these units are fragmentary, but such information as is available is shown in Tables VII and VIII below.

TABLE VII
Rank and File Strengths (Monthly Averages),
New York Frontier and Sullivan Expedition,
July, 1778-October, 1779

Regiment	Nov., 1778		Dec., 1778-May, 1779		June-Oct., 1779	
	Pa. Rgtl. Strength	Pa. Rgt./ Non-Pa. Av.	Pa. Rgtl. Strength	Pa. Rgt./ Non-Pa. Av.	Pa. Rgtl. Strength	Pa. Rgt./ Non-Pa. Av.
4th Pa.	190	.62	218	.69	181	.70
"New" 11th Pa.	(B)	(B)	331	1.05	104	1.17
Pa. Av.	190	.62	275	.87	243	.93
Non-Pa. Av.	308	—	315	—	260	—

Even though the November, 1778, strength of the 4th Pennsylvania had increased considerably over its average for the preceding period (157—see Table V), it was sharply below the strength of the average non-Pennsylvania regiment in the New York frontier area in the same period. It experienced a further build-up for the Sullivan Expedition, but even when the larger "New" 11th Pennsylvania is added, the Pennsylvania contingent is still found to be substantially smaller than the average for non-Pennsylvania regiments. No figures are available for the expedition itself, the June-November, 1779, figures in Table VII being based on returns submitted at the end of the operation; at that stage, the Pennsylvania average approximated the non-Pennsylvania average, but only because of a larger decline in the latter. The above-average strength of the "New" 11th Pennsylvania probably reflects the fact that, like the other larger Pennsylvania units, it actually consisted of the remnants of two regiments.

TABLE VIII
Rank and File Strengths (Monthly Averages),
Western Department, December, 1778-November, 1779

Regiment	Dec., 1778-May, 1779		June-Nov., 1779	
	Pa. Rgtl. Strength	Pa. Rgt./ Non-Pa. Av.	Pa. Rgtl. Strength	Pa. Rgt./ Non-Pa. Av.
8th Pa.	389	1.51	159	.57
Non-Pa. Av.	257	—	280	—

Table VIII illustrates the dramatic drop in the strength of the 8th Pennsylvania on the completion of the original three-year enlistments, which occurred in the summer of 1779. Returning from Valley Forge to its home region during the summer of 1778, it had grown from a monthly average of 351 men during the 1777-1778 winter encampment to a peak higher than its greatest previous level (379, in the April-May, 1777, period). However, from being approximately one and a half times the average strength of the other regiments in the Western Department, it dropped to little more than half their average strength.

After the Sullivan Expedition, the 4th and "New" 11th Pennsylvania regiments joined Washington's Command in the northern New Jersey-Hudson Highlands area. Table IX portrays their average strengths from that time until the mutiny of the Pennsylvania Line brought an end to the regiments as they had existed up to that time.

TABLE IX
Rank and File Strengths (Monthly Averages),
Washington's Command, December, 1779-November, 1780

Regiment	Dec., 1779-May, 1780		June-Nov., 1780	
	Pa. Rgtl. Strength	Pa. Rgt./ Non-Pa. Av.	Pa. Rgtl. Strength	Pa. Rgt./ Non-Pa. Av.
1st Pa.	210	.86	239	.98
2d Pa.	361	1.47	303	1.24
3d Pa.	280	1.14	257	1.05
4th Pa.	156	.64	218	.89
5th Pa.	264	1.08	233	.95
6th Pa.	179	.73	227	.93
7th Pa.	178	.73	230	.94
9th Pa.	162	.66	227	.93
10th Pa.	289	1.18	245	1.00
"New" 11th Pa.	240	.98	236	.96
Pa. Av.	232	.95	241	.98
Non-Pa. Av.	245	—	245	—

Between the 1779 campaign season and the winter encampment of 1779-1780, the strengths of the Pennsylvania units of Washington's Command declined by anything from the six per cent of the 5th and 10th regiments to the almost fourteen per cent of the 4th and 9th regiments, for an average of approximately twelve per cent. During the same time-frame, the strength of the average non-Pennsylvania regiment, however, dropped by some twenty per cent, so that the average Pennsylvania regiment's strength, relative to that of the average non-Pennsylvania regiment, increased fairly significantly. The reductions were largely due to the expiration of the enlistments entered into in 1777. The increases realized by the Pennsylvania regiments in the final period reflect the arrival of militia levies, called in to compensate for the departure of time-expired men. The fact that the Pennsylvania regiments finally reached fairly uniform size (varying only from a low of 218 to a high of 303) makes it seem evident that the levies were deliberately assigned to fill the greatest gaps, and reflects an attempt by the authorities to maintain the full organizational structure of ten regiments. However, this effort had to be abandoned. It is obvious that, during the June-November, 1780, period, the average monthly strength of the individual Pennsylvania regiments closely approximated that of the average non-Pennsylvania regiment; but that average had dropped to so low a level that the authorities decided on a general consolidation: the proposed combination of the ten Pennsylvania regiments into six was only one part of a more comprehensive plan, which affected the units of several states.

Table X shows such figures as are available for the Western Department.

TABLE X
Rank and File Strengths (Monthly Averages),
Western Department, December, 1779-November, 1780

Regiment	Dec., 1779-May, 1780		June-Nov., 1780	
	Pa. Rgtl. Strength	Pa. Rgt./ Non-Pa. Av.	Pa. Rgtl. Strength	Pa. Rgt./ Non-Pa. Av.
8th Pa.	153	.65	136	.83
Non-Pa. Av.	234	—	164	—

Here again, strength of both Pennsylvania and non-Pennsylvania regiments continued to decline. Even though the reduction in non-Pennsylvania units was proportionally greater, the strength of the Pennsylvania regiment in the Western Department was still almost eighteen per cent lower than that of the non-Pennsylvania average.

Assessment of the preceding tables suggests a number of general conclusions.

One, mentioned earlier, is that as a rule, something less than half of the veterans of the twelve-month battalions were willing to re-enlist—at least, immediately—in the three-year regiments.

A second is that, despite variations up and down throughout the period after the three-year regiments were formed, the average monthly strength of the Pennsylvania regiments of Washington's Command, after their initial organization was completed, remained relatively constant: the average for October-November, 1777, was 239; that for June-November, 1780, was 241. Their lowest average occurred during the Valley Forge encampment (195); but in general, the season of the year does not seem to have been an important determining factor, for the following winter encampment (December, 1778-May, 1779) saw these regiments reach their peak average monthly strength of their entire service (287). Although the Pennsylvania regiments as a whole closely approximated the average strengths for the non-Pennsylvania regiments of Washington's Command during five of the eight periods examined, they fell marginally below that average even then; and during the remaining three periods, their average strength was significantly below (by fifteen to twenty-nine per cent) the average for other regiments of the command.

A similar pattern occurs with regard to the Pennsylvania contingent on the New York frontier and on Sullivan's Expedition.

In the Western Department, the one Pennsylvania regiment did outnumber the non-Pennsylvania regiments until the summer of 1779, when over half of its men left at the end of their first enlistments; unable to obtain replacements, the regiment thenceforth existed at a level drastically below the average of the other units of the Department until the final period, when their strengths also began to drop.

Considering only the eight Pennsylvania regiments which served uninterruptedly with Washington's Command, their average monthly strength for the entire period from early 1777 until the mutiny is shown in Table XI, which lists the regiments in descending order of strength, and compares each with the average for all non-Pennsylvania regiments of the command.

TABLE XI

Average Monthly Strengths, Washington's Command,
April, 1777-November, 1780

Regiment	Pa. Rgtl. Strength	Pa. Rgt./ Non-Pa. Av.
2d Pa.	298	1.10
1st Pa.	278	1.02
5th Pa.	268	.99
10th Pa.	263	.97
3d Pa.	248	.91
7th Pa.	195	.72
9th Pa.	193	.71
6th Pa.	191	.70
Pa. Av.	242	.89
Non-Pa. Av.	272	—

On the average, therefore, the regiments of the Pennsylvania contingent were eleven per cent below the typical non-Pennsylvania regiment. When the Pennsylvania regiments are examined individually, only the 1st and 2d were above the non-Pennsylvania average, but the 3d, 5th, and 10th were below the average by relatively small amounts. The 6th, 7th, and 9th, however, were significantly weaker, being approximately thirty per cent under what could be considered normal regimental strength.

SICK RATES, RANK AND FILE

Sick rates shown in the following tables are based on total rank and file reported sick, expressed as a percentage of total rank and file assigned. The returns do not distinguish between sick and wounded. However, on the basis of such casualty figures as are available—see Howard H. Peckman, ed., The Toll of Independence (Chicago: University of Chicago Press, 1974)—and considering the fact that few of the tables cover periods marked by sizable combat, it is probable that the vast majority, if not necessarily all, of the men reported as sick were indeed sick and not wounded.

Phase I—August, 1775-December, 1776

Table XII presents sick rates during the siege of Boston.

TABLE XII
Rank and File Sick Rates, August, 1775-February, 1776

Unit	Aug.	Sept.	Oct.	Nov.	Dec.	Jan.	Feb.	Av.
A. Sick, Present								
Thompson's Bn.	2.2	4.9	5.6	10.7	10.1	11.7	10.7	8.0
Av. Non-Pa. Units	11.9	9.8	7.2	7.5	7.2	10.3	14.4	9.8
Pa./Non-Pa. Av.	.19	.50	.78	1.43	1.40	1.14	.74	.82
B. Sick, Absent								
Thompson's Bn.	2.5	4.3	6.0	9.6	9.0	7.7	3.3	6.1
Av. Non-Pa. Units	6.5	5.4	5.7	4.7	3.4	1.8	2.3	4.3
Pa./Non-Pa. Av.	.39	.80	1.05	2.04	2.65	4.28	1.44	1.42
C. Total Sick								
Thompson's Bn.	4.7	9.2	11.6	20.3	19.1	19.4	14.0	14.0
Av. Non-Pa. Units	18.4	15.2	12.9	12.2	10.6	12.1	16.7	14.0
Pa./Non-Pa. Av.	.26	.61	.90	1.67	1.80	1.60	.84	1.00
Sick Present/ Sick Absent, Pa.	.88	1.14	.93	1.11	1.12	1.52	3.24	1.31
Sick Present/ Sick Absent, Non-Pa.	1.83	1.81	1.26	1.60	2.12	5.72	6.26	2.28

Taking as a whole the seven months addressed by Table XII, the *total* sick rate for Thompson's Battalion was identical with that of the non-Pennsylvania average. Examination on a month-by-month basis, however, gives a somewhat different picture. Table XII shows that from August through October, sickness in Thompson's Battalion was less prevalent than in the command as a whole, although the difference became progressively less great. By contrast, from November through January, the sick rate in Thompson's Battalion exceeded by a substantial proportion the average for the other units of the command. A similar pattern is found if rates for sick, present and sick, absent are examined individually, with the higher incidence of illness in Thompson's Battalion being especially pronounced with regard to sick, absent (presumably, the sick, absent were more seriously ill than the sick, present).

The average non-Pennsylvania organization consistently reported more men sick, present than sick, absent. Thompson's Battalion, by contrast, had a higher rate of sick, absent than sick, present in August and October. Even after this trend was reversed, the proportion of sick, absent to sick, present was consistently greater in Thompson's Battalion than in the non-Pennsylvania units. Since the non-Pennsylvania element of the force consisted almost exclusively of New Englanders, it seems reasonable to conclude that the Pennsylvanians' higher sick rates in November, December, and January reflect greater difficulty in adjusting to conditions of climate to which the New England troops were already accustomed.

Table XIII deals with the sick rates of the Continental organizations serving under Washington from the initial concentration around New York City in April through the operations along the Pennsylvania-New Jersey border in December, 1776.

TABLE XIII
Rank and File Sick Rates, Washington's Command, April-December, 1776

Unit	Apr.	May	June	July	Aug.	Sept.	Oct.	Nov.	Dec.	Av.
A. Expressed as Total Rates										
1. Sick, Present										
Thompson's Bn.	2.2	2.6	3.5	(A)	(A)	(A)	(A)	(A)	(A)	2.8
1st Pa. Rgt.	(B)	(B)	(B)	8.5	(C)	10.1	7.0	11.0	6.9	8.7
3d Pa. Bn.	(D)	(D)	2.7	9.8	(C)	13.4	(C)	(E)	(E)	8.6
5th Pa. Bn.	(D)	(D)	7.3	10.7	(C)	14.1	(C)	(E)	(E)	10.7
Prov'l State Bn.	(D)	(D)	(D)	(D)	(C)	16.4	4.8	(C)	(C)	10.6
Pa. Av.	2.2	2.6	4.5	9.7	(C)	13.5	5.9	11.0	6.9	8.2
Non-Pa. Av.	6.6	6.8	8.9	18.1	(C)	15.2	13.1	13.8	7.8	11.3
2. Sick, Absent										
Thompson's Bn.	4.5	3.9	1.4	(A)	(A)	(A)	(A)	(A)	(A)	3.3
1st Pa. Rgt.	(B)	(B)	(B)	3.0	(C)	8.2	10.9	14.3	40.6	15.4
3d Pa. Bn.	(D)	(D)	1.9	2.0	(C)	16.5	(C)	(E)	(E)	6.8
5th Pa. Bn.	(D)	(D)	2.6	5.7	(C)	21.7	(C)	(E)	(E)	10.0
Prov'l State Bn.	(D)	(D)	(D)	(D)	(C)	19.3	20.2	(C)	(C)	19.8
Pa. Av.	4.5	3.9	2.0	3.6	(C)	16.4	15.6	14.3	40.6	11.0
Non-Pa. Av.	6.7	3.3	2.2	2.8	(C)	13.0	17.2	15.9	28.7	11.2
3. Total Sick										
Thompson's Bn.	6.7	6.5	4.9	(A)	(A)	(A)	(A)	(A)	(A)	6.0
1st Pa. Rgt.	(B)	(B)	(B)	11.5	(C)	18.3	17.8	25.3	47.5	24.1
3d Pa. Bn.	(D)	(D)	4.6	11.8	(C)	30.0	(C)	(E)	(E)	15.5
5th Pa. Bn.	(D)	(D)	9.9	16.4	(C)	35.9	(C)	(E)	(E)	20.7
Prov'l State Bn	(D)	(D)	(D)	(D)	(C)	35.7	25.0	(C)	(C)	30.4
Pa. Av.	6.7	6.5	6.5	13.3	(C)	29.9	21.4	25.3	47.5	19.2
Non-Pa. Av.	13.3	10.1	11.1	20.9	(C)	28.2	30.3	29.7	36.5	22.5
B. Expressed as Percentage of Corresponding Month's Non-Pennsylvania Average										
1. Sick, Present										
Thompson's Bn.	.33	.38	.39	(A)	(A)	(A)	(A)	(A)	(A)	.38
1st Pa. Rgt.	(B)	(B)	(B)	.47	(C)	.66	.53	.80	.88	.64
3d Pa. Bn.	(D)	(D)	.30	.54	(C)	.88	(C)	(E)	(E)	.61
5th Pa. Bn.	(D)	(D)	.82	.59	(C)	.93	(C)	(E)	(E)	.76
Prov'l State Bn.	(D)	(D)	(D)	(D)	(C)	1.08	.37	(C)	(C)	.75
Pa. Av.	.33	.38	.51	.54	(C)	.89	.45	.80	.88	.73
2. Sick, Absent										
Thompson's Bn.	.67	1.18	.64	(A)	(A)	(A)	(A)	(A)	(A)	.80
1st Pa. Rgt.	(B)	(B)	(B)	1.07	(C)	.63	.63	.90	1.41	.99
3d Pa. Bn.	(D)	(D)	.86	.71	(C)	1.27	(C)	(E)	(E)	1.13
5th Pa. Bn.	(D)	(D)	1.18	2.04	(C)	1.67	(C)	(E)	(E)	1.67
Prov'l State Bn.	(D)	(D)	(D)	(D)	(C)	1.48	1.17	(C)	(C)	1.31
Pa. Av.	.67	1.18	.91	1.29	(C)	1.26	.91	.90	1.41	.98

Unit	Apr.	May	June	July	Aug.	Sept.	Oct.	Nov.	Dec.	Av.
3. Total Sick										
Thompson's Bn.	.50	.64	.75	(A)	(A)	(A)	(A)	(A)	(A)	.52
1st Pa. Rgt.	(B)	(B)	(B)	.55	(C)	.65	.59	.85	1.30	.83
3d Pa. Bn.	(D)	(D)	.41	.56	(C)	1.06	(C)	(E)	(E)	.77
5th Pa. Bn.	(D)	(D)	.89	.78	(C)	1.27	(C)	(E)	(E)	1.03
Prov'l State Bn.	(D)	(D)	(D)	(D)	(C)	1.27	.83	(C)	(C)	1.04
Pa. Av.	.50	.64	.59	.64	(C)	1.06	.71	.85	1.30	.85
Sick Present/ Sick Absent, Pa.	.49	.67	2.25	2.69	(C)	.82	.38	.77	.17	.75
Sick Present/ Sick Absent, Non-Pa.	.99	2.06	4.05	6.46	(C)	1.17	.76	.87	.27	1.01

So far as total sick rates are concerned, the Pennsylvania unit average for the period as a whole was some fifteen per cent below the average for other units of the command. This was due to a substantially lower overall rate for sick, present, as the rates for sick, absent were almost identical.

Average rates for total sick for both Pennsylvania and non-Pennsylvania units rose dramatically, and remained at high levels, after the Battle of Long Island. Aside from the fact that during that period there was a seasonal deterioration of weather, the Army was much of the time in retreat, which would have depressed morale, with a consequent effect on the sick rate.

With regard to total sick rates on a month-by-month basis, the average for all Pennsylvania units was significantly below the average for the other units of the command in all months except September and December. In September, however, three of the four Pennsylvania units were above the non-Pennsylvania average; only the exceptionally low rate in the 1st Pennsylvania Regiment brought the Pennsylvania average below the average for non-Pennsylvania units. In December, figures exist only for the 1st Pennsylvania Regiment, which reported over forty per cent of its assigned rank and file as sick, absent—conceivably, a reflection of the possibility that, being actually in Pennsylvania, many men went home with ailments that would not normally have called for their hospitalization.

In terms of the relationship between sick, present and sick, absent, the Pennsylvania units consistently had a substantially higher percentage of their sick in the sick, absent category than did the average non-Pennsylvania organization. This may indicate a higher incidence of more serious illness among the Pennsylvanians than among the soldiers from other states, but without independent evidence it is not possible to explain this difference with assurance.

Comparing the individual Pennsylvania units' average rates with the rates for corresponding months for the average non-Pennsylvania unit, all Pennsylvania organizations are found to have a lower rate of sick, present than the rest of the command. The 3d and 5th Pennsylvania battalions and the Provisional State Battalion exceeded that average, however, in sick, absent; and the 5th Pennsylvania Battalion and the Provisional State Battalion also exceeded it in terms of rates of total sick.

One point worthy of particular note is the difference between the February and April sick rates for Thompson's Battalion. Despite a rise of 1.2 per cent in the sick, absent rate, the drop in sick, present was so dramatic that the unit's total sick rate in April was less than half of what it had been in February. This could be due partly to improving weather; possibly, too, the climate of New York was better than that of Boston. A factor which cannot be discounted, however, is the change of command which took place on March 1, 1776. Edward Hand, who replaced William Thompson as colonel, was not only a physician but had served as a surgeon's mate in the British Army. It seems possible that he introduced and, as commanding officer, enforced field hygiene procedures which were of direct benefit to the health of the battalion. This possibility is reinforced by the fact that this organization had significantly lower sick rates than the other units in New York, at least until after the Battle of Long Island, even though it was exposed to the same conditions of weather and climate.

Sick rates for the other four Pennsylvania battalions, serving in the Northern Department, are shown in Table XIV.

TABLE XIV
Rank and File Sick Rates, Northern Department, May-November, 1776

Unit	May	June	July	Aug.	Sept.	Oct.	Nov.	Av.
A. Expressed as Total Rates								
1. Sick, Present								
1st Pa. Bn.	7.5	2.4	(C)	16.3	9.0	.4	(A)	7.1
2d Pa. Bn.	9.4	6.9	(C)	20.3	16.9	35.1	25.2	19.0
4th Pa. Bn.	17.3	7.3	(C)	26.6	24.5	30.0	38.2	24.0
6th Pa. Bn.	3.7	5.0	(C)	19.3	34.0	38.7	52.9	25.6
Pa. Av.	9.5	5.4	(C)	20.6	21.1	26.1	38.8	19.4
Non-Pa. Av.	10.3	20.9	(C)	21.4	35.3	24.3	18.4	21.8
2. Sick, Absent								
1st Pa. Bn.	4.1	8.8	(C)	18.2	34.0	31.4	(A)	19.3
2d Pa. Bn.	2.9	8.8	(C)	17.2	20.8	13.7	13.6	12.8
4th Pa. Bn.	.6	.5	(C)	3.1	3.4	4.6	4.9	2.9
6th Pa. Bn.	1.4	.5	(C)	8.0	4.1	13.2	15.1	7.1
Pa. Av.	2.3	4.7	(C)	11.6	15.6	15.7	11.2	10.1
Non-Pa. Av.	7.2	12.2	(C)	14.0	8.6	12.9	3.4	9.7

Unit	May	June	July	Aug.	Sept.	Oct.	Nov.	Av.
3. Total Sick								
1st Pa. Bn.	11.6	11.2	(C)	34.5	43.1	31.8	(A)	26.4
2d Pa. Bn.	12.3	15.7	(C)	37.5	37.7	48.7	38.7	31.8
4th Pa. Bn.	17.9	7.8	(C)	29.7	27.8	34.6	43.1	26.8
6th Pa. Bn.	5.1	5.5	(C)	27.3	38.1	51.9	68.0	32.7
Pa. Av.	11.7	10.1	(C)	32.3	36.7	41.8	49.9	29.5
Non-Pa. Av.	17.5	33.1	(C)	35.4	43.9	37.2	21.8	31.5
B. Expressed as Percentage of Corresponding Month's Non-Pennsylvania Average								
1. Sick, Present								
1st Pa. Bn.	.73	.11	(C)	.76	.25	.02	(A)	.32
2d Pa. Bn.	.91	.33	(C)	.95	.48	1.44	1.37	.87
4th Pa. Bn.	1.68	.35	(C)	1.24	.69	1.23	2.08	1.10
6th Pa. Bn.	.36	.24	(C)	.90	.96	1.59	2.90	1.17
Pa. Av.	.92	.26	(C)	.96	.60	1.07	2.11	.89
2. Sick, Absent								
1st Pa. Bn.	.57	.72	(C)	1.30	3.95	2.43	(A)	1.75
2d Pa. Bn.	.40	.72	(C)	1.23	2.42	1.06	4.00	1.32
4th Pa. Bn.	.08	.04	(C)	.22	.40	.36	1.44	.30
6th Pa. Bn.	.19	.04	(C)	.57	.48	1.02	4.44	.73
Pa. Av.	.32	.39	(C)	.83	1.81	1.22	3.29	1.04
3. Total Sick								
1st Pa. Bn.	.66	.34	(C)	.97	.98	.85	(A)	.84
2d Pa. Bn.	.70	.47	(C)	1.06	.86	1.31	1.78	1.01
4th Pa. Bn.	1.02	.24	(C)	.84	.63	.93	1.98	.85
6th Pa. Bn.	.29	.17	(C)	.77	.87	1.40	3.12	1.04
Pa. Av.	.67	.31	(C)	.91	.84	1.12	2.29	.94
Sick Present/ Sick Absent, Pa.	4.13	1.15	(C)	1.78	1.35	1.66	3.46	1.92
Sick Present/ Sick Absent, Non-Pa.	1.43	1.71	(C)	1.53	4.10	1.88	5.41	2.25

For the period as a whole, the Pennsylvania battalions in the Northern Department had a marginally lower rate for total sick than did the non-Pennsylvania units. However, when this rate is broken into its component elements, it develops that while the Pennsylvanians' sick, present rate was considerably lower than the average for the other organizations, their rate of sick, absent was somewhat higher. At the same time, both the Pennsylvania and non-Pennsylvania averages show a higher proportion of the total being in the sick, present rather than the sick, absent category. This may indicate limitations of facilities for hospital-type care in what was, compared to the operational area of Washington's Command, a relatively sparsely settled and undeveloped region, and not a difference in the incidence of more serious illness. One point which is obvious, however, is that average sick rates for both Pennsylvania and non-Pennsylvania units were much higher, in each corresponding month as well as over all, in the Northern Department than in Washington's Command.

A further examination of the monthly averages shows that the same phenomenon of a dramatic jump in sick rates occurred in the Northern Department in the period after the retreat from Canada as occurred in Washington's Command in the months of retreat from Long Island. In the Northern Department, this increase was more marked in the Pennsylvania battalions' average than in the average non-Pennsylvania unit.

The month of November brought the Pennsylvania units their highest total sick rate, which was more than twice as great as the non-Pennsylvania average for that month, and was almost five times their lowest rate, which they experienced in the preceding June.

As for individual Pennsylvania units, the 2d and 6th battalions had the highest total sick rates, differing from each other only by approximately one per cent. The 1st and 4th Pennsylvania battalion rates were approximately five per cent below those of the other two Pennsylvania organizations, but differed from each other by only four-tenths of a per cent.

One curious point is that although the 1st and 2d Pennsylvania battalions had comparatively low rates for sick, present, they had high rates for sick, absent, whereas the exact reverse is true for the 4th and 6th battalions. Except for the 6th Battalion, which spent the period from July through September providing an outpost force at Crown Point, all the Pennsylvania battalions served in the same locations, subjected to the same conditions. Perhaps the high rate of sick, present for the 6th Battalion is due partly to its assignment, which presumably required a man who would have been hospitalized if the unit were in garrison to be kept with the battalion as "sick in quarters." It is also noteworthy that prior to August, this battalion had experienced one of the lowest sick, present rates of any of the four Pennsylvania battalions. During that same period, its sick, absent rates had also been extremely low. It may be significant that the battalion commander, Col. William Irvine, was a physician by profession, and that he was taken prisoner at Three Rivers on June 9; conceivably, while he was with the command he had been able to enforce proper field hygiene practices by his troops, without succeeding in convincing them of the importance of such practices.

Another noteworthy point is that the 4th Pennsylvania Battalion, while showing the distinctly lowest sick, absent rate, consistently had by far the greatest number of sick, present in proportion to sick, absent. Its commander was Col. Anthony Wayne, who traditionally had been noted as a disciplinarian. On a purely speculative basis, it might be suggested that his troops viewed him as a martinet, and resorted to one of the few refuges available to enlisted men under such circumstances, which in modern military slang is known as "riding the Sick Book," or reporting sick with minor or imaginary ailments.

Phase II—April, 1777-May, 1778

Sick rates for this phase will be examined in terms of the same time periods that were used for strengths. Table XV lists the rates for the periods from the initial concentration of Washington's Command after the formation of the three-year regiments through the last complete month of the Valley Forge encampment.

TABLE XV
Rank and File Sick Rates (Monthly Averages),
Washington's Command, April, 1777-May, 1778

Regiment	April-May, 1777		Oct.-Nov., 1777		Dec., 1777-May, 1778	
	Pa. Rgtl. Rate	Pa. Rgt./ Non-Pa. Av.	Pa. Rgtl. Rate	Pa. Rgt./ Non-Pa. Av.	Pa. Rgtl. Rate	Pa. Rgt./ Non-Pa. Av.
A. Sick, Present						
1st Pa.	9.0	.81	6.1	.85	6.3	.37
2d Pa.	3.1	.28	7.1	.99	9.2	.53
3d Pa.	8.8	.79	15.7	2.18	10.6	.62
4th Pa.	9.7	.87	7.6	1.06	7.5	.44
5th Pa.	16.9	1.52	7.3	1.01	8.3	.48
6th Pa.	(C)	(C)	2.9	.40	6.4	.37
7th Pa.	(C)	(C)	8.1	1.13	9.7	.56
8th Pa.	8.7	.78	7.1	.99	10.8	.63
9th Pa.	2.6	.23	5.1	.71	7.5	.44
10th Pa.	17.3	1.56	4.9	.68	7.1	.41
"Old" 11th Pa.	9.4	.85	4.9	.68	7.2	.42
12th Pa.	17.8	1.60	5.8	.81	11.7	.68
13th Pa.	(C)	(C)	5.6	.78	10.8	.63
German Rgt.	8.0	.72	3.1	.43	7.2(J)	n/a
Patton's Additional	12.9	1.16	3.7	.51	10.8	.63
Hartley's Additional	6.5	.59	7.3	1.01	5.7(K)	n/a
Pa. Av. (L)	10.1	.91	6.4	.89	8.9	.52
Non-Pa. Av.	11.1	—	7.2	—	17.2	—
B. Sick, Absent						
1st Pa.	11.3	.49	17.4	.73	10.6	.66
2d Pa.	1.5	.07	8.6	.36	6.3	.39
3d Pa.	1.8	.08	27.0	1.13	18.3	1.14
4th Pa.	4.6	.20	17.9	.75	13.7	.86
5th Pa.	10.4	.45	24.9	1.04	17.8	1.11
6th Pa.	(C)	(C)	29.8	1.24	23.9	1.49
7th Pa.	(C)	(C)	27.2	1.13	16.0	1.00
8th Pa.	17.7	.77	18.3	.76	14.4	.90
9th Pa.	3.1	.13	28.7	1.20	18.1	1.13
10th Pa.	2.1	.09	33.2	1.38	23.3	1.46
"Old" 11th Pa.	0	0	35.2	1.47	25.5	1.59
12th Pa.	13.4	.58	24.2	1.01	17.1	1.07
13th Pa.	(C)	(C)	14.3	.60	15.3	.96
German Rgt.	15.3	.67	9.0	.38	13.4(J)	n/a
Patton's Additional	4.8	.21	19.7	.82	24.5	1.53
Hartley's Additional	2.6	.11	23.9	.99	25.4(K)	n/a
Pa. Av. (L)	11.8	.51	20.8	.87	16.5	1.03
Non-Pa. Av.	23.0	—	24.0	—	16.0	—

Regiment	April-May, 1777		Oct.-Nov., 1777		Dec., 1777-May, 1778	
	Pa. Rgt. Rate	Pa. Rgt./ Non-Pa. Av.	Pa. Rgtl. Rate	Pa. Rgt./ Non-Pa. Av.	Pa. Rgtl. Rate	Pa. Rgt./ Non-Pa. Av.
C. Total Sick						
1st Pa.	20.3	.84	23.4	.75	16.9	.51
2d Pa.	4.6	.19	15.6	.50	15.4	.46
3d Pa.	10.6	.44	42.8	1.37	28.9	.87
4th Pa.	14.3	.59	25.5	.81	21.2	.64
5th Pa.	27.2	1.12	32.2	1.03	26.1	.79
6th Pa.	(C)	(C)	32.6	1.04	30.2	.91
7th Pa.	(C)	(C)	35.3	1.13	25.6	.77
8th Pa.	26.4	1.09	25.3	.81	25.2	.76
9th Pa.	5.7	.24	33.8	1.08	25.6	.77
10th Pa.	19.4	.80	38.1	1.22	30.4	.92
"Old" 11th Pa.	9.4	.39	40.1	1.28	32.6	.98
12th Pa.	31.2	1.29	30.1	.96	28.8	.87
13th Pa.	(C)	(C)	19.9	.64	26.1	.79
German Rgt.	23.3	.96	12.1	.39	20.6(J)	n/a
Patton's Additional	17.7	.73	23.5	.75	35.3	1.06
Hartley's Additional	9.0	.37	31.2	.99	31.1(K)	n/a
Pa. Av. (L)	20.7	.86	27.0	.86	25.3	.76
Non-Pa. Av.	24.2	—	31.3	—	33.2	—
Sick Present/ Sick Absent, Pa.	.86		.31		.54	
Sick Present/ Sick Absent, Non-Pa.	.48		.30		1.08	

Total sick rates for the Pennsylvania regiments rose over six per cent between the April-May and October-November periods, but during the Valley Forge encampment actually dropped slightly (approximately two per cent) from the October-November level. The non-Pennsylvania average, however, rose consistently, increasing some seven per cent from the first to the second of these periods, and rising slightly (2.1 per cent) between the second and third periods. On a comparative basis, the Pennsylvania average maintained the same level (fourteen per cent below the non-Pennsylvania average) in April-May and October-November, but dropped to twenty-four per cent below the non-Pennsylvania average at Valley Forge.

As for the breakdown between sick, present and sick, absent, the Pennsylvania regiments had more sick, absent than sick, present during all three periods. The same is true for the non-Pennsylvania regiments only during the April-May and October-November periods. During the winter encampment, they reported eight per cent higher rates of sick, present than sick, absent, whereas the Pennsylvania regiments' rates show almost twice as many men sick, absent as sick, present during that period. The explanation probably lies in the fact that the Pennsylvanians were serving in their own state, and ailing soldiers could readily be sent home for care instead of having to be treated in camp.

With regard to individual Pennsylvania regiments, only three out of thirteen—the 5th, 8th, and 12th—had total sick rates above the average non-Pennsylvania rate during the April-May period; but seven out of sixteen (the 3d, 5th, 6th, 7th, 9th, 10th, and "Old" 11th) were above the non-Pennsylvania average in October-November. By contrast, during the winter encampment all Pennsylvania regiments except Patton's were below the non-Pennsylvania average, by amounts ranging from two to fifty-four per cent.

On an absolute scale, sick rates were high in all periods. The reports for April-May show only four of the thirteen Pennsylvania regiments with total sick rates of less than ten per cent. Four others ranged between ten and twenty per cent, another four were in the twenty per cent bracket, and one experienced an average monthly sick rate of over thirty per cent. For the October-November period, the lowest rate among the sixteen regiments reporting was twelve per cent; only two others were below twenty per cent; four were between twenty and thirty per cent; seven had rates between thirty and forty per cent; and two listed over forty per cent of their rank and file as sick. At Valley Forge, eight of the fourteen Pennsylvania regiments completing the entire encampment had average monthly sick rates between twenty and thirty per cent; only two regiments had lower rates (the lowest of all being fifteen per cent); but none of the remaining four had an average sick rate of much over thirty-five per cent.

No one regiment can be said to have had consistently the lowest or the highest rates. However, the sick rate of the 10th Pennsylvania was in the higher half for all Pennsylvania regiments in all three periods; and the 3d, 5th, "Old" 11th, and 12th regiments were in the upper half during two of the three periods. By comparison, both the 2d and 4th regiments consistently had sick rates that were in the lower half for Pennsylvania regiments, and the 1st and 8th regiments had lower-half rates during two of the three periods.

Table XVI presents the sick rates for the Pennsylvania regiments of Washington's Command during the eighteen months after the Valley Forge encampment.

TABLE XVI
Rank and File Sick Rates (Monthly Averages), Washington's Command, June, 1778-November, 1779

Regiment	June-Nov., 1778		Dec., 1778-May, 1779		June-Nov., 1779	
	Pa. Rgtl. Rate	Pa. Rgt./ Non-Pa. Av.	Pa. Rgtl. Rate	Pa. Rgt./ Non-Pa. Av.	Pa. Rgtl. Rate	Pa. Rgt./ Non-Pa. Av.
A. Sick, Present						
1st Pa.	4.9	.72	4.8	.70	4.3	.91
2d Pa.	6.3	.93	6.3	.91	5.3	1.13
3d Pa.	7.2	1.06	6.9	1.00	7.3	1.15
5th Pa.	8.0	1.18	7.3	1.06	10.8	2.30
6th Pa.	4.3	.63	4.9	.71	7.8	1.49
7th Pa.	7.1	1.04	6.4	.93	6.6	1.40
9th Pa.	7.8	1.15	7.1	1.03	10.6	2.26
10th Pa.	3.8	.56	3.4	.49	4.1	.87
Pa. Av.	6.2	.91	5.9	.87	7.1	1.51
Non-Pa. Av.	6.8	—	6.9	—	4.7	—
B. Sick, Absent						
1st Pa.	6.8	.41	3.1	.38	3.6	.69
2d Pa.	9.0	.54	6.6	.80	4.2	.81
3d Pa.	20.0	1.20	7.7	.94	5.0	.96
5th Pa.	15.1	.91	6.9	.84	5.1	.98
6th Pa.	15.9	.96	7.7	.94	3.2	.62
7th Pa.	6.3	.38	3.5	.43	2.3	.44
9th Pa.	19.4	1.17	6.6	.80	5.6	1.08
10th Pa.	8.5	.51	5.6	.68	3.4	.65
Pa. Av.	12.6	.76	6.0	.73	4.1	.79
Non-Pa. Av.	16.6	—	8.2	—	5.2	—
C. Total Sick						
1st Pa.	11.7	.50	7.9	.52	7.9	.80
2d Pa.	15.3	.65	12.9	.85	9.5	.96
3d Pa.	27.2	1.16	14.6	.97	12.3	1.24
5th Pa.	23.1	.99	14.2	.94	15.9	1.61
6th Pa.	20.2	.86	12.6	.83	11.0	1.11
7th Pa.	13.4	.57	9.9	.66	8.9	.90
9th Pa.	27.2	1.16	13.7	.91	16.2	1.64
10th Pa.	12.3	.53	9.0	.60	7.5	.76
Pa. Av.	18.8	.80	11.9	.79	11.2	1.13
Non-Pa. Av.	23.4	—	15.1	—	9.9	—
Sick Present/ Sick Absent, Pa.	.49		.98		1.73	
Sick Present/ Sick Absent, Non-Pa.	.41		.84		.90	

The most immediately striking feature of the period covered by Table XVI is the major reduction in sick rates from the period covered by Table XV. The rate of total sick for the Pennsylvania regiments dropped 6.5 per cent between the 1777-1778 winter encampment and the 1778 campaign season; it dropped approximately seven per cent more during the 1778-1779 winter encampment; and then dropped still again, although by less than one per cent, during the 1779 campaign season. Consistent percentage reductions of even greater magnitude occurred in the non-Pennsylvania averages (approximately nine, eight, and five per cent, respectively, for the three periods). On a relative basis, the average total sick rate for Pennsylvania regiments was below that of the non-Pennsylvania regiments by some twenty per cent during both the 1778 campaign season and the 1778-1779 winter encampment; the Pennsylvania rate was thirteen per cent higher than the non-Pennsylvania average during the 1779 campaign season, but this reflects a greater degree of reduction in the sick rates in the non-Pennsylvania regiments, not an increase in the Pennsylvania sick rate. What caused the decline of the Pennsylvania sick rate to be markedly slowed was a sharp increase during the June-November, 1779, period in the rate of sick, present, which was one and a half times the rate for non-Pennsylvania regiments. No outstanding reason for this upsurge of illness among the Pennsylvania troops is evident.

Except for that period, the Pennsylvania contingent's sick, present rate was lower than its sick, absent rate, which is consistent with its previous record.

During the 1778 campaign season, only the 3d and 9th Pennsylvania regiments experienced total sick rates above the non-Pennsylvania average. While encamped for the 1778-1779 winter, all Pennsylvania regiments had total sick rates below that average. The 1779 campaign season, however, saw the 3d, 5th, 6th, and 9th Pennsylvania regiments—half of all the Pennsylvania regiments of the command—all with above-average total sick rates.

Comparing the Pennsylvania regiments with each other, the 3d, 9th, and 5th regiments had relatively high sick rates in all three periods, and the 1st, 7th, and 10th had consistently lower rates. The remaining two Pennsylvania regiments (the 2d and 6th) had comparatively high sick rates during two of the three periods.

Data for the Pennsylvania regiments on the New York frontier and with the Sullivan Expedition are extremely sparse. Table XVII presents such information as is available.

TABLE XVII
Rank and File Sick Rates (Monthly Averages),
New York Frontier and Sullivan Expedition,
July, 1778-October, 1779

Regiment	Nov., 1778		Dec., 1778-May, 1779		June-Oct., 1779	
	Pa. Rgtl. Rate	Pa. Rgt./ Non-Pa. Av.	Pa. Rgtl. Rate	Pa. Rgt./ Non-Pa. Av.	Pa. Rgtl. Rate	Pa. Rgt./ Non-Pa. Av.
A. Sick, Present						
4th Pa.	5.8	1.32	5.0	1.04	3.1	.63
"New" 11th Pa.	(B)	(B)	4.8	.71	3.0	.61
Pa. Av.	5.8	1.32	4.9	.72	3.1	.63
Non-Pa. Av.	4.4	—	6.8	—	4.9	—
B. Sick, Absent						
4th Pa.	22.6	1.42	10.8	1.86	4.8	.62
"New" 11th Pa.	(B)	(B)	.9	.16	8.6	1.12
Pa. Av.	22.6	1.42	5.9	1.02	6.7	.87
Non-Pa. Av.	15.9	—	5.8	—	7.7	—
C. Total Sick						
4th Pa.	28.4	1.40	15.8	1.26	7.9	.63
"New" 11th Pa.	(B)	(B)	5.7	.46	11.6	.92
Pa. Av.	28.4	1.40	10.8	.86	9.8	.78
Non-Pa. Av.	20.3	—	12.5	—	12.6	—
Sick Present/ Sick Absent, Pa.	.26		.83		.46	
Sick Present/ Sick Absent, Non-Pa.	.28		1.17		.64	

To the extent that the limited number of months for which figures exist permits a comparison, Table XVII shows that the experience of the Pennsylvania regiments on the New York frontier and during Sullivan's Expedition was similar to that of the Pennsylvania regiments of Washington's Command during the same period: the total sick rates were about the same, and they showed a parallel decline; the only marked difference is that the Table XVII units consistently had more men sick, absent than sick, present, whereas the Pennsylvania regiments of Washington's Command had more sick, absent than sick, present in the 1778 campaign season and the 1778-1779 winter encampment, but not in the 1779 campaign season.

Except for the November, 1778, figure (based only on the 4th Pennsylvania), the Pennsylvania contingent treated in Table XVII suffered total average sick rates that were substantially lower than the non-Pennsylvania average. As between the two Pennsylvania regiments considered, during the two periods for which data on both are available, each had a high rate and a low rate, on a reciprocal basis. On the whole, however, the 4th Pennsylvania's sick rate was about thirty-seven per cent greater than that of the "New" 11th.

Sick rates for the Western Department are set forth in Table XVIII.

TABLE XVIII
Rank and File Sick Rates (Monthly Averages),
Western Department, December, 1778-November, 1779

Regiment	Dec., 1778-May, 1779		June-Nov., 1779	
	Pa. Rgtl. Rate	Pa. Rgt./ Non-Pa. Av.	Pa. Rgtl. Rate	Pa. Rgt./ Non-Pa. Av.
A. Sick, Present				
8th Pa.	3.5	.81	6.3	.89
Non-Pa. Av.	4.3	—	7.1	—
B. Sick, Absent				
8th Pa.	2.7	6.75	0	n/a
Non-Pa. Av.	.4	—	0	—
C. Total Sick				
8th Pa.	6.2	1.32	6.3	.89
Non-Pa. Av.	4.7	—	7.1	—
Sick Present/ Sick Absent, Pa.	1.30		n/a	
Sick Present/ Sick Absent, Non-Pa.	10.75		n/a	

On an absolute scale, the 8th Pennsylvania's sick rates as reported during this period were very low, and remained virtually unchanged despite a drastic reduction in numerical strength of the regiment between the winter encampment and the campaign season. Although a considerable proportional difference exists between the 8th Pennsylvania's total sick rates and the non-Pennsylvania averages, the *finite* differences are quite small. The failure of any Western Department units to report any men as sick, absent during the 1779 campaign season may be an omission rather than an indication that no men fell into the sick, absent category during that period.

Moving on to the final period, Table XIX depicts sick rates in Washington's Command during the twelve months preceding the mutiny of the Pennsylvania Line.

TABLE XIX
Rank and File Sick Rates (Monthly Averages),
Washington's Command, December, 1779-November, 1780

Regiment	Dec., 1779-May, 1780		June-Nov., 1780	
	Pa. Rgtl. Rate	Pa. Rgt./ Non-Pa. Av.	Pa. Rgtl. Rate	Pa. Rgt./ Non-Pa. Av.
A. Sick, Present				
1st Pa.	5.5	.83	4.2	.98
2d Pa.	6.3	.95	3.6	.84
3d Pa.	10.9	1.65	6.6	1.53
4th Pa.	6.9	1.05	2.9	.67
5th Pa.	10.4	1.58	4.0	.93
6th Pa.	9.3	1.41	3.7	.86

Regiment	Dec., 1779-May, 1780		June-Nov., 1780	
	Pa. Rgtl. Rate	Pa. Rgt./ Non-Pa. Av.	Pa. Rgtl. Rate	Pa. Rgt./ Non-Pa. Av.
7th Pa.	6.5	.98	5.5	1.28
9th Pa.	14.6	2.21	5.4	1.26
10th Pa.	4.2	.64	4.2	.98
"New" 11th Pa.	6.3	.95	3.3	.77
Pa. Av.	8.1	1.23	4.3	1.00
Non-Pa. Av.	6.6	—	4.3	—
B. Sick, Absent				
1st Pa.	2.8	.51	7.6	1.49
2d Pa.	3.5	.64	6.9	1.35
3d Pa.	2.3	.42	6.9	1.35
4th Pa.	4.0	.73	4.3	.84
5th Pa.	4.2	.76	6.2	1.22
6th Pa.	1.4	.25	4.4	.86
7th Pa.	1.7	.31	5.2	1.02
9th Pa.	4.8	.87	8.0	1.57
10th Pa.	3.7	.67	5.4	1.06
"New" 11th Pa.	3.2	.58	7.4	1.45
Pa. Av.	3.2	.58	6.2	1.22
Non-Pa. Av.	5.5	—	5.1	—
C. Total Sick				
1st Pa.	8.3	.69	11.8	1.26
2d Pa.	9.8	.81	10.5	1.12
3d Pa.	13.2	1.09	13.5	1.44
4th Pa.	10.9	.90	7.2	.77
5th Pa.	14.6	1.21	10.2	1.09
6th Pa.	10.7	.88	8.1	.86
7th Pa.	8.2	.68	10.7	1.14
9th Pa.	19.4	1.60	13.4	1.43
10th Pa.	7.9	.65	9.6	1.02
"New" 11th Pa.	9.5	.79	10.7	1.14
Pa. Av.	11.3	.93	10.6	1.13
Non-Pa. Av.	12.1	—	9.4	—
Sick Present/ Sick Absent, Pa.	2.53		.69	
Sick Present/ Sick Absent, Non-Pa.	1.20		.84	

Table **XIX** shows that the total sick rates of the Pennsylvania regiments of Washington's Command varied very little during the final year of the regiments' service from what had prevailed since the December, 1778-May, 1779, winter encampment. As compared with the non-Pennsylvania regiments, however, the Pennsylvania average during the December, 1779-November, 1780, period tended to approximate the non-Pennsylvania averages somewhat more closely than had been the case during the preceding year. Again, the total sick rate is seen to be lower during the winter encampment than during the campaign season.

Another difference noticeable between the two seasons is that whereas the Pennsylvania units had a considerably higher rate of sick, absent than sick, present during the campaign season, the reverse was true during the winter encampment of 1779-1780. That high ratio of sick, present to sick, absent may be a continuation and intensification of the situation prevailing (for whatever reasons) during the immediately preceding (1779) campaign season. These are the only two instances after the formation of the three-year regiments when the Pennsylvania contingent of Washington's Command had more sick, present than sick, absent.

For the 1779-1780 winter encampment, three of the ten Pennsylvania regiments (the 3d, 5th, and 9th) had total sick rates exceeding the non-Pennsylvania average, but only the 4th and 6th Pennsylvania regiments failed to exceed that average during the 1780 campaign season. For the most part, this reflects the distortion resulting from calculating percentages from numbers which are quite small. Viewed in absolute terms, the sick rates for most of the Pennsylvania units as well as the average for non-Pennsylvania units during the months covered by Table XIX were comparatively low. The increase which occurred in individual regiments' sick rates during the June-November, 1780, period is almost certainly due in considerable measure to the arrival of the reinforcements mentioned earlier—men who were not, as a whole, inured to field service, and who, compared with the men they replaced, were untrained in caring for themselves.

Once again the 10th Pennsylvania, this time joined by the 2d, had consistently low total sick rates, while the 3d and 9th regiments continued to have high rates.

Sick rates for the Western Department during this same time-span are shown in Table XX.

TABLE XX
Rank and File Sick Rates (Monthly Averages),
Western Department, December, 1779-November, 1780

Regiment	Dec., 1779-May, 1780		June-Nov., 1780	
	Pa. Rgtl. Rate	Pa. Rgt./ Non-Pa. Av.	Pa. Rgtl. Rate	Pa. Rgt./ Non-Pa. Av.
A. Sick, Present				
8th Pa.	3.3	.80	3.4	1.10
Non-Pa. Av.	4.1	—	3.1	—
B. Sick, Absent				
8th Pa.	.7	1.80	0	n/a
Non-Pa. Av.	.4	—	0	—
C. Total Sick				
8th Pa.	4.0	.89	3.4	1.10
Non-Pa. Av.	4.5	—	3.1	—
Sick Present/ Sick Absent, Pa.	4.7		n/a	
Sick Present/ Sick Absent, Non-Pa.	10.3		n/a	

Sick rates reported for the 8th Pennsylvania for the final twelve months considered were even lower than before—in fact, the total rate for the June-November, 1780, period (during which no men were listed as sick, absent) is the lowest rate reported by any Pennsylvania organization for any period during the entire war. The men of the 8th Pennsylvania were either exceptionally healthy or reporting was somewhat lax. The situation is rendered even more noteworthy because of the low assigned strength to which the regiment had sunk, for a relatively small number of men reported sick would represent a larger sick *rate* than would be the case for an equal number of sick men in a larger unit.

Considering the entire health record of the Pennsylvania Continental organizations, the figures which have been brought out justify a number of observations.

With regard to total sick rates, most of the time the average of Pennsylvania units was lower than the average for all non-Pennsylvania units of the same major command. The only exceptions were in Washington's Command during the campaign seasons of 1779 and 1780; on the New York frontier during the campaign season of 1778; and in the Western Department during the winter encampment of 1778-1779 and the campaign season of 1780. In all these cases except the New York frontier, the Pennsylvania total sick rate exceeded the non-Pennsylvania average by only marginal amounts.

The highest Pennsylvania average rate of total sick (29.5) occurred in the Northern Department in the May-November, 1776, period. The next highest (28.4) was on the New York frontier during the campaign season of 1778. The other two exceptionally high rates were in Washington's Command—27.0 during the 1777 campaign season, and 25.3 during the Valley Forge encampment which followed it. The lowest total sick rates were registered in the Western Department.

The bulk of the Pennsylvania regiments saw all or most of their service in Washington's Command. Their average total sick rates rose steadily through the 1777 campaign season, then began a decline— sharp after the Valley Forge encampment during the following twelve months, and then leveling off at between eleven and twelve per cent for the remainder of their service. The stabilization of the sick rate at this fairly low level probably reflects a combination of several influences: the less hardy men had been eliminated by death or discharge; the troops had become disciplined, thereby observing camp hygiene regulations more conscientiously; and the conditions of service had become less severe—the period of low sick rates coincides with the period when active, large-scale campaigning had ceased, the troops being employed solely in scouting and patrolling, punctuated occasionally by a skirmish or a moderate-size raid.

So far as individual Pennsylvania units are concerned, their average monthly total sick rates ranged from a low of 3.4 for the 8th Pennsylvania during the campaign season of 1780 to a high of sixty-eight for the 6th Pennsylvania Battalion in November, 1776. After the reorganization of July 1, 1778, when the Pennsylvania Line took what was essentially its permanent form, the 10th Pennsylvania had the lowest total sick rates, relatively speaking, among the Pennsylvania regiments; while the 3d and 9th regiments had the highest.

Viewing as a whole the entire period of the three-year regiments' service, and considering only those regiments consistently with Washington's Command (as was done for strengths in the preceding section), the monthly average total sick rates, by regiment in descending order, are as shown in Table XXI.

TABLE XXI
Average Monthly Total Sick Rates,
Washington's Command, April, 1777-November, 1780

Regiment	Pa. Rgtl. Rate	Pa. Rgt./ Non-Pa. Av.
3d Pa.	20.4	1.03
5th Pa.	20.4	1.03
9th Pa.	19.4	.98
6th Pa.	17.9	.90
10th Pa.	16.8	.85
7th Pa.	16.0	.81
1st Pa.	13.5	.68
2d Pa.	11.7	.59
Pa. Av.	17.0	.86
Non-Pa. Av.	19.8	—

The regiments of the Pennsylvania contingent, together, averaged fourteen per cent fewer total sick per month than the non-Pennsylvania average. Only two Pennsylvania regiments (the 3d and 5th) were above that average, and only marginally so at that. The 6th and 9th were also close to the non-Pennsylvania average, but slightly below. The remaining four regiments—the 1st, 2d, 7th, and 10th—were well below the average sick rate, by anything from fifteen to over forty per cent.

In summary, the incidence of illness in the Pennsylvania units as a whole appears with a marked degree of consistency to have been lower than the average for the other units with which they were serving.

DESERTIONS

In speaking of desertion in the Continental Army, it is important to remember that no distinction was made between true desertion—that is, unlawful departure with the intention not to return—and absence without leave. Consequently, without minimizing the scandalous rates of actual desertions which occurred, the fact remains that the desertions reported do not all represent desertions in the modern sense of the term.

Data on desertions, moreover, were not systematically recorded until the Valley Forge encampment. These data, expressed as percentages of rank and file assigned, will be presented in as close conformity as possible with the chronological sequence employed for strength figures and sick rates.

Table XXII addresses the desertion rates during the 1777-1778 winter encampment.

TABLE XXII
Desertion Rates (Monthly Averages),
December, 1777-May, 1778

Regiment	Pa. Rgtl. Rate	Pa. Rgt./ Non-Pa. Av.
1st Pa.	2.20	2.16
2d Pa.	2.44	2.39
3d Pa.	1.34	1.31
4th Pa.	4.56	4.47
5th Pa.	2.22	2.18
6th Pa.	1.98	1.94
7th Pa.	4.04	3.96
8th Pa.	.81	.79
9th Pa.	3.02	2.96
10th Pa.	1.98	1.94
"Old" 11th Pa.	2.19	2.15
12th Pa.	.90	.88
13th Pa.	2.13	2.09
German Rgt.	.33(J)	n/a
Patton's Additional	1.50	1.47
Hartley's Additional	1.75(K)	n/a
Pa. Av. (L)	2.24	2.20
Non-Pa. Av.	1.02	—

Among the forces at Valley Forge during the winter encampment of 1777-1778, the Pennsylvania regiments as a whole (excluding the German Regiment and Hartley's Regiment) had a desertion rate two and a fifth times as high as the average for non-Pennsylvania regiments! This was not due to an extremely high rate in one regiment outweighing moderate rates in others; in fact, desertion rates in every Pennsylvania regiment except the 8th and 12th exceeded the non-

Pennsylvania average during this period. The highest Pennsylvania desertion rates during this period were registered by the 4th and 7th regiments.

In part, the high incidence of desertion among the Pennsylvania troops may be due to their being in their own state, making unauthorized visits home more feasible and therefore more tempting. In this connection, it may be significant that the two regiments with the lowest desertion rates—the 8th and 12th—were from parts of Pennsylvania remote from Valley Forge, and that the 4th Pennsylvania, with one of the two highest rates, had four companies from areas adjacent to the campsite.

The next phase presented deals with Washington's Command during the period after the Valley Forge encampment through the campaign season of 1779.

TABLE XXIII
Desertion Rates (Monthly Averages),
Washington's Command, June, 1778-November, 1779

| Regiment | June-Nov., 1778 | | Dec., 1778-May, 1779 | | June-Nov., 1779 | |
	Pa. Rgtl. Rate	Pa. Rgt./ Non-Pa. Av.	Pa. Rgtl. Rate	Pa. Rgt./ Non-Pa. Av.	Pa. Rgtl. Rate	Pa. Rgt./ Non-Pa. Av.
1st Pa.	.65	.70	1.35	1.32	2.81	3.12
2d Pa.	.91	.98	1.29	1.26	1.06	1.18
3d Pa.	.41	.44	1.00	.98	.95	1.06
5th Pa.	.66	.71	.68	.67	1.13	1.26
6th Pa.	1.00	1.08	.67	.66	1.95	2.17
7th Pa.	.35	.38	1.19	1.17	2.04	2.27
9th Pa.	1.83	1.97	1.83	1.79	2.77	3.08
10th Pa.	1.49	1.60	.57	.56	.92	1.02
Pa. Av.	.91	.98	1.07	1.05	1.70	1.89
Non-Pa. Av.	.93	—	1.02	—	.90	—

In the 1778 campaign season, the Pennsylvania regiments' average desertion rate dropped dramatically from its level during the preceding six months. This reduction occurred not only in absolute terms, but also in relation to the average for non-Pennsylvania regiments, although it fell only marginally below that average. Only three of these eight Pennsylvania regiments (the 6th, 9th, and 10th) exceeded the non-Pennsylvania average; and of these, the excess was not significant in the case of the 6th.

During the 1778-1779 winter encampment there was an increase in desertion rates in both the Pennsylvania contingent and the average non-Pennsylvania regiment, but the increase was slightly greater among the Pennsylvanians. The impression given by this minor increase is somewhat deceptive, for treating the Pennsylvania rates as an average conceals significant reductions in the 6th and 10th regiments and significant increases in the 1st, 2d, 3d, and 7th regiments. The rate for the 5th Pennsylvania remained low and that for the 9th remained high.

The campaign season of 1779 brought a marked increase in the Pennsylvania average desertion rates with a simultaneous reduction in the non-Pennsylvania average, with the result that the Pennsylvania regiments as a whole had a rate eighty-nine per cent above that of the other regiments of the command. Only the 3d Pennsylvania's rate was lower than it had been during the preceding period, and even then it exceeded the non-Pennsylvania average. All other Pennsylvania regiments registered increases over the 1778-1779 winter encampment, and the desertion rates of all Pennsylvania regiments were above the average of non-Pennsylvania regiments; the 1st and 9th Pennsylvania regiments had rates more than three times as great as the command average, and the 6th and 7th Pennsylvania regiments' rates were more than double that average; the 2d and 5th were significantly above the average, although by lesser amounts.

There is no obvious explanation for this upsurge in Pennsylvania desertions. While it is true that the campaign season of 1779 also was the one period during which the average total sick rate for the Pennsylvania three-year regiments exceeded the average for non-Pennsylvania regiments, this relative rise was due to a reduction in the non-Pennsylvania sick rate rather than an increase in the Pennsylvania sick rate.

Insufficient information is available to justify any attempt to analyze desertion rates of the Pennsylvania regiments serving on the New York frontier and with the Sullivan Expedition. Some figures are available, however, for the Western Department during the 1778-1779 winter encampment season.

TABLE XXIV
Desertion Rates (Monthly Averages),
Western Department, December, 1778-May, 1779

Regiment	Pa. Rgtl. Rate	Pa. Rgt./ Non-Pa. Av.
8th Pa.	.26	1.37
Non-Pa. Av.	.19	—

As was the case for sickness, desertion rates in the Western Department were very low during this period. Perhaps the fact that during much of this period the troops were operating in small detachments deep in hostile territory inhibited desertion or made reporting incomplete, or both.

During the final year of the Pennsylvania regiments' service, desertion rose to new heights for both the Pennsylvania and non-Pennsylvania regiments of Washington's Command.

TABLE XXV
Desertion Rates (Monthly Averages),
Washington's Command, December, 1779-November, 1780

| Regiment | Dec., 1779-May, 1780 | | June-Nov., 1780 | |
	Pa. Rgtl. Rate	Pa. Rgt./ Non-Pa. Av.	Pa. Rgtl. Rate	Pa. Rgt./ Non-Pa. Av.
1st Pa.	1.75	.93	1.68	1.17
2d Pa.	1.85	.98	2.04	1.42
3d Pa.	1.73	.92	1.43	.99
4th Pa.	2.78	1.48	.92	.64
5th Pa.	2.15	1.14	2.08	1.44
6th Pa.	2.24	1.19	1.17	.81
7th Pa.	2.91	1.55	1.45	1.01
9th Pa.	2.67	1.42	2.28	1.58
10th Pa.	2.14	1.14	2.04	1.42
"New" 11th Pa.	4.23	2.25	1.20	.83
Pa. Av.	2.45	1.30	1.63	1.13
Non-Pa. Av.	1.88	—	1.44	—

Table XXV shows that the 1779-1780 winter encampment saw the Pennsylvania average desertion rate reach the highest peak recorded during the war. In contrast to the previous high point for Pennsylvania regiments (at Valley Forge), however, the non-Pennsylvania average was also at a high point, so that the Pennsylvania rate was not as much greater, relatively, as it had been during the 1777-1778 winter encampment.

To a degree, the high Pennsylvania average in the December, 1779-May, 1780, period was due to an abnormally high rate for the "New" 11th Pennsylvania. At the same time, except for the 1st Pennsylvania, all Pennsylvania regiments had increases in desertion rates over the 1779 campaign season, and all but the 1st, 2d, and 3d regiments (whose rates were slightly below the non-Pennsylvania average) were well above the command average.

On a speculative basis, it might be suggested that the high desertion rates reflected a deterioration of morale at a point when the troops had become tired and dispirited from lengthy service but were still many months short of their scheduled discharge dates, and at the same time saw no end to the war in sight.

The final six months before the mutiny of the Pennsylvania Line, corresponding to the 1780 campaign season, brought a reduction in desertions, but only to levels that still were high compared to most of the previous months. Again, the Pennsylvania rate was substantially greater than the non-Pennsylvania average, although not dramatically so. Except in the case of the 2d Pennsylvania, whose desertion rate increased over the preceding period, the rates for all Pennsylvania regiments declined. Only for the 3d, 4th, 6th, and "New" 11th, however, were these reductions sufficient to bring the rates below the non-Pennsylvania average. The highest desertion rates were in the 2d, 5th, 9th, and 10th regiments.

Western Department desertions for this period are shown in Table XXVI.

TABLE XXVI
Desertion Rates (Monthly Averages),
Western Department, December, 1779-November, 1780

Regiment	Dec., 1779-May, 1780		June-Nov., 1780	
	Pa. Rgtl. Rate	Pa. Rgt./ Non-Pa. Av.	Pa. Rgtl. Rate	Pa. Rgt./ Non-Pa. Av.
8th Pa.	1.96	.98	2.70	.95
Non-Pa. Av.	1.99	—	2.85	—

Throughout this period, desertions in the Western Department rose to rates comparable to those in Washington's Command. In the Western Department, however, the 8th Pennsylvania's rates closely approximated the non-Pennsylvania average. The Western Department's desertion rates are in sharp contrast both to the sick rates for this period and the desertion rates for the previous period recorded (December, 1778-May, 1779).

Reviewing the desertion record of the Pennsylvania regiments in Washington's Command, the only period in which they did not exceed the non-Pennsylvania average was the 1778 campaign season, when their rate was slightly below the average. In all other periods, Pennsylvania desertions were above the command average, and in most instances significantly so. A possible explanation for the extremely high rate during the 1777-1778 winter encampment has been suggested, but the same reasoning cannot apply to the other periods, during all of which these regiments were serving outside of Pennsylvania, almost exclusively in the area bounded by Morristown, New Jersey, and West Point, New York.

As for specific regiments, considerable variation in relative desertion rates occurred from one period to the next. Only the 3d Pennsylvania consistently registered rates that were among the lowest for the Pennsylvania Line. The 5th and the 10th, however, had comparatively low rates for all but two of the six periods. At the other extreme, the 9th Pennsylvania experienced high desertion rates for all six periods; the

7th regiment had high rates during all but one period; and the 1st and 2d during all but two.

The average monthly desertion rates for the eight Pennsylvania regiments which served throughout the entire period with Washington's Command are shown, in descending order, in Table XXVII.

TABLE XXVII
Average Monthly Desertion Rates,
Washington's Command, December, 1777-November, 1780

Regiment	Pa. Rgtl. Rate	Pa. Rgt./ Non-Pa. Av.
9th Pa.	2.40	1.76
7th Pa.	2.00	1.47
1st Pa.	1.74	1.41
2d Pa.	1.60	1.30
10th Pa.	1.52	1.24
6th Pa.	1.50	1.22
5th Pa.	1.49	1.21
3d Pa.	1.14	.93
Pa. Av.	1.67	1.36
Non-Pa. Av.	1.23	—

Over all, therefore, desertion occurred in the Pennsylvania contingent of Washington's Command at a rate over a third greater than in the average non-Pennsylvania regiment. Except for the 3d Pennsylvania, whose rate was slightly below the non-Pennsylvania average, all Pennsylvania regimental desertion rates exceeded that average by twenty-one to seventy-six per cent. According to tradition, the units of the Pennsylvania Line were among the best disciplined in the Continental Army. To the extent that desertion rates represent an index of discipline, the traditional view appears to be open to challenge.

SUMMARY

In terms of size, the twelve-month Pennsylvania battalions tended to be larger than the non-Pennsylvania units. Reorganization into three-year regiments altered that situation, however, as most of the Pennsylvania regiments were consistently below the average strength of the other regiments.

Sick rates in the Pennsylvania units were below the average for non-Pennsylvania units almost without exception throughout the entire period examined. The worst period of sickness for the Pennsylvania troops occurred in 1776 in the Northern Department, particularly between August and November. The next worst was registered during the campaign season of 1777, closely followed by the Valley Forge encampment of 1777-1778.

Desertion rates for the Pennsylvania units ran high, and only once failed to exceed the non-Pennsylvania average. Peak periods were the Valley Forge encampment and the winter encampment of 1777-1778.

Footnotes

Introduction

¹Thomas Lynch Montgomery (ed.), *Pennsylvania Archives* (Harrisburg, Pa.: Harrisburg Publishing Company, State Printer, 1906), Fifth Series, Volume II, page 4. All subsequent references to the *Pennsylvania Archives* will use the initials, PA, followed, in parentheses, by an arabic number indicating the series, a Roman numeral for the volume, and the page number in arabic numerals. Thus, the foregoing citation would be given as PA(5), II, 4.

²Fred Anderson Berg, *Encyclopedia of Continental Army Units* (Harrisburg: Stackpole Books, 1972), p. 52.

³PA(5), II, 56.

⁴Berg, pp. 52-53.

⁵*Ibid.*, p. 53.

⁶See Eric I. Manders, "Notes on Troop Units in the Flying Camp, 1776," *Military Collector & Historian*, XXVI, No. 1 (Spring, 1974), 9-13.

⁷Berg, pp. 54-55.

⁸See *The Military System of Pennsylvania During the Revolutionary War* (Pennsylvania Historical and Museum Commission Information Leaflet No. 3).

CHAPTER I. THE PENNSYLVANIA CONTINENTALS: FROM CAMBRIDGE TO SAVANNAH

No Notes

CHAPTER II. THE PENNSYLVANIA RIFLE BATTALION/1ST PENNSYLVANIA REGIMENT

¹PA(5), II, 3-4.

²PA(5), II, 15.

³Francis B. Heitman, *Historical Register of Officers of the Continental Army During the War of the Revolution* (Baltimore: Genealogical Publishing Co., Inc., 1973), p. 272.

⁴*Ibid.*, p. 149.

⁵PA(5), II, 15.

⁶PA(5), II, 16.

⁷PA(5), II, 5-7.

⁸PA(5), II, 19.

⁹PA(5), II, 22.

¹⁰PA(5), II, 22-24.

¹¹PA(5), II, 8.

¹²PA(5), II, 25.

¹³PA(5), II, 5-7.

¹⁴PA(5), II, 7.

¹⁵PA(5), II, 26.

¹⁶PA(5), II, 26-29.

¹⁷PA(5), II, 29-30.

¹⁸Herbert C. Bell, *History of Northumberland County, Pennsylvania* (Chicago: Brown, Runk & Co., Publishers, 1891), p. 101.

¹⁹PA(5), II, 35.

²⁰PA(5), II, 5.

²¹PA(5), II, 37.

²²PA(5), II, 10.

²³PA(5), II, 12.

²⁴PA(5), II, 37-38.

²⁵PA(5), II, 41.

²⁶PA(5), II, 9-11.

²⁷PA(5), II, 12-13.

²⁸PA(5), II, 43.

²⁹PA(5), II, 6-7.

³⁰PA(5), II, 7.

³¹PA(5), II, 8.

³²PA(5), II, 43-46.

³³PA(5), II, 6.

³⁴PA(5), II, 12-13.

³⁵PA(5), II, 13.

CHAPTER II (continued

[36]PA(5), II, 6.

[37]PA(5), II, 627.

[38]Heitman, p. 149.

[39]*Ibid.*, p. 474.

[40]*Ibid.*, p. 137.

[41]PA(5), II, 627.

[42]Heitman, p. 137.

[43]PA(5), II, 627.

[44]Heitman, p. 392.

[45]*Ibid.*, p. 399.

[46]PA(5), II, 628-32.

[47]PA(5), II, 16-22, 24-25, 26-29, 31-34, 35-40, 41-42, 43-46, 641-42, 643-46, 647-50, 651-53, 658-60.

[48]Heitman, p. 262.

[49]PA(5), II, 628-29.

[50]PA(5), II, 668-69.

[51]PA(5), II, 627.

[52]PA(5), II, 670-71.

[53]PA(5), II, 669-70.

[54]Heitman, p. 599.

[55]PA(5), II, 616.

[56]Heitman, p. 427.

[57]PA(5), II, 648-50, 673-74, 675.

[58]Heitman, p. 498.

[59]PA(5), II, 35-37, 643-44.

[60]Heitman, p. 175.

[61]PA(5), II, 628, 672.

[62]Heitman, p. 175.

[63]*Ibid.*, p. 275.

[64]PA(5), II, 647-48, 676-77.

[65]Heitman, p. 599.

[66]PA(5), II, 41-42, 651-53, 673.

[67]Heitman, p. 270.

[68]*Ibid.*, p. 611.

[69]PA(5), II, 628.

[70]Heitman, pp. 505-506.

[71]*Ibid.*, p. 296.

[72]*Ibid.*, p. 365.

[73]Berg, p. 94.

[74]PA(5), II, 6.

[75]PA(5), II, 6.

[76]PA(5), II, 9.

[77]PA(5), II, 6-7.

[78]PA(5), II, 8-9.

[79]PA(5), II, 11.

[80]PA(5), II, 11-12.

[81]PA(5), II, 13.

[82]PA(5), II, 13-14.

[83]John Joseph Henry, *Account of Arnold's Campaign Against Quebec* (Albany: Joel Munsell, 1877), p. 13.

[84]*Ibid.*, pp. 58-59.

[85]*Ibid.*, p. 74.

[86]PA(5), II, 609.

[87]PA(5), II, 610-11.

[88]PA(5), II, 612.

[89]PA(5), II, 613-14.

[90]PA(5), II, 610.

[91]PA(5), II, 741.

[92]Bell, p. 103.

[93]Samuel Stelle Smith, *The Battle of Trenton* (Monmouth Beach, N.J.: Philip Freneau Press, 1965), p. 28.

[94]*Ibid.*, p. 23.

[95]*Ibid.*, p. 24.

[96]*Richard M. Ketchum, The Winter Soldiers* (Garden City, N.Y.: Doubleday & Company, Inc., 1973), pp. 341-43.

[97]Samuel Stelle Smith, *The Battle of Princeton* (Monmouth Beach, N.J.: Philip Freneau Press, 1967), p. 27.

[98]Lt. Charles M. Lefferts, *Uniforms of the American, British, French, and German Armies in the War of the American Revolution 1775-1783*. Edited by Alexander J. Wall. (Old Greenwich, Conn.: WE Inc., [1971]), pp. 50, 73.

[99]PA(5), II, 712.

[100]PA(5), II, 617.

[101]PA(5), II, 619.

[102]Charles J. Stille, *Major-General Anthony Wayne and the Pennsylvania Line in the Continental Army* (Philadelphia: J. B. Lippincott Company, 1893), p. 62.

[103]Bell, p. 103.

[104]PA(5), II, 621-22.

CHAPTER II (continued)

[105]Bell, p. 104.

[106]PA(5), II, 622.

[107]Ray Thompson, *Washington at Whitemarsh* (Fort Washington, Pa.: The Bicentennial Press, 1974), p. 67.

[108]Samuel Stelle Smith, *The Battle of Monmouth* (Monmouth Beach, N.J.: Philip Freneau Press, 1964), pp.22-23.

[109]*Ibid.*, p. 32.

[110]Bell, p. 104.

[111]Glenn Tucker, *Mad Anthony Wayne*

and the New Nation (Harrisburg: Stackpole Books, 1973), p. 135.

[112]Bell, p. 103.

[113]PA(5), II, 581.

[114]Stille, p. 212.

[115]Tucker, pp. 168-69.

[116]*Ibid.*, p. 169.

[117]*Ibid.*, p. 170.

[118]Stille, p. 233.

CHAPTER III. 1st PENNSYLVANIA BATTALION/2d PENNSYLVANIA REGIMENT

[1]PA(5), II, 56-57.

[2]John Lacey, "Memoirs of Brigadier-General John Lacey, of Pennsylvania," *Pennsylvania Magazine of History and Biography*, XXV (1901), 499.

[3]PA(5), II, 61.

[4]PA(5), II, 66.

[5]Heitman, p. 69.

[6]PA(3), XIV, 153.

[7]PA(3), XXVI, 28.

[8]PA(5), II, 67.

[9]PA(3), XXVI, 61.

[10]Heitman, p. 187.

[11]See, for example, PA(3), XIV, 197, 348, 374, 388.

[12]PA(3), XXVI, 329.

[13]PA(5), II, 64.

[14]PA(5), II, 65.

[15]PA(3), XIV, 225.

[16]PA(5), II, 61.

[17]PA(5), II, 65.

[18]PA(3), XIV, 262.

[19]PA(5), II, 63.

[20]Heitman, p. 319.

[21]PA(5), II, 782.

[22]"Minutes of the Committee of Safety of Bucks County, Pennsylvania, 1774-1776," *Pennsylvania Magazine of History and Biography*, XV (1891), 264.

[23]PA(5), II, 64.

[24]PA(5), II, 63.

[25]PA(5), II, 64.

[26]PA(5), II, 67.

[27]Lefferts, p. 50.

[28]PA(5), II, 773.

[29]Heitman, p. 192.

[30]*Ibid.*, p. 314.

[31]PA(5), II, 781.

[32]Heitman, p. 521.

[33]PA(5), II, 781.

[34]Heitman, p. 325.

[35]PA(5), II, 781.

[36]Heitman, p. 392.

[37]*Ibid.*, p. 408.

[38]PA(5), II, 781-82.

[39]Heitman, p. 187.

[40]*Ibid.*, p. 201.

[41]*Ibid.*, p. 593.

[42]*Ibid.*, p. 325.

[43]*Ibid.*, p. 274.

[44]PA(3), XIV, 247, 266, 277, 432.

[45]Heitman, p. 429.

[46]PA(3), XIV, 159.

[47]Heitman, p. 85.

[48]PA(5), II, 840.

[49]PA(5), II, 806.

CHAPTER III (continued)

[50]PA(3), XIV, 266-67.

[51]PA(5), II, 782.

[52]PA(5), II, 498.

[53]PA(5), II, 782.

[54]Heitman, p. 304.

[55]*Ibid.*, p. 516.

[56]PA(5), II, 804.

[57]PA(5), II, 820-21, 833-35.

[58]PA(5), II, 782.

[59]PA(5), II, 833.

[60]PA(3), XIV, 153.

[61]Heitman, p. 318.

[62]PA(5), II, 316.

[63]PA(5), III, 693.

[64]PA(5), II, 781.

[65]PA(5), II, 782.

[66]PA(5), II, 831.

[67]PA(5), II, 782.

[68]PA(3), XIV, 94, 334.

[69]PA(5), II, 67.

[70]PA(5), II, 791-93.

[71]PA(5), II, 804-805.

[72]PA(5), II, 782.

[73]PA(5), II, 838-40.

[74]Heitman, p. 162.

[75]PA(5), II, 782.

[76]PA(5), II, 836-37.

[77]PA(5), II, 782.

[78]Heitman, p. 513.

[79]PA(5), II, 251.

[80]PA(5), II, 332.

[81]PA(5), II, 512.

[82]PA(5), III, 693.

[83]Heitman, p. 380.

[84]PA(5), II, 825-27.

[85]PA(5), II, 782.

[86]PA(5), II, 781.

[87]PA(5), II, 701.

[88]PA(5), II, 547-50.

[89]PA(5), II, 276, 279.

[90]PA(5), II, 781.

[91]PA(5), II, 843.

[92]PA(5), II, 782.

[93]Lefferts, p. 126.

[94]PA(5), II, 789-800.

[95]PA(5), II, 843-44.

[96]PA(5), II, 61-62.

[97]PA(5), II, 62-63.

[98]PA(5), II, 63.

[99]Tucker, pp. 38-39.

[100]PA(5), II, 63.

[101]PA(5), II, 195.

[102]Tucker, pp. 40-42.

[103]*Ibid.*, p. 43.

[104]PA(5), II, 64.

[105]PA(5), II, 89-90.

[106]PA(5), II, 89.

[107]PA(5), II, 64-65.

[108]PA(5), II, 773.

[109]Smith, *Battle of Princeton*, p. 35.

[110]Stille, p. 100.

[111]PA(5), II, 875.

[112]PA(5), II, 807.

[113]Stille, p. 100.

[114]PA(5), II, 784.

[115]PA(5), II, 807.

[116]PA(5), II, 774.

[117]Thompson, p. 67.

[118]Smith, *Battle of Monmouth*, p. 21.

[119]*Ibid.*, p. 32.

[120]PA(5), II, 775.

[121]PA(5), II, 581.

[122]Stille, p. 212.

[123]PA(5), II, 784.

[124]PA(5), II, 874.

[125]Tucker, pp. 168-69.

[126]PA(5), II, 783.

[127]Tucker, p. 170.

[128]Stille, p. 233.

[129]Carl Van Doren, *Mutiny in January* (New York: The Viking Press, 1943), p. 46.

Chapter IV. 2d Pennsylvania Battalion/3d Pennsylvania Regiment

[1]PA(5), II, 80.

[2]PA(5), II, 92.

[3]PA(5), II, 92.

[4]Edward F. De Lancey, "Chief Justice William Allen," *Pennsylvania Magazine of History and Biography,* I (1877), 207.

[5]Heitman, p. 69.

[6]De Lancey, p. 209.

[7]Heitman, p. 603.

[8]*Ibid.,* p. 175.

[9]*Ibid.,* p. 138.

[10]PA(5), II, 93.

[11]PA(5), II, 102.

[12]PA(5), II, 95.

[13]PA(5), II, 106.

[14]PA(5), II, 98.

[15]PA(3), XXIII, 332.

[16]Heitman, p. 121.

[17]PA(3), XVI, 291.

[18]PA(5), II, 93.

[19]PA(5), II, 102.

[20]PA(5), II, 110.

[21]PA(5), II, 103-105.

[22]PA(5), II, 106.

[23]PA(3), XIV, 257.

[24]PA(5), II, 108.

[25]PA(3), XVIII, 67.

[26]PA(3), XVIII, 102.

[27]PA(5), II, 108-109.

[28]PA(5), II, 109-11.

[29]PA(3), XIV, 435, 453.

[30]PA(5), II, 109-10.

[31]PA(5), II, 111-15.

[32]PA(3), XXII, 73.

[33]Heitman, p. 576.

[34]PA(5), II, 111.

[35]PA(5), II, 90-91.

[36]Lefferts, pp. 123-24.

[37]PA(5), II, 909.

[38]PA(5), II, 911.

[39]Heitman, p. 603.

[40]PA(5), II, 92.

[41]Heitman, p. 175.

[42]PA(5), II, 911.

[43]PA(5), II, 911-12.

[44]PA(5), II, 927.

[45]PA(5), III, 671.

[46]PA(5), II, 672.

[47]PA(5), II, 912.

[48]Heitman, p. 462.

[49]*Ibid.,* p. 121.

[50]PA(5), II, 945-47.

[51]PA(5), II, 931.

[52]PA(5), II, 911-12.

[53]PA(5), II, 108.

[54]PA(5), II, 931.

[55]PA(5), II, 912.

[56]PA(5), II, 106.

[57]PA(5), II, 93.

[58]PA(5), II, 912.

[59]Heitman, p. 207.

[60]PA(5), II, 912.

[61]PA(5), II, 97.

[62]PA(5), II, 912.

[63]PA(5), II, 912.

[64]PA(5), II, 971.

[65]PA(5), II, 913.

[66]Heitman, p. 138.

[67]PA(5), II, 912.

[68]PA(5), II, 912.

[69]PA(5), II, 971.

[70]PA(5), II, 911.

[71]Lefferts, p. 127.

[72]PA(5), II, 80-81.

[73]PA(5), II, 111.

[74]PA(5), II, 82.

[75]Tucker, pp. 40-43.

[76]PA(5), II, 89.

[77]Heitman, p. 603.

[78]PA(5), II, 90-91.

[79]PA(5), II, 91-92.

[80]PA(5), II, 91, 909.

[81]Stille, p. 62.

CHAPTER IV (continued)

[82]PA(5), II, 1005.

[83]Heitman, p. 141.

[84]PA(5), II, 911.

[85]Thompson, p. 67.

[86]PA(5), II, 909.

[87]Smith, *Battle of Monmouth*, pp. 22-23.

[88]William S. Stryker, *The Battle of Monmouth* (Princeton: Princeton University Press, 1927), p. 211.

[89]Smith, *Battle of Monmouth*, p. 32.

[90]PA(5), II, 999.

[91]PA(5), II, 581.

[92]Stille, p. 212.

[93]PA(5), II, 910.

[94]Tucker, p. 168.

[95]Stille, p. 233.

[96]Van Doren, p. 47.

CHAPTER V. 3D PENNSYLVANIA BATTALION/4TH PENNSYLVANIA REGIMENT

[1]PA(5), II, 122.

[2]PA(5), II, 125.

[3]Heitman, p. 122.

[4]PA(5), II, 125.

[5]PA(5), II, 126.

[6]PA(5), II, 126.

[7]PA(5), II, 126.

[8]PA(5), II, 126.

[9]PA(5), II, 126-27.

[10]PA(5), II, 126.

[11]PA(5), II, 126.

[12]PA(5), II, 124.

[13]Lefferts, p. 124.

[14]PA(5), II, 1026.

[15]Heitman, p. 138.

[16]PA(5), II, 1031.

[17]Heitman, p. 487.

[18]PA(3), XXV, 147, 149-50.

[19]PA(5), II, 276.

[20]Heitman, p. 258.

[21]*Ibid.*, p. 227.

[22]PA(5), II, 127.

[23]Heitman, p. 102.

[24]PA(5), II, 258.

[25]Heitman, p. 370.

[26]*Ibid.*, p. 101.

[27]PA(5), II, 1032.

[28]Van Doren, pp. 46-47.

[29]PA(5), II, 19.

[30]Heitman, p. 133.

[31]PA(5), II, 1032.

[32]Heitman, p. 550.

[33]PA(5), II, 1061.

[34]Heitman, p. 550.

[35]PA(5), II, 43.

[36]Heitman, p. 179.

[37]PA(5), II, 1033.

[38]PA(3), XXV, 97.

[39]Heitman, p. 167.

[40]PA(5), II, 1031.

[41]Heitman, p. 124.

[42]*Colonial Records of Pennsylvania* (Harrisburg: Printed by Tho. Fenn & Co., 1853), XII, 357. (Cited hereafter as *Colonial Records.*)

[43]PA(5), II, 1033.

[44]Lefferts, p. 127.

[45]PA(5), II, 1070-71.

[46]Ketchum, pp. 127-29.

[47]PA(5), II, 122.

[48]PA(5), II, 122-23.

[49]PA(5), II, 123.

[50]Ketchum, pp. 145-56.

[51]PA(5), II, 124.

[52]Smith, *Battle of Princeton*, p. 35.

[53]PA(5), II, 1078.

[54]PA(5), II, 1025.

[55]PA(5), II, 1031, Note.

[56]PA(5), II, 1025.

[57]Thompson, p. 67.

[58]Smith, *Battle of Monmouth*, p. 28.

CHAPTER V (continued)

59*Ibid.*, p. 32.

60PA(5), II, 1026-28.

61PA(5), II, 1026.

62PA(5), II, 1029-30.

63Thomas C. Amory, *The Military Services and Public Life of Major-General John Sullivan* (Port Washington, N.Y.: Kennikat Press, Inc., 1968), pp. 121-24.

64PA(5), II, 1055.

65Gregory B. Keen, "The Descendants of Joran Kyn, The Founder of Upland," *Pennsylvania Magazine of History and Biography*, VII (1883), 98.

66PA(5), II, 1030.

67Stille, p. 233.

68Van Doren, pp. 46-47.

CHAPTER VI. 4TH PENNSYLVANIA BATTALION/5TH PENNSYLVANIA REGIMENT

1PA(5), II, 136.

2PA(5), II, 140.

3Heitman, p. 322.

4PA(5), II, 141.

5PA(5), II, 142.

6"Some Extracts from the Papers of General Persifor Frazer," *Pennsylvania Magazine of History and Biography*, XXXI (1907), 130. (Cited hereafter as "Frazer Papers," PMHB.)

7PA(5), II, 142.

8Heitman, p. 450.

9PA(5), II, 137.

10PA(5), II, 138.

11Lacey, p. 499.

12*Ibid.*, p. 12.

13*Ibid.*, pp. 191-92.

14*Ibid.*, p. 353.

15PA(5), II, 136-37 and Note, 137.

16PA(5), II, 138 and Note.

17Lacey, p. 201.

18PA(5), II, 151.

19PA(5), II, 152.

20Lacey, p. 192.

21PA(5), II, 136.

22PA(5), II, 82-85.

23PA(5), II, 154.

24PA(5), II, 155.

25Lacey, p. 193.

26*Ibid.*, p. 341.

27PA(5), II, 156.

28PA(5), II, 138.

29PA(5), II, 140.

30Lacey, p. 192.

31Lefferts, p. 124.

32Heitman, p. 322.

33PA(5), III, 7.

34"Frazer Papers," PMHB, p. 131.

35Heitman, p. 236.

36*Ibid.*, p. 389.

37*Ibid.*, p. 471.

38PA(5), III, 7.

39PA(5), III, 33.

40PA(5), III, 8.

41Heitman, p. 526.

42PA(5), III, 8.

43Heitman, p. 450.

44PA(5), II, 142-46; III, 43-44, 57-58.

45Heitman, p. 89.

46*Ibid.*, p. 322.

47PA(5), III, 17-19, 35-36.

48Heitman, p. 371.

49PA(5), III, 61-62.

50Heitman, p. 560.

51*Ibid.*, p. 87.

52PA(5), III, 57.

53Heitman, p. 154.

54PA(5), III, 8

55Heitman, p. 507.

56PA(5), III, 8.

57PA(5), III, 33.

CHAPTER VI (continued)

[58]Heitman, p. 262.

[59]PA(5), III, 8.

[60]PA(5), III, 33.

[61]Heitman, p. 488.

[62]PA(5), III, 36.

[63]PA(5), III, 57.

[64]Heitman, p. 488.

[65]PA(5), III, 33.

[66]Heitman, p. 111.

[67]PA(5), III, 41.

[68]PA(5), III, 8.

[69]Heitman, p. 111.

[70]*Ibid.*, p. 560.

[71]Lefferts, pp. 127-28.

[72]PA(5), III, 53.

[73]PA(5), II, 136.

[74]Lacey, p. 12.

[75]PA(5), II, 136.

[76]Lacey, p. 12.

[77]PA(5), II, 136.

[78]Stille, p. 28.

[79]Lacey, p. 193.

[80]PA(5), II, 81-82.

[81]Tucker, pp. 39-42.

[82]Lacey, p. 201.

[83]Tucker, pp. 43-44.

[84]PA(5), II, 89.

[85]Lacey, p. 203.

[86]PA(5), II, 89.

[87]PA(5), II, 138.

[88]Lacey, p. 342.

[89]PA(5), II, 140.

[90]"Frazer Papers," PMHB, p. 131.

[91]PA(5), III, 3.

[92]PA(5), III, 10.

[93]PA(5), III, 87, 92.

[94]PA(5), III, 3.

[95]Thompson, p. 67.

[96]Smith, *Battle of Monmouth*, p. 32.

[97]PA(5), II, 581.

[98]Stille, p. 216.

[99]Van Doren, p. 47.

[100]PA(5), III, 73, 79.

CHAPTER VII. 5TH PENNSYLVANIA BATTALION/6TH PENNSYLVANIA REGIMENT

[1]Berg, pp. 95, 96.

[2]PA(5), II, 167.

[3]PA(5), II, 15.

[4]Heitman, p. 435.

[5]PA(5), II, 167.

[6]PA(5), II, 37.

[7]Heitman, p. 409.

[8]PA(5), II, 167.

[9]Heitman, p. 95.

[10]PA(5), II, 168-71.

[11]PA(5), II, 168.

[12]PA(5), II, 171-73.

[13]PA(5), II, 171.

[14]PA(5), II, 173-75.

[15]PA(5), II, 175-77.

[16]PA(5), II, 177.

[17]PA(5), II, 179-82.

[18]PA(5), II, 182-84.

[19]PA(5), II, 184-86.

[20]Lefferts, pp. 124-25.

[21]PA(5), II, 167.

[22]Heitman, p. 102.

[23]*Ibid.*, p. 274.

[24]PA(5), III, 103.

[25]PA(5), II, 166.

[26]Heitman, p. 99.

[27]PA(5), III, 103.

[28]PA(5), III, 104.

[29]Heitman, p. 355.

[30]PA(5), III, 116.

[31]Heitman, p. 355.

[32]*Ibid.*, p. 203.

Chapter VII (continued)

[33]PA(5), III, 101.

[34]Heitman, p. 482.

[35]PA(5), III, 104.

[36]PA(3), XII, 37.

[37]Heitman, p. 308.

[38]PA(5), III, 104.

[39]PA(3), XII, 118.

[40]Heitman, p. 112.

[41]PA(5), III, 104.

[42]PA(3), XII, 98.

[43]PA(5), II, 175.

[44]Heitman, p. 592.

[45]PA(5), III, 104.

[46]PA(5), III, 101.

[47]PA(5), III, 104.

[48]PA(5), II, 24.

[49]Heitman, p. 179.

[50]PA(5), III, 104.

[51]Heitman, p. 577.

[52]PA(5), III, 104.

[53]Heitman, pp. 404-405.

[54]PA(5), III, 672.

[55]PA(5), III, 104.

[56]PA(3), XIX, 67.

[57]Heitman, p. 122.

[58]PA(5), III, 102.

[59]PA(5), III, 104.

[60]PA(3), XIV, 166, 302.

[61]Heitman, p. 203.

[62]PA(5), III, 105.

[63]Heitman, p. 369.

[64]PA(5), III, 105.

[65]Heitman, p. 556.

[66]*Ibid.*, p. 482.

[67]PA(5), III, 135.

[68]Heitman, p. 132.

[69]Lefferts, p. 128.

[70]See, for example, Ketchum, pp. 126, 132.

[71]PA(5), II, 165-66.

[72]PA(5), II, 166.

[73]Ketchum, p. 132.

[74]*Ibid.*, pp. 133-34; PA(5), II, 164-65.

[75]PA(5), II, 167.

[76]Heitman, p. 507.

[77]PA(5), III, 186-87.

[78]PA(5), III, 174.

[79]PA(5), III, 108, 173, 179, 181.

[80]Thompson, p. 67.

[81]PA(5), III, 185.

[82]PA(5), III, 102.

[83]PA(5), II, 581.

[84]PA(5), III, 106, 150, 152, 162.

[85]PA(5), III, 179.

[86]PA(5), III, 179.

[87]Van Doren, p. 47.

Chapter VIII. 6th Pennsylvania Battalion/7th Pennsylvania Regiment

[1]PA(5), II, 194.

[2]Heitman, p. 314.

[3]PA(5), II, 199.

[4]Heitman, p. 207.

[5]*Ibid.*, p. 262.

[6]PA(5), II, 230.

[7]PA(5), II, 205.

[8]PA(5), III, 206.

[9]PA(5), II, 208.

[10]PA(5), II, 236.

[11]PA(5), II, 216.

[12]Heitman, p. 599.

[13]PA(5), II, 89.

[14]PA(5), II, 226.

[15]Heitman, p. 64.

[16]PA(5), II, 226.

[17]PA(5), II, 220.

[18]PA(5), II, 221.

[19]PA(5), II, 213.

[20]PA(5), II, 85.

CHAPTER VIII (continued)

[21]Heitman, p. 365.

[22]PA(5), II, 213.

[23]PA(5), II, 194.

[24]Lefferts, p. 125.

[25]Heitman, p. 314.

[26]PA(5), III, 199.

[27]Heitman, p. 278.

[28]*Ibid.*, p. 262.

[29]*Ibid.*, pp. 167-68.

[30]*Ibid.*, p. 274.

[31]PA(5), III, 206.

[32]Heitman, p. 281.

[33]PA(5), III, 206.

[34]Heitman, p. 427.

[35]PA(5), III, 206.

[36]PA(5), II, 202.

[37]Heitman, p. 501.

[38]*Ibid.*, p. 65.

[39]PA(5), III, 206.

[40]Heitman, p. 397.

[41]PA(5), III, 206.

[42]PA(5), III, 219.

[43]Heitman, p. 314.

[44]PA(5), III, 206.

[45]Heitman, p. 468.

[46]*Ibid.*, p. 424.

[47]PA(5), III, 206.

[48]PA(5), III, 203.

[49]Heitman, p. 599.

[50]PA(5), III, 206.

[51]PA(5), III, 203.

[52]Heitman, p. 118.

[53]*Ibid.*, p. 393.

[54]PA(5), III, 243.

[55]Heitman, p. 66.

[56]PA(5), III, 207.

[57]Heitman, p. 329.

[58]PA(5), III, 206.

[59]Heitman, p. 365.

[60]*Ibid.*, p. 368.

[61]PA(5), III, 206.

[62]Heitman, p. 393.

[63]PA(5), III, 207.

[64]Heitman, p. 136.

[65]PA(5), III, 206.

[66]Heitman, pp. 360-61.

[67]Lefferts, p. 129.

[68]PA(5), II, 80.

[69]PA(5), II, 81-83.

[70]PA(5), II, 198.

[71]PA(5), II, 196-97.

[72]Lacey, p. 201.

[73]PA(5), II, 88-89.

[74]Lacey, p. 204.

[75]PA(5), II, 89-90.

[76]PA(5), II, 198.

[77]PA(5), III, 201-202.

[78]PA(5), III, 283.

[79]PA(5), III, 202-203 and Note, 202.

[80]Heitman, p. 129.

[81]PA(5), III, 286, 288, 291.

[82]PA(5), III, 203-204.

[83]Thompson, p. 67.

[84]Smith, *Battle of Monmouth*, p. 22.

[85]PA(5), III, 1018.

[86]Captain John B. Landis, "Investigation into American Tradition of Woman Known as 'Molly Pitcher,'" *The Journal of American History*, V (1911), 85-86.

[87]PA(5), II, 581.

[88]Heitman, p. 129.

[89]Harry Emerson Wildes, *Anthony Wayne, Trouble Shooter of the American Revolution* (New York: Harcourt, Brace and Company, 1941), p. 209.

[90]Van Doren, p. 47.

CHAPTER IX. 8TH PENNSYLVANIA REGIMENT

[1]PA(5), III, 305.

[2]PA(5), III, 313.

[3]PA(5), III, 311.

[4]Heitman, p. 371.

[5]PA(5), III, 313.

[6]PA(5), III, 305.

[7]PA(5), III, 313.

[8]Heitman, p. 474.

[9]PA(5), III, 311.

[10]Heitman, p. 92.

[11]PA(5), III, 313.

[12]Heitman, p. 92.

[13]PA(5), III, 313.

[14]PA(3), XXII, 34.

[15]Heitman, p. 331.

[16]*Ibid.*, p. 306.

[17]PA(5), III, 318-19.

[18]Heitman, p. 306.

[19]PA(3), XXII, 27, 31.

[20]PA(5), III, 325.

[21]Heitman, p. 393.

[22]PA(5), III, 327.

[23]Heitman, p. 529.

[24]PA(5), III, 314.

[25]PA(5), III, 312.

[26]Heitman, p. 529.

[27]PA(5), III, 312.

[28]Heitman, p. 529.

[29]PA(5), III, 325, 327, 333-34.

[30]Heitman, p. 177.

[31]*Ibid.*, p. 442.

[32]*Ibid.*, p. 226.

[33]*Ibid.*, p. 378.

[34]PA(5), III, 314, 318-19, 323, 327.

[35]PA(5), III, 314.

[36]Heitman, p. 378.

[37]*Ibid.*, p. 169.

[38]PA(3), XXII, 28.

[39]Heitman, p. 422.

[40]*Ibid.*, pp. 522-23.

[41]PA(5), III, 314.

[42]Heitman, p. 146.

[43]*Ibid.*, p. 315.

[44]PA(5), III, 314.

[45]Heitman, p. 397.

[46]PA(5), III, 318-19, 325.

[47]PA(5), III, 314.

[48]Heitman, p. 203.

[49]*Ibid.*, p. 117.

[50]*Ibid.*, p. 189.

[51]PA(5), III, 314.

[52]Heitman, p. 399.

[53]*Ibid.*, p. 157.

[54]*Ibid.*, p. 144.

[55]*Ibid.*, pp. 226-27.

[56]PA(5), III, 305-306.

[57]Lefferts, p. 129.

[58]PA(5), III, 306.

[59]PA(5), III, 307.

[60]PA(5), III, 308.

[61]PA(5), III, 309.

[62]PA(5), III, 308.

[63]PA(5), III, 312.

[64]Thompson, p. 67.

[65]PA(5), III, 308.

[66]PA(5), III, 308.

[67]PA(1), VI, 666.

[68]PA(5), III, 309.

[69]PA(2), XII, 110.

[70]PA(2), XII, 146.

[71]PA(5), III, 309.

[72]PA(2), XII, 107.

[73]PA(2), XII, 108.

[74]PA(2), XII, 155.

[75]PA(2), XII, 130-32.

[76]PA(2), XII, 155-56.

[77]PA(2), XII, 156-57.

[78]PA(2), XII, 155.

[79]PA(5), III, 309.

CHAPTER X. 9TH PENNSYLVANIA REGIMENT

[1]Berg, p. 98.

[2]PA(5), III, 380.

[3]Heitman, p. 402.

[4]PA(5), III, 380.

[5]Heitman, p. 137.

[6]PA(5), III, 380.

[7]Heitman, pp. 505-506.

[8]*Ibid.*, p. 413.

[9]PA(5), III, 381.

[10]PA(3), XX, 87.

[11]Heitman, p. 218.

[12]PA(5), III, 408-409, 427, 430-31.

[13]PA(5), III, 381.

[14]Heitman, pp. 519-20.

[15]PA(5), III, 381.

[16]Heitman, p. 284.

[17]PA(5), III, 410-11, 428-29.

[18]PA(3), XXV, 260.

[19]PA(5), II, 27.

[20]Heitman, p. 413.

[21]PA(5), III, 411.

[22]PA(5), III, 381.

[23]PA(3), XIV, 233.

[24]Heitman, p. 411.

[25]PA(5), III, 381.

[26]Heitman, p. 411.

[27]PA(5), III, 381.

[28]Heitman, p. 256.

[29]PA(5), III, 381.

[30]PA(5), III, 412.

[31]PA(5), II, 332.

[32]Heitman, p. 255.

[33]PA(3), XII, 81.

[34]Heitman, p. 365.

[35]PA(3), XI, 512.

[36]Heitman, p. 112.

[37]PA(5), III, 433.

[38]PA(5), III, 441.

[39]Heitman, p. 188.

[40]PA(5), III, 407, 435-36.

[41]PA(3), XII, 10.

[42]Heitman, p. 432.

[43]*Ibid.*, p. 139.

[44]*Ibid.*, p. 372.

[45]Lefferts, pp. 129-30.

[46]PA(5), III, 435-36.

[47]PA(5), III, 379.

[48]PA(5), III, 383, 456.

[49]PA(5), III, 383.

[50]Thompson, p. 67.

[51]PA(5), III, 451, 461.

[52]Stryker, p. 78.

[53]Smith, *Battle of Monmouth*, pp. 11-13.

[54]*Ibid.*, pp. 16-17.

[55]*Ibid.*, p. 13.

[56]*Ibid.*, p. 32.

[57]Stille, p. 180.

[58]*Ibid.*, p. 190.

[59]PA(5), III, 452-53.

[60]PA(5) III, 379.

[61]PA(5), II, 581.

[62]PA(5), III, 445.

[63]PA(5), III, 457.

[64]PA(5), III, 463.

[65]Van Doren, p. 29.

[66]*Ibid.*, p. 47.

[67]PA(5), III, 379.

CHAPTER XI. 10TH PENNSYLVANIA REGIMENT

[1]PA(5), III, 467.

[2]Berg, p. 98.

[3]PA(5), III, 469.

[4]Heitman, p. 149.

[5]PA(5), III, 469.

[6]PA(5), III, 469.

[7]PA(5), III, 470. See also John C. Fitzpatrick (ed.), *The Writings of George*

CHAPTER XI (continued

Washington From the Original Manuscript Sources, 1744-1789 (Washington, D.C.: United States Government Printing Office, 1933), X, 485; XI, 234.

[8]PA(5), III, 470.

[9]PA(5), III, 471.

[10]Heitman, p. 517.

[11]*Ibid.*, p. 430.

[12]*Ibid.*, p. 288.

[13]PA(5), III, 487-88.

[14]PA(5), III, 503-504, 511-12.

[15]PA(5), III, 526.

[16]Heitman, p. 480.

[17]PA(5), III, 533.

[18]PA(5), III, 534-35, 563-64.

[19]Heitman, p. 517.

[20]PA(5), III, 502-503, 512-13, 530-32, 548, 552-53.

[21]PA(3), XXV, 95-96.

[22]PA(5), III, 470.

[23]PA(5), III, 526.

[24]PA(3), XVII, 122.

[25]PA(5), III, 499-500, 517-18.

[26]PA(5), III, 535-37.

[27]PA(5), III, 542-43.

[28]PA(5), III, 548-49.

[29]Heitman, p. 524.

[30]*Ibid.*, p. 430.

[31]PA(5), III, 470.

[32]Heitman, p. 339.

[33]PA(5), III, 506-507, 515-16, 526, 535-37, 559-60.

[34]PA(3), XVII, 63.

[35]PA(3), XVII, 175, 318.

[36]PA(3), XVII, 381, 402.

[37]Heitman, p. 514.

[38]*Ibid.*, p. 577.

[39]PA(5), III, 470, Note.

[40]PA(5), III, 565-66.

[41]Heitman, p. 577.

[42]*Ibid.*, p. 146.

[43]*Ibid.*, p. 374.

[44]Lefferts, p. 130.

[45]Smith, *Battle of Princeton*, p. 35.

[46]PA(5), III, 582.

[47]PA(5), III, 468.

[48]PA(5), III, 467.

[49]PA(5), III, 471, 473, 582.

[50]PA(5), III, 583.

[51]PA(5), III, 576.

[52]PA(5), III, 582.

[53]PA(5), III, 468.

[54]Thompson, p. 67.

[55]Smith, *Battle of Monmouth*, p. 32.

[56]PA(5), III, 468.

[57]PA(5), III, 510.

[58]Heitman, p. 281.

[59]PA(5), II, 581.

[60]PA(5), III, 545.

[61]PA(5), III, 557, 562, 567.

[62]Van Doren, p. 47.

CHAPTER XII. "OLD" 11TH PENNSYLVANIA REGIMENT

[1]Berg, p. 98.

[2]PA(5), III, 588.

[3]Heitman, p. 309.

[4]*Ibid.*, p. 205.

[5]*Ibid.*, p. 416.

[6]*Ibid.*, p. 389.

[7]PA(3), XI, 34.

[8]Heitman, p. 189.

[9]PA(5), III, 589.

[10]Heitman, p. 161.

[11]PA(5), III, 589.

[12]PA(5), III, 608.

[13]Heitman, p. 432.

[14]*Ibid.*, p. 284.

[15]PA(5), III, 607.

[16]PA(5), III, 608.

CHAPTER XII (continued

[17]Heitman, p. 372.

[18]PA(3), XIV, 784.

[19]Heitman, p. 116.

[20]PA(5), III, 608.

[21]PA(5), II, 93.

[22]Heitman, p. 474.

[23]PA(3), XVIII, 93.

[24]Heitman, p. 487.

[25]PA(3), XIV, 230.

[26]PA(3), XII, 52, 141.

[27]Heitman, p. 285.

[28]PA(5), III, 608.

[29]Heitman, p. 199.

[30]PA(3), XVII, 212, 224.

[31]Heitman, p. 202.

[32]*Ibid.*, p. 373.

[33]Lefferts, pp. 130-31.

[34]Heitman, p. 470.

[35]Smith, *Battle of Princeton*, p. 35.

[36]PA(5), III, 587.

[37]Wildes, p. 98.

[38]PA(5), III, 589-90.

[39]PA(5), III, 625-28.

[40]Tucker, p. 86.

[41]Quoted in Stille, p. 87.

[42]John F. Reed, *Campaign to Valley Forge* (Philadelphia: University of Pennsylvania Press, 1965), p. 173.

[43]Tucker, p. 86.

[44]Reed, *Campaign*, p. 175.

[45]PA(5), III, 627.

[46]Reed, *Campaign*, p. 173.

[47]Tucker, p. 89; Wildes, p. 131.

[48]Heitman, p. 359.

[49]PA(5), III, 623, 628.

[50]PA(5), III, 587.

[51]Thompson, p. 67.

[52]Smith, *Battle of Monmouth*, p. 21.

[53]*Ibid.*, p. 32.

Chapter XIII. 12th Pennsylvania Regiment

[1]Berg, p. 98.

[2]PA(5), III, 672.

[3]PA(5), III, 671.

[4]PA(5), III, 672.

[5]Fitzpatrick, XII, 7-8.

[6]Heitman, p. 258.

[7]*Ibid.*, p. 177.

[8]PA(5), III, 673.

[9]Heitman, p. 177.

[10]PA(5), III, 673.

[11]Heitman, p. 602.

[12]*Ibid.*, p. 463.

[13]PA(5), III, 673.

[14]Heitman, p. 393.

[15]Bell, p. 111.

[16]PA(5), III, 673.

[17]PA(5), III, 671-72.

[18]Heitman, p. 110.

[19]Bell, p. 111.

[20]PA(5), III, 673.

[21]Heitman, p. 117.

[22]Bell, p. 111.

[23]Heitman, p. 276.

[24]*Ibid.*, p. 149.

[25]Bell, p. 111.

[26]PA(5), III, 673.

[27]Heitman, p. 372.

[28]PA(5), III, 673.

[29]Heitman, p. 429.

[30]*Ibid.*, p. 606.

[31]*Ibid.*, p. 351.

[32]Lefferts, p. 131.

[33]PA(5), III, 671.

[34]Smith, *Battle of Princeton*, p. 35.

[35]PA(5), III, 671.

[36]Howard H. Peckham (ed.), *The Toll*

CHAPTER XIII (continued)

of Independence: Engagements & Battle Casualties of the American Revolution (Chicago: The University of Chicago Press, 1974), p. 33.

[37]PA(5), III, 673.

[38]Peckham, p. 34.

[39]PA(5), III, 674.

[40]PA(5), III, 686-87.

[41]PA(5), III, 671.

[42]Heitman, p. 286.

[43]PA(5), III, 686.

[44]PA(5), III, 687-88.

[45]PA(5), III, 672.

[46]Heitman, p. 114.

[47]PA(5), III, 672.

[48]Heitman, p. 145.

[49]PA(5), III, 672.

[50]PA(5), III, 686, 688.

[51]Thompson, p. 67.

[52]Heitman, p. 369.

[53]PA(5), III, 687.

[54]PA(5), III, 672.

CHAPTER XIV. HARTLEY'S "ADDITIONAL" CONTINENTAL REGIMENT

[1]PA(5), III, 737.

[2]PA(5), III, 738.

[3]Heitman, p. 278.

[4]PA(5), III, 737-38.

[5]Heitman, p. 592.

[6]*Ibid.*, pp. 167-68.

[7]*Ibid.*, p. 305.

[8]*Ibid.*, p. 136.

[9]*Ibid.*, p. 212.

[10]*Ibid.*, p. 213.

[11]PA(5), III, 749.

[12]PA(5), II, 217.

[13]Heitman, p. 136.

[14]*Ibid.*, p. 529.

[15]Lefferts, p. 79.

[16]PA(5), II, 221.

[17]Heitman, p. 414.

[18]*Ibid.*, p. 188.

[19]*Ibid.*, p. 522.

[20]PA(1), VII, 8.

[21]Heitman, p. 136.

[22]PA(5), II, 213.

[23]Heitman, p. 300.

[24]*Ibid.*, p. 474.

[25]PA(3), XI, 669, 686.

[26]Heitman, p. 362.

[27]PA(5), III, 748.

[28]Heitman, p. 223.

[29]*Ibid.*, p. 329.

[30]PA(3), XII, 69, 74.

[31]PA(3), XVII, 180, 467.

[32]Heitman, p. 328.

[33]PA(5), III, 748.

[34]Heitman, p. 426.

[35]*Ibid.*, p. 564.

[36]*Ibid.*, p. 143.

[37]PA(1), VII, 8.

[38]Lefferts, p. 79.

[39]Berg, p. 49.

[40]PA(5), III, 737.

[41]PA(5), III, 752.

[42]PA(5), III, 752-53.

[43]Heitman, p. 136.

[44]*Ibid.*, p. 300.

[45]*Ibid.*, p. 347.

[46]*Ibid.*, p. 197.

[47]*Ibid.*, p. 522.

[48]Wildes, pp. 131-33.

[49]PA(5), III, 752.

[50]PA(5), III, 753.

[51]Thompson, p. 67.

[52]PA(5), III, 737.

[53]PA(1), VII, 5.

[54]Bell, p. 124.

[55]PA(1), VII, 5.

[56]PA(1), VII, 5-6.

CHAPTER XIV (continued)

[57]PA(1), VII, 6-7.
[58]PA(1), VII, 7.
[59]PA(1), VII, 7-8.
[60]PA(1), VII, 8.
[61]Bell, p. 124.

[62]PA(1), VII, 3.
[63]PA(1), VII, 81-82.
[64]Bell, p. 125.
[65]PA(1), VII, 86-87.
[66]PA(5), III, 737-38.

CHAPTER XV. PATTON'S "ADDITIONAL" CONTINENTAL REGIMENT

[1]PA(5), III, 737.
[2]PA(5), III, 757.
[3]PA(5), II, 257.
[4]Heitman, p. 430.
[5]PA(5), III, 758.
[6]Berg, p. 93.
[7]Heitman, p. 424.
[8]*Ibid.*, p. 487.
[9]PA(5), III, 758.
[10]Heitman, p. 454.
[11]PA(5), III, 758.
[12]Heitman, pp. 327-28.
[13]PA(5), II, 396.
[14]PA(5), II, 38.
[15]PA(5), II, 396.
[16]Heitman, p. 264.
[17]*Ibid.*, p. 193.
[18]*Ibid.*, p. 159.
[19]*Ibid.*, p. 373.
[20]PA(5), III, 760.

[21]Heitman, p. 134.
[22]Lefferts, p. 80.
[23]PA(5), III, 761.
[24]PA(5), III, 760.
[25]Smith, *Battle of Monmouth*, p. 28.
[26]Heitman, p. 430.
[27]PA(5), III, 760.
[28]Heitman, p. 193.
[29]Thompson, p. 67.
[30]Gilbert S. Jones (comp.), *Valley Forge Park* (Valley Forge Park Commission, 1947), p. 22.
[31]Smith, *Battle of Monmouth*, p. 28.
[32]*Ibid.*, p. 13.
[33]*Ibid.*, pp. 18-19.
[34]*Ibid.*, p. 20.
[35]PA(5), III, 652.
[36]Heitman, pp. 115-16.
[37]PA(1), VII, 86-87.
[38]PA(5), III, 737-38.

CHAPTER XVI. "NEW" 11TH PENNSYLVANIA REGIMENT

[1]PA(5), III, 737-38.
[2]Heitman, p. 139.
[3]*Ibid.*, p. 203.
[4]*Ibid.*, p. 592.
[5]PA(5), III, 663.
[6]Berg, p. 130.
[7]PA(3), XIV, 302.
[8]See PA(3), XI, 7, 38, 67, 113; XIV, 160, 363; XVII, 35, 318.
[9]PA(3), XXIV, 758.
[10]PA(5), III, 665.
[11]See PA(5), III, 644-62.

[12]Heitman, p. 278.
[13]*Ibid.*, pp. 305-306.
[14]*Ibid.*, pp. 167-68.
[15]PA(5), III, 637.
[16]Heitman, p. 454.
[17]*Ibid.*, p. 212.
[18]*Ibid.*, p. 188.
[19]*Ibid.*, p. 316.
[20]PA(5), III, 642, 758.
[21]Heitman, p. 316.
[22]*Ibid.*, p. 134.
[23]PA(5), III, 642.

CHAPTER XVI (continued)

[24]Heitman, p. 368.

[25]PA(5), III, 644-46.

[26]PA(5), III, 759-60.

[27]PA(5), III, 130-31.

[28]PA(5), III, 666.

[29]Heitman, p. 212.

[30]PA(5), III, 646-48.

[31]PA(5), III, 759-60.

[32]PA(5), III, 663-64.

[33]PA(5), III, 666.

[34]Heitman, p. 136.

[35]PA(5), III, 643.

[36]PA(5), III, 639.

[37]PA(5), III, 649-50.

[38]PA(5), III, 745-46.

[39]PA(5), III, 759-60.

[40]Heitman, pp. 327-28.

[41]PA(5), III, 651-52.

[42]PA(5), III, 759-60.

[43]PA(5), III, 663-64.

[44]PA(5), III, 666.

[45]Heitman, p. 233.

[46]*Ibid.*, p. 316.

[47]PA(5), III, 658-60.

[48]PA(5), III, 745-46.

[49]PA(5), III, 759-60.

[50]PA(5), III, 666.

[51]Heitman, p. 564.

[52]PA(5), III, 653-54.

[53]PA(5), III, 130-31.

[54]Heitman, p. 159.

[55]PA(5), III, 655-57.

[56]PA(5), III, 745-46.

[57]PA(5), III, 759-60.

[58]PA(5), III, 666.

[59]Heitman, p. 529.

[60]PA(5), III, 642.

[61]Heitman, p. 134.

[62]PA(5), III, 657-58.

[63]Heitman, p. 143.

[64]PA(5), III, 658-60.

[65]PA(5), III, 745-46.

[66]PA(5), III, 663-64.

[67]PA(5), III, 666.

[68]Lefferts, p. 131.

[69]See, for example, Van Doren, p. 43.

[70]PA(5), III, 631.

[71]PA(5), III, 638.

[72]John W. Jordan (ed.), "Adm Hubley, Jr., Lt Colo. Comdt 11th Penna. Regt, His Journal, Commencing at Wyoming, July 30th, 1779," *Pennsylvania Magazine of History and Biography*, XXXIII (1909), 131-32. (Cited hereafter as "Hubley's Journal," PMHB.)

[73]*Ibid.*, p. 134.

[74]*Ibid.*, p. 136.

[75]*Ibid.*, pp. 137-41.

[76]*Ibid.*, pp. 141-43.

[77]*Ibid.*, pp. 143-46.

[78]New York Division of Archives and History, *The Sullivan-Clinton Campaign in 1779* (Albany: The University of the State of New York, 1929), p. 131. (Cited hereafter as *Sullivan-Clinton Campaign.*)

[79]Hubley's Journal," PMHB, p. 146.

[80]PA(2), XV, 234.

[81]"Hubley's Journal," PMHB, pp. 279-83.

[82]*Ibid.*, pp. 285-86.

[83]*Ibid.*, PP. 286-88.

[84]PA(2), XV, 237.

[85]*Sullivan-Clinton Campaign*, P. 137.

[86]*Ibid.*, p. 139.

[87]"Hubley's Journal," PMHB, pp. 289-90.

[88]*Ibid.*, pp. 300-302, 409-11.

[89]PA(2), XV, 239.

[90]"Hubley's Journal," PMHB, pp. 300-302, 409-11.

[91]PA(2), XV, 244.

[92]PA(2), XV, 243.

[93]"Hubley's Journal," PMHB, p. 416.

[94]PA(2), XV, 248.

[95]"Hubley's Journal," PMHB, p. 416.

[96]PA(2), XV, 248.

CHAPTER XVI (continued)

[97]"Hubley's Journal," PMHB, pp. 416-18.

[98]PA(2), XV, 248.

[99]"Hubley's Journal," PMHB, p. 417.

[100]PA(2), XV, 249.

[101]"Hubley's Journal," PMHB, p. 418.

[102]PA(2), XV, 249.

[103]"Hubley's Journal," PMHB, pp. 419-20.

[104]*Ibid.*, pp. 421-22.

[105]PA(5), II, 597.

[106]PA(5), II, 595.

[107]Van Doren, p. 43.

CHAPTER XVII
PENNSYLVANIA STATE RIFLE REGIMENT
PENNSYLVANIA STATE BATTALION OF MUSKETRY
PENNSYLVANIA STATE REGIMENT
13TH PENNSYLVANIA REGIMENT

[1]PA(5), II, 250-51.

[2]PA(5), II, 256.

[3]Heitman, p. 391.

[4]PA(5), II, 256.

[5]Heitman, p. 443.

[6]PA(5), II, 256.

[7]PA(5), II, 253.

[8]Heitman, p. 122.

[9]*Ibid.*, p. 595.

[10]PA(5), II, 257.

[11]Heitman, p. 430.

[12]PA(5), II, 258.

[13]Heitman, p. 490.

[14]PA(5), II, 258.

[15]Heitman, p. 370.

[16]PA(5), II, 276.

[17]Heitman, p. 580.

[18]PA(5), II, 297.

[19]Heitman, p. 127.

[20]PA(5), II, 297.

[21]Heitman, p. 399.

[22]PA(5), II, 310.

[23]Heitman, pp. 64-65.

[24]PA(5), II, 251.

[25]Heitman, p. 408.

[26]*Ibid.*, p. 380.

[27]PA(5), II, 356.

[28]Heitman, p. 433.

[29]PA(5), II, 372.

[30]Heitman, p. 154.

[31]PA(5), II, 391.

[32]Heitman, p. 218.

[33]PA(5), II, 396.

[34]Heitman, p. 264.

[35]PA(5), II, 414.

[36]Heitman, p. 222.

[37]PA(5), II, 433.

[38]Lefferts, p. 122.

[39]PA(5), II, 250-51.

[40]PA(5), II, 466.

[41]Heitman, p. 78.

[42]*Ibid.*, p. 427.

[43]*Ibid.*, p. 449.

[44]PA(5), II, 467.

[45]Heitman, p. 71.

[46]PA(5), II, 355.

[47]PA(3), XIV, 244.

[48]Heitman, p. 355.

[49]PA(5), II, 471.

[50]Heitman, p. 355.

[51]PA(5), II, 475.

[52]Heitman, p. 408.

[53]PA(5), II, 475.

[54]Heitman, p. 243.

[55]PA(5), II, 481.

[56]See PA(3), XIV, 656; XV, 96, 354, 475.

Chapter XVII (continued)

[57]Heitman, p. 380.

[58]PA(5), II, 481.

[59]Heitman, p. 365.

[60]PA(5), II, 483.

[61]Heitman, p. 286.

[62]PA(5), II, 489.

[63]Heitman, p. 192.

[64]PA(5), II, 494.

[65]PA(3), XIV, 337, 341, 400, 451.

[66]Heitman, p. 413.

[67]PA(3), XIV, 267.

[68]Heitman, p. 304.

[69]Lefferts, pp. 122-23.

[70]*Colonial Records*, X, 743.

[71]*Ibid.*, X, 766-67.

[72]PA(5), II, 511.

[73]PA(2), I, 745-46.

[74]Heitman, p. 131.

[75]*Colonial Records*, XI, 215-16.

[76]PA(5), II, 514.

[77]Heitman, pp. 520-21.

[78]*Ibid.*, p. 222.

[79]*Ibid.*, p. 408.

[80]PA(5), II, 516-19.

[81]Heitman, p. 144.

[82]PA(5), II, 550-53.

[83]PA(5), II, 391.

[84]Heitman, p. 468.

[85]PA(5), II, 276.

[86]PA(5), II, 547-50.

[87]Heitman, p. 486.

[88]PA(5), II, 526-29.

[89]PA(5), II, 356.

[90]Heitman, p. 399.

[91]PA(5), II, 297.

[92]PA(5), II, 530-34.

[93]PA(5), II, 520-24.

[94]PA(5), II, 525-26.

[95]PA(5), II, 434.

[96]Heitman, p. 510.

[97]PA(5), II, 535-38.

[98]PA(5), II, 332.

[99]Heitman, p. 157.

[100]PA(5), II, 539-41.

[101]Heitman, p. 258.

[102]PA(5), II, 542-46.

[103]*Coloniul Records*, XI, 215-16.

[104]See PA(3), XII, 68, 91, 103.

[105]Lefferts, pp. 52, 125.

[106]PA(1), V, 715.

[107]Berg, p. 99.

[108]PA(5), III, 692.

[109]Heitman, pp. 520-21.

[110]*Ibid.*, p. 222.

[111]PA(5), III, 692.

[112]Heitman, p. 408.

[113]*Ibid.*, p. 454.

[114]PA(1), V, 714.

[115]Heitman, p. 71.

[116]*Ibid.*, p. 144.

[117]*Ibid.*, p. 468.

[118]*Ibid.*, p. 486.

[119]*Ibid.*, p. 399.

[120]*Ibid.*, p. 380.

[121]*Ibid.*, p. 413.

[122]*Ibid.*, p. 510.

[123]PA(2), XV, 217.

[124]Heitman, p. 157.

[125]*Ibid.*, p. 258.

[126]Lefferts, p. 131.

[127]PA(5), II, 250.

[128]PA(2), I, 519.

[129]PA(2), XV, 195.

[130]PA(2), I, 519.

[131]PA(5), II, 251.

[132]PA(2), I, 520.

[133]PA(5), II, 251.

[134]PA(1), V, 21.

[135]PA(2), I, 512-13.

[136]PA(2), I, 520-21.

[137]PA(1), V, 21-22.

[138]PA(2), I, 513-16.

CHAPTER XVII (continued)

[139]PA(2), I, 521-22.

[140]PA(1), V, 22.

[141]PA(5), II, 253.

[142]PA(2), XV, 199.

[143]PA(5), II, 253-54.

[144]PA(5), II, 255.

[145]PA(5), II, 391.

[146]PA(2), XV, 201.

[147]PA(5), II, 256.

[148]PA(2), XV, 201-202.

[149]PA(5), II, 256.

[150]PA(2), XV, 202.

[151]Smith, *Battle of Trenton*, p. 28.

[152]PA(2), XV, 202.

[153]Smith, *Battle of Trenton*, p. 20.

[154]PA(2), XV, 203.

[155]Smith, *Battle of Princeton*, pp. 20-23.

[156]PA(2), XV, 203.

[157]PA(2), XV, 204.

[158]PA(5), II, 256.

[159]PA(2), XV, 205.

[160]PA(5), II, 513.

[161]PA(2), XV, 205-206.

[162]PA(5), II, 514.

[163]PA(2), XV, 206-10.

[164]PA(2), XV, 210-11.

[165]PA(5), III, 694.

[166]PA(5), II, 373; III, 716.

[167]PA(5), III, 716.

[168]PA(2), XV, 211-12.

[169]Alfred C. Lambdin, "Battle of Germantown," *Pennsylvania Magazine of History and Biography*, I (1877), 400.

[170]PA(2), XV, 213.

[171]PA(1), V, 713-14.

[172]PA(5), III, 694.

[173]PA(5), II, 392.

[174]PA(5), II, 393; III, 717.

[175]PA(1), V, 716.

[176]PA(2), XV, 213-16.

[177]PA(2), XV, 216.

[178]Smith, *Battle of Monmouth*, pp. 14-15.

[179]*Ibid.*, p. 16.

[180]*Ibid.*, p. 19.

[181]*Ibid.*, p. 32.

CHAPTER XVIII, 4TH CONTINENTAL ARTILLERY

[1]*Colonial Records*, X, 368.

[2]Benjamin M. Nead, "A Sketch of General Thomas Procter, With Some Account of the First Pennsylvania Artillery in the Revolution," *Pennsylvania Magazine of History and Biography*, IV (1880), 454.

[3]Heitman, p. 453.

[4]W. A. Newman Dorland, "The Second Troop Philadelphia City Cavalry," *Pennsylvania Magazine of History and Biography*, XLVI (1922), 167, Note 185.

[5]*Colonial Records*, X, 389-90.

[6]*Ibid.*, X, 423-24.

[7]PA(5), III, 944.

[8]*Colonial Records*, X, 437.

[9]*Ibid.*, X, 438.

[10]Heitman, p. 497.

[11]PA(5), III, 943.

[12]Heitman, p. 497.

[13]PA(5), III, 944.

[14]PA(5), III, 945.

[15]PA(5), III, 944.

[16]Heitman, p. 525.

[17]PA(5), III, 947-50.

[18]*Colonial Records*, X, 685.

[19]PA(5), III, 957.

[20]Heitman, p. 525.

[21]*Ibid.*, p. 233.

[22]Newman Dorland, PMHB, XLVII (1923), 371, Note 349.

[23]PA(5), III, 943.

[24]*Colonial Records*, X, 773.

[25]PA(5), III, 943-44.

[26]*Colonial Records*, XI, 116.

[27]*Ibid.*, XI, 136-37.

Chapter XVIII (continued

28*Ibid.*, XI, 215.

29PA(5), III, 961.

30*Colonial Records*, X, 470.

31*Ibid.*, X, 479.

32Stille, p. 473.

33PA(5), III, 954.

34Berg, p. 106.

35Heitman, p. 473.

36*Ibid.*, p. 324.

37PA(5), III, 954-55.

38Heitman, pp. 453-54.

39*Ibid.*, p. 525.

40*Ibid.*, p. 233.

41PA(5), III, 972.

42William A. Porter, "A Sketch of the Life of General Andrew Porter," *Pennsylvania Magazine of History and Biography*, IV (1880), 290.

43Heitman, pp. 446-47.

44*Ibid.*, p. 233.

45*Ibid.*, p. 218.

46*Ibid.*, p. 175.

47*Ibid.*, p. 453.

48PA(1), IX, 121.

49Heitman, pp. 194-95.

50PA(5), III, 945.

51PA(5), III, 947.

52PA(5), III, 957.

53Heitman, p. 551.

54PA(5), III, 947.

55PA(5), III, 973.

56Heitman, p. 173.

57"Orderly Book of General Edward Hand, Valley Forge, January, 1778," *Pennsylvania Magazine of History and Biography*, XLI (1917), 202.

58Fitzpatrick, XI, 19-20.

59Heitman, p. 173.

60PA(5), III, 945.

61PA(5), III, 947.

62PA(5), III, 958.

63Heitman, p. 206.

64PA(5), III, 974.

65Heitman, p 206.

66*Ibid.*, p. 202.

67*Ibid.*, p. 453.

68John W. Jordan (ed.), "Orderly Book of the Second Pennsylvania Continental Line Col. Henry Bicker. At Valley Forge, March 29,—May 27, 1778," *Pennsylvania Magazine of History and Biography*, XXXVI (1912), 246.

69Heitman, p. 225.

70PA(5), III, 945.

71PA(5), III, 946.

72PA(5), III, 957.

73Heitman, p. 561.

74*Ibid.*, p. 120.

75PA(5), III, 974.

76Heitman, p. 172.

77*Ibid.*, p. 175.

78*Ibid.*, p. 450.

79*Ibid.*, p. 453.

80*Ibid.*, p. 382.

81PA(5), III, 973.

82Heitman, p. 465.

83PA(5), III, 957.

84Heitman, p. 216.

85PA(1), IX, 121.

86Berg, p. 23.

87Heitman, p. 592.

88Porter, p. 290.

89Heitman, pp. 446-47.

90*Ibid.*, p. 366.

91PA(5), III, 977.

92Heitman, pp. 497-98.

93PA(5), III, 978-83.

94PA(5), III, 1044-45.

95Lefferts, p. 84.

96*Ibid.*, p. 10.

97*Ibid.*, p. 38.

98Nead, p. 464.

99PA(5), III, 971.

100PA(5), III, 948.

101Ketchum, p. 139.

102*Ibid.*, p. 141.

CHAPTER XVIII (continued)

[103]*Ibid.*, p. 148.

[104]*Colonial Records*, XII, 34.

[105]Webb Garrison, *Sidelights on the American Revolution* (New York: Abingdon Press, 1974), p. 92.

[106]Nead, pp. 456-57.

[107]PA(1), V, 141-42.

[108]PA(1), V, 142.

[109]PA(5), III, 943.

[110]Ketchum, p. 342.

[111]Smith, *Battle of Princeton*, p. 27.

[112]*Ibid.*, p. 35.

[113]*Ibid.*, p. 28.

[114]*Ibid.*, p. 34.

[115]*Ibid.*, pp. 23-25.

[116]*Ibid.*, pp. 27-28.

[117]*Ibid.*, pp. 28-29.

[118]PA(5), III, 943-44.

[119]PA(5), III, 961.

[120]Nead, pp. 457-59.

[121]*Ibid.*, p. 460.

[122]Tucker, p. 70.

[123]PA(5), II, 621-22.

[124]PA(5), III, 1056.

[125]William Summers (collector), "Obituary Notices of Pennsylvania Soldiers of the Revolution," *Pennsylvania Magazine of History and Biography*, XXXVIII (1914), 443-44.

[126]Nead, p. 461.

[127]PA(5), III, 961.

[128]Nead, p. 461.

[129]PA(5), III, 1014.

[130]PA(5), III, 1027.

[131]Heitman, p. 119.

[132]Thompson, p. 67.

[133]Nead, p. 461.

[134]PA(5), III, 974.

[135]Stryker, p. 74.

[136]Nead, p. 462.

[137]PA(5), III, 963.

[138]Nead, p. 462.

[139]"Hubley's Journal," PMHB, p. 141.

[140]*Ibid.*, p. 287.

[141]*Sullivan-Clinton Campaign*, p. 137.

[142]PA(5), III, 1027.

[143]PA(5), III, 965.

[144]PA(5), III, 968-69.

[145]Nead, p. 463.

[146]PA(5), III, 1027.

[147]Van Doren, p. 47.

[148]Nead, p. 465.

[149]Van Doren, pp. 234-36.

[150]Porter, p. 260.

[151]Wildes, pp. 247-48.

[152]Stille, p 267.

[153]Wildes, p. 256.

[154]Tucker, p. 148.

[155]PA(5), III, 974.

[156]PA(5), III, 1021.

[157]PA(5), III, 971.

[158]PA(5), III, 1026.

[159]PA(5), III, 1016.

[160]PA(5), III, 1038.

[161]Porter, p. 290.

[162]PA(5), III, 971.

[163]Berg, p. 24.

[164]*Ibid.*, p. 26.

CHAPTER XIX. 4TH CONTINENTAL LIGHT DRAGOONS

[1]Berg, pp. 27-28.

[2]*Ibid.*, pp. 28-29.

[3]*Ibid.*, p. 31.

[4]Heitman, p. 406.

[5]*Cf.* PA(5), III, 835-36, and entries in Heitman for the individuals named.

[6]PA(1), VII, 666.

[7]Martin I. J. Griffin, *Stephen Moylan* (Philadelphia: The Author, 1909), p. 52.

[8]PA(5), III, 835; Heitman, p. 536.

[9]Heitman, p. 223.

[10]PA(1), IX, 752.

[11]PA(5), III, 837-39.

[12]Heitman, p. 223.

CHAPTER XIX (continued)

13*Ibid.*, p. 505.

14*Ibid.*, p. 300.

15*Ibid.*, p. 598.

16PA(5), III, 836.

17Heitman, p. 422.

18*Ibid.*, p. 201.

19*Ibid.*, p. 283.

20*Ibid.*, p. 444.

21*Ibid.*, p. 378.

22*Ibid.*, p. 303.

23*Ibid.*, p. 175.

24*Ibid.*, p. 442.

25*Ibid.*, p. 248.

26*Ibid.*, p. 236.

27Quoted, Griffin, p. 51.

28Lefferts, p. 18.

29Griffin, p. 51.

30Lefferts, p. 10.

31Berg, p. 31.

32PA(5), III, 835.

33PA(1), IX, 321.

34PA(5), III, 845-51.

35Griffin, pp. 52-54.

36*Ibid.*, p. 54.

37*Ibid.*, pp. 56-57.

38*Ibid.*, pp. 58-59.

39*Ibid.*, p. 61.

40*Ibid.*, p. 63.

41Thompson, p. 67.

42Griffin, pp. 67-68.

43*Ibid.*, pp. 73-74.

44Stryker, p. 73.

45*Ibid.*, p. 91.

46Griffin, p. 76.

47*Ibid.*, p. 77.

48*Ibid.*, pp. 77-80.

49*Ibid.*, pp. 84-85.

50*Ibid.*, pp. 85-86.

51*Ibid.*, p. 88.

52Heitman, p. 248.

53Griffin, pp. 92-95.

54*Ibid.*, p. 99.

55*Ibid.*, p. 103.

56*Ibid.*, pp. 106-107.

57Berg, p. 31.

58Griffin, p. 108.

59*Ibid.*, p. 119.

60Van Doren, p. 36.

61Griffin, pp. 117-18.

62*Ibid.*, p. 117.

63*Ibid.*, p. 120.

64PA(5), III, 837-39.

65Griffin, pp. 120-21.

66*Ibid.*, pp. 123-24.

67Stille, p. 287.

68Griffin, p. 128.

69Berg, p. 31.

CHAPTER XX. MISCELLANEOUS ORGANIZATIONS

1PA(5), III, 765.

2PA(5), III, 855.

3PA(5), III, 885.

4PA(5), III, 895.

5PA(5), III, 785.

6Berg, p. 47.

7PA(5), III, 785.

8Berg, p. 47.

9PA(5), III, 787.

10Heitman, p. 280.

11PA(5), III, 787.

12Samuel W. Pennypacker, "Samuel John Atlee," *Pennsylvania Magazine of History and Biography*, II (1878), 80.

13Heitman, p. 525.

14*Ibid.*, p. 581.

15PA(5), III, 787.

16Heitman, p. 133.

17PA(5), III, 787.

18Heitman, p. 306.

19PA(5), III, 807-15.

20PA(5), III, 816-20.

CHAPTER XIX (continued)

[21]Heitman, p. 133.

[22]PA(5), III, 787.

[23]Heitman, p. 114.

[24]PA(5), III, 787.

[25]Heitman, p. 306.

[26]*Ibid.*, p. 84.

[27]*Ibid.*, p. 132.

[28]*Ibid.*, p. 579.

[29]*Ibid.*, p. 464.

[30]*Ibid.*, p. 602.

[31]*Ibid.*, p. 288.

[32]*Ibid.*, p. 258.

[33]*Ibid.*, p. 306.

[34]PA(5), III, 788.

[35]Heitman, p. 484.

[36]Lefferts, p. 81.

[37]Heitman, p. 139.

[38]PA(5), III, 829.

[39]Smith, *Battle of Trenton*, p. 28.

[40]Ketchum, p. 341.

[41]PA(5), III, 827.

[42]Smith, *Battle of Princeton*, p. 35.

[43]PA(5), III, 795.

[44]PA(5), III, 789.

[45]PA(5), III, 829.

[46]"A Partial List of Pennsylvania Troops Killed, Wounded, and Captured at the Battle of Germantown, October 4, 1777," *Pennsylvania Magazine of History and Biography*, XL (1916), 242.

[47]PA(5), III, 826, 830-32.

[48]Heitman, p. 12.

[49]Berg, p. 47.

[50]PA(5), III, 785.

[51]Heitman, p. 230.

[52]*Ibid.*, p. 360.

[53]Berg, p. 11.

[54]Heitman, p. 472.

[55]*Ibid.*, p. 414.

[56]Berg, p. 11.

[57]Heitman, p. 314.

[58]PA(5), III, 1101.

[59]Berg, p. 11.

[60]Heitman, p. 424.

[61]*Ibid.*, p. 171.

[62]Berg, pp. 11-12.

[63]Heitman, p. 171.

[64]Berg, p. 12.

[65]Heitman, p. 609.

[66]*Ibid.*, p. 326.

[67]*Ibid.*, p. 424.

[68]PA(5), III, 1086.

[69]Heitman, p. 424.

[70]PA(5), III, 1086.

[71]Heitman, p. 247.

[72]PA(5), III, 1099-1100.

[73]PA(5), III, 1094-95.

[74]PA(5), III, 1063-67.

[75]Lefferts, p. 85.

[76]PA(5), III, 1089.

[77]PA(5), III, 1108-10.

[78]PA(5), III, 1107-1108.

[79]PA(5), III, 1119-22.

[80]PA(5), III, 1095-96.

[81]PA(5), III, 917.

[82]Heitman, p. 561.

[83]PA(5), III, 917.

[84]PA(5), III, 923-25.

[85]PA(1), IX, 486-87.

[86]Berg, p. 133.

[87]Lefferts, p. 10.

[88]PA(5), III, 917.

[89]Berg, p. 133.

Appendix A. Regional Origins of Organizations

No Notes

Appendix B. The Individual Soldier

[1]Heitman, p. 691.

[2]Berg, pp. 52-53.

[3]PA(5), II, 843-44.

[4]PA(5), II, 33.

[5]PA(5), III, 179.

[6]PA(5), III, 924, 927.

[7]PA(5), II, 186.

[8]PA(5), III, 187.

[9]PA(5), III, 1056.

[10]Summers, PMHB, XXXVIII (1914), 443-44.

[11]"Some Extracts from the Papers of General Persifor Frazer," PMHB, XXXI (1907), 134.

[12]PA(5), II, 705.

[13]PA(5), III, 654.

[14]PA(5), III, 435.

[15]PA(5), III, 924, 927.

Appendix C. Battles and Engagements

No Notes

Appendix D. Casualties

No Notes

Appendix E. Personnel Data

No Notes

Bibliography

Although the original manuscripts of many of the primary sources cited in the following bibliography and in footnotes are available in a number of libraries (conspicuously, at the Historical Society of Pennsylvania, 1300 Locust Street, Philadelphia), all references have been restricted to published collections of these documents, on the theory that the more widespread availability of such publications would make research more feasible for any individual wishing to conduct further research into specific matters mentioned in the text of this book.

AMORY, THOMAS C. *The Military Services and Public Life of Major-General John Sullivan.* Port Washington, N.Y.: Kennikat Books, 1968 (originally published in 1868).

BELL, HERBERT C. *History of Northumberland County, Pennsylvania.* Chicago: Brown, Runk & Co., 1891.

BERG, FRED ANDERSON. *Encyclopedia of Continental Army Units.* Harrisburg: Stackpole Books, 1972.

Colonial Records of Pennsylvania. Harrisburg: Printed by Tho. Finn & Co., 1853. Volumes X-XII.

CRIST, ROBERT GRANT. *Captain William Hendricks and the March to Quebec.* Carlisle, Pa.: The Hamilton Library and Historical Association of Cumberland County, 1960.

DELANCEY, EDWARD F. "Chief Justice William Allen." *Pennsylvania Magazine of History and Biography,* I (1877), 202-11.

FITZPATRICK, JOHN C. (ed.). *The Writings of George Washington From the Original Manuscript Sources, 1744-1799.* Washington, D.C.: United States Government Printing Office, 1933. Volumes X-XII.

GARRISON, WEBB. *Sidelights on the American Revolution.* New York: Abingdon Press, 1974.

GRIFFIN, MARTIN I. J. *Stephen Moylan.* Philadelphia: The Author, 1909.

HEITMAN, FRANCIS B. *Historical Register of Officers of the Continental Army During the War of the Revolution.* Baltimore: Genealogical Publishing Co., Inc., 1973.

HENRY, JOHN JOSEPH. *Account of Arnold's Campaign Against Quebec.* Albany: Joel Munsell, 1877.

JONES, GILBERT S. (comp.). *Valley Forge Park.* Valley Forge Park Commission, 1947.

JORDAN, JOHN W. (ed.). "Adm Hubley, Jr., Lt Colo. Comdt 11th Penna Regt, His Journal, Commencing at Wyoming, July 30th, 1779." *Pennsylvania Magazine of History and Biography,* XXXIII (1909), 129-46, 279-302, 409-22.

————— (ed.). "Orderly Book of the Second Pennsylvania Continental Line Col. Henry Bicker. At Valley Forge, March 29, May 27, 1778." *Pennsylvania Magazine of History and Biography,* XXXVI (1912), 30-59, 236-53, 329-45.

KATCHER, PHILIP R. N. *Encyclopedia of English, Provincial, and German Army Units, 1775-1783.* Harrisburg: Stackpole Books, 1973.

KEEN, GREGORY B. "The Descendants of Joran Kyn, The Founder of Upland." *Pennsylvania Magazine of History and Biography,* VII (1883), 94-100.

KETCHUM, RICHARD M. *The Winter Soldiers.* Garden City, N.Y.: Doubleday & Company, Inc., 1973.

LACEY, JOHN. "Memoirs of Brigadier-General John Lacey, of Pennsylvania." *Pennsylvania Magazine of History and Biography,* XXV (1901), 1-13, 191-207, 341-54, 498-515; XXVI (1902), 101-11, 265-70.

LAMBDIN, ALFRED C. "Battle of Germantown." *Pennsylvania Magazine of History and Biography,* I (1877), 368-403.

LANDIS, CAPTAIN JOHN B. "Investigation into American Tradition of Woman Known as 'Molly Pitcher.'" *The Journal of American History*, V (1911), 83-95.

LEFFERTS, LT. CHARLES M. *Uniforms of the American, British, French, and German Armies of the War of the American Revolution, 1775-1783*. Old Greenwich, Conn.: WE Inc., [1971]. Edited by Alexander J. Wall.

LESSER, CHARLES H. (ed.). *The Sinews of Independence: Monthly Strength Reports of the Continental Army*. Chicago: University of Chicago Press, 1976.

MANDERS, ERIC I. "Notes on Troop Units in the Flying Camp, 1776." *Military Collector & Historian*, XXVI, No. 1 (Spring, 1974), 9-13.

The Military System of Pennsylvania During the Revolutionary War. Pennsylvania Historical and Museum Commission Information Leaflet No. 3.

"Minutes of the Committee of Safety of Bucks County, Pennsylvania, 1774-1776." *Pennsylvania Magazine of History and Biography*. XV (1891), 257-90.

NEAD, BENJAMIN M. "A Sketch of General Thomas Procter, With Some Account of the First Pennsylvania Artillery in the Revolution." *Pennsylvania Magazine of History and Biography*, IV (1880), 454-70.

NEWMAN DORLAND, W. A. "The Second Troop Philadelphia City Cavalry." *Pennsylvania Magazine of History and Biography*, XLVI (1922), 57-77, 154-72, 262-71, 346-65.

New York Division of Archives and History. *The Sullivan-Clinton Campaign of 1779*. Albany: The University of the State of New York, 1929.

"Orderly Book of General Edward Hand, Valley Forge, January, 1778." *Pennsylvania Magazine of History and Biography*, XLI (1917), 198-223, 257-73, 458-67.

"A Partial List of Pennsylvania Troops Killed, Wounded, and Captured at the Battle of Germantown, October 4, 1777." *Pennsylvania Magazine of History and Biography*, XL (1916), 241-43.

PECKHAM, HOWARD H. (ed.). *The Toll of Independence: Engagements & Battle Casualties of the American Revolution*. Chicago: The University of Chicago Press, 1974.

Pennsylvania Archives. Harrisburg: State Printer. Old Series, Volumes V-VII, IX; Second Series, Volumes I, XII, XV; Third Series, Volumes XI, XII, XIV, XV, XVII-XX, XXII-XXVI; Fifth Series, Volumes II, III.

PENNYPACKER, SAMUEL W. "Samuel John Atlee." *Pennsylvania Magazine of History and Biography*, II (1878), 74-84.

PETERSON, HAROLD L. *The Book of the Continental Soldier*. Harrisburg: Stackpole Books, 1968.

PORTER, WILLIAM A. "A Sketch of the Life of General Andrew Porter." *Pennsylvania Magazine of History and Biography*, IV (1880), 261-301.

REED, JOHN F. *Campaign to Valley Forge*. Philadelphia: University of Pennsylvania Press, 1965.

_____. *Valley Forge, Crucible of Victory*. Monmouth Beach, N.J.: Philip Freneau Press, 1969.

SMITH, SAMUEL STELLE. *The Battle of Monmouth*. Monmouth Beach, N.J.: Philip Freneau Press, 1964.

_____. *The Battle of Princeton*. Monmouth Beach, N.J.: Philip Freneau Press, 1967.

_____. *The Battle of Trenton*. Monmouth Beach, N.J.: Philip Freneau Press, 1965.

"Some Extracts from the Papers of General Persifor Frazer." *Pennsylvania Magazine of History and Biography*, XXXI (1907), 129-44, 311-19, 447-51.

STILLE, CHARLES J. *Major-General Anthony Wayne and the Pennsylvania Line in the Continental Army*. Philadelphia: J. B. Lippincott Company, 1893.

STRYKER, WILLIAM S. *The Battle of Monmouth*. Princeton: Princeton University Press, 1927.

SUMMERS, WILLIAM (comp.). "Obituary Notices of Pennsylvania Soldiers of the Revolution." *Pennsylvania Magazine of History and Biography,* XXXVIII (1914), 443-460.

THOMPSON, RAY. *Washington at Whitemarsh.* Fort Washington, Pa.: The Bicentennial Press, 1974.

TUCKER, GLENN. *Mad Anthony Wayne and the New Nation.* Harrisburg: Stackpole Books, 1973.

VAN DOREN, CARL. *Mutiny in January.* New York: The Viking Press, 1943.

WILDES, HARRY EMERSON. *Anthony Wayne, Trouble Shooter of the American Revolution.* New York: Harcourt, Brace and Company, 1941.

WILLIAMS, GEORGE H. *History of the Negro Race in America from 1619 to 1880.* 2 vols. New York: G. P. Putnam's Sons, 1883.

Index